Gender, Education, and Employment Developments in South Asia: A Review of Progress in Afghanistan and Pakistan

Bahaudin G. Mujtaba

ILEAD Academy, LLC
Davie, Florida. United States of America
www.ileadacademy.com

Bahaudin G. Mujtaba, 2015. *Gender, Education, and Employment Developments in South Asia: A Review of Progress in Afghanistan and Pakistan*

Cover Design by: Cagri Tanyar

Cover photo by Bahaudin Mujtaba in Rahm-Abad, Logar.

ISBN-13: 978-1-936237-11-1
ISBN-10: 1-936237-11-3

Subject Code & Description

1:	EDU032000	Education: Leadership
2:	EDU046000	Education: Professional Development
3:	BUS072000	Business & Economics : Development - Sustainable Development

Printed in the United States of America by ILEAD Academy, LLC. Davie, Florida.

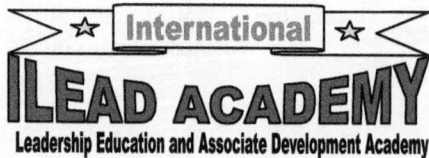

☆ **International** ☆
ILEAD ACADEMY
Leadership Education and Associate Development Academy

Dedication

We dedicate this book to those who advance the equality of education and gender across the globe.

"You reap what you sow. Don't plant anything but love."
- Rumi

Table of Contents

Acknowledgements

There are many individuals that have contributed to this volume; *first,* I would like to thank the following colleagues and coauthors for their contributions to the content of this book:

- Adiqa Kiani
- An Quoc Nguyen
- Ayesha Zahid
- Belal A. Kaifi
- Cagri Tanyar
- Ch. Abdul Rehman
- Danai Cheretis
- Daria Prause
- Farzana Rahman Safi
- Frank J. Cavico
- Eleanor Marschke
- Ikwukananne I. Udechukwu
- Katie M. Gordon

- Kiran Pari Razzaq
- Janice M. Karlen
- Jatuporn Sungkhawan
- Mario E. Delgado
- Maike Emmi Lina Koehler
- Memoona Zareen
- Navid Reza Ahadi
- Qudsia Batool
- Razia Begum
- Sumaira Rehman
- Tipakorn Seanatip
- Wajma Aslami

Second, I would like to extend special appreciations and thanks to Professor Frank Cavico for reading the chapters and suggesting great improvements for the organization of this book.

Third, all the contributors of this book and I would like to thank all those professional organizations, such as the Academy of Management, and our family members who helped us get to this point. Overall, I would like to thank you for reading this material; and we trust you will find this book interesting, thought-provoking, useful, and beneficial.

Overall, the content of this book is diverse, as it covers many issues related to gender and education across the globe. Each author is responsible for his/her own writing and the copyright ownership for his/her submission. This book is based on the papers prepared for, and presented at, the annual Academy of Management (AoM) conference in Philadelphia, PA, United States of America, on August 1, 2014.

Bahaudin

Preface

This book provides a great deal of relevant cross-cultural knowledge regarding gender and education developments for all students, academicians, business owners, entrepreneurs, and policy-makers, especially if they are working in South Asia's Afghanistan and Pakistan. However, as once emphasized by the actor and martial artist, Bruce Lee, "knowing is not enough, we must apply…willing is not enough, we must do"; and following this advice is the socially responsible thing to do in order to make our society a little better every single day.

Knowledge and application of diverse and relevant ideas, concepts, and philosophies regarding gender and educational developments are important to all politicians and business leaders; and also they must act in an ethical and socially responsible manner by being fair to males and females alike in order for society to become progressively better. As such, political, business and educational leaders must act for the greater good, treat all stakeholders with dignity and respect, and be socially responsible by supporting the community in civic and philanthropic efforts toward equality in gender and education for everyone. Acting in a responsible way will require leaders to be cognizant of all stakeholder interests and values as well as to attempt to balance them in a fair and just way.

The author and contributors hope that this book serves as a tool for ethical conduct, true gender equality, stakeholder responsibility, and organizational and societal sustainability.

Bahaudin!

CHAPTER 1

Challenges Women Face in the Workplace

By: Bahaudin G. Mujtaba and Katie M. Gordon
Nova Southeastern University

This chapter opens with a discussion on some of the challenges women face in the modern workplace. The chapter provides an overview of leadership, and discusses the traits and characteristics needed to lead in the 21st century. Studies indicate numerous commitments have been made over the past three decades to promote gender equality and eliminate discrimination toward women in the workplace. Governments have enacted laws to help with these commitments; however the disparity and inequality of pay and promotional opportunities still seem to exist in the business world for many women across the globe. The chapter discusses the disparities of wages and the inequity for women in today's society.

In this chapter, other discussions include the challenging global forces that leaders should be prepared to address. The focus in the future will be on innovative technology and economic forces. Women must be educated and trained in these fields to obtain and maneuver in the business world. The chapter also explores external forces such as global outsourcings and competition and how they will affect women in business. The discussion includes information on value driven management and concludes with recommendations on policies and procedures organizations can implement to create gender equality in the workplace.

Introduction

The history of women in leadership roles dates back to the beginning of time; their roles are inclusive of community leaders, leaders in their family, in public service and in society. Some of the stereotypes to be discussed in academic literature include if women are too friendly, social, and whether they are good mediators. Women have their own perceptions or preconceived thoughts as to why they are being stereotyped in the workplace. One such perception is that women are better in supportive roles while men are seen as best in the leadership roles.

Leadership in the 21st Century continues to be one of the most challenging arenas for women such as supervisors and managers. The number of women in leadership roles is rising but is still relatively low in the top levels of management. As the number of women in leadership increases, so will the challenges for women in the workplace. Most would say the traditional challenges such as work-life balance, parenting, multi-tasking, sexual harassment, and discrimination are not limited to women; research supports that male employees face the same challenges.

According to Mary Joe Frug in *Women and the Law*, women-owned businesses are growing 50 percent faster than male-owned businesses. The perception is that women make better business owners and leaders because they have better communication skills, have a higher degree of emotional intelligence, and are more likely to take initiative.

To drill down even further within the wage gap, another disparity is between black and white women in the United States. In the early 1980s, the wage differences between black and white women was relatively small mainly because of affirmative action and anti-discrimination laws. Although black women's educational attainment has increased since 1980, by the close of the twentieth century, employed white women were over 13% more likely than employed black women to have attended some college. As the economic opportunities of the college educated diverge from those with less education, we should expect a growing wage gap between white and black women (Pettit & Ewert, 2009).

As women of any race graduate from college, the expectations are for them to transition into professional positions in the business world with their expertise. Some of these women might initially be naïve as to what to expect, and some will think they should be able to move through the ranks with ease. Eventually they too will see that sitting alongside men in the boardroom and becoming top executives, earning the same or more than men will not only be a challenge, but sometimes the opportunity may not exist at all.

The Equal Pay Act of 1963 in the United States was intended to eradicate unequal wages for women; however it doesn't appear to have worked in all companies or locations across the country. Representative Rosa L. DeLauro told a Senate hearing that "paycheck fairness has become a family issue now that women make up half the workforce, and two thirds of women are either the sole breadwinner or the co-breadwinner of their families" (McMillion, May 2010). (Rothkopf, 2013) states,

> UC Davis published a study in 2011 that examined the 400 largest companies in California. This study showed that only 9.7% of board room seats or top paying executive positions are held by women. Thirty-four percent had no women on their executive board and none of the companies in the study had an all-female board. In addition, none of the companies had a gender-balanced board or management team (pp. 103-104).

This information would lead one to believe that women are still underrepresented in top leadership roles in business. This is not a problem that exists only in the United

States; rather it also exists in other countries. For instance, Afghanistan, Australia, China, India, Norway, Iran, Pakistan, and Thailand, to name a few, are experiencing the same problems. In Norway, the underrepresentation of women in the boardroom has become such a problem that they have given consideration to several options to circumvent the challenge. Norway has considered instituting a quota system which provides for every major corporation to have at least 30% of women on their board. This will equate to about three women on every board of directors in the country of Norway. This is an indication that although there are laws in place, they believe they have to take it a bit further to ensure that women are equally represented and given a fair chance for advancement opportunities.

According to the U.S. Bureau of Labor Statistics (BLS) and Catalyst Inc., statistics about women in business as of 2013 shows women account for 2.2 percent of chief executive officers (CEO) among Fortune 500 companies. Among the top earners in Fortune 500 companies, 7.6% are women. There is one area that continues to be directed only toward women, and that is the wage gap. According to Jones and George (2011), American women's average weekly earnings are about $160.00 dollars less than men. It is indicated that women make up 51% of employees in managerial and professional positions, however only 6.7% of the top earners are women. Thus the gender pay gap appears to be alive and well as the glass ceiling. Women workers account for 46.7% of the labor force of the U.S. According to the U.S. Bureau of Labor Statistics, "in 2007, women who were full-time wage and salary workers had median weekly earnings of $614, or about 80 percent of the $766 median for their male counterparts. This ratio has grown since 1979 (the first year for which comparable earnings data are available), when women earned about 62 percent as much as men." As quoted by President Obama during his State of the Union Speech in January 2014,

> You know, today, women make up about half our workforce, but they still make 77 cents for every dollar a man earns. That is wrong, and in 2014, it's an embarrassment. Women deserve equal pay for equal work. You know, she deserves to have a baby without sacrificing her job. A mother deserves a day off to care for a sick child or sick parent without running into hardship. And you know what, a father does too. It is time to do away with workplace policies that belong in a "Mad Men" episode. This year let's all come together, Congress, the White House, businesses from Wall Street to Main Street, to give every woman the opportunity she deserves, because I believe when women succeed, America succeeds.

President Barak Hussain Obama also made a reference to the fact that women hold a majority of lower-wage jobs, but they are not the only ones stifled by stagnant wages. The President summed it up by saying everyone deserves a chance and an opportunity to earn or achieve his/her dream. This sounds very profound and noble, but we must realize that women in the workplace face certain challenges that men do not. Even with this presidential speech and the mandated laws, women still have not experienced a significant change.

Challenges in the workplace

Women in the workplace have faced and continue to face many obstacles in the past and still do today. Women starting and operating their own business will face the challenge of lack of cash flow and getting or qualifying for government contracts. Sexual harassment and gender bias that began as far back as elementary school as well as covert discrimination are other challenges that women are facing in the workplace. The reasons why women opt for teaching and/or social work positions could be because of what the parents are teaching in the household which practice is commonly known as covert discrimination. In most cases covert discrimination begins many years before a woman enters the workforce. Parents are responsible for being role models for their children and it is clear that parents are modeling the roles of caregivers and nurturers to the girls, at the same time boys are learning from their parents and others to be competitive and tough. This type of discrimination is done in a way that is not obvious in the beginning; however as an adult it is clear the path that has permeated in the minds of those that have been exposed to this type of parenting. Parents tend to separate and push their male and female children in directions that they feel are most beneficial based on their sexual orientation.

Many companies tout that they offer work-life balance, but what the companies perceive as work-life balance and what the women in the workforce perceive as work life balance are not synonymous. An example is the Family Medical Leave Act (FMLA) that allows for both women and men to have time off for maternity; however they are subjected to financial setbacks because most companies are not required by the law to compensate the employee for taking the time.

Women continue to deal with *glass ceiling* (meaning invisible barriers that prevent women and minorities from promotional and advancement opportunities), unequal pay for the same work, and unwarranted stereotypical barriers. Gender discrimination is among the challenges that exist in many organizations despite legislation against them. According to Jones and George (2011, p. 188), the Glass Ceiling Commission Report indicated that African-Americans have the hardest time being promoted and climbing the corporate ladder, that Asians are often stereotyped into technical jobs, and that Hispanics are assumed to be less well educated than other minority groups. Women as well as men in management must empower employees to speak out if they observe other employees being unfairly treated or being discriminated against. They can accomplish this laudable goal by setting the precedent in being the first to take classes or bring in diversity experts to teach awareness and increase understanding on how to appreciate other cultures and perspectives. According to Greenlaw & PKJ (1996, p. 4),

> More than 50% of women who work can expect to be sexually harassed sometime during their careers. In 1993 approximately 8% of all cases

filed before the Equal Employment Opportunity Commission (EEOC) and state human rights commissions involved charges of sexual harassment, with the vast majority of claims continuing to involve working women. Although sexual harassment can occur to both sexes, only 10% of sexual harassment complaints filed with the EEOC in 1994 were from men. Sexual harassment continues to be a problem in the 21st century and women must figure out ways to address it head on, otherwise it will continue to be a challenge for the women behind them.

A poll conducted from November 9-13, 2011 by the Washington Post found that one in four women report having experienced sexual harassment in the workplace; however, this is predicated only on the number of women that have reported it. Ten percent of the men polled believed their actions were misconstrued, and they did not perceive their interactions as sexual harassment. According to a 2009 study by the University of Minnesota, women in positions of authority are more likely to be victims of sexual harassment. The researchers discovered that women in supervisory positions were 137% more likely to be harassed than women not in these positions.

Offering support for emotional challenges others are facing is one area that women can be there for each other; the other area is mentorship for women in business, and especially for the ones that are graduating from business schools. There are legal obligations by employers to maintain a safe and harassment free workplace, of course, and not adhering to the laws can result in lawsuits, poor morale, and low productivity. A leader's strategy in preventing workplace harassment of any kind should be visible, known to all employees, and effective.

Leadership is a Must for Success
Leadership is defined as the process, by which an individual exerts influence over other people, inspires, motivates, and directs their activities to help achieve group or organizational goals (Jones & George, 2011, pp. 463-464). Effective leadership increases an organization's ability to meet all the contemporary challenges, including the need to obtain a competitive advantage, the need to foster ethical behavior, and the need to manage a diverse workforce fairly and equitably.

According to Robert Preziosi (1996), management in the 21st century will need to focus on a well-documented values-based theory of leadership. The connection between leader values and high performance is what the leader "believes" and what the leader "does" to promote high performance. Preziosi has determined a list of principles that will motivate and inspire the follower behavior. Just to list a few: build on success by identifying those elements and consciously repeat them, champion the shared vision and act as an energizing force behind that vision, and generate renewal by being creative and by encouraging creativity on the part of the followers. Women leaders must incorporate these examples of practical impact to arrive at the end result of high performance and competitive advantage in the organization.

Leadership that makes subordinates aware of the importance of their jobs, the performance to the organization, their own needs for personal growth, as well as leadership that motivates subordinates to work for the good of the organization is known as transformational leadership. Women leaders are often more transformational leaders because of their supportive and considerate behavior. These behaviors are advantageous for women and may allow them to be outstanding leaders (according to Esther Lopez-Zafra, at the University of Spain).

It is an understatement to think that men can do things women cannot; accordingly, organizations should equip women with the assistance of role models and mentors if they expect to see change. The lack of role models in leadership for women is still very hard to come by and therefore makes it a conundrum for young women graduating from colleges in business.

An article in *The Wall Street Journal*, (2013) speaks on developing a leadership style that is a challenge for most young managers, but particularly for young women. Leadership experts say they must navigate a "double-bind": If they assert themselves forcefully, people may perceive them as not acting feminine enough, triggering a backlash. But if they act in a stereotypically feminine way, they are not seen as strong leaders. "This is a particularly challenging process for women early in their careers," says Herminia Ibarra, a Professor at Insead, a business school with campuses in France and Singapore, who has studied women's leadership styles. "It's one of their big hurdles."

Julie Steinberg, a reporter, says there are nine rules women must follow to get ahead. They include work hard, do work no one else wants to do, cultivate the people in charge, know what you want and go after it, promote yourself legitimately, network with peers, make your own career, leave to get ahead, and dress well and play golf. In an article in *Talent Management*, called "Uncovering the Secrets of Leadership", Matthew Such is quoted as saying "to identify who has the potential to be a great leader, organizations should assess skills, experience and motivation. Doing so can help to improve operational efficiency, revenue and employee engagement".

Evolution of Women in leadership
Research indicates that more women are seen as workers rather than as business leaders or business owners. As stated by Walsh (1998, p. 189), much of business history has been written in terms of earnings, success, size, achievement, upward mobility, power and organization. How does running a convent, a school, a restaurant or the dairy side of a farm fit into a firm-centered approach to economic growth? Until recently it has not. The "walls" in the corporate and professional worlds have thus, for the most part, excluded women. Some have managed to scale these walls by adapting to the male model of business behavior. In so doing they have often forgotten, ignored, or downgraded their family ties. As stated by Worldwide Guide to Women in Leadership (2013),

Only one and three women entered the workforce in 1950, whereas in 1998 the number had increased to three in five women entering the workforce. In 2006, women comprised 46 percent of the workforce. Over the last 30 years, women in the workforce has influenced economic factors such as productivity, average family income, and consumer behavior.

An article in *New York Times* discussed the disparity of women in national positions; it speaks of a study that concludes women are well behind men in two crucial areas; economic equality and political power. The Gender Gap Report 2011 indicated that women hold fewer than 20 percent of all decision making national positions. Klaus Schwab, founder and executive chairman of the Geneva based World Economic Forum, said that a world where women professionals make up less than 20 percent of the global decision makers is a world that is missing a huge opportunity for growth and peace while ignoring an untapped reservoir of potential (Torregrosa, 2011). It is apparent that women have experienced some growth in executive positions over the last decade; however there are statistics that show the glass ceiling still exist. According to statistics posted by the Labor Force, 14.6% of women held executive officers positions, and 16.9% held board seats in Fortune 500 companies.

Traits, Characteristics and Stereotypes
It has been stated that effective leaders should have certain personal qualities that separate them from non-leaders. Being successful in business requires a strong sense of purpose, a willingness to learn, and a belief in yourself. Intelligence in a leader helps managers understand complex issues and solve problems. Research conducted by researchers in the last four decades tend to conclude that men are more likely to use task-oriented and autocratic leadership styles than women, whereas women are more likely than men to use interpersonally oriented and democratic leadership styles.

Emotional intelligence may play a particularly important role in leadership effectiveness. This type of intelligence will assist leaders with developing a vision for their organizations, motivate their subordinates to commit to the vision, and energize them to enthusiastically work to achieve this vision (Jones & George, 2011, p. 483). Effective leaders need to be able to influence their employees to achieve the goals of the organization. They must also have the ability to understand and manage one's own moods and emotions. With the many high demands and uncertainties women face, they will definitely need high energy and tolerance for stress. Of course, as usual and regardless of one's gender, honesty is the single most important trait any leader can have.

When a leader is credible and honest, employees feel more secure and trusting around him/her. An article in *The Wall Street Journal* (2013) stated research from three different CFO's providing insight into some common traits and values of a CFO. Courage, perseverance to mastery, self-assurance, and ethical responsibility were listed; however some of them are innate, and others were developed over time. The article also listed other steps female leaders that aspire to become top executives can incorporate in their journey, such as evaluate and envision what you want to be, proactively own your career and invest in broad experiential learning.

Cultural stereotypes (such as women are not as smart as men in technical subjects) can make it seem as though women do not have what it takes in the science and technology fields. These types of stereotype also tend to hinder women for important leadership roles. Cultural stereotypes add to the obstacle that women faces in getting positions that produce important power and authority. Stereotyping can exist without a person realizing that is what they are doing, which is why it is important to educate managers, personnel and employers.

Instituting educational programs that will teach individuals how to recognize and monitor their own perceptions is one way of dealing with stereotypes. Other ways to reduce gender stereotyping includes implementing a check and balance system, placing employees in gender diversified groups, and portraying images that contradict such stereotypes. Finally, according to an article written by Paula Brantner in *Today's Workplace*, "this type of stereotyping leads to discrimination that unfairly provides challenges to women's success in the workplace." To remain competitive in the global business world, stereotyping must be eradicated.

Just as there are different types of leaders, there are different kinds of action logic, ways which leaders interpret their surroundings and how they react when their power or safety is tested. David Rooke and William R. Tolbert describe seven transformations of leadership in an article from *Harvard Business Review*. The following list of transformation leadership styles will improve as leaders grow with their skills. As stated by Rooke and Torbert (2005), an *opportunist* is characterized as one who wins any way possible, *diplomat* avoids overt conflict, *expert* rules by logic and expertise, *achiever* meets strategic goals, *individualist* interweaves competing personal and company action logic, *strategist* generates organizational and personal transformations, or *alchemist* generates social transformations. Women tend to have strong commitment to values, community and trust, therefore supporting the theory that their strengths are based on skills they were socialized to develop. In general women value association, relationship, and dialogue instead of debating. It is important for leaders to experiment with different styles to find what is best suited for them and their organization. It is also necessary to continue to develop and become self-aware to reach their leadership goals.

Unstable economic times makes it imperative for women to use the transformational style of leadership which research says is consistent with their values and skills. Maintaining a competitive edge technologically is essential for women in the future, especially with the pace of change in computers, information technology and cyber changes.

Technological and Economic Forces

Economic forces produce many opportunities and threats for male and female managers alike. The opportunities such as low levels of unemployment and falling interest rates allows more money to be spent, and organizations to sell more goods and services. Poor economic conditions make the environment more complex and managers' jobs more difficult and demanding. Being able to predict the future would be an ideal talent for anyone who is managing or doing business, however, that is not realistic. It is realistic to understand that as we gradually rebound from the economic downturn, leaders will need to have a plan in place to facilitate economic growth.

Being a forward thinking manager that challenge oneself to devise a strategic plan that include discovering new resources, and implementing innovated technology is must for the 21st century manager. Women leaders must keep abreast of what is occurring in the economy at the national and regional levels to respond appropriately. According to some research, women tend to shy away from fields such as technology and science, mathematics, and engineering. Since these fields traditionally are dominated by males, women should consider pursuing an education and/or career in fields that are underrepresented by women. Some organizations and schools offer incentives such as scholarships and grants to women who are interested in these fields. Taking advantage of this prospect will increase the position of role models and mentors in any one of these fields.

Dr. Cynthia McDaniels, Professor of Educational Leadership at Southern Connecticut State University, concluded that information technology has gender neutral aspects that can bring big advantages of the "good ole boys" and "glass ceilings". It is suggested that newer and faster changing field of the IT culture is less entrenched, technical competency is more "clear cut" in IT than in insurance and banking, and gender is less obvious in contacts over the Internet.

The increase in business activities through the Internet is a challenge for managers. Managers are facing the responsibility of constantly updating and improving their use of advanced IT to increase organizational performance. They must work to adopt the most effective IT solutions for their employees and customers or risk being surpassed by more effective rivals who have developed superior IT competencies (Jones & George, 2011). To successfully plan, lead, organize, and control effectively, managers must have access to information to assist with making the right decisions both internally and externally. Having access to advanced technology provides managers with information that is needed to make competitive strategic decisions.

Technological changes have grown greatly in the last decades and are still increasing by large scale. One of the most important innovations in transportation technology that opened the global environment has been growth of commercial jet travel. In addition to speeding travel, and modern communications, transportation technologies have also helped reduce the cultural distance between countries. The internet and its millions of Web sites facilitate the development of global communications networks and media that are helping to creature a worldwide culture above and beyond unique cultures.

Changes in this area can threaten an organization; create a host of new opportunities for designing, making, or distributing new and better kinds of good and services (Jones et al.,(2011). Changes in IT such as teleconferencing, videoconferencing, and telecommuting allows managers to supervise and coordinate geographically. Managers face increasing coordination problems in managing their global supply chains to take advantage of national differences in production costs. As stated by Jones and George (2011), information technology and communication advancements have dramatically increased managers' abilities to communicate with others as well as to quickly access information to make decisions. The impact that the advances are having on managerial communication include the Internet, intranets groupware, and collaboration software. Regardless of the volumes of communications facilitated by information technology, managers must remember communication is essentially a human endeavor. As a result, managers must adopt ever more sophisticated IT that helps them coordinate the flow of materials, semi-finished goods, and finished products throughout the world.

Effective communication skills by managers will have barriers that originate from both the sender and the receiver. If managers are not in tune to the conversation, not listening to the messages, and not trying to understand the meaning of the message, it can cause ineffective communication. If the sender is communicating, it is necessary to make sure the message is clear and complete, eliminate jargon unless you are speaking to someone that is in the same field, and choose the correct medium in which to relay the message. When communicating as the receiver, it is important to pay attention to the message received, be a good listener by making eye contact, engaged posture, and being focused, and being empathetic to the feeling of the sender. As managers recognize the differences in communication skills and style of communication of others, it is beneficial to adjust the way you relate and be open-minded to others and their way of communicating. It is just as important to have an educated IT team that will communicate changes, safeguard systems and keep management abreast of technological changes. Therefore managers must not only embrace the digital technology age, but take leadership roles so they can formulate policy in the U.S. and global workplace.

Global Outsourcing and Competition
Global outsourcing is defined as the purchase or production of inputs of final products from overseas suppliers to lower costs and improve product quality or design. It occurs when a company contracts with supplier in other countries to make the various outputs or components that go into its products or to assemble the final products to reduce costs. The most threatening force that managers have to deal with is rivalry between competitors. The difference between intense rivalry and low rivalry is whether managers will have access to resources more readily. As an effective manager, you want to make sure you understand outsourcing and what is being outsourced. Also, important questions are whether the decision to outsource

will bring value to the organization, as well as whether the investment is beneficial to undertake. Having the operational experience and knowledge to determine if your company will receive the desired results, how to get the organization prepared, and knowing how to gauge the company's capabilities is imperative to attain success.

Over the last decades, global outsourcing has grown tremendously in preparation for national differences in cost and quality resources such as labor or raw materials. A manager's job is more challenging in a dynamic global environment because of the increased intensity of competition that goes hand in hand with the lowering of barriers to trade and investment. These types of global exchanges are becoming more complex to the everyday leader. Women must have "hands on" experience, and the ability to negotiate effectively in making global deals with global businesses. The leader will need to be educated in the law, rules and regulations, and most importantly the cultural differences of those countries to be an effective leader in the 21st century. As stated by Jones and George (2011, pp. 200-203),

> The basic building blocks of national culture are values and norms. Cultural differences are important implications to managers because of the differences that exist from one country to the next. Managers will need to keep in mind that management practices must be tailored to suit the cultural contexts within which an organization operates.

An approach that is effective in the United States may not be effective in another country. It is imperative that managers are sensitive to the value systems and norms of that country and behave accordingly. Managers must realize that organizations and organizational members reflect their national culture's emphasis on individualism or collectivism. For example, Japanese culture values collectivism and the U.S. values individualism.

There are several reasons why differences in national cultures have important implications for managers. Because of cultural differences, management practices in the U.S. might be totally different in other countries or cultures. When doing business with other cultures, management practices must be tailored to the culture you are doing business in. It is said "when in Rome, do as the Romans." Not only must managers be sensitive to the value systems and norms of the other country, they also must act accordingly. Finally, a cultural diverse management team can be a source of strength for an organization participating in a global marketplace.

Educating managers in diversity can help managers and subordinates gain a better understanding of how people may interpret communication differences. Managers are required to increase their efforts to focus on diversity skills to help them communicate and interact with diverse workforce. Managers must be open to different approaches and perspectives and must possess the flexibility needed to understand and appreciate diverse perspectives (Jones & George, 2011, pp. 166, 171).

Diversity in the workplace is a great opportunity to increase competitiveness in the global economy and capitalize on the unique talents and contributions that diverse groups bring to the table (Kerby & Burns, 2013). Women of color own 1.9 million firms which generate annually $165 billion in revenue and employ over 1.2 million people. Kirby and Burns stated that by 2050, there will not be a racial or ethnic majority in the United States; therefore it stands to reason that the makeup of the boardrooms will need to change to reflect the demographics.

Irene Dorner, CEO of HSBC, USA, stated in a *New York Times* article, "As she sees it, diversity is not just a moral issue, but also a good business decision. I think that you are insane commercially if you run any corporation and you turn down the opportunity for different views, innovation and a different way of thinking." Achieving diversity in the workplace is not limited to the women vying for top executive positions, it is the very essence of what is required if a company is expected to take advantage of achieving success in today's business environment. When the company does not recognize the benefits of diversity, the effects of that can negatively impact the development of growth in talent, and eliminate the possibility of the company being competitive in the economic market.

The new "crop" of talent coming from law schools and medical schools indicates that between 40 to 50 percent are women. Over 35 percent of American MBA degrees are awarded to women (Hill, 1993, p. 26). This is a great opportunity for organizations to select from the best and brightest, and achieve greater diversity in the workplace. Although women are receiving the education needed to handle these types of concerns, education alone will not suffice, great negotiations skills is a must.

Negotiation is an effective method of conflict resolution in which parties consider various alternative ways to allocate resources to come up with a solution acceptable to all of them. Managers can use various strategies to facilitate integrative bargaining. They are emphasizing superordinate goals; focus on the goal not the people; focusing on interest, not demands; creating new options for joint gain; and focusing on what is fair. Competition that exists for both men and women in the 21st century is indirect and direct competition. Direct competitors are those who are in the same industry as the company under consideration. Indirect competitors are businesses that offer the same product or service, but not as their primary service. Either type will require a leader that is sophisticated in negotiation skills, market savvy, and who is able to anticipate advances in technology.

Having great negotiation skills is not limited to successfully bargaining for contracts for the company, you can also use the same skills to bargain for pay equality for yourself. Negotiation skills are a must if you expect to accomplish your personal and professional goals as they relate to pay equality. Women should know their worth as it relates to pay, and be able to effectively negotiate by selling their skills, qualifications and achievements. Some steps women can take to improve their negotiation skills:

- Doing your homework and research is imperative in helping you make decisions in determining what equal pay is for you. Research should encompass taking a look at what others in similar positions are earning.
- Instead of accepting the first offer, you can negotiate by communicating any positive contributions you have made or are making to the company, and also articulate any recent problems you have solved for the company and/or ideas that have brought value to the company.
- Most importantly having confidence and portraying yourself as confident is crucial to your negotiation skills both personally and professionally.

Language barriers are one of the most common barriers and language capability has a direct impact on their negotiation skills. Words such as assertive, ambitious, decisive, are commonly associated with positive qualities of managers and negotiators; however if a woman has these same qualities it is sometimes perceived as negative and can remove their chances of future promotions. With confidence in their own abilities and strengths, and a desire to succeed, women have the potential to be great negotiators by overcoming any internal and external barriers they are faced with. In an effort to maximize value over time, women can build on their negotiation skills by being knowledgeable to increase productivity and profit, and thus strengthen their competitive position.

Microsoft CEO's Comment on Pay Raises
Due to the widespread presence of the invisible "glass ceiling" in the workplace, women continue to face more challenges in rising management ranks as quickly as men, and wage equality is another major obstacle since many female professionals in the United States earn about 20-22% less than their male colleagues. In other words, American women earn about $11,000 less each year than their male colleagues. So business leaders and politicians need to do more to equalize this compensation inequality in the workplace. The first step is awareness that this problem exists and then modeling what needs to be done through his or her words and behaviors in order for the system to be fair to female employees in the workplace. Sadly, even top leaders make grave mistakes when they are not fully aware of the challenges and how to best minimize gender compensation inequality.

During an interview on October 9, 2014, Microsoft's South-Asian born CEO from India, Satya Nadella became under enormous scrutiny and criticism for his comments about women not asking for a raise being good Karma. Nadella was interviewed by Maria Klawe, who is the President of Harvey Mudd College as well as a Microsoft director, at the Grace Hopper Conference of Women in Computing. In this interview, Nadella was asked about his suggestion to female professionals who are not comfortable asking for a salary raise in the workplace. Nadella, who became CEO of the world's largest software maker in February 2014, said that not asking for a raise can be "one of the additional superpowers that, quite frankly, women who don't ask for a raise have. Because that's good karma. It'll come back because somebody's going to know that's the kind of person that I want to trust."

Nadella said "It's not really about asking for the raise, but knowing and having faith that the system will actually give you the right raises as you go along." Taking advantage of this "teachable moment", President Klawe, immediately disagreed with Nadella, politely recommending that women should ask for a raise when they are not being paid fairly.

Upon some reflection and to do some damage control, Nadella later said he believes men and women should get equal pay and that the industry must eliminate the gender gap. He continued to say that he wholeheartedly supports programs at Microsoft and in the industry that bring more women into the technology field and those initiatives that close the pay gap for women. He confirmed his belief that men and women should get equal pay for equal work in all industries.

So if you think you deserve a raise in your job, then you should just ask for a raise. Regardless of your gender, you must be prepared to ask for a raise by planning properly and to do it at the right time and in the right manner. As President Klawe recommended during this interview with Microsoft CEO, do your homework to make sure you know what the right salary should be for your job in the industry and then role play asking for a specific amount of raise with a friend that you trust. Then go and ask for it at the right time.

Asking for the Compensation that You Deserve
As a male or female professional in the workplace, keep in mind that you are your brand and should get every professional accolade you deserve. However, salary and compensation discussions are often a sensitive and uncomfortable issue for most people (both males and females) because they do not want to appear egotistical and materialistic, or they simply do not want their bosses to be embarrassed. However, it is important to reflect on how to ask for a raise or promotion you truly deserve. Now we will discuss the importance of receiving a fair salary and asking for an earned raise or promotion at the best time and with the right approach to maximize the probability of achieving one's goal.

Compensation and Raises
A brand is built over time through one's education, knowledge, behavior, character, and overall vision. For example, the Coca Cola's brand is worth around 70 billion dollars; the McDonald's brand is worth over 25 billion dollars; and the Oprah Winfrey's brand's value is estimated to be near 3 billion dollars. The creation of these strong brand values for products, companies and individuals did not just happen overnight, but rather came about through years of deliberate effort to grow their name and image.

In today's competitive workplace for top jobs, personal branding will continue to be a very important consideration in the recruitment of leaders. Perhaps, in some cases when it comes to job hunting, personal branding will be more important than Company or Product Branding. Your personal brand ultimately emerges from the search for your identity and meaning in life. A clear personal brand can provide you with positive energy and confidence in the workplace. In general, people with a strong brand usually believe that they have a personal mission or duty to succeed in their calling or what they deem to be important. As such, they learn everything about their "calling" and work hard to make contributions in that area. Whether it is the building of one's personal brand or professional corporate image for a product, one must strive toward excellence, improve continuously, and make sure that he or she lives up to the expectations in both the real and ideal worlds. In the workplace, if you think you have lived up to the expectations of your superiors, colleagues, and customers, then you should be getting what you are truly worth to the company.

Compensation is an important topic for workers and managers of all organizations. Workers need their salaries to support their families and hobbies. Managers use compensation strategies to achieve the goals of their departments and organizations. Traditionally though, most companies have provided employee reviews and raises either annually or more often based on their rules and policies. While this might still be the case in many firms, raises are not always offered to employees on a regular basis and this is especially true during recessionary times. Therefore, employees have to build the courage to ask for a raise at the right time. If you think you deserve more money for the work you do, then you should ask for it before it negatively impacts your overall morale toward your job or the organization. So it is best to have a frank talk with your boss, ask for the raise, and/or understand the facts surrounding your case. It is understandable that asking for a raise can be uncomfortable and stressful for everyone, and even more challenging for those who come from collective and high-context cultures where patronage relationships are the norm. In patronage relationships where power distance between managers and employees are high, a paternalistic or reciprocal relationship is expected where the managers take care of their employees and the workers remain loyal in return. It could be even more embarrassing, awkward, and challenging to ask for a raise in such an environment since managers carry their positions in the community and employees do not want them to be embarrassed or "lose face" when wishes regarding raises cannot be granted on an individual basis. So employees continue to do their work and managers try to remain fair by giving everyone an increase when profits are high.

Whether you are living in an individualistic or collective society, work is a reality of life for building a fair living and for making worthwhile and purposeful contributions to good causes in society. Some people work very hard and others hardly work. Whether you hardly work or work very hard, you deserve to be fairly compensated for your time, skill, knowledge, and overall output. For most people, one purpose of work is to earn a fair salary for the output of their skill or expertise and a secondary reason would be to do something that contributes to the enhancement of one's skills as well as the well-being of the society. While the secondary reason becomes more important as one's need for monetary income diminishes, a fair compensation often remains a very important concern, even for people who are financially rich.

You can get a "free lunch" every now and then from the generosity of others in society. However, there is no "free lunch" when you expect it every day or every week, especially when you do not deserve it. The same is true for increasing your income and salary. If you work hard and enhance your overall value, then you are likely to be deserving of more income in the marketplace. Conduct some research to see if you deserve a raise by looking at what similar jobs at your company or other firms are currently paying in your area. You can type the word "salary surveys" on popular search engines and get a number of credible places that can offer information about salaries in your profession. There are many firms and online resources such as PayScale or Monster.com that provide salary information for different jobs. Before asking for the raise, make sure you deserve it and/or are ready for more responsibilities. If your output is worth less than the salary you are getting, then you probably do not deserve a raise and asking for it might be a waste of time. Assume that you are the boss to honestly assess your performance and clarify why a manager would give you a raise. The theory or law of compensation states that you would be directly and proportionally compensated according to the following three variables: 1) the market need for what you do and your overall skills; 2) your ability to fill this market need, and 3) your substitutability or the ease with which you can be replaced by internal or external candidates. If others can get your work done for less income, then why would a firm pay you more money than the market value? So measure your contributions, assess your true market value, enhance your skills so you can contribute more, and make sure you are producing more than you are getting paid before asking for a raise. Then, plan to ask for a raise and be prepared to make suggestions on what additional responsibilities you can perform to become more valuable to the department and organization. You can follow the "Steps in Asking for a Raise / Promotion Model" presented in Figure 1.1 which starts with self-assessment.

Prior to asking for a raise, one must understand the manager's side and ask for a raise at the right time, in the right way, and in the right place. Managers are often limited by budgetary constraints as well as minimum and maximum wage levels for different job titles and job categories. In some cases, getting more money means moving into a new job or department which can enable one to make more money. It should be remembered that receiving a raise is not just about getting more money since additional opportunities and benefits can come in different forms such as promotions, cross-functional training and skill building, having a vacation, getting a bonus, getting stock options, extra days off, leaving work early, receiving better healthcare benefits, etc. Remain flexible and open-minded to take good notes of your manager's suggestions which can lead to future raises and promotions.

If you can demonstrate or provide evidence that you have earned a raise, then more income or additional benefits will definitely be in your future. The best way to get the raise you deserve is to exceed the goals and expectations of your boss and higher administrators. One can focus on enhancing the bottom-line by increasing revenues, improving quality, decreasing cost, and adding value in whatever ethical means possible. You should always work for the greater good and long-term success of the organization. There are many approaches and steps involved in asking for more income or a promotion. Of course, what you actually do depends on such factors as your readiness, your relationship with the boss, the financial status of the organization, your personal and professional worth to the department or the company, and your future potential for value creation in the organization. If you are a valuable member of the organization, then you also need to know the needs of your boss, department, and the organization in order to ask for a raise in the appropriate manner and time.

Figure 1.1 - Steps in Asking for a Raise / Promotion Model

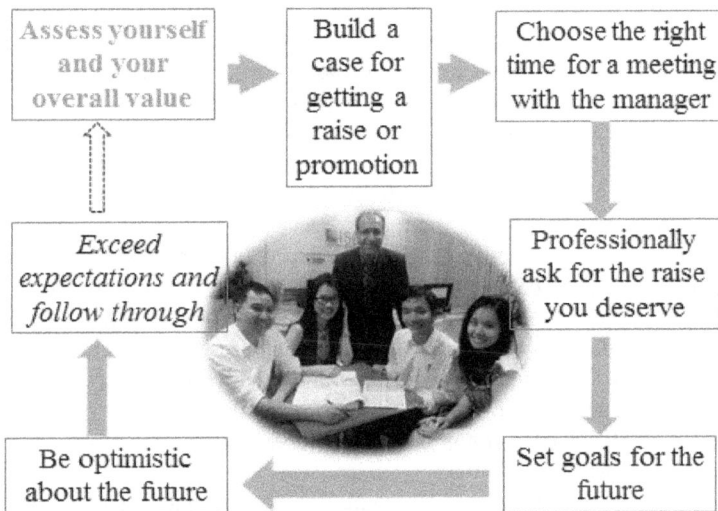

Before asking for a raise, educate yourself as much as possible about the status and financial well-being of your organization, and whether your boss can actually award an increase in your salary at this time. If you do many great things for the organization, do not forget to "toot your own horn" when needed –as they say, if you don't "toot your own horn" then others may simply use it as a spittoon. Make your accomplishments clear to your colleagues and your boss. If you are doing well, mention it and make sure your boss knows about your overall contributions because effective leaders want to retain productive and cooperative employees. When layoffs are a necessity in the organization, this situation can create opportunities for a raise for those who have to pick up the extra work of employees who are laid off. While there are many things you can do to have a better chance of getting a salary increase that you supposedly deserve, the following are some considerations for your reflection in this process:

Assess yourself and your overall value. You get paid based on what your expertise and time are worth to others in the market. Based on this concept, you can increase your salary by increasing your overall worth or value to others in society. Be good at what you do and try to become better than the best so you can be a value-added member of the organization. Not only will this help in preventing you from getting laid off during recessionary times, but it can also lead to raises and promotions. There is no real substitute for hard work, skill and dedication to one's passion. You can increase your salary by working more hours, getting a second job, and/or increasing your overall worth and value to others. The third option is usually a great way to also earn a raise. Assess your situation to make sure you have earned a raise or promotion. The manager might ask "What have you done for me lately?" Be ready to answer this question immediately and provide the "value-added" aspect of your work. So if you truly think you have earned a raise, then a raise you shall get sooner or later. Think of yourself as a company and make sure you know the KPIs (key performance indicators) for your job and your overall results for the past week, month, and year(s). If you do not know how you have contributed to the success of your organization, then you are likely to lose the job at any time. Assess your overall contribution or life-time value (LTV) to the organization so you can give it to your boss during the meeting and this will make it easier for him/her to lean toward an affirmative response. Plan to discuss why you deserve a raise or promotion. Plan to be a professional and tactful throughout the process to negotiate your way to the desired amount of income or promotion that you deserve. Using salary data in the city, state or industry, compare your work and your output with others who have similar qualifications and jobs. Have data and facts to provide to the manager during your scheduled meeting about the raise or promotion.

Build a case for getting a raise or promotion. Track your success and document it as this will make it easier for your boss to see your contributions and consider giving you the raise. In some departments and organizations, hard work is not always recognized or rewarded; therefore you will need to formally campaign and ask for the reward or raise you deserve. Build a business case for getting a raise so you can campaign like the politicians for your goals. You should be able to thoroughly and confidently explain why you deserve a raise or promotion. If you think you are poor and getting poorer in society, then this might be a discussion you should have with your financial advisor or therapist, not your boss. If you are near bankruptcy or will soon lose your house or car if you don't make the monthly payments, then try to borrow money from a friend. This unfortunate situation means you truly need more money to become financially healthier, but it does not mean that you deserve a raise. You should not go to your boss and say you need a raise since your upcoming wedding is costing more money than originally planned. A desperate need for money does not equate to being worthy of a raise. If you need more money, then get a second job or ask to work more hours. Do not confuse what you need with what you are worth in the marketplace. You might be worthy of a raise if you are adding more value to the firm than most others within and outside of the company. So it is very important that you keep the discussion with your manager about your work performance, your qualifications for more income, and your overall value to the organization.

Choose the right time for a meeting with the manager. Choose the right time to have a discussion about the raise or promotion with your boss. You might be deserving of a raise when you have been successfully doing about twenty percent more work than what you were hired to do, or if you are doing twenty percent more work since your last raise. A best time to ask for a raise might be when you have just received good news or if the company received good news and you had a part in it. Perhaps Thursdays or paydays might be a good time to schedule a meeting for discussing the raise. The end of the fiscal year is probably not the right time for a raise since this might be the time when most managers are preparing their budgets for the next year or are answering for their spending of the past year. Therefore managers might be a bit too stressed in such days and weeks when they are dealing with annual budgets.

Ask for what you deserve. Ask for what you want in a realistic and sincere manner. Tell your boss that "I would like to explain some of my major accomplishments and why I believe I deserve a raise." Explain the facts about why you deserve a raise and then ask for a specific increase. If you do not ask for it, then the chances of getting a raise is very small. Even though most managers are fair and want to be just, they are busy individuals who are guided by budgetary constraints. So ask for the raise if you think you deserve it. While you should expect a positive answer, be prepared for a "no" answer as well as to effectively and professionally negotiate alternatives to a raise when extra income is not an option due to budget limitations. Keep in mind that in many cases a "no" response is getting you one step closer to the affirmative answer. The "no" answer should lead to the question of "Why and/or what can I do to earn a raise in the next opportunity?" Remember that people like to know what is in it for them. So explain to your boss the benefits of you receiving a raise or promotion.

Set goals for the future. Strategically partner with your manager to get the raise or promotion you deserve or would like to have in the future. Volunteer to help when new and upcoming challenging or time-consuming projects. Agree to work on projects and times that nobody likes to work on. When possible, befriend the manager as your mentor or coach and jointly set goals for the upcoming quarter and year. The best way to get what you want is to be clear about your desired objectives, write it down, create a process or a road map for getting there, and then follow the road map in a step-by-step process until you achieve it.

Be optimistic about the future. Be positive and respond appropriately to the answers given by the manager. Don't "burn your bridges" since a raise and promotional opportunities might be available in the coming months or year(s). Do not leave with hurt feelings. It is important that you become very clear on future opportunities for getting more income or the job responsibilities / promotion you want. Remember and reflect on the fact that increasing your compensation can be done through more salary or gaining additional benefits (vacation, stock options, extra days off, etc.). Show that you truly care about the organization and the success of your boss. Treat the organization as if you are the owner. Demonstrate that money is the means to an end and not necessarily the ultimate objective—show that you truly love what you do. Be a cheerleader at the office, especially in difficult economic times.

Exceed expectations and follow through. Be appreciative of the guidance, goals and expectations provided by the manager. Exceed the expectations of your boss by doing more than you jointly agreed upon, and complete everything ahead of the expected due dates. When you know that you definitely deserve a raise or promotion based on your assessment and credentials, then schedule a time for another meeting with the manager to follow up on getting a raise or promotion.

When you are asking for a raise, demonstrate confidence, multitasking ability, the intention of volunteerism, professional appearance because when you feel better you will also look better, and being a morale booster in the department. Volunteer to do more tasks before the start of your day, during your lunch times, and after work hours. Volunteering toward worthwhile causes is a great way to enhance your skills and chances of getting noticed by colleagues and managers in your department. It should be noted that colleagues play a critical role in one's advancement in the department. You do not have to befriend or like your colleagues or even agree with them on all issues; however, it is very important that your colleagues respect you and believe in your true intentions toward the betterment of the organization. If your colleagues see that you are working hard, they will recommend you for raises and promotional opportunities—or at least they will not stand in your way when an advancement opportunity presents itself. Managers think about employees who are respected by their colleagues when they are making layoff, salary and promotional decisions. So make sure to respect your coworkers for their knowledge and wisdom, hear their thoughts, cooperate with them especially when it is in the best interest of the organization, and ask for their guidance when you need it.

The selection of the appropriate time is another important issue for the discussion of getting a raise or promotion with managers. What days and times are best for discussing the money issue with your boss? Mondays and Fridays are usually busy times for managers and employees. Also, most mornings are hectic for department managers as they might have meetings to deal with revenue and sales issues from the day before. Thursdays seem to be one best day for setting an appointment with the manager to discuss getting a raise since this is often a payday for some firms. Therefore, try to choose an appropriate time for this important discussion. Make sure there is about a thirty-minute window of idle time for the interaction or goal-setting process of this discussion. The best time to ask for a raise is right when you have been given more responsibilities and soon after you have completed an important task or project. So plan the timing based on your achievements, the manager's schedule and his/her availability. Schedule the meeting and ask for the raise. Expect to get the raise but be prepared for a "no" response. Since you know your market value or BATNA (best alternative to a negotiated agreement), if and when relevant, have an exit strategy. Know that you have the choice of staying or simply leaving to the next best available offer when it is the right time. If your manager or employer does not recognize and reward you fairly for your overall output, then find another organization that will compensate you more justly based on your real or perceived expertise and market value.

Simply Ask for the Raise You Deserve
In recessionary times when salaries are lower than ever and prices are higher than most previous years, a little boost in weekly or monthly earnings for most families could be very helpful. Instead of seeing a recession as an impediment, you can see this as an opportunity to do more work in creative or cost-saving manner which can enhance your opportunities for getting a raise. With a new paradigm and a positive mental attitude, visualize prosperity and imagine yourself getting a raise that you rightly deserve. Think and speak affirmatively with statements such as "promotion and money flow smoothly to me at all times. I deserve a raise and I will receive a raise." By mentally repeating such positive statements, your mind will automatically think of different ways to enhance your skills and ability to do more so you can receive the well-deserved raise or promotion in due time. When you truly believe that you definitely deserve a raise, then you can easily use the following steps as a guide:
1. Assess yourself and your overall value.
2. Build a case for getting a raise or promotion.
3. Choose the right time for a meeting with the manager.
4. Ask for what you deserve.
5. Set goals for the future.
6. Be optimistic about the future.
7. Exceed expectations and follow through.

Regardless of the immediate outcome, realize that a "no" answer today does not mean a "no" answer tomorrow, next month, or next year. Circumstances and situations can change in your favor and you can influence decisions toward a raise for you by being a value-creating employee and a good role-model in the organization. So always work hard and continue to do an excellent job to energize or impress yourself, your colleagues, and your boss by working diligently to create a competitive advantage for your team, department and company. Learn more, do more tasks, and energize others to look positively toward the future. Go beyond the requirements of your job description. By doing this, your manager will be more likely to notice your performance and positive contributions to the organization; and s/he will have to recognize and honor your value-added work in order to reinforce such good behavior throughout the department and organizational culture. If your hard work makes extra revenues and money for the company, then you are enhancing and influencing your own future for getting a raise or the promotion. Enhancing the competitiveness of the organization is a great way to guarantee a raise and/or promotion. Start with the ABCs of getting a raise: assess your market value; build a case to get more income; and choose or create the right opportunity to ask for a raise.

The key element of getting a raise that you rightfully deserve is to plan for it, practice asking for it, and then tactfully ask for it. The last step is very important because "if you ask, you shall eventually receive." Ask for what you want and then be open to hear what your manager has to say about the raise and promotion. Be thankful and implement your manager's suggestions in a timely manner. Try to do something that you enjoy doing while making this world a little better. If you leave this world a little better than you found it while doing something that earned you a fair salary, then that is the ultimate or ideal type of work. Always aim for the ideal job that you would love to have, and once you get it make sure to do a great job, and a fair salary will be its natural corollary. Aim strategically and realistically, eventually you will get there.

Value Driven Management
Value Driven Management is a concept which claims that what a person values is likely to have a great influence over his or her thinking, feelings and behaviors. In both their professional and personal life, women value inclusivity in the workplace, freedom from stereotyping, working conditions that support work-life balance, and opportunities for advancement. They are also concerned with and value relationships in the workplace, equity, respect, fairness and open communication and collaboration. Basic everyday values that are used in our daily lives tend to not have the same power in the workplace. Skills such as multitasking come natural for most women because they use it daily to address family needs. Women are considered to be active listeners, which make them more customer-oriented; with their participative decision making skills, they are good mentors to their subordinates and who are able to build teams by "letting go", as their self-esteem is multifaceted.

A workplace culture that is positive and agreeable to women adds value over time because it helps the business retain the skilled talents, compete effectively in the diverse markets, improve decision making skills by having different opinions, and reduce turnover costs. Women in business are obligated to bring value adders to their organizations, such as continuous improvement opportunities, a formula that goes beyond product and services and provide customer delight, and concern for their employees that will ultimately bring immeasurable achievements. Other value adders will be in the form of being a part of a company that is socially and corporately responsible, and a leader that can utilize the company's resources effectively and efficiently. Increasing the number of women in the workforce to help drive innovation and operational improvements is definitely adds value. To improve corporate performance and help raise national productivity, you will need to hire top skilled women with talent to enhance job productivity. The success of any business is predicated on whether or not it has the right people doing the right jobs. The business has to be able to retain and attract those with skills and talents to help take the business to the next level. From the personal perspective of adding value, women have innate qualities that are instrumental in helping them with their career endeavors. As leaders, they tend to have strong people skills which enable them to see situations from all sides and weigh them appropriately. Studies have shown that women are much more inclusive than men; and they seem to be more effective in the team building style of leadership.

Women will need to maintain their belief in themselves and their qualifications and continue to make contributions to the organization. As stated by Barsh and Yee (2013), transitioning women from individual contributors to next level management is a positive for the company and for women. Women that have moved to the next level management tier have already shown they are a value to the organization by working hard to get to that level. When companies take advantage of those opportunities to promote those highly skilled women, this will put women in a position to become mentors or role models for "up and coming" women executives. Taking advantage of these opportunities will also help companies rebalance their executive board, which may increase the possibility of satisfying gender diversity.

Some studies have shown that gender diversity on the boards can lead to improved shareholder return growth. Other suggested benefits include a fresh perspective to the norms and add value to the overall success of the organization. A recent survey by RSA, the executive search firm, looked at the UK life sciences industry and found that "women bring empathy and intuition to leadership" with nearly two-thirds of respondents (62 per cent) thinking that women contribute differently in the boardroom, compared to their male colleagues. While other research by Herminia Ibarra, *Professor of Leadership and Learning at Insead Business School*, suggests men and women network differently – men are more likely to network upwards, whereas women try to network with other women.

Value-destroyers include not promoting women with skills to leadership roles, lack of female role models high in the organization, lack of colleagues' support to help them achieve their goals and provide opportunities, and lastly stereotypically imbedded institutional and individual mindsets.

It is imperative for any organization to make sure the make-up of the board is indicative of the customer base. It would be counterintuitive to think that an all men board will understand the needs and wants of a female dominated product or service. Gender diversity on the board will point out to shareholders and those alike that management supports the organizational structure, and values that are necessary to effect positive changes. One way to effect change is to have a commitment by top executives to implement programs to develop women as leaders, and create an environment that is supportive of coaching and mentoring women for top positions in their company.

Market-based Management
According to Gable and Ellig (993), market-based management focuses on discovering organizational structures, responsibilities, values, and incentives that motivate people to advance a common mission. Perhaps leaders can implement

some of the philiosophies of market-based management into their business by creating an environment that rewards employees for being creative and innovative. Although there are several concepts to the philiosophy, knowledge generation and communication are a couple that will be discussed briefly. These two would be a great place to start especially since many businesses have not taken advantage of these concepts.

The purpose of knowledge generation is to empower employees to freely communicate their ideas to management. To accomplish this task, we suggest having several available channels (not just a specific person) to disburse information. To employ an example of empowerment in this area is to set up a scheduled time for women that are interested in sharing their input; this will make them feel as though they are adding value to the organization. Being flexible in their style of management will eliminate reluctancy on the part of the selected employees to participate, and offer ideas. This will in turn encourage employees to participate in programs that will eventually benefit the employee and the organization by increasing revenue and improving morale. Managers that are able to show flexibility in their management style will encourage employees to share their ideas and give them a sense of pride in being a part of the organziation.

Communicating the vision of the organization in a way that everyone can understand will prove beneficial in the long term. The vision of the organization should be known by every employee and should be visible. In most organization the vision is articulated from the top down; however the success of that vision is not limited to the sharing, leaders must emulate that vision to all. According to Cato and Jean (2013) of Walden University,

> The alignment of the strategic vision to employee productivity is a key contributor to the success of an organization. This alignment encourages and stimulates employees' creativity so that they can perform more effectively to realize the organizational goals and objectives. A synergistic effort of employees' work effort, along with management best business practices that align with the vision, would yield positive results for an academic institution or an organization.

The value of implementing these concepts are employee increased satisfaction, operational improvements, ideas freely shared by employees, and a sense of pride and fulfillment to the organization. To take advantage of the benefits women bring to the organization, there are several opportunities and recommendations listed below.

Recommendations

- *Executive sponsorship and role models.*

As an executive and leader of the organziation, your responsibility is not limited to handing down orders or exercising power over others. The preferred goal of an executive should be to empower others to achieve their best for themselves and for the company. One way of doing that is to establish an internal department which is responsible for connecting the best and talented skilled personnel with board members and members of the executive team. Matching an executive as a sponsor will help to boost confidence, lead to an increase desire to advance and possibly create opportunities that will not ordinarily exist between upper management and the potential candidate. Another possibility is an opportunity for the candidate to "give back". This can be accomplished by having a candidate that has successfully completed his/her time with a sponsor and has shown proficiency in a particular area, then becoming a sponsor for other candidates that maybe in the employement pool.

- *Cultural change in organization.*

To change the culture of an organization, you must first address the mindset and the behaviors of employees from the top down. This is definitely a difficult feat to say the least; however a successful organization can incorporate simple steps to initiate the process. To effect a cultural change in an organization, leadership must move outside of their current behavioral model and labor together in innovative ways. It will be solely up to the level of commitment by all involved to change. This process to produce change can be a short or a long term endeavor. The first area to be addressed is to make certain the vision of the company is inclusive of change and the vision is reiterated to all employees. When an employee shows reluctance to support the direction of the organization, sometimes it could be as simple as reiterating so that the vision is clear. The commitment is transparent when the leaders are able to model the behavior that is expected and by supporting the vision, values, and objectives of the organization. Make sure the vision is communicated and demonstrated in a way that everyone can understand it and everyone wants to support it. Lastly, management at all levels is encouraged to act with integrity, make sound decisions, and show competence in what they are doing.

- *Identify talented women through a systematic approach and train them.*

Involve HR in the quest to develop programs that will attract women of integrity, dedication, commitment to excellence and the knowledge and skills visible to be considered as an executive. HR can develop or create a testing or skills database where women can test themselves to better understand where their skills are better served. Continued education is a "must" for women that want to contribute on a corporate level. Organizations can offer internal classes geared to improve the skillset of the ambitious, and well qualified women which in turn will increase productivity and overall satisfaction of those interested. Women that are trained and developed, as well as provided real time coaching and feedback will only expand the pool of available women in leadership. Identifying potential leaders can be challenging for any organization, the following are a few things to use when indentifying a potental leader: combine the traditonal format (skills assessments, interviews etc.) along with technology based tools, career goals, proven track records of successful performance, and a high potential to add value to the organization. These combinations should greatly improve your organization's chance of attracting the "best and the brightest".

Summary

Women should attain the highest level of education possible and also should use their networking skills to continue to build relationships that will help take them to the next level. Women that are starting their own business or interested in becoming entrepreneurs may find it more beneficial to focus those new ventures in the area of technology or economic forecasting. In the 21st century, women may need to consider moving away from the notion that in order to be successful; the characteristics of a "shark" are needed to do business with men; perhaps it is time to embark on your own business where you can still do great business and still act like a woman. Women owned businesses are making a huge impact on the economy and continues to grow in numbers and in size.

Although women are better educated than ever, they are still paid less than men. In determining why this is happening, one area we do not give much credence to is that women tend to opt for teaching and social work positions. In the scheme of pay, traditionally these are low paying positions in comparisons to management positions.

Tackling the challenges in the workplace women will need to have confidence in themselves and their ideas. Societies will benefit more by economically empowering and educating women so they will be prepared for leadership. It is imperative that women continue to make progress in promotions and pay, especially for performing the same job as men. It is suggested that if women want to achieve equal pay, they will need to ask for it and negotiate for better compensation packages and recognition. Carol Frohlinger, author of The Shadow Negotiation says, "The reality is that women aren't negotiating money because most women are reluctant to negotiate for themselves."

The success of any organization is predicated on how well the management team handles changes, challenges and obstacles. Top management need to consider executing change in a fair and concise manner, and making sure the level of competency is equal. Businesses need to make it clear that men and women are afforded the same opportunities regardless of gender, decisions are respected, and contributions are recognized. To establish and maintain an open work environment, companies must increase women in the position of leadership, and in turn this visibility will show other women they have someone to advocate for them.

If one lacks the necessary behaviors or skill to attain their goals, B.F. Skinner suggests operant conditioning theory. In this theory people learn to perform behaviors that lead to desired consequences and learn not to perform behaviors that lead to undesired consequences. In other words, if women are to move to the next level in management and sit alongside men at the head of the boardroom table, they must be motivated to perform at a level where performance and goal attainment brings them to the desired outcome. Of course if the executives are offering positive reinforcement for these individuals, it would make it more likely that the desired behavior would be repeated more often to get to their goal.

Something as simple as reading books written by successful women leaders in the field of your interest can be beneficial in improving your skill-set. Figure out what successful women such as Sheryl Sandberg, author of *"Lean In"* Hillary Clinton, Former Secretary of State, and Anne Marie Slaughter, Princeton Professor did right, then use that knowledge to work out a career plan. In *Lean In,* Sheryl Sandberg examines why women's progress in achieving leadership roles has stalled, explains the root causes, and offers compelling, commonsense solutions that can empower women to achieve their full potential. The concept of "Leaning In" may be a powerful way of getting where you want to go, but keep in mind that too much "leaning in" can cause dysfunctions in other areas of your life. Learn how to achieve a balance between *"leaning in"* and enjoying your life, the ability to accomplish this enormous feat is far better than ending up wondering what happened to your personal life.

In preparation for the changes in the 21st Century, women will need to prepare to launch out into the deep and present themselves as a force to be reckoned with. Women must display and own their talents, skills and abilities, speak up for themselves, have confidence in their level of knowledge and stand for what they believe it. Women must maintain their level of integrity in the workplace and focus on ways to effectively deal with the changes and challenges that will impact our society and economy.

References

Barsh, J., & Yee, L. (2013, August 24). *Unlocking the full potential of women in the U.S. economy.* Retrieved from Wall Street Journal McKinsey & Company: http://online.wsj.com

Cato, S. T., & Jean, G. (2013, December). *Relationship of the strategic vision alignment to employee .* Retrieved from Research in Higher Education Journal Walden University: http://www.aabri.com

Charles Koch Institute. (2013, July 14). Retrieved from Charles Koch Institute Management: http://www.charleskochinstitute.org/mbm/

Gable, W. & Ellig, J. (1993). Introduction to Market-Based Management. Fairfax, Virginia, United States of America.

Greenlaw, P. S., & P, K. J. (1996). Creative Thinking and Sexual Harrassment. *SAM Advancement Management Journal*, 4.

Hill, R. J. (1993, July 26). Women and work - is the glass ceiling coming down? *Risk Management.*

Jones, G. R. & George, J. M. (2011). *Contemporary Management .* New York: McGraw-Hill Irwin.

Kerby, S. & Burns, C. (2013, July 12). *American Progress.* Retrieved March 24, 2014, from The Top 10 Economic Facts of Diversity in the Workplace: http://www.americanprogress.org/issues/labor/news

McMillion, R. (May 2010). Payday Equality: ABA Urges Congress to Bolster Laws Curbing Gender-based Wage Discrimination. *ABA Journal*, 67.

Mujtaba, B. G. (2007). *Cross Cultural Management and Negotiation Practices.* Florida: ILEAD Academy Publications.

Pettit, B. & Ewert, S. (2009). Employment Gains And Wage Declines: The Erosion Of Black Women's Relative Wages Since 1980*. *Demography (Pre-2011), 46*(3), 469-92.

Preziosi, R. C. (1996). *Value-Based Leadership for the 21st Century.* San Diego, CA.: Pfeiffer & Company .

Rooke, D., & Torbert, W. R. (2005, April 1). *Harvard Business Review*. Retrieved from Seven
	Transformations of Leadership: http://aliainstitute.org
Rothkopf, D. (2013). The Balance of Power. *Foreign Policy*, 104-103.
The Wall Street Journal. (2013, July 23). Retrieved from CFO Journal: http://deloitte.wsj.com/cfo
Torregrosa, L. L. (2011, November 1). *Progress for Women, but a Long Way to Go*. Retrieved from The
	New York Times: http://www.nytimes.com
Walsh, M. (1998). In M. Walsh, *Incorporating Women: A History of Women and Business in the United
	States*. New York: Twayne Publishers.
Worldwide Guide to Women in Leadership. (2013, July 13). Retrieved July 23, 2013, from
	Guide2Women Leaders: http://www.guide2womenleaders.com/

CHAPTER 2
Sophists and Machiavellianism in Society

By: Frank J. Cavico and Bahaudin G. Mujtaba
Nova Southeastern University

Introduction

The word "sophist" originally carried neither negative connotation nor disparaging reference. It merely meant teacher, professor, intellectual, disseminator of ideas, or practitioner of wisdom. The Sophists emerged with distinction in the latter decades of the fifth century B.C. in Greece, a period marked by substantial political and social transformation. Democracy was politically rising, but the affluence and authority of the old aristocratic families had not yet receded. The ascendance and expansion of democracy afforded many political opportunities, provided one possessed not only intelligence and ambition but also the knowledge and skills to prevail over one's adversaries. The possessors of such intelligence and ambition were mostly men who acquired the lessons which are still being practiced to get ahead, often at a cost to other equally qualified females.

The Sophists traveled from city to city, offering schooling and supplying education to those who could afford to pay. They professed a wide variety of skills and knowledge; those essential to success in law and politics were most in demand. Since most of their paying clients were men who wanted to be in charge and in powerful positions through learning and what came to be known as "Machiavellianism", men became the better educated gender in networking, politicking and getting what they wanted in the workplace. Some of these "power" tactics and practices are still present in the modern society. As such, this chapter focuses on understanding the history of Sophists and the meaning of Machiavellianism in the modern society.

The Sophists as Teachers

As the Sophists journeyed throughout Greece and the Mediterranean, they came to know of and report on the many peoples and cultures of the ancient world; they perceived diverse customs, practices, religions, governments, laws, beliefs, and values. The Sophists' own views were far from uniform, but one can sense a predilection toward relativism permeating their thinking. To Socrates, the Sophists conveyed ideas which he believed should be condemned as false and dangerous ones.

The Sophists did not establish any particular philosophical school or even hold one set of opinions; rather, they came into prominence as a profession of itinerant teachers. Some were in fact well versed in philosophy; others knew science, astronomy, mathematics, music, rhetoric, language, grammar, and memory training. In fifth century B.C. Greece there were no universities, law schools, colleges, adult education centers, and no public provision for education. There were no professional lawyers. The parties to a lawsuit appeared in person and made their own presentation and argumentation to a panel of judges composed of lay persons. There clearly was a need for professional instruction. The Sophists were the first professional teachers in Greece. The emphasis in their teaching was to impart practical knowledge and to inculcate practical skills, especially in the areas of law and politics. They taught material that would be useful to their fee-paying students. They concentrated on the knowledge and skills that were essential to advance one's position in society. Rhetoric, for example, was a leading subject for aspiring politicians and potential "lawyers." The methodologies of the Sophists also varied. Some conducted conventional classes; others gave lectures to large or small groups; others employed discussion groups or seminars; and some held question and answer sessions. They spoke on prepared themes from a written text, invited questions and commentary from the audience, and conducted rhetorical exercises (especially structured to show how the most unpromising position could be maintained). Many young ambitious adults with the means to pay attended their presentations and were educated in this new "school" of self-awareness, self-satisfaction, self-realization, and ultimately "sophistication."

Rhetoric
The study of rhetoric was particularly useful in a society where a great deal depended upon the ability to influence public opinion and to advocate a position in the law courts. Persuasive public speaking was, and still is, an essential component to success, advancement, and the attainment of power. Rhetoric, therefore, was one subject that practically all the Sophists taught. They stressed the important lesson of speaking and arguing with equal clarity and cogency on both sides of an issue. The Sophists instructed their students to see both sides to a question, to recognize the virtues and defects of each position, to approve and disapprove with commensurate vigor, and especially to bolster up the weaker side so that it would seem stronger. Life was in good part a "verbal battle," said the Sophists, and one must win the contest by the "power of words." Therefore, it was a prime necessity to master the art of speaking well and persuasively.

Although the Sophists emphasized the art of disputation, they did not restrict their teaching to mere form and style. In showing how to argue for or against any position, the Sophists also treated the substance of what was being disputed, but only to the extent that such substantive knowledge would be efficacious to the art of argumentation. The Sophists were convinced that people could be persuaded of anything. The emphasis on rhetoric flowed naturally from this cynical sounding and potentially subversive belief. Yet today, one very well might assign to rhetoric the place now occupied by advertising. As the ancient Greeks had the Sophists and "schools" of rhetoric, modern society has its business schools and courses in marketing and advertising.

Although the Sophists were cognizant of ethics and philosophy, their ultimate objective was neither to make the student "good" in the moral sense of the term, nor to assist the student in searching for and attaining the "truth" on any matter. Their aim was to help the student become a good speaker and a good debater and to master all the skills that would make the student successful and dominant in whatever sphere he or she endeavored to enter. The Sophists, viewed in this "sophisticated" light, conceivably can be pictured as the first business consultants, political promoters, and public relations specialists!

The Sophists as Relativists
Protagoras (born 500 B.C.), an important figure in the Sophist fellowship, is credited with the saying: "Man is the measure of all things, seen and unseen." This statement was interpreted to mean that everything is relative to each individual person; that everything is as it seems to each individual person; and that each person has the right to determine for oneself what is good and bad; and that what one considers good, another may consider bad. Such an interpretation leads one down a relativistic path. Morality is relative to the particular perceiver. There are no absolute values, general principles, fundamental rules, or objective standards as to what is right and wrong. When people differ on moral issues, there are no impersonal criteria to decide who is right and who is wrong.

Such relativism engenders a profound mistrust in the possibility of ever attaining absolute knowledge and truth. If there are no rational grounds for knowledge and truth, how can one expect to find any absolute moral values and standards? One consequently becomes skeptical, and skepticism was in fact an attitude shared by the Sophists. If knowledge and truth are only relative to the perceiving subject, then all truth is ephemeral and no one knows anything for certain. Truth, moral or otherwise, is individual and temporary, not universal and eternal. Truth for any person is simply what he or she believes for the moment or what he or she could be convinced of, and the Sophists maintained that it was possible to persuade anyone of anything.

Skepticism led some Sophists to cynicism. If right and wrong, good and bad, and just and unjust are subjective and unreal concepts, they are simply empty words; the Sophists counseled that at times it is prudent and expedient to act as if these notions actually existed. One now can discern the more modern definition of the term "sophist" emerging, with its negative connotations of overly clever but false argumentation and disingenuous reasoning. Relativism, however, did lead some Sophists to more conventional ethical theories. Ethical relativism, a morality based on custom and convention, with moral rules relative to the group that believed in them, can be traced to Sophist thinking. Legal positivism, a morality based on the laws promulgated by a particular group, with the laws serving as the arbiter as to what to accept and observe, also can be traced to the Sophists.

Justice as Power

Thrasymachus, a Sophist described in the first book of Plato's *Republic*, was defiant toward all conventional opinions of justice. He denied that morality and law have anything to do with justice. He admitted that law exists; but what is law, said Thrasymachus, but a set of rules that the ruler (or ruling few or class) imposes on its subjects. Even in a democracy, the law is simply what the majority decides. In every situation, the ruler, whether individual, few, class, or majority, prescribes the law, composes it in its own interest and advantage, and enforces the law with its power. As a consequence, Thrasymachus claimed that there is no justice except the desires and interests of the stronger. In essence, "might makes right." Power becomes the highest virtue; and there are no impersonal objective standards to which to appeal in the struggle for power. Thrasymachus, therefore, repudiated all accepted views of law, morality, and ethics, as well as obedience to a law made only in the interests of the stronger. Act in one's own interest, if one can, and regardless of the law, advised Thrasymachus. The stronger one is, the surer one is of obtaining what one wants.

What about the people who do act conventionally "good" and do abide by the law? They are stupid or weak. Mere conformity, in the sense of submissive obedience, exposes defects in intelligence or character. These people cannot or will not see that morality and law do not serve their interest. Traditionally just people always come off worse than the unjust, both in private transactions and in their relations with government. They thus should violate moral and legal norms when it is advantageous, expedient, and safe to do so. Get what one can, and get what one can get away with; and then worry about one's reputation, since "virtue comes from having money," which is the "ethics" of the Sophist Thrasymachus.

As one can perceive, the Sophists shocked people, especially people for whom philosophy, ethics, morality, and law were a way of life closely tied to religion. To many people, the Sophists seemed to be overly clever and cynical contrivers who made use of specious and disingenuous disputations. To some people, they appeared as utterly immoral; and these perceptions, perhaps, were the origins of the odium that the Sophists incurred and the reasons for the negative connotations of the term "sophistry." Egoism and self-interest generate conflict when people pursue their own, often clashing, interests, but ethical egoism does not resolve these contests. As a consequence, life deteriorates into a long series of conflicts, with each person struggling to win. What then is the "solution"? Do one's very best to prevail! Consequently, any resolution occurs not by the application of any objective ethical principles and moral rules, but by one person "winning" the struggle. Actions, therefore, are not good or bad in themselves but only relatively as they augment or diminish one's power. Virtue and power thereby become one.

Machiavelli

Niccolo Machiavelli (1469-1527), the Italian political philosopher, set out to discover, from history, contemporary events, and his own experience, how principalities are founded, won, held, and lost. Machiavelli's philosophy is regarded as "scientific" in the sense that it is empirical, pragmatic, and rational. For the first time in political theorizing, Machiavelli attempted to look at his materials from a scientific perspective. His attention clearly is on the "what is." What he is accused of leaving out is the "what should be," that is, ethics and morality. His focus is on the manner in which people behave and how society is run, not on expounding the good way to behave or how society should be run. His purposes were to discover how principalities are won, how they are held, and how they are lost; how one becomes a ruler and how a ruler must behave if the ruler wishes to survive and prosper. Machiavelli's most notable work, *The Prince*, is a disturbing book, both for what it says and for the deliberately provocative way Machiavelli says it. *The Prince*, although clearly prefigured in the thinking of the Sophists, is rightfully regarded as a post-medieval philosophical assault launched against traditional ethics and morality.

Machiavelli's Two Key Questions

In *The Prince*, Machiavelli poses two seminal questions: First, what do people strive for? This aim, whatever it is, is their "good." Second, what acts will produce this good? These acts, whatever they are, are "virtues." Machiavelli's answer to the first question is "power." Ultimately, the question becomes one of power. Reality is power. Everyone endeavors to obtain, maintain, and expand one's power. This aim, then, is the "good." Machiavelli does not expect the work of founding a principality or any great enterprise to be undertaken from purely unselfish motives; rather, the impetus stems from the desire for power and the success, fame, and glory that power can achieve. To attain any significant end, power of one kind or another is essential, although this evident fact often is concealed by philosophical slogans to the effect that right, good, and justice will prevail. As to the question, what are the best techniques for securing and maintaining one's power? Machiavelli sets forth and describes the "virtuous" means to the assigned end, regardless of whether the means are considered traditionally good or bad. In order to ascertain these means, it was necessary for Machiavelli to examine human nature.

Machiavelli's Conception of Human Nature and the "Traditional" Virtues

Machiavelli's conception of human nature is an important postulate in his theorizing and an essential aspect of his view of public affairs. Machiavelli's major premise is that people are predominantly egoistic and selfish, unscrupulous and treacherous, envious and greedy, fearful and cowardly, passionate and irrational, and, above all, short-sighted, gullible, and stupid. These are the characteristics that one must take into account when founding a principality or attempting any great enterprise. Machiavelli replaces an optimistic view of human nature with a pessimistic one; human nature is treated, at least for the purpose of public affairs, as "bad." Since people are incapable of governing themselves intelligently, and since their self-seeking drives spawn only disharmony, a strong power is necessary to guide and regulate people and to prevent them from destroying themselves and others.

Observation of the real world in which people live, particularly the world of public affairs, disclosed to Machiavelli so much upheaval, strife, and injustice as to amount to a "moral jungle." A traditionally good virtuous person simply cannot survive, let alone prosper, in a world where most people are not good. Moral standards, therefore, are merely snares for fools. A founder cannot succeed, and a ruler cannot endure, if he or she is always traditionally good. The traditional classical virtues, such as good faith, integrity, temperance, forbearance, charity, and even at times prudence, are contrary to self-interest. They are severe hindrances when dealing with those who ignore any constraints on their self-interest. Machiavelli, consequently, repudiates traditional morality and justice, especially when the conduct of a founder or a ruler is concerned. Machiavelli, in essence, converts the traditional virtues into vices, a "vice" appearing as any behavior that impedes, diminishes, or destroys power. One who pursues the "good" goal of power by moral means in bound to fail. Machiavelli very clearly explains his "real-world" view in Chapter XV of the *Prince*:

> Since I intend to write something useful to an understanding reader, it seemed better to go after the real truth of the matter than to repeat what people have imagined. A great many men have imagined states and princedoms which nobody ever saw or knew in the real world, for there's such a difference between the way we really live and the way we ought to live that the man who neglects the real to study the ideal will learn how to accomplish his ruin, not his salvation. Any man who tries to be good all the time is bound to come to ruin among the great number who are not good. Hence, a prince who wants to keep his post must learn how not to be good, and use that knowledge, or refrain from using it, as necessity requires....For if you look at matters carefully, you will see that something resembling virtue, if you follow it, may be your ruin, while something else resembling vice will lead, if you follow it, to your security and well-being (Machiavelli, *The Prince*, translated and edited by Robert M. Adams, 1977, pp. 44-45).

The Machiavellian "Virtues"
Machiavelli's advice to a founder or ruler, particularly an aspiring one, is to employ the Machiavellian virtues of astute, sharp, cold-blooded calculation of self-interest, readiness to take a risk, and use of whatever means are available to promote the acquisition and maintenance of one's power. One, for example, can use deceit, disguise one's character, and employ hypocrisy. Break promises; do not keep faith when it is against one's interest. Engage in manipulation and propaganda; play upon the passions and stupidity of human beings. Manage others so as to serve one's advantage. Win people over. Persuade them that the one is devoted to their welfare,

yet avoid making any real concessions. Above all, appear more virtuous than one's rivals. So, counseled Machiavelli, in Chapter XVIII of the *Prince* – The Way Princes Should Keep Their Word: "...You must be a great liar and hypocrite. Men are so simple of mind, and so much dominated by their immediate needs, that a deceitful man will always find plenty who are ready to be deceived" (Machiavelli, *The Prince*, translated and edited by Robert M. Adams, 1977, p. 50).

Yet, if all else fails, make oneself feared, even at the risk of being hated (which is nonetheless better than being loved). Force, of course, is "expensive"; so use other means first, but always be prepared to back them up with force and to deal very firmly with those who are not easily deceived or readily manipulated. Only by these "virtues" can the "good" end of power be secured. Machiavelli, in Chapter XVIII of the *Prince*, tellingly titled "The Way Princes Should Keep Their Word," again clearly explains what the shrewd prince should do regarding making promises: "How praiseworthy it is for a prince to keep his word and live with integrity rather than by craftiness, everyone understands; yet we see from recent experience that those princes have accomplished most who paid little heed to keeping their promises, but who knew how craftily to manipulate the minds of men. In the end, they won out over those who tried to act honestly" (Machiavelli, *The Prince*, translated and edited by Robert M. Adams, 1977, p. 49).

As such, pursuant to Machiavellian ethics, a "virtue" is a means to effectuate a given end. No means is rejected if it is necessary to achieve the desired result; any means that diverts or hinders one from pursuing the objective is rejected. The result is a consequentialist type of ethics. If the end is "good," then one must use whatever means is required to achieve a successful result, regardless of how many ethical principles are violated and regardless of whether the means are designated conventionally as good or bad. Any fastidiousness about the means employed is not only inappropriate, but also may be a dereliction of duty. The "means" issue must be treated in a purely pragmatic manner. A "bad" means is nothing more than an ineffective or inadequate one; a "good" means is an efficacious one. Thus, counseled Machiavelli, the Prince "...has to have a mind ready to shift as the winds of fortune and varying circumstances of life may dictate. And as I said..., he should not depart from the good if he can hold to it, but he should be ready to enter on evil if he has to" (Machiavelli, *The Prince*, Chapter 18, translated and edited by Robert M. Adams, 1977, p. 50). Accordingly, for Machiavelli, the only relevant moral criterion for an enterprise is success. Success is right; failure is wrong. Attainment of purpose, acquiring power, wealth, prestige, continuing strength and prosperity, personal and organizational dominance, and, ultimately, fame and glory measurable by the historian, are all part of the Machiavellian value of success.

Public v. Private Morality
Machiavelli does draw a distinction between public morality, appropriate for great enterprises, and private morality, suitable for personal relations. When dealing with personal relationships, such as family and friends, one's egoism, in principle, can be

transcended. One is assumed to regard the good of others as a sufficient reason for acting or not acting. These relationships are based on recognized commitments, distinct duties, and special values; they may claim a measure of altruistic conduct. One may be called upon to suspend or even to sacrifice one's own good for the good of these special others. In the public sphere, however, individuals predominantly are valued only as means to certain ends. These ends, however, may not solely pertain to one person, because if one is involved in public affairs and is undertaking public responsibilities, these ends can, and should be, in the interests of the community. A person acting in a public policy capacity, therefore, shoulders an enlarged burden, because the consequences of public policies are more weighty, more enduring, and affect a greater number of people than mere personal interactions. Accordingly, one playing a public role is obligated to support, protect, and advance the interests of those whom one in some sense represents.

As a result, it may be stupid and irresponsible to apply to public action the traditional moral standards that are appropriate for private life and personal relations. Public policies are evaluated by their outcomes and not by the innate quality of the actions necessary for their successful implementation. The tenets of traditional morality, therefore, may not apply to a public person. Since he or she serves the community as a whole, he or she is empowered to do whatever is warranted to fulfill and to further the community's objectives. The need for unscrupulous tactics may arise in the public arena. If one is unable or unwilling to be manipulative, deceitful, ruthless, and coercive in pursuit of public policy goals, one is betraying the trust of these people who have placed their fate in the hands of their representative.

Machiavelli and Management

The Political Corporation
A corporation is perceived as an organized, structured, rational, goal-oriented, and efficient entity. There is a great deal of corporate behavior, however, that is highly politicized. These political features of the corporation reflect a more Machiavellian view of the corporation. Corporate officers and employees, for example, may be engaged in intrigues for influence, struggles for career advancement, controversies over corporate goals, and disagreements concerning strategies. There may be feuding among cliques, battles for corporate benefits and resources, and disputes regarding management. The corporation, therefore, can be considered a system of competing individuals and groups who enter into power coalitions and who engage in power tactics, both formal and informal and overt and covert, to exert their influence over others and to advance their aims. As a result of these power arrangements, the goals of the corporation actually may be those established by the most powerful and dominant individual or group.

The Fundamental Corporate Reality for Management

The fundamental corporate reality, therefore, emerges as power. Power is the capability of an individual or group to control the behavior of others within the corporation. In addition to the formal system of controls and rewards and punishments, the corporation contains many informal avenues and sources of power that do not appear on the corporation's organizational charts, and the uses of this power may be covert and perhaps not recognized as legitimate. Serious moral questions arise with regard to the acquisition and exercise of corporate power. What moral limits are there, if any, on the use of power within the corporation? What moral constraints should be placed on the use of power within the corporation? The Machiavellian answer to these questions is clear. A person should seek power. One should aim for power in one's life, including, and perhaps especially, one's corporate life. Power emerges not only as a tool for the successful corporate manager, but also as the goal of a manager intent on advancing his or her career. The means to acquiring this "good" end of power, and the application of power for one's benefit, are justifiable according to Machiavellian empowerment ethics.

Entrepreneurial Applications

In the modern world, founding a political principality or conquering a kingdom is a problematic undertaking. Entrepreneurship and corporate empire building, however, are excellent opportunities for a person with "princely" ambitions. Machiavelli's "lessons" for aspiring entrepreneurs are clear: be tough, smart, single-minded, and dedicated; be cruel and exploitative if forced to; bend and break the rules if necessary; pursue business success and attain the ultimate goals of wealth, fame, and glory; and do not be overly concerned with traditional notions of ethics and morality. Majority of the suggestions were targeted toward men that would do all relevant acts to get what they wanted.

In *The Prince*, Machiavelli discusses at length and attempts to solve the problems confronting as aspiring "founder." This examination makes Machiavelli's book very relevant to an enterprising individual. The many practical examples Machiavelli cites for founding a political entity can be translated into modern entrepreneurial and corporate terms. Machiavelli's commentary on the manipulation of people, and the orientation and tactics employed by manipulators, certainly are subjects the aspiring entrepreneur should be motivated to study. The entrepreneur can start a business, as the prince could found a principality; an entrepreneur can conquer markets, as the prince could subjugate cities. How should the entrepreneur manage a taken-over firm? The same way the prince handles subject cities. Machiavelli recommends the interjection of clusters of adherents, acting as small management teams, to represent the prince. These supporters will be capable, loyal, and indebted to the prince. Those displaced will be few and easily removed from the scene; everyone else will be docile and anxious to avoid the same fate. Machiavelli advises the prince to either treat people well or destroy them, because people can and will retaliate for less serious injuries, but they cannot avenge themselves of the more serious debilitating ones. The entrepreneur, therefore, instead of demoting taken-over top executives, should discharge them outright. Furthermore, the entrepreneur as well as any business manager should never trust a sycophant. The worst and most dangerous advisor is the "yes man" or "yes woman," because all he or she can offer the manager and entrepreneur is fawning information which prevents one from making realistic and wise decisions.

Machiavellian Management Practices

In the pursuit of corporate power, conduct within the corporation can readily become "Machiavellian." Abusive tactics, such as lying, deception, manipulation, and exploitation, can be employed to advance individual interests at the expense of organizational or group interests. Such tactics also can seriously harm those who themselves possess little or no power, knowledge, or expertise. One, for example, can sabotage the careers of one's co-workers by anonymously making false charges on the firm's ethic's "hot line," by acquiring control of scarce resources needed by others, or by withholding, distorting, or overwhelming a party with information. In order to obtain information about one's competitors, one can create and advertise for a fake job position, meet with the "duped" applicants, and get them to talk about their employers; and the reverse is also true, that is, one can interview with a job at a rival company to gain information about the firm. One can feign power, expertise, friendship, concern, favor, or respect and thereby manipulate others to show deference, loyalty, indebtedness, and trust and persuade them to perform actions for one's benefit that they ordinarily would not do. One can exploit particular personal vulnerabilities, such as vanity, gullibility, sense of responsibility, or generosity, which unknowingly can place a person in a position of dependency and servility. One can associate with the influential, ingratiate oneself with one's superiors, build one's image, and develop a base of support for one's ideas. If competitors challenge entrepreneurs, attack the competitors, blame them for any failures, and denigrate their accomplishments as unimportant, self-serving, poorly timed, or just lucky. Undo, obliterate, or minimize one's own association with policies that are failing. Always remember, appearances are essential; one must seem to be important, intelligent, confident, honest, ethical, sensitive, personable, and popular.

Commercial and legal negotiations, warns Reilly (2009), are rife with the Machiavellian practices of deception and lying. People lie; lawyers lie; business people lie; and they lie especially in negotiations, declares Reilly (2009). Negotiations, in fact, require a "talent" for deception (Reilly, 2009, p. 484). Deception encompasses "lies," that is, false statements which are known to be false and uttered with the intent to deceive another, as well as the broader category of "deception," that is, other means to conceal the truth or create a false impression, including silence (Reilly, 2009). The most common "dirty trick," as well as the "oldest form of negotiating trickery," is to make a knowingly false statement (Reilly, 2009, p. 490). Moreover, "a major difficulty…is that although some lies (such as the existence of competing bidders or the substantive strength of a given lawsuit) can usually be proven false by consulting with independent sources and experts, many lies (such as person's priorities, underlying interests, or reservation point) simply cannot be detected, unless one is good at mind-reading" (Reilly, 2009, p. 493). Negotiators are also confronted with what Reilly (2009, p. 496) deems to be the "Negotiator's Dilemma," that is, how much information should a negotiator reveal to an opposing party, and when should the negotiator reveal it. Reilly (2009, p, 501) consequently asserts that in negotiations, "Two things…are clear. The most important is that we cannot say as a general matter that honesty is the best policy for individual negotiators to pursue if by 'best' we mean most effective or most profitable. In those bargaining situations…and virtually all negotiations, lying is a coherent and often effective strategy. In these same circumstances, a policy of never lying may place a negotiator at a systemic and sometimes overwhelming disadvantage." Machiavelli would be proud, but would add that if the "best" means "effective" and "profitable, it also means "moral"! Reilly (2009, p. 525) does have a "possible solution" to the prevalence of lying and deception in negotiations, to wit: "…Simply assume that lying and deception sometimes occur, and therefore arm all negotiation participants (lawyers and non-lawyers alike) with mindsets, strategies and techniques that will enable them to defend themselves against the liars and deceivers." Some of those defensive strategies and tactics proposed by Reilly (2009) encompass conducting thorough background research, networking and researching potential negotiator counterparts, creating rapport and a collegial environment, insisting on the use of objective standards whenever possible, limiting the disclosure of information in a strategic manner, recognizing and trying to thwart tactics of evasion, watching for signs of deception, and establishing long-term relationships (and thereby especially watching for changes in normal behavior). By employing these strategies and tactics, advises Reilly (2009), one will minimize the risks of being the victim of lies and deceptions and thus being exploited and taken advantage of; but, nonetheless, he warns that it will be "impossible to prevent lying in the context of negotiations" (Reilly, 2009, p. 534). And Machiavelli would certainly appreciate and "second" this "real-world" view.

Spying certainly could be considered as another Machiavellian tactic. In the Hewlett-Packard "spy" case of 2006-2007 (Cavico and Mujtaba, 2013), any corporate power tactics appeared justified, and viewed as "good," by management to preserve stability and to maintain power. The company was under suspicion that several employees, as well as members of the company's board of directors, were leaking very sensitive and highly confidential information to the media. The nature of the leaks suggested that the leaks were occurring at a very high management and governance level in the company. So, in true Machiavellian fashion, the executives resorted to "any and all" means available to find the "traitors." The fact that the investigation utilized certain illegal and unethical tactics to uncover the source of the leaks was not germane. Since the tactics were construed as absolutely necessary, the conventionally "immoral" nature of the means was not an issue. These tactics were necessary to protect the organization; and the constituents of the organization could well expect that the managers would take these actions to protect the company. Invading people's privacy, assuming their identity, and deceiving them and others were all perceived as necessary, and thus "good," actions to preserve the collective entity, though these actions traditionally have been condemned as "bad." However, Machiavelli would also advise, of course, that if one is going to use "Machiavellian" tactics, such as "pre-texting" (fraudulently assuming people's identities in order to obtain private phone information and computer records), to ascertain which members of the company's board of directors and management were "leaking" confidential information to the media, one should do so very, very carefully, or else one (for example, H-P's former CEO and ethics officer) might find oneself indicted for fraud, identity theft, and illegal use of computer data. The true Machiavellian response would be to do what was necessary to find the leak, but not, as Machiavelli counseled, be "hated," that is, in the H-P case, not being prosecuted and being condemned as unethical. Unfortunately, here, at least in the Machiavellian context, the HP investigative tactics were exposed; the company was fined; the company's top executives were implicated; they were held accountable in the criminal justice system as well as the "court of public opinion" in the Hewlett-Packard "spy scandal." One would think that Machiavelli would have said that if the company had to be traditionally "bad," do it craftily and well.

Machiavellianism can also emerge in job interviews. To illustrate, Hogue, Levashina, and Hang (2013) found a correlation between job interview "faking behaviors" and "Machiavellianism." They divided "faking behaviors" into four types: 1) Extensive Image Creation, defined as the "complete invention of an image of a good job applicant," for example, telling fictional stories about one's credentials or claiming to have skills one does not have; 2) Image Protection, defined as "protecting the image of a good job applicant," for example, not mentioning that one needed more training to do the job, or trying to hide one's "true" personality; 3) Slight Image Creation, defined as "enhancing personal qualities to present the image of a good job applicant," such as saying that one is an "expert" though one is only familiar with a field, or inflating the "fit" between one's values and goals and the values and goals of the organization; and 4) Ingratiation, defined as "gaining favor with the interviewer to improve the appearance of being a good job applicant, for example, agreeing outwardly with the interviewer even when one disagrees inwardly, or complementing the organization on something though one believes it is not important (Hogue, Levashina, and Hang, 2013, p. 403). They described a person who exhibited a "Machiavellian" style as having the following characteristics: "pursuit of self-interest at any expense," "aggressive and devious in pursuit of goals," engaging in "unabashed self-promotion," withhold(ing) information about personal imperfections," "be(ing)" confident in their lie-telling," "more willing to be deceptive during interviews," and "view(ing) deception as an appropriate interview strategy" (Hogue, Levashina, and Hang, 2013, pp. 401-02). In order to determine who possessed these Machiavellian traits they used a Machiavellian scale which measured respondents' intentions to particular behaviors. Sample questions would ask whether a respondent would be prepared to "walk all over people" to get what they wanted, and whether at work or in business they would prefer to "get on quietly" with their work or get involved in "political maneuvering" which might get them a better position (Hogue, Levashina, and Hang,

2013, p. 404). They sampled 125 undergraduate business students (approximately divided between men and women) at a large mid-western university in the United States (Hogue, Levashina, and Hang, 2013, p. 403). Their research, as noted, showed a correlation between being a Machiavellian and engaging in "faking behaviors" in job interviews. Hogue, Levashina, and Hang (2013) emphasized that a Machiavellian job interviewee will exhibit the principal traits of selfish motives, deception, and manipulation (p. 408). They also warned that "interviewers are often unable to detect deception during the employment interview" and, significantly, that "faking can lead to interview success" (Hogue, Levashina, and Hang, 2013, p. 407). And, in what they deemed to be an "interesting" implication, they pointed out that though the "construct" of being a Machiavellian has a "negative connotation," the research indicates that being a Machiavellian "often leads to life success" (Hogue, Levashina, and Hang, 2013, p. 408).

Another area rife with Machiavellianism is the management practice of obtaining foreign government contracts and other benefits in return for making payments or transferring things of value to foreign government officials, that is, bribery. Bribery, of course, is a federal crime (a felony) as well as a civil wrong in the United States pursuant to the Foreign Corrupt Practices Act (FCPA) (Cavico and Mujtaba, 2011). There are serious criminal and civil penalties against a company and its officers, agents, and employees who violate the law, including imprisonment and the payment of substantial fines. The essence of the legal wrong of bribery is the transfer of "anything of value," directly or indirectly, to a foreign government official with a "corrupt" or bad motive, that is to unduly influence the official to wrongfully award a contract or grant certain business to one's firm (Cavico and Mujtaba, 2011). Davis (2012), however, emphasizes that primary motivations for the statute was "moralism" and accordingly for the U.S. Congress to make a "moral statement" (pp. 500-01); nevertheless, "…Congress was not completely oblivious to the FCAP's potential impact on U.S. economic interests" (p. 501). There is, therefore, a "tension," says Davis (2012, p. 506), between the moral aspects of the law and self-interest; and one way to reconcile this tension is "the idea of enlightened self-interest" on the part of the business community as well as the government (p. 507). The manner which the statute is written, moreover, may provide an opportunity for both the business community and the government to exercise their self-interest.

The FCPA is a very vaguely written statute, which, perhaps paradoxically, gives greater discretionary power to government prosecutors and regulators, but also may provide "cover" for a "sophisticated" defense effort. "Bribery," of course, is a pejorative term, as is "grease money," though the latter actually may be legal, as will be seen. Yet, there is nothing wrong with a little culturally appropriate good will gift to the foreign government official, is there? Or is there! Similarly, a bribe is "bad," but a little "tip" or "gift" to show appreciation, or to use the Middle Eastern term, "baksheesh," is good, right? To complicate matters – legally, morally, and practically – bribery is intrinsically bound up with the cultural norms and social practices of a society, which the shrewd international business manager must be cognizant. In particular, gift-giving in many cultures is an integral way of doing business. To illustrate, in Greece, "baksissi" is equivalent to baksheesh, which typically is construed as a little and proper gift or tip; whereas "fakelaki," roughly translated to "little envelopes," connotes doing expensive political favors and thus likely would be construed as a bribe. In Nigeria, a "kola nut," which is a caffeine-laden nut, is a traditional offering of hospitality in that country is also construed as a small gift or tip; whereas a "Ghana-Must-Go-Bag," which is a colorful woven satchel used in the 1980's when the government pressured residents from Ghana to return home, represents a substantial cash bribe to a government official, which very likely would be deemed an illegal bribe. In South Korea, payments of "ttokkap" or "rice case expenses" are typical gifts given during the Korean Thanksgiving and on New Year's Day. They are considered to be a social courtesy and are an established local cultural practice. Yet whether "ttokkap" to a South Korean government official is viewed as an illegal bribe would depend on the amount of the "expenses" compared to what is considered to be socially acceptable levels. Similarly, in Afghanistan, "bakhshish," which is comparable to bahsheesh, as well as "shookrana," which is a token present of cash or something of value to say "thank you" should be proper; but the greater the amounts or value of the presents the greater the likelihood for the government to interpret the payments as an illegal bribe, which in Afghanistan is called "roshwat khoory" (based on the word "khoordan," which literally means "eating." The culturally competent business manager is thus well-advised to become aware of these local societal norms and practices and in particular their legal, ethical, and practical ramifications (Cavico and Mujtaba, 2011).

There are exceptions and defenses in the FCPA, moreover, that is, legal "bribes" (or rather "payments" to foreign government officials. One exception deals with "facilitating and expediting" payments; that is, relatively small payments to lower-level foreign government officials to motivate them to perform more quickly and more smoothly routine government services, such as turning on utilities and processing paperwork, which one's firm is legally entitled to. An affirmative defense allows reasonable, legitimate, and *bona fide* payments to foreign government officials related to the demonstration and explanation of one's firm's products or services. This latter exception allows the reimbursement of travel, lodging, and meals expenses as well as the giving of "good will" gifts (Cavico and Mujtaba, 2011). Good will gifts, moreover, should be modest, never lavish, and given at culturally appropriate times. Regarding payments related to the demonstration and explanation of products and services, Pacini (2012), however, warns that "the government strictly construes this defense, knowing that firms will use it as a means of hiding excessive payments under the guise of reasonable promotional expenses" (p. 572). Furthermore, regarding gifts, Earle and Cava (2013) point out that "Congress understood when enacting the FCPA that corruption often takes the form of small 'gifts' or payments made repeatedly over time. A stream of benefits is often part of a larger scheme. Moreover, a review of enforcement action shows small gifts made over time have never been the primary basis for FCPA actions, which instead focus on larger payments" (p. 150). And Stein (2012) adds that the mere payment of a gift to a public official is insufficient for liability; rather, the gift must be tied to the public official doing a particular, identifiable, and improper official act to benefit the gift-giver.

The legal wrong of bribery, furthermore, has an intent element; that is, the government must prove (and in a criminal case the standard is "beyond a reasonable doubt") that the person or business paying the bribe did so with "bad" or "evil" intent, that is, to wrongfully induce the foreign government official to award the contract or bestow some benefit to the company that the entity did not merit (Cavico and Mujtaba, 2011). The second exception to the FCPA as well as the intent requirement will emerge as critical factors in the next bribery case to be discussed.

A "classic" modern case of Machiavellianism in the context of international bribery is the Salt Lake City Olympic bribery scandal (Cavico and Mujtaba, 2011). In December 1998, the U.S. Justice Department announced that it was reviewing allegations that Olympic organizers in Salt Lake City might have engaged in bribery of International Olympic Committee members as part of a successful effort to bring the 2002 games to Utah. Attorney General Janet Reno at the time acknowledged that Justice's Criminal Division has launched an inquiry after the Salt Lake Organizing Committee (SLOC) admitted paying tuition, expenses, and fees for several relatives of IOC members. Investigators at Justice are trying to determine whether the SLOC violated the Foreign Corrupt Practices Act, which prohibits the bribery of foreign officials. In addition, tax fraud could be part of the case if the Justice Department investigators were to determine that tax exempt money had been misused by buying gifts or funding scholarships for relatives of members of the IOC. The issue of vote buying arose because of the disclosure of scholarship payments made to six relatives of IOC members by Salt Lake City officials during their successful bid to play host to the 2002 winter games. The SLOC has said the payments, which amounted to slightly less than $400,000, came from a privately financed fund that was started in 1991. Moreover, Justice investigated Intermountain Health Care, Utah's largest health care provider, which confirmed that it gave free surgical services worth $28,000 to at least two people associated with the IOC. The surgery included knee replacement surgery for an IOC member, and plastic surgery to smooth the bags under the eyes of one person associated with the IOC. The price to stage the 2002 Winter Games was at the time already up to $1.4 billion; and the SLOC's bid process cost $13 million. Tax forms filed by the SLOC did not include entries for the scholarship program. Cash payments ranging from $5,000 up to $70,000 to IOC members from Africa and Latin America also were investigated, as well as a Utah land deal, arranged by Committee officials that turned a quick $60,000 profit for IOC member Jean-Claude Ganga of the Republic of Congo. Expensive gifts, including a pair of shotguns, worth $2,000, for IOC President, Juan Antonio Samaranch, were also reportedly given. Finally, a Salt Lake ethics panel looked into possible use of Committee credit cards to pay for "female escorts" for IOC members. IOC rules forbid members from accepting anything worth more than $150 from bidders.

Marc Holder, an 80 year old lawyer, a Swiss IOC member, member of the IOC's Executive Board, and former head of the International Ski Federation, stated that he believed that several IOC members and their agents had been involved in vote buying the past 10 years; and he said he thought 5 to 7 percent of IOC members, at the time numbering 115, were open to bribery. He also said that there was one agent of an IOC member who boasts that "no city has ever won the Olympic Games without his help." Agents promise, according to Holder, to deliver blocs of IOC votes. Frank Joklik, president of the SLOC, apologized and accepted full responsibility for the scholarship program run by the group that won the bid for the games. The program provided the $400,000 in tuition and other assistance to 13 individuals, including six relatives of IOC members, mostly from Africa. Only one recipient of the scholarship fund had been identified so far, the daughter of an IOC member from Cameroon, Africa. It was also reported that the son of a Libyan IOC member listed the Salt Lake bid committee's address on his application to Brigham Young University.

Holder, in fact, had used the word "bribe" to describe the scholarship fund. "With hindsight, I believe this program should not have been part of the bid campaign," Joklik said. Yet, he said he still supported giving academic aid and athletic training to youngsters from developing countries, professing the "humanitarian" and "educational" purposes thereto; but acknowledged that "it should not be done in a way that might possibly appear to influence improperly the voting of IOC members." Nonetheless, Joklik steadfastly maintained that it was not the SLOC's intent to bribe IOC members. In January of 1999 Jolik, and Dave Johnson, the committee's senior vice-president, resigned under pressure. Both denied personal knowledge of these activities. Holder, moreover, raised the scandal to global proportions when he claimed irregularities in the election campaigns awarding the Summer Games to Atlanta in 1996 and Sydney in 2000 and the Winter Games to Nagano in 1998. He charged that the Olympic selection process is riddled with corruption, with agents demanding up to $1 million to deliver votes. Officials in Beijing, moreover, accused Sydney of buying the 2000 vote.

According to interviews and news accounts, Salt Lake City decided it would concentrate its courting of delegates from Africa and Latin America. The feeling was that finalists, Ostersund, Sweden, and Sion, Switzerland, likely had the support of most European IOC members, and that Quebec's bid might neutralize Salt Lake City's support in North America. A Quebec City newspaper quoted a 2002 bid official who said at least three agents claiming IOC ties offered to swing the vote away from Salt Lake City, which eventually won by a 54-14 vote margin. Ironically, Salt Lake City did not need the African votes; and because the balloting is secret, SLOC could not even be sure it had gotten the votes it is accused of paying for.

The scandal tarnished the reputations of Salt Lake City and Utah, ignited opposition to letting the city play host to the Games, and has provoked "second thoughts" by at least one major corporate sponsor. The allegations already have jeopardized a $50 million pledge of sponsorship from US West Inc., a telecommunications company, which withhold its first payment of $5 million, until it gained more information on the scandal. Local organizers and the U.S. Olympic Committee feared that it would be difficult to raise the remaining $200 million needed to meet the budget. After an extensive Justice Department investigation, two former executives of the SLOC were indicted in the summer of 2000 on fraud, bribery (for violating the Foreign Corrupt Practices Act), and conspiracy theories for orchestrating a wide-ranging bribery scheme of Olympic officials in order to secure the Winter 2000 games for Salt Lake City, Utah. Thomas Welch and David Johnson were the Salt Lake City Olympic Organizing Committee officials named in the indictment; and they were accused of paying more than $1 million in cash and bogus contracts to IOC officials in an effort to "buy" votes. Welch was the head of the committee of civic leaders that put together the city's bid for the winter Olympics, and Johnson was his deputy.

However, less than three months before the Games began, a federal judge dismissed all the charges. An internal IOC probe did lead to the dismissal of 10 IOC members. Nonetheless, the federal government appealed the judge's decision, and in April of 2003, a federal appeals court reinstated the case against Welch and Johnson, stating that the government deserved a chance to put the case before a jury. However, in December of 2003, another federal judge dismissed the criminal case against the two Salt Lake civic leaders. This judge, U.S. District Court Judge David Sam, was especially bitter to the federal government. He declared that in his 18 years on the federal bench, he had never seen a case so devoid of "criminal intent or evil purpose." The judge further stated that the evidence never met the legal standard for bribery, and that the case "offends my sense of justice." The judge formally acquitted the two men, which means the government cannot appeal again, because retrying them would amount to illegal "double jeopardy." The two men had faced up to 75 years in prison, although they probably would have received far less if actually convicted. Even if the case had reached a jury, the prosecution would have had a difficult time, since proof of evil intent or bad motive is an indispensable element to a case of bribery and fraud; and the Salt Lake City principals insisted to the end that their intent was "good" and socially responsible, as manifested by their "educational" and "humanitarian" purposes (Cavico and Mujtaba, 2011).The legal case, as well as the "scandal-plagued" Salt Lake City Winter Olympics, was finally over; the Olympics was a success; and the Sophists and Machiavelli, one would think, would be proud!

Other very recent manifestations of Machiavellianism in the context of bribery and international business involve some major corporations. JPMorgan is being investigated by the Securities and Exchange Commission for allegedly violating the FCPA by bribing (indirectly) Chinese government officials of state-owned companies by hiring their children and other relatives in order to secure lucrative consulting and other contracts. The company denied any corrupt intent since it claimed it was merely engaged in proper networking activities in a good faith attempt to curry favor with the officials and that the people hired were otherwise qualified for the jobs, which were legitimate positions (Palazzolo,

Matthews, and Ng, 2013; Silver-Greenberg, Protess, and Barboza, 2013). The government, of course, will need proof of corrupt intent, which will be difficult to establish as merely seeking to create good will with foreign officials is not a crime if the hiring of their relatives is otherwise appropriate. Nepotism, though carrying a negative connotation, is not in and of itself a crime; and also may be a "good" Machiavellian business tactic.

Another manifestation of Machiavellianism involved the pharmaceutical company GlaxoSmithKline, which is being investigated by the U.S. as well as Chinese government for allegedly bribing Chinese doctors, who are considered civil servants, for prescribing (and purportedly over-prescribing) the company's drugs. The company is accused of taking the Chinese doctors and their families on junkets to prime tourist attractions in China and elsewhere as well as paying them money to prescribe the company's drug in violation of the FCPA. The company, however, insists that the trips were not illegal bribes but in addition to the tourism element had educational and training components. Moreover, the company contends that the money paid to some of the doctors were merely "honorariums" and speaking fees for their legitimate educational services. And the "rewards" that the company gave to certain doctors, who prescribed the largest amounts of the company's drugs, were not illegal bribes, the company asserted, but merely "continuing education" credits or money to obtain such credits, which the doctors needed to fulfill hospital requirements (Burkitt and Matthews, 2013). Consequently, as with the Salt Lake City case, the intent is claimed to be not "corrupt" but "good," as evidenced by the providing and enhancing of education and training. Also, a "junket," though too carrying a negative connotation, is not necessarily a crime in and of itself; and it also may be another "good" Machiavellian business practice. Time, and government investigations, will tell!

In order for the Machiavellian business manager to take advantage of the "looseness" in the wording of the Foreign Corrupt Practices Act and consequently make arguably legal and culturally appropriate payments foreign government officials, and thus to secure contracts and business, as well as personal "fame and fortune," the authors advise that gifts, honorariums, and entertainment be modest, certainly not lavish, and given at culturally appropriate times and places and given with the intent to merely establish "good will." The authors also advise that any reimbursement to foreign government officials for travel, meals, and lodging be directly related to the firm's demonstration and explanation of its products and/or services and be legitimate and reasonable.

The Machiavellian Manager
A Machiavellian manager strives to attain power, riches, rank, fame, and above all, personal eminence and grandeur. In order to achieve these lofty and exalted goals, the Machiavellian manager first must be cognizant certainly as to the true nature of people. Most people, stressed Machiavelli, are ignorant, unmindful, and stupid, self-interested, selfish, and petty, suspicious and envious, ungrateful, disagreeable, and malcontented, readily deceived and misled, merely satisfied and even impressed by

superficial appearances and show than substance and reality, and too weak and disabled to be either completely good or bad, though venal and easily corruptible and more prone to evil. If anarchy is to be avoided, and order and progress are to be obtained, the majority obviously cannot rule; but rather the people need a strong manager to discipline and control them and to convince, persuade, manipulate, command, or frighten them into acting prudently for their common good.

In order to be a successful manager of the people and to secure one's own position, wealth, and glory, the Machiavellian manager must be well aware that management definitely does not consist of adhering to any objective, universal, veritable, or ethical code, law, or principles of management. True management, rather, is a relative, situational, contingent, suitable, adaptive, and amoral conception; that is, the manager must do, and has the right to do, depending on the circumstances, whatever the manager deems necessary, fit, and proper to get the people to perform correctly, to maintain the manager and to advance the manager's objectives, and to achieve the manager's greatness. The manager, moreover, must do whatever it takes to fulfill these purposes, repudiating any notion of any higher law as well as eliminating any questions as to the conventional rightness or wrongness of the means used. Management, therefore, is simply a matter of expediency, which Machiavelli advocates as the one true and inviolable principle of management.

In purely private matters, for example, dealings with family and friends, the conventional virtues, values, and moral standards perhaps can be sustained, but when one enters the domain of public affairs and concerns, one must leave behind any notions of conventional morality, goodness, or rightfulness, because such "good" thoughts and precepts are irrelevant, and perhaps even "bad," for the ambitious manager, who must take on an amoral approach.

The overriding issue for the manager, therefore, plainly is not whether a particular action is good, right, or moral, or bad, wrong, and immoral; rather, the overruling principle is whether the circumstances require the use of a specific efficacious means. Any traditional "badness" of the proposed method must be weighed carefully against the anticipated desirable consequences of achieving the objective. It is thus quite possible that a customarily "bad" means will be outweighed by the prospects of securing a sufficiently "good" end, as defined and calculated by the manager, of course. Immorality and vice, as well as morality and virtue, all have their uses, and the sharp manager keenly can alternate between good and bad. Such actions as fraud, deceit, dissimulation, manipulation, cunning, intrigue, strategem, disrespect, and abuse are not necessarily bad; rather, they are merely instruments to be used if the situation demands their use, and they actually may rise to the level of laudable virtuous actions, depending on the "good" ends they serve. If the situation requires, for example, that the manager's followers (or perhaps employees in a corporate setting), be lied to, misused, or even betrayed, and these "bad" actions are indispensable to the manager's personal success, then so be it! Machiavelli counseled, for example, that a reputation for morality is an important ingredient to the manager's formula for mastery; and if it is necessary for the manager to deceive the people as to the manager's true character, such deception not only is permissible, but good too! The goodness or badness of any action just depends on the particular circumstances and consequences involved; traditional moral norms are irrelevant; and actions become disassociated not only from moral standards but also from the actors performing them. The manager thereby is licensed completely to perform actions that do not conform to the exemplar of the virtuous ruler, and also is enjoined not to render conventionally good deeds if to do so would thwart the manager's "good" purposes. Good and bad are merely seemingly good or bad, and the manager is not bad by using an expedient "bad," that is, good, means. To illustrate, Daimler-Chrysler Chairman Jurgen E. Schrempp admitted that he had lied to Chrysler executives and employees regarding their status in the merged company; and specifically that he had never intended the combined auto company to be "a merger of equals"; rather, he stated that he chose to be "misleading" for psychological reasons since if he had been truthful there would have been no merger, and he could not have made Chrysler into merely another Daimler operating unit. Since lying was absolutely necessary to get the deal done, lying was moral, at least according to Machiavellian "ethics" (Cavico and Mujtaba, 2013). Yet, the way things worked out between Daimler and Chrysler, with the former selling the latter at a considerable loss in 2007, perhaps it would have been better for chairman Schrempp to have told the truth!

Intelligence, reason, judgment, and prudence thus emerge as truly virtuous qualities for the successful manager. Realizing that traditionally good acts neither may serve the public good nor the "princely" good, the astute and calculating manager cautiously will alternate between good and bad, virtue and vice, and moral and immoral. The manager may have to use a means, traditionally classified as "bad," which due to its efficaciousness in a particular situation now may be deemed a good action. In certain circumstances, for example, it may be counterproductive to be kind and compassionate, and thus good to be severe and cruel. If innocent people have to be dishonored, betrayed, or abandoned for a greater good, so be it. Yet, Machiavelli warns that the manager must be careful, circumspect, and proportionate in employing conventionally bad means. Do not indulge or tolerate disproportionate or pointless badness, admonishes Machiavelli, or else one will become subject to hatred and contempt and one's purposes ultimately will be frustrated. Bad means are temporary expedients that must be used in appropriate, direct, and expeditious ways and to accomplish great goals, of course. The manager, moreover, who is obliged to apply bad methods naturally should attempt to appear as conventionally good, and otherwise actually may be quite conventionally good, but always ready and willing to change to the contrary if circumstances dictate. Carefully alternating between good and bad and eschewing extremes, however, does not mean that the manager should give way to feeble half-measures, weak compromises, and granting concessions. Irresolution, vacillation, and continually choosing the middle course must be rejected. Such signs of weakness and indecision surely will undermine the manager's power. The manager, instead, should opt for a bold course of action; and plan it and execute it well. Such a Machiavellian manager hence will be able to cause change, whether by reason and common sense, persuasion and manipulation, or command and coercion.

A fundamental question concerning a Machiavellian approach to management is whether Machiavelli really is teaching evil. Machiavelli, in fact, does abjure traditional moral virtue and goodness, and instead sanctions the Machiavellian virtues of ambition, expedience, and the prudent use of good and bad. Yet, for the manager to attain and maintain power and authority and ultimately to achieve great glory, must not the manager also consider the needs and aspirations of the manager's followers, the community, as well as society as a whole? That is, must not the manager's personal ambitions and "princely" goals be advanced and achieved fully in the context of benefiting the public; and, therefore, does not the common good become the ultimate, almost utilitarian, criterion for the Machiavellian manager?

Perhaps the arrival of a crisis allows a manager to act in an absolutely Machiavellian manner. A manager confronting an emergency may be impelled to take swift, decisive, strong, even draconian measures to save the organization; and in such a situation the manager must do quickly whatever is necessary to ensure survival, without the consultation or participation of followers or managers, even though the manager's determination directly affects them, and without the niceties of ethical evaluation or moral justification. Yet, if there is a true crisis and the manager has forged bonds of trust with his or her followers, then one's followers will rely on the manager's judgment and accept, and perhaps welcome, the manager's prompt unilateral exercise of power.

Machiavelli, therefore, would view the acquisition of corporate power as the "good" objective to be attained by any means. Power drives the corporate manager and the entrepreneur because power is not only an end but also a means, because if one uses and wields power correctly, one will be rewarded with success, wealth, fame, and glory.

Problems with Machiavellian Management
In the short term it may be expedient for a manager to be Machiavellian, but is it efficacious in the long term for a manager to be Machiavellian in the sense of being deceptive and manipulative and disrespectful and abusive? Dissimulation cannot be concealed forever, and eventually one will run out of people to mistreat; and this type of "raw power," coercive, intimidating management ultimately will fail as it cannot sustain itself indefinitely. People simply will neither follow nor labor for individuals they mistrust or detest; and thus such a Machiavellian immoral or amoral "boss" will not be able to motivate or direct activity.

A manager, therefore, must be very careful in asserting Machiavelli's rationales as the pretense for expedient, short-term, or crisis-caused authoritarian conduct. Once one acknowledges that Machiavellian behavior is acceptable, one risks falling into the trap of portraying present circumstances as fittingly critical, problematical, exceptional, or tactical for swift, arbitrary, "tough," Machiavellian handling, and thereby steadily sanctioning autocratic conduct. Moreover, regardless of the unsettled, troublesome, or exiguous nature of a situation, is it ever morally permissible or appropriate for a manager to act in a despotic and tyrannical manner?

It is never permissible or appropriate to mistreat, disrespect, betray, deceive, manipulate, or exploit people. It is always immoral to behave in such a wrongful manner and to contravene fundamental natural rights and no crisis, real or perceived, no short term advantage, can ever justify such misconduct. True management, as well as successful long-term management, is built on certain fundamental, inviolable ethical principles, such as integrity, honesty, trust, and respect, which are constant, permanent, non-contingent, and categorical norms. Effective management, of course, will require at times course corrections and changes in strategy and tactics, yet management also demands steadfast adherence to ethical principles and moral rules. A person who is ethically deficient thus lacks the necessary predicate for successful management, and when such a person confronts a crisis or is tempted by short term advantage, or for that matter, simply faces the unavoidable problems of authority and administration, he or she will act in such a way as to destroy any management effectiveness.

A manager who is demanding, and even exacting, may well be acceptable as well as efficacious, but one who is abusive and coercive is never acceptable, and in the long term such managers will be failures. Trying to lead by fear, suspicion, and manipulation hinders genuine communication and interaction, breeds apathy and mistrust, suppresses motivation, undermines commitment and loyalty, prevents empowerment, and eventually engenders serious problems and wrong decisions. If leading by fear, manipulation, and paternalism is neither morally acceptable nor practically efficacious, are there feasible management techniques for the results-oriented individual? Successful, long-term management always comes down to certain essential attributes - morality, honesty, and integrity. Treating one's followers and one's employees with dignity and respect, trusting and empowering them, as opposed to coercing and controlling them, will create not heedless, mindless, enervated automatons, but rather knowledgeable, energetic, and motivated associates who wholeheartedly believe in the manager and who are enthusiastically committed to achieving the manager's vision. Such management is principle centered, values based, and vision inspired; and the only type of management capable of producing and sustaining transformational and beneficial change.

The risk of underscoring the value of power is that that power becomes an end in itself. This goal of power, however, may be unattainable. Possessing and maintaining power over others may require one to constantly strive to increase the power that one possesses. The power that one has thus cannot be used to achieve any notable purposes; rather, it is merely a means to obtain more power, which is the means to secure every further power, and so on indefinitely. The result is an incessant, repetitive, naked power struggle with an endless deferring of goals. The liberation from traditional moral restraints and the granting of moral legitimacy to self-interest may make some people more energetic and creative, but a concomitant decline in moral standards might engender increasing malaise, suspicion, distrust, perfidy, social disunity, and inevitably anarchy.

A personal acting in a public affairs capacity should be able to do whatever he or she desires, Machiavelli counsels, so long as the action is for the community as a whole, and not solely for that person's own satisfaction and aggrandizement. How realistic is such a scenario? Machiavelli himself saw the problems with his own reasoning. He notes how difficult it is to find a good person willing to employ bad means, even though the ultimate goal is good. He also observes how infrequently a bad person, after having acquired power, is willing to use it for good ends. If a person cannot succeed by moral means, perhaps it is preferable that he or she not succeed at all, because if successful the objective would no longer be the same cause for which the person initially sought to attain. Perhaps Machiavelli is too much the realist and gives too much emphasis to material and "scientific" factors. His "crime" may not be one of amorality or immorality, but an underestimation of the moral factor in public and business affairs.

One also must consider the long-term consequences of using "Machiavellian" tactics on oneself, others, and an organization. Prolonged use of such tactics can engender debilitating outcomes. One who exercises power in such a manner, and aggressively seeks to secure and use even more power, can find himself or herself corrupted thereby. The use of power can routinize not only the control, but also the undignified and abusive treatment of less powerful individuals. Those controlled and so treated perhaps feel like failures and may regress to a depressed and apathetic state or perhaps feel frustrated and become aggressive and hostile. Capable corporate employees might leave the organization, or their performance could deteriorate, when a manager uses unscrupulous tactics over a prolonged period of time. An organization can become plagued by ruthless competition, antagonistic rivalries, and conflict. Society's economic and social health and the livelihoods of many people are dependent on business. Thus, to regard business as some type of Machiavellian" power game" is both fallacious and dangerous.

Admittedly, building a power base is important in establishing or conducting a business, but gaining power as one's ultimate goal is not a license for the practice of a spurious or specious code of ethics. There is not a separate set of moral standards for business or for a manager acting in a corporate capacity. One is not relieved of moral responsibility by acting in a public affairs or business capacity. One cannot hide behind and attempt to operate under a separate, unique, and dual system of ethics applicable only to business and public affairs. There should be one system of ethics, one set of moral rules, and one ethical code that applies to everyone alike, including business. A pernicious potential consequence of a "dual system" type of thinking is the acceptance or acquiescence by some in the business and political community that the "public" system or code can be, is, and should be, morally inferior to the "private" code.

Summary
Egoism and self-interest generate conflict when people pursue their own, often clashing, interests, but ethical egoism does not resolve these contests. As a

consequence, life deteriorates into a long series of conflicts, with each person struggling to win. What then is the "solution"? Do one's very best to prevail! Consequently, any resolution occurs not by the application of any objective ethical principles and moral rules, but by one person "winning" the struggle. Actions, therefore, are not good or bad in themselves but only relatively as they augment or diminish one's power. Virtue and power thereby become one in the Machiavellian mind-set.

Machiavelli is regarded as a well-known exponent of public morality and power tactics. His name is used to symbolize a sinister "real-world" view. Machiavelli, however, does expose the internal contradiction between traditional morality and real business and public "ethics." Comprehending this contradiction and resolving it is not merely an abstract theoretical challenge, but a very concrete and practical one. It is simplistic, however, to use Machiavelli as a synonym for wicked realism. Machiavelli does recognize traditional moral standards; he does not deny the intrinsic value of moral rules and virtues. He also recognizes, and wants his readers to understand, that the real world of values is not a homogeneous one. There is not just a world of moral values that alone exists in reality. Recognizing this fact does not mean that the Machiavellian solution is simply a matter of recommending deception, manipulation or coercion; rather, Machiavelli is urging that people confront the real world, know what real-world tactics they and others are using, and realize that some of these tactics are evil.

Machiavelli never regards "badness" as a tactic to be used continually and regularly, but rather as a temporary means to secure and maintain power more firmly. In the real world, it will be impossible to act in compliance with traditional moral standards at all times and all places. Such compliance is contrary to human nature and hardly a new discovery. Machiavelli's point is that the contravention of traditional morality (though in a moral sense adjudged as "bad"), can act as the necessary means, in certain concrete circumstances, to effectuate a greater "good." Machiavelli clearly recognizes and it is extremely important for his readers to recognize, that certain means, although regarded as necessary, are in fact bad and immoral. The moral character of the means remains unchanged, even though they are used for a good purpose. One must not only recognize a bad means as a bad means, but also only the extent necessary to employ such means. Then one can dispose of the bad means as soon as the good end is achieved. One must be true and honest to oneself and to others, admit that one does not have "clean hands" by having used such means, and ought to accept that reality.

The acquisition of power and the assumption of a public affairs role afford one the opportunity to change other people's lives on a large scale. Since power possesses instrumental as well as intrinsic value in Machiavelli's scheme, men and woman can use power for "good" ends, such as establishing one's authority in moral matters and using power to administer standards of right and wrong to people. Power and public affairs entail enlarged responsibility, accountability, and gravity in the use of power. Significant potential public consequences thus compel male and female professionals to formulate carefully and seriously, calculate cleverly, intelligently justify, and prudently implement public policies.

References

Barker, E. (1959). *The Political Thought of Plato and Aristotle*. New York: Dover Publications, Inc.

Beauchamp, Tom L. (1982). *Philosophical Ethics*. New York: McGraw-Hill Book Company.

Briton, Crane (1990). *A History of Western Morals*. New York: Paragon House.

Burkitt, Laurie and Matthews, Christopher M. (August 19, 2013). Glaxo Junkets Highlight Ills of Chinese Medical System. *The Wall Street Journal*, pp. B1, B7.

Camerer, M. (2006). Measuring Public Integrity. *Journal of Democracy*, Vol. 17(1), pp. 152-165.

Cavico, F.J. and Mujtaba, B.G. (2011). *Baksheesh or Bribe: Cultural Conventions and Legal Pitfalls*. Florida: ILEAD Academy.

Cavico, F.J. and Mujtaba, B.G. (2013). *Business Ethics: The Moral Foundation of Leadership, Management, and Entrepreneurship* (3rd edition). Boston: Pearson Custom Publishing.

Davis, Kevin E. (2012). Why Does the Unites Dates Regulate Foreign Bribery: Moralism, Self-Interest, or Altruism. *New York University Annual Survey of American Law*, Vol. 67, pp. 497-507.

DeGrazia, Sebastian (1989). *Machiavelli in Hell*. Princeton, New Jersey: Princeton University Press.

Earle, Beverly and Cava, Anita (2013). When Is a Bribe Not a Bribe? A Re-Examination of the FCPA in Light of Business Reality. *Indiana International & Comparative Law Review*, Vol. 23, pp. 111-146.

Frankena, William K. (1973). *Ethics* (2d edition). Englewood Cliffs, New Jersey: Prentice-Hall, Inc.

Garver, Eugene (1987). *Machiavelli and the History of Prudence*. Madison Wisconsin: The University of Wisconsin Press.

Ghazanfar, S.M. and May, K.S. (2000). Third World Corruption: A Brief Survey of the Issues. *The Journal of Social, Political, and Economic Studies*, Vol. 24(3), pp. 351-368.

Guthrie, W.K.C (1971). *Socrates*. Cambridge: Cambridge University Press.

Guthrie, W.K.C (1975). *The Greek Philosophers*. New York: Harper & Row, Publishers.

Guthrie, W.K.C (1978). *The Sophists*. Cambridge, England: Cambridge University Press.

Hogue, Mary, Levashina, Julia, and Hang, Hongli (2013). Will I Fake It? The Interplay of Gender, Machiavellianism, and Self-monitoring on Strategies for Honesty in Job Interviews. *Journal of Business Ethics*, Vol. 117, pp. 399-411.

Hulliung, Mark (1983). *Citizen Machiavelli*. Princeton: Princeton University Press.

Jay, Anthony (1994). *Management and Machiavelli*. Oxford: Pfeiffer and Company.

Jones W.T. (1975). *A History of Western Philosophy* (2d edition revised). New York: Harcourt, Brace, Jovanovich Publishers.

Kelman, S. (2000). Corruption and Government: Causes, Consequences, and Reform. *Journal of Policy Analysis and Management*, Vol. 19(3), p. 448f.

MacIntyre, Alasdair (1966). *A Short History of Ethics*. New York: Macmillan Publishing Company.

Machiavelli (1950). *The Prince and Discourses*. New York: Random House, Inc.

Machiavelli (1977). *The Prince*. Translated and Edited by Robert M. Adams. New York: W.W. Norton & Company.

Machiavelli (1985). *The Prince* (2d edition). Translated and with an Introduction by Harvey C. Mansfield. Chicago: University of Chicago Press.

Mansfield, Harvey C. (1995). *Machiavelli's Virtue*. Chicago: University of Chicago Press.

Matthews, Christopher M. and Ovide, Shira (August 22, 2013). Microsoft Bribe Probe Reaches Into Pakistan, Russian Deals. *The Wall Street Journal*, p. B1.

Mattingly, Garret (1965). "Machiavelli" in *Renaissance Profiles*. Plumb, J. H. (editor). New York: Harper & Row, Publishers.

Mujtaba, B.G. (2014). *Managerial Skills and Practices for Global Leadership*. Florida: ILEAD Academy.

Mujtaba, B.G. (2014). *Capitalism and its Challenges Across Borders* (edited). Florida: ILEAD Academy.

Mujtaba, B.G., Tajaddini, R., and Chen, L.Y. (2011). Business Ethics Perceptions of Public and Private Sector Iranians. *Journal of Business Ethics*, Vol. 104(3), pp. 433-447.

Norman, Richard (1991). *The Moral Philosophers: An Introduction to Ethics*. Oxford: Clarendon Press.

Pacini, Carl (2012). The Foreign Corrupt Practices Act: Taking a Bite Out of Bribery in International Business Transactions. *Fordham Journal of Corporate & Financial Law*, Vol. 17, pp. 545-592.

Palazzolo, Joe, Matthews, Christopher M., and Ng, Serena (August 20, 2013). Nepotism: When Is It a Crime. *The Wall Street Journal*, pp. B1, B2.

Prahalad, C.K. (2010). The Responsible Manager, *Harvard Business Review*, Vol. 88(1) p. 36.

Rachels, James (1986). *The Elements of Moral Philosophy*. New York: McGraw-Hill Publishing Company.

Reilly, Peter (2009). Was Machiavelli Right? Lying in Negotiations and the Art of Defensive Self-Help. *Ohio State Journal of Dispute Resolution*, Vol. 24, pp. 481-515.

Russell, Bertrand (1972). *A History of Western Philosophy*. New York: Simon & Schuster.

Silver-Greenberg, Jessica, Protess, Ben, and Barboza, David (August 18, 2013). Hiring in China by JPMorgan under scrutiny. *The Miami Herald*, p. 4A.

Stein, Alex (2012). Adjudicating the Guilty Mind: Corrupt Intentions: Bribery, Unlawful Gratuity, and Honest-Services Fraud. *Law and Contemporary Problems*, Vol. 75, pp. 61-109.

Strauss, Leo (1958). *Thoughts on Machiavelli*. Chicago: The University of Chicago Press.

Williams, Bernard (1985). *Ethics and the Limits of Philosophy*. Cambridge, Massachusetts: Harvard University Press.

CHAPTER 3
Education Progress in Afghanistan

By: Bahaudin G. Mujtaba
Nova Southeastern University

There is an old proverb which states: "Sow a thought, and you reap an act; Sow an act, and you reap a habit; Sow a habit, and you reap a character; Sow a character, and you reap a destiny." Many of the academic professionals, elders, and leaders today in Afghanistan have sown the seeds of wisdom, and thus created powerful destinies for themselves and other Afghans through their involvement in paving the way toward a brighter society. While having an advanced degree or formal specialization on the part of each official is not a solution for all of Afghanistan's challenges, it is great to see that the Afghan Constitution has made the credentials of relevant higher education a requirement for selecting ministers, deputy ministers and other such senior leadership officials. Such requirements will certainly encourage learning, creativity, and continuous pursuit of knowledge among all those who want to serve the country and society by using their mental faculties through peaceful means.

This chapter discusses the Afghan culture, the challenges facing people throughout the country, and the progress of education and gender equality over the past few decades.

The Afghan History and Politics

Afghanistan is located at the heart of Central Asia and is bounded on the north by Tajikistan, Uzbekistan, Turkmenistan at the Amu River, on the east and south by Pakistan, in the northeast by the Republic of China, and on the west by Iran. Afghanistan is a mountainous country with most of it about 4,000 feet above the sea level and only about 20 percent of the land is arable. The Hindu Kush Mountains reach a height of 25,000 feet (about 6,000 meters); Hindu Kush is said to be the second highest mountain in the world. Other mountains include the mountains of Paghman, Salang, Salt, Suleiman, Khwaja Amran, Doshak, Prapamisus or Safed Kuh, and Kuhi Baabah.

Afghanistan was known as Ariana during the ancient times, which later became known as Khorasan during the middle-ages. Eventually, the name was changed to Afghanistan. Afghanistan is a small country located in southwest Asia in the northwest of the Indian subcontinent with an area of 253,861 square miles (637,397 square kilometers). The nearest seaport to Afghanistan is in Karachi, Pakistan, about 1,170 kilometers away. Its farthest length from west to east is about 1,240 kilometers, and its extreme width from north to south is about 565 kilometers.

Afghanistan has an approximate population of 32,000,000 people. The last official population count was in June 15th to July 4th of 1979 which resulted in a figure of about 15,500,000 people. The ratio of men to women has always been higher, as for every 100 women there has been 106 or higher number of men. Life expectancy of males in Afghanistan is around 46 and female life expectancy is about 45 years of age. Infant mortality is estimated to be about 15.3 percent, which is alarmingly high. Literacy rate is about 30 percent, and about 88 percent of Afghans have no formal schooling experience, so some of the literacy has come from Mosque attendance.

There are people of different ethnic backgrounds in Afghanistan; and some of the common ethnicities are Pushtuns, Tajiks, Hindus, Baluchis, Nuristanis, Uzbeks, Khirghiz, Hazaras, and Turkmans. As can be seen from the various reports, Pushtuns and Tajiks make up the largest groups of Afghans. There are more than twenty different languages being spoken in Afghanistan, with the main ones being Persian (Dari or Farsi) spoken by at least 60% of Afghans and Pushtu spoken by about 38% of Afghans. An interesting fact is that most Afghans speak two or more languages (such as Dari, Pushtu and Urdu; or Uzbekie, English and Dari). Afghanistan also has about 2.5 million Kuchis (nomads) who travel, sometimes thousands of miles, to different parts of the country as the seasons change. Historically, the nomads used to bring and pass information from one place to another; however, technology has diminished their information transfer role. The dominant religion is Islam, practiced by about 99% of the population, with the other one percent making up the minority religions such as Hindus, Christians and others. The climate of the country varies from place to place ranging from below zero to 120 degrees in some deserts.

Afghanistan's flag has three distinct colors of black, red, and green. *Black* color represents the occupation of foreigners, the *Red* portion represents the blood of those who protect the country, and the *Green* part represents freedom and faith.

There have been many great leaders, yet some that were not able to keep peace in Afghanistan in the past century. It is assumed that all leaders intended to create a peaceful Afghanistan, while industrializing it so it could become a powerful force economically, spiritually, physically, and militaristically. However, historically, great leaders are not judged or measured just by what they intended to do, but rather they are judged by what they actually achieved (or caused to be achieved in the coming years) while they were in power. One characteristic of good leaders is to see the condition they left the government and the country upon their departure. Their goal is, and should be, to leave it better than they found it. Table

3.1 describes some of Afghanistan's political leaders or heads of state as organized by Afghan-land and other historians.

Table 3.1 – Afghanistan's Political Leaders

Date	Head of State, King, President
1919-1929	King Amanullah Khan
1929	Habibullah Kalakani (Bachai Saqao)
1929-1933	King Mohammad Nader Shah
1933-1973	King Mohammad Zahir Shah
1973-1978	Prince Mohammad Daud Khan
1978-1979	Noor Mohammad Taraki
1979	Hafizullah Amin
1979-1986	Babrak Karmal
1986-1992	Najibullah Ahmadzai
1992	Sebghatullah Mojadedi
1992-1995	Burhanuddin Rabbani
1995-2001	Mullah Mohammad Omar
2001-2002	Hamid Karzai Interim Leader
2002-2004	Hamid Karzai Transitional Leader
2004-2009	President Hamid Karzai
2000-2014	President Hamid Karzai
2014-2017	President Ashraf Ghani Ahmadzai

Afghanistan has always welcomed tourists, investors, entrepreneurs, and other visitors to the country. It was a country of beautiful sceneries and ancient artwork. It was a country of peace, quiet, caring, and friendly neighborhoods. Afghanistan is still a beautiful country and, as a natural corollary of stability and peace, more of the visitors will be returning for tourism and entrepreneurship at an increasing rate.

The common foods in the country consist of various forms of rice, tomatoes, potatoes, carrots, stew, chicken, lamb (sheep meat), beef (cow meat), goat, and other agricultural products. Major crops are wheat, corn, rice, cotton, various vegetables, nuts, and other fresh and dry fruits. Agriculture industry is the largest employer, about 60%, of the labor force. Livestock includes approximately 2 million cattle and 14 million sheep. Much of the country is cold and snowy during the three months of the winter season, with dry summers in most of the region and warm in a few provinces (i.e. Jalalabad, Qandahar) during the summer. Many of the villages in Afghanistan still do not have electricity or modernized irrigations systems. At any given time, around 30 to 50 percent of the people enjoy electricity on regular basis. Throughout the history, most major industries have been government owned; however, privatization has been increasing over the past decade. About ten percent of the labor force has been employed for knitting and sewing clothes and carpets. Major industries include natural gas, furniture, cement, textiles, mining, farming, livestock, and fresh dry food processing. Most of the service industry includes trade, transportation, government, and military agencies.

Some of the natural resources are gas, oil, coal, copper, zinc, iron, chrome, barite, lapis lazuli, and others. Other resources include wool, hides, and *qaraqul* pelts. Major exports have been natural gas, dried fruits, carpets, rugs, and animal skins. Major imports have been in the areas of manufacturing, machinery, certain foods, and refined petroleum products.

Kindergarten, if available, starts at age five and elementary school starts at age seven in first grade which continues till eighth grade. Some areas have a middle school for grades seventh through ninth. High school, usually, includes students from ninth or tenth grade through twelfth. Colleges and universities range from two to seven years. At least two years of college education are needed for elementary school teaching and six to seven years for medical students.

Education Progress: An Interview with Dr. Saif Samady[1]

The people of Afghanistan have experienced nearly four decades of war and turmoil, and there does not seem to be an end to the mismanagement of political resources and strategies by local, domestic, and international players. The lack of a strong police force to enforce local norms and existing laws has limited foreign direct investment opportunities from multinational firms. Furthermore, the existence of widespread corruption in getting paperwork done through various public agencies has put local and domestic small business entrepreneurs at a disadvantage as they cannot always compete by paying large amounts of cash in "grease" or "facilitating" payments. All these challenges for the country are further exacerbated by a lack of sufficient educational institutions as well as the fact that the international community is no longer going to be providing funds for non-governmental agencies (NGOs) and other development initiatives beyond 2015.

While there are many political challenges that are facing Afghan politicians and their international colleagues, the key is to focus on the one principal variable that will enable the country of Afghanistan to stand on its own in the decades to come. That principal variable is education, which is considered to be the enabler of peace, growth, development, and prosperity in a moral, ethical, and legal business environment.

Afghanistan is now going through its most critical transition period in its history and having an educated population and workforce is the key to its long-term development, peace and prosperity when the international community leaves the country in 2014. Education is not just important for the success of developing and developed countries, but it is crucial for survival in the modern twenty-first century's globally competitive environment. As part of the education and

---

[1]   Originally published in the *Journal of Applied Management and Entrepreneurship*:

•   Mujtaba, B. G. (January 2014). Education Status and Development Strategies in Afghanistan: A Perspective from Dr. Saif R. Samady, Former Deputy Minister and Chairman of the Independent High Commission of Education. *Journal of Applied Management and Entrepreneurship*, 19(1), 110-120.

performance management processes, modern leaders in Afghanistan and neighboring region must also focus on the reduction of corruption by integrating ethics and morality modules in their regular academic curriculums through spiritual and faith-based teachings.

Kaifi (2014) explains that the progress toward capitalism in Afghanistan over the past one decade has created high levels of corruption and this damaging situation can be reduced by integrating local values, and spirituality-based morality into the education process for college students and working adults. Consequently, most experts are advocating the proper education of young Afghans, continuous training and development of working adults through effective coaching and leadership in the business environment, and timely management of peace by military and political leaders throughout the country.

Since education is the foundation of any measurable and noticeable progress, let us interview a respected and long-time leader from Afghanistan to see what his suggestions are based on a lifetime of productive experience in Afghanistan and other countries around the globe. In this interview, Dr. Saif Samady offers a reality of the current education process in Afghanistan along with excellent historical reflections and prescriptive remedies that can be used by educators, administrators, managers, business leaders, and politicians inside Afghanistan and those outside of the country who are helping during this transition period.

Biography[2]. Dr. Saif Samady completed his secondary education from Habibia High School in Kabul, in Afghanistan, and earned his undergraduate degree in chemical engineering from the University of Illinois, and a doctoral degree in chemistry from the University of Colorado. He has done research at the American Potash and Chemical Company (Trona, CA) and at the University of Durham in the United Kingdom. In terms of employment in Afghanistan, he was an associate professor in Faculty of Science, Kabul University, and served as the President of department of vocational education and teacher training, and deputy minister of education. During the last decade (2002/2003), he was an elected Chairman of the Independent High Commission of Education for Afghanistan.

Dr. Samady is a well-known educator in Afghanistan. He has served as Deputy Minister of Education and the President of the department which included technical education. In this capacity he has been involved in the administration of technical schools. Many of the current engineers and technicians, especially those who have graduated from Afghan Institute of Technology may have learned about his leadership. Besides being a knowledgeable and respected person, Dr. Samady is one of the most experienced and well-informed educators around the globe.

[2] This interview was originally published as an Executive Interview in the *Journal of Applied Management and Entrepreneurship* (JAME). Special thanks go to the Executive Committee at the Society of Afghan Engineers (SAE) who involved the author and initiated this interview with Dr. Saif Samady for SAE e-Newsletter. I am thankful to everyone at SAE, at JAME, and to Dr. Samady for their time in granting me this interview.

Internationally, he has served as UNESCO Regional Education Advisor (Bangkok, Thailand), Director of UNRWA/UNESCO Department of Education (Beirut, Lebanon), and Director of Division of Science, Technical and Environmental Education in UNESCO (Paris, France).

You have been an educator for many years in Afghanistan. How are things different now?
It should be recognized that the development of modern education in Afghanistan was slow due to government policy, cultural constraints and limited resources. In the 1960s and 1970s some progress was made in development of education according to government policy and strategies in the context of a democratic movement, peace and stability. The role of dedicated education leaders, Afghan experts and teachers was significant. The war and conflicts of the 1980s and 1990s devastated the social and economic infrastructure including the education system in the country. In 1980, there were 1.2 million students including (18 %) girls in all levels and types of education in Afghanistan. After twenty years at the end of the century the total enrolment in the education system was less than one million with only (7 %) girls. During this period the quality of education suffered and the system did not function effectively due to conflicts and instability. Since 2002, with the assistance of the international community, efforts have been made to develop the education system. There has been significant expansion of education. In 2012 the enrolment in general education was 8.6 million including 2.9 million girls (38 %). The enrolment in higher education was 110,000 including 19,200 female students (19 %). However, the quality and efficiency of education continue to be a major challenge. There has been no significant progress in adult literacy which remains under 30%.

The Afghan government established an Independent High Commission of Education in 2002. What was the role of the Commission?
The Commission was established, with the support of UNESCO, to propose policy, objectives and strategies for the revival and development of education in Afghanistan. It was composed of 23 Afghan educators and experts from within the country, Europe and the USA. The Commission completed its report in August 2003, which contained recommendations concerning modernization and development of the education system. The education of girls and women and promotion of education for peace and human rights were emphasized. The Commission also made specific proposals concerning future education policy and objectives which were reflected in the new Constitution of Afghanistan. The report of the Commission under the title 'The Revival and Development of Education in Afghanistan' is available on UNESCO website.

What is the status of general education in Afghanistan now?
The development of education requires resources. In Afghanistan the education system is financed through the government budget, contribution of the international

community and public participation. Currently the development of education depends largely on external assistance and support. To make the best use of available resources, it is necessary to develop relevant strategies and ensure the efficiency of the system. This requires proper management, transparency and accountability. The support of communities and civil society, professional organizations such as teachers' associations and school councils will contribute in the improvement of quality and efficiency of education. The use of new technologies and innovative methods such as distance education can increase educational opportunities. There has already been significant development of private vocational and higher education in Afghanistan. This trend can be further encouraged and facilitated by the authorities. The enterprises can participate in the training of young people. According to the Education Law in Afghanistan, education in government schools and institutions is free. Ways and means should be explored to encourage voluntary participation and contribution of the people in education.

The literacy rate for Afghans who are in the age of 15 and above appears to be less than 30%. What should Afghan leaders do to help more adults become literate in a shortest period of time?

Adult literacy has been a major problem in Afghan society. The main reasons are limitation of resources for an effective literacy program and lack of schooling for a significant portion of school age population. In order to improve the situation, it is necessary to undertake a national campaign for adult literacy with appropriate strategies and adequate resources, and continue efforts for achievement of basic education of all children. Substantial private and public resources will have to be mobilized, large number of teachers from the formal and non-formal education systems and volunteers including university students should be trained and innovative methods and relevant materials developed for functional literacy. The use of technology and distance learning could be explored. The national program for eradication of illiteracy should be decentralized and conducted in cooperation with all governmental and non-governmental organizations, agencies, institutions, enterprises, development projects, and communities. Realistically, at present it seems unlikely that adequate resources could be mobilized for an accelerated national program of adult literacy. There are also social and cultural constraints for literacy program especially for women. Furthermore, in 2012 only 58% of school age children were in basic education. The out of school children and young people will impact literacy efforts. Nevertheless, in addition to governmental measures, the communities and voluntary groups could play an important role in literacy efforts. The non-governmental organizations and private sector should be engaged.

What can be done to increase the number of qualified master's and doctoral degree educators in Afghanistan?

I believe the training of faculty for higher education in Afghanistan is of utmost importance, which could be organized by developing graduate studies and sending qualified candidates abroad for higher degrees. The ministry of higher education has undertaken such programs, largely through scholarships to USA, Europe and other countries. Currently 175 faculty members study abroad for the master's and doctoral degrees. There are also 16 master's programs in several faculties of the universities in Kabul and another 7 programs have been approved in 2013. I understand the ministry of higher education intends to expand these programs as soon as the conditions permit. It is important to ensure the quality and standards of graduate studies. It is also necessary to make the employment conditions (salary, opportunity for research and professional growth) of the higher education faculty more attractive and interesting to encourage trained Afghans return home. Peace and security is also a factor. In general Afghans love their country, and in the 1960s and 1970s the majority of Afghans who were trained abroad came back to Afghanistan.

What are your thoughts regarding technical education in Afghanistan?
Technical education is very important for economic development in Afghanistan. Engineers and technicians need to be trained for all sectors of development. In 2012 a total of 18,112 students including 893 female students were enrolled in the Faculties of Engineering, computer science, geology and mining, and agriculture. There were also 350,000 trainees in about 600 public and private technical and vocational centers. A survey of 420 centers found that 58% of trainees are in computers, mechanics, electronics, and construction, and 17% received training in business. The quality of teachers and facilities are not always at desired standards. The government departments, agencies and the private sector have developed separate strategies, and there is a need for coordination and a comprehensive national strategy for the training of engineers and technicians. The application of technologies in the management of education has been very limited and used primarily for data collection and statistics, communication, libraries, etc. The application of new technologies initially in higher education and teacher training in Afghanistan will improve the quality of education. The gradual provision of appropriate facilities including hardware and software and necessary training programs will be required.

What do you think about online or distance education in Afghanistan?
Virtual education or e-learning have developed extensively in the United States, Europe and many developing countries. The first successful distance teaching university was the Open University, which was established in 1970 in London. There are many advantages in virtual education, as it provides flexible distance education for working people, who may not have access to standard universities. It is assumed that the cost of on-line education will be less than the cost of standard education. Virtual education depends largely on computers and telecommunication. There is a need to plan and manage effectively this new mode of teaching and learning. While hundreds of thousands of students receive education through distance and virtual mode around the world, questions remain about accreditation and the quality of assessment. In Afghanistan distance education was used for

teacher training as early as the 1960s. In recent years some higher education institutions have made limited use of e-learning. At present the technical capacity (computers and internet facility) and managerial experience for virtual education in Afghanistan is very limited. But it is important that higher education institutions and teacher training colleges consider the development of distance education modalities in their system.

What are your thoughts regarding the privatization of education as for-profit institutions in Afghanistan?
According to the Constitution of Afghanistan the government has a responsibility to provide education. The Constitution and Education Law allow private education, and that is why a number of private institutions have been developed in the last few years especially in economics, business and management, computer science, engineering, medical technology, journalism, etc. Not all private education institutions are for-profit. For example the American University of Afghanistan is a non-profit private institution. I believe the number and capacity of private higher education institutions will rapidly increase. Hopefully the majority will be non-profit or minimum-profit to allow young Afghans have higher education and contribute in the development of the country. Many private universities in Europe and the USA find additional funds from philanthropic foundations, charities and private contributions from individuals and enterprises in order to keep the cost to students as minimum. The concept of making significant profit in universities is not generally appreciated by public. In Afghanistan, the ideal situation will be for government to increase the capacity of university education as much as feasible and for the private sector to offer higher education at reasonable cost. The wealthy people and enterprises have a moral responsibility to contribute in the education of young people. The government should provide incentive for enterprises and private individuals through the tax system for their contribution to education. Ways and means should be explored to help qualified needy students with scholarships or low interest loans.

Over the past decade, higher education enrollment has increased threefold to over 101,000 students in Afghanistan and 19% of them are females. What are your thoughts regarding the education of all those who are eligible to attend college?
In Afghanistan education at all levels is free in public schools and educational institutions. Private higher education institutions charge tuition fees. The public universities at present can admit about 40,000 new students. Last year 130,000 students graduated from secondary schools. It is estimated that about 5000 joined private institutions, several thousand students were admitted to post-secondary teacher training and technical and vocational training programs. The remaining presumably joined the labor force or they are waiting for opportunities next year. The number of secondary school graduates will substantially increase in the years to come. It is necessary that greater efforts should be made to expand post-secondary and higher education. The ministry of higher education intends to develop

community colleges. Measures should be taken to develop part-time and distance education as well. The possibility of virtual education also needs to be explored. Unless substantial resources become available, it seems unlikely that all eligible students will be absorbed in higher education. Flexible higher and post-secondary education and increasing participation of private sector will be essential to meet this need.

Should all colleges begin teaching their curriculums in English? Would this transition even be doable with the existing teachers in higher education of Afghanistan?
The English language is important in higher education especially for studies such as science, technology, business, and management. Afghan students should learn English to be able to study English texts and communicate with fluency in this international language. It would be very useful and efficient in terms of quality if science and technology subjects and business courses could be taught in English. However, the teaching of all subjects in English is neither doable nor advisable. In India and Pakistan the English language as the medium of instruction in colleges is part of their colonial heritage. The great majority of Afghan students and faculty will not be able to use English as a means of instruction and learning effectively. It would be highly desirable to be able to make use of available English textbooks, references and resource materials. They should also be able to study abroad when the opportunity comes up. In this perspective efforts should made to provide intensive English language training to university students. It is also important that textbooks and educational resource materials are prepared in our national languages (Pashto and Dari). These are important languages with rich literature, which should be further developed and used to produce texts in all areas of modern knowledge including science and technology.

It is my understanding that many graduates are still looking to find jobs. What should be the government's role and responsibilities in this area?
In reality the number of current university graduates is much smaller than the development needs of the country. If many graduates are unable to find jobs, and companies hire professionals from outside the country, it is a question of matching qualifications with jobs and perhaps a problem of management as well. At present there is no national strategy for human resource development. The number and qualification of manpower needed for the country has not been established. There is currently no mechanism for communication and effective cooperation between universities and enterprises. The employment system for recruitment of new graduates is also inadequate. Companies with foreign participation find it convenient to hire experienced professionals from neighboring countries. The English language ability and experience could also be in favor of foreign professionals. It should be recognized that the country has experienced very significant social and economic changes during the last few years. There are many deficiencies in the administration and management of human resources including

training and employment of graduates. The government should encourage and if necessary regulate that companies in their employment policies give preference to Afghan nationals, based on qualification.

What is the role of science and technology in social and economic development of Afghanistan?

Science and technology play an important role in economic development and improvement of standard of living. The application of science and technology, development of scientific infrastructure, education and training are essential for sustainable development and progress in modern societies. The teaching of science and technology to children and young people, training of engineers and scientists, and promotion of public understanding of science and technology facilitate the application of science and technology to development. During the last decade some efforts have been made in developing science and technology education and training in the country. However greater resources and efforts are needed to promote the application of science and technology not only in education and training but in all sectors of the economy. I have advocated the development of a national policy and long term strategic plan for science and technology. Special attention needs to be given to applied research and development of appropriate infrastructure and mechanism such as a National Council for Science and Technology. The promotion of scientific literacy and public understanding of science and technology will contribute to modernization and development of Afghanistan.

I believe non-formal programs of science education and information such as a science museum can be an effective means for inspiring children and young people in science and technology. I hope the Afghan scientists and engineers support a science museum in Afghanistan.

Given the current situation of education in Afghanistan, what are the future challenges for educational development in the country?

One of the most important constraints in the development of education in Afghanistan is lack of resources. The education system is largely funded through international contributions. It is hoped that with exploitation of natural resources including minerals and other economic activities, the country will be able to finance its development. The important challenges are not only lack of capacity in the education system, but also the quality and efficiency of education. These challenges include shortage and qualification of teachers and university faculty, lack of adequate physical and learning facilities such as laboratories and libraries, outdated curricula and lack of appropriate textbooks especially in vocational and higher education. The achievement of a basic education for all children, which according to the Constitution should be compulsory up to middle school level, and adult literacy will be a continuing challenge in education. Social and cultural constraints for the education of girls and women especially in the South and East of the country will affect the development of education. Peace and stability will be the most important factor for progress in education.

Learning and Changing
High literacy rates, training, and equipping the workforce with the right skills to become industrialized as well as continuous education are critical elements to the region's progressive development and growth. Efforts geared toward such personal developments of the workforce generations can speed up the process of economic development and independence of Afghanistan from foreign aid. All such efforts should be accompanied strategically with effective management and strategy. Since no two situations are likely to be similar in all variables, it is best to apply effective skills in order to deal with each challenge. Many experts tend to agree that one major change in today's corporate and political environment in the region might be the transformation and creation of a culture with regard to honest "service" to customers, suppliers, employees, and one's colleagues. Of course, before describing the remedy, leaders need to diagnose the problems, illnesses and pains caused by the decades of war and conflict.

The term *"Afghan,"* represents all individuals who were born in Afghanistan, descendants of Afghans, and those who were official citizens of the country, as agreed upon by the country's constitution. Symbolically, the term Afghan stands for love, courage, devotion, dignity, commitment, loyalty, and the desire to make sacrifices for one's country and people. It further symbolizes endurance, patriotism, dedication to the Afghan land and flag, and the freedom to soar in the beautiful mountains and deserts which are considered to be their ancestors' gleaned and protected backyards. In general, Afghans are people of honor, hospitality, and are committed to being masters of their own destiny. Various types of patriotism and conditioning to keep the country independent are weaved into the culture. We must realize that independency is not the solution to all of the country's challenges and in today's environment all people need to work through "interdependent" relationships with other countries and allies. "Dependence" must be converted to "independence" and simultaneously to "interdependent relationships" with other countries so Afghanistan can benefit from certain comparative advantages which are afforded to it through its natural resources.

The conditioning of "independence" can lead to ethnocentricity, as well as xenophobic thinking and paradigm, that is, when one is thinking or reflecting only at the "surface level" with regard to receiving international assistance and help from foreigners in the rebuilding process. High illiteracy rates in the country may be causing some individuals to only think at the surface level, since they may not have access to more material for inductive and deductive reasoning for cause and effect analysis. As such, progress requires chancing our perspective and paradigms toward learning and living interpedently with everyone in the world, especially those in the South Asian region.

As human beings, we know and acknowledge that the past cannot be changed but we can most certainly influence what happens now and in the future. Change is most effective when it starts from within, and thus each person should take personal responsibility for his or her own personal as well as professional growth and development. We must all be productive individuals and good leaders in order to effectively contribute to the team's goal toward the creation of a peaceful environment for all. Of course, being productive individuals, and becoming effective leaders, is a good start for each person in Afghanistan since individuals have the most control over their own behaviors. We can say that improving one's life, knowledge and the community is a personal and professional obligation. Imam Ali said, "Persist in your action with a noble end in mind...Failure to perfect your work while you are sure of the reward is injustice to yourself."

Many of the children and adults in Afghanistan are currently making great contributions with a noble end in mind...to improve Afghanistan. There are at least three ingredients in one's progress toward the achievement of good life: learning, earning, and yearning. Afghan people have done, and are doing, all three as they yearn for a peaceful country and region. Each person has the choice to constantly "move" toward worthwhile and predetermined ethical goals with integrity, thereby making his/her life, and that of their family members' and colleagues' more interesting and joyful throughout Afghanistan and the region. Every person has the power for making great contributions toward peace and prosperity in serving their fellow human beings. The process of development, nation-building, and prosperity needs educated citizens, resources, and creativity to make the most out of what is available.

Progress and economic development are basically like a race without a finish line, and consequently every citizen must participate in this rewarding process. Many talented and educated individuals are doing all they can as they know that they have one life in this world, and they must make the best of it while they have the opportunity to do so because life is short. They know that there is:

"Only one life that soon will pass – Only what is done with love will last."

Instead of being too focused on the past, we need to take actions with good intentions and true love, while being forward-looking and anchored toward the future that we all desire for ourselves and our offspring. Productive individuals and effective leaders are forward-oriented and, at challenging times, use professionalism to create synergy with people of diverse backgrounds, ethnicities, religions, and languages.

When government officials and corporate leaders do become an integral part of the responsibility involved in leading these major worldly issues, they will realize that diagnosis must come before prescription if people are to bypass or evade much rework and wasted efforts. As such, we can begin by understanding who Afghans are and their desire for "independency." For ordinary Afghans, and especially their leaders and educators, continuous learning and "adjusting" to the existing needs and demands of local citizens will be the key to simultaneously help the country become independent and interdependent with the international community. In order for this to happen, Afghans must go beyond complying with the simple definition of literacy and thus must help more people become more than merely functionally literate. We must understand that the modern workplace has different rules and higher expectations. Just becoming literate in reading, writing and mathematics is no longer sufficient for global success. In order to work toward a globally prosperous country and region, a nation's people must soar above the average requirements since being average will not give you an "edge". The illiterate of the 21st century workplace will not be those who cannot read and write, but those who cannot learn, unlearn, and relearn. So, it is the power of deciding to learn new methods or techniques for individual and workplace success, unlearning what is no longer working or valid, and relearning new knowledge and relevant strategies, in order to make the lives of people a little better each month and each year. Overall, human development and capacity building become critical for learning, unlearning, and relearning and thus to make society a little better as a result of us having had the opportunity to live in it.

Summary
This chapter provided a brief introduction to the Afghan culture, the latest figures regarding student enrollments and educational challenges facing people throughout Afghanistan. Developing countries need resources, education, and continuous development of both their male and female populations if they are to effectively transition and take full advantage of internationalization trends in this global economy. Fortunately, Afghanistan has begun to stake out its position on important educational issues for both males and females in the country. To be successful in this effort, government officials and the working people of Afghanistan must assess and take seriously their own level of readiness to lead these important agendas. Being educated and a peaceful individual, and becoming an effective leader is a good start for each person in Afghanistan as well as for those around the world since people have the most control over their own behaviors.

The past cannot be changed by anyone; however, we can change what happens now and in the future. Change must start from within each citizen in each community, country, and region; therefore, each person must take full responsibility for his or her own physical, mental, spiritual, and psychological developments.

References
Cavico, F. J. and Mujtaba, B. G. (2013). *Business Ethics: The Moral Foundation of Leadership, Management, and Entrepreneurship (3rd edition)*. Pearson: Boston.

Kaifi, B.A. (2014). *Afghanistan's Conundrum: Capitalism in a Dependent Nation, pp. 29 – 37*, Chapter 4 in "Capitalism and its Challenges Across Borders". Edited by Bahaudin G. Mujtaba. Florida: ILEAD Academy.

Mujtaba, B. G. (2014a). *Managerial Skills and Practices for Global Leadership*. ILEAD Academy: Florida.

Mujtaba, B. G. (2014b). *Capitalism and its Challenges across Borders (edited)*. Florida: ILEAD Academy.

Mujtaba, B. G. (2008). *Coaching and Performance Management: Developing and Inspiring Leaders*. ILEAD Academy Publications; Davie, Florida, USA.

Mujtaba, B. G. (2007a). *Afghanistan: Realities of war and rebuilding (2nd edition)*. LEAD Academy, LLC, Florida; United States.

Mujtaba, B. G. (2007b). *The ethics of management and leadership in Afghanistan (2nd edition)*. ILEAD Academy: Florida - USA.

Mujtaba, B. G. (2006). *Privatization and Market-Based Leadership in Developing Economies: Capacity Building in Afghanistan.* Llumina Press and Publications, Florida.

Mujtaba, B.G. and Kaifi, B.A. (2010). Business ethics and morality in Afghanistan. *Business and Professional Ethics Journal,* 29(1-4), 32-63.

Mujtaba, B. G. and Preziosi, R. C. (2006). *Adult Education in Academia: Recruiting and Retaining Extraordinary Facilitators of learning.* 2nd Edition. Information Age Publishing. Connecticut.

CHAPTER 4
WOMEN AND ISLAM IN AFGHANISTAN

By: Belal A. Kaifi and Wajma Aslami

Afghanistan's strategic location has always connected the rest of the world to the country, dating back to the Silk Road. According to Ewans (2002), "Afghanistan has also over its long history been a highway of conquest between west, central and southern Asia" (p. 10). Different empires have traveled throughout Afghanistan, from China in the East to Italy in the West resulting in many distractions, quandaries, and unwanted circumstances that have impaired and faltered the society in a number of different ways.

This chapter provides both direct and indirect constructs, recommendations, and mechanisms for promoting gender equality, reversing the brain-drain, and embracing capacity building endeavors to help with the development process of Afghanistan.

Introduction
Over the years, the struggle for a unified Afghanistan has been an arduous situation because of belligerent neighbors, dependency on Western empires, sub-optimal leadership, and tribalocracy. One main reason for this unfortunate situation is that Afghanistan is located in a strategic location in Asia which has caused many conflicts. In fact, throughout Afghanistan's history, there has been involuntary conflict. Ewans (2002) explains, "Although never colonized, Afghanistan is part of the colonial history of Tsarist Russia and British India" (p. 9). Throughout the late 1800s and early 1900s, the British attempted to colonize Afghanistan on three different occasions and were unsuccessful. Throughout the late 1970s and 1980s, the Russians invaded Afghanistan hoping to spread communism, and were also defeated by the Afghan resistance. Afghans have never surrendered to an outside invader. "Uniquely among the nations of Eurasia, Afghanistan has steadfastly resisted conquest, despite being a crossroads for ambitious empires throughout ancient and medieval times and a battleground in the modern age during the Great Game and Cold War" (Tanner, 2009, p. 26). In 1996, the Taliban aggressively invaded and controlled many parts of the country. After the Taliban were defeated

in 2001, a liberal democratic Afghanistan emerged and has played a pivotal role in the future of this nation. Afghanistan currently has a very young population with a median age of about 18 years. Furthermore, several generations of Afghan boys and girls have grown into adults knowing and seeing nothing but continuous war (Frank, 2002, p. 82). While universal education is a legal requirement, due to economic realities, only a small percentage of the population is literate (Mujtaba, 2007). For several decades, Afghanistan has become dependent on the international community for assistance in all matters. "As a result of this long-term foreign assistance and dependence, Afghanistan has regressed" (Kaifi, 2008, p. 17).

Afghanistan's unique profile would lead one to assume that this largely rural, poor population embodies the characteristics of a collective culture that remains close to its tribal and village based lifestyle. According to one study, "The schools generally requested help from students' fathers for renovations and improvements to classrooms and schools, which accorded with traditional gender roles and expertise" (Hoodfar, 2007, p. 280). Furthermore, school teachers and educational officials in rural parts of the country tend to rely more on tribal and community leaders to educate their students. While women might show more empathy toward people and lead with a care orientation, it is evident from modern research that males and females will be equally effective in leadership roles (Jones & George, 2009). Since Afghanistan has been economically depressed due to three decades of intense and destructive war and violence, fewer women have had educational opportunities which would qualify them to reach higher ranks of management and leadership positions (Mujtaba, 2007). As such, Afghan managers and government officials should strategize to provide more educational and management development opportunities to this underrepresented group. In Afghanistan, there was a transformational leader (King Amanullah from 1919-1929) who embraced the importance of independence, modernization, education, and equality. With the 2014 presidential elections quickly emerging, it is imperative for the Afghan people to elect a President who will embrace and implement what King Amanullah envisioned almost 100 years ago.

Afghanistan's King Amanullah

There was a visionary leader named King Amanullah (1919-1929), the son of King Habibullah and the grandson of King Abdur Rahman who had a dream for Afghanistan to progress. As documented in history, "On February 27, 1919, Amanullah was formally crowned" (Ewans, 2002, p. 87). King Amanullah and his soldiers defeated the British in a month long war and gained complete independence of Afghanistan during the third Anglo-Afghan war and soon after became a national hero. King Amanullah was a strategic-forward thinker and a change agent, and was able to properly evolve the country into a modernized society.

During King Amanullah's reign, Afghanistan flourished into an independent nation that focused on enhancing human rights, education, and promoting modernization. He understood the inequalities faced by women in Afghanistan and quickly worked toward granting them equal rights. The King's ability to enhance the quality of life in the Afghan society will always be commendable and admirable. "For the first time [in Afghan history], a written constitution was written up, implemented, and promulgated" (Evans, 2002, p. 93). The public was both astonished and surprised by his bold endeavors to make positive changes.

King Amanullah went on a grand tour with his wife Queen Soraya where he spent time in India, Egypt, France, Germany, Britain, the former Soviet Union, Turkey, and Iran. This notorious tour allowed him to be exposed to different cultures, lifestyles, and ideologies. Being a charismatic and visionary leader allowed him to accept, adapt, and enjoy the differences that he and his wife encountered.

King Amanullah understood the importance of education and the positive impact education has on a society. He established a number of schools, including some for girls with the help of Queen Soraya, and started to "send young Afghans abroad for higher studies" (Evans, 2002, p. 93). Suddenly, Afghans were immersed in their studies and worked hard to receive scholarships to study abroad. Many Afghans traveled to the west during his time and received advanced degrees and returned to Afghanistan to help with the development process. King Amanullah influenced the people of Afghanistan by empowering them to be visionary, proactive, and an active part of the global community. After King Amanullah's reign in 1929, all of his successors neglected his progressive reforms and instead, were manipulated and influenced by foreign powers and became dependent on foreign resources, support, and aid.

Dependency Theory and Afghanistan
Afghanistan throughout the millennia has been a place of rich culture and a junction of civilizations from multiple continents (Mujtaba, 2007). This has led the country to become dependent on the international community for survival and the prospect of a peaceful future. Of course, "Dependency theory concludes that poverty in the developing nations is the result of their dependence on high-income nations" (Tregarthen & Rittenburg, 2000, p. 675). Influence is exerted over Afghanistan by many other nations. According to Tregarthen and Rittenburg (2000), "Dependency theory holds that the industrialized nations control the destiny of the developing nations, particularly in terms of being the ultimate markets for their exports, serving as the source of capital required for development, and controlling the relative process and exchange rates at which market transactions occur" (p. 675).

Despite much foreign aid, Afghanistan still lacks in many professional and technological fields (Mujtaba, 2005). This is perhaps normal as well since "the benefits of trade between a rich country and a poor country will go almost entirely to the rich country" (Tregarthen & Rittenburg, 2000, p. 675). Even though the majority of the benefits are going to the richest countries, poor countries do not have many options if they want to live peacefully with the international community. The good news is that "Dependency theory, like Marxian economic analysis, promises prosperity, equity, and justice once the political obstacles to economic transformation have been overcome" (Ahiakpor, 1985, p. 538). In this case, the future does look brighter if the citizens of the developing country educate themselves and become self-reliant key players in the global community. Ultimately, the people of a country must help themselves if they want to prosper and to be key players in the global community. However, it has been suggested that the people of each country must realize that "Capital and technology from the West do not lead to development but can only deepen underdevelopment" (Munck, 1999, p. 58).

Poor countries are often stuck in the cycle of oppression until they are able to put an end to this cycle through entrepreneurship, development, and education. According to Perraton (2007), "dependency theory not only argued that the nature of peripheral countries' insertion into the global economy perpetuated their subordinate status but also that it reinforced domestic inequality with a 'comprador' bourgeoisie unable to play a developmental role leading to the type of capitalist transformation seen historically in Western countries" (p. 32).

Such countries must develop a comparative advantage for themselves to trade with their regional neighbors and globally. Gradually, they must strive to escape the dependency trap since dependency is said to be a theory of underdevelopment: "Poor countries exiled to the periphery of the world economy could not develop as long as they remained enslaved by the rich nations of the center" (Velasco, 2002, p. 44). Long-term dependence cannot be sustained. Dos Santos (1970) explains that, "By dependence we mean a situation in which the economy of certain countries is conditioned by the development and expansion of another economy to which the former is subjected" (p. 231). Dependency can be best converted into sustainable development through equal and speedy education of all citizens of a country. Equal and public access to a speedy education can help avoid the disparity between the upper and lower classes. As stated by researchers, "dependency theory holds that economic development widens the gap between the rich and the poor because most new jobs are for educated middle-class and skilled blue-collar workers rather than for unskilled workers" (Tensey & Hyman, 1994, p. 31). Independency is part of the journey toward the ultimate goal of living interdependently with the global community. However, over-emphasizing nationalism, culture, and historical literature can certainly lead people of a society to desire absolute independence from the global community. This, however, is not a long-term solution in today's interconnected global community. Today's economic productivity and work environment are dependent on an "open system" where people can receive resources from anywhere worldwide and sell them globally, rather than functioning in a "closed system" which requires independency on all fronts. Overall, dependence is especially harmful when the nation is forced to rely upon less-developed countries. As presented in the previous chapter by Bahaudin Mujtaba, "dependence" must be converted to "independence" and then to "interdependent relationships" globally; in this way, Afghanistan can benefit from certain comparative advantages which are afforded to it through its natural resources. The continuous conditioning of "independence" can also lead to ethnocentricity, as well as xenophobic thinking and paradigms. This "surface level" mentality can negatively impact a country who is receiving international assistance in the rebuilding process. High illiteracy rates in the country may be causing this mentality since they cannot perform proper cause and effect analysis due to the lack of knowledge on inductive and deductive reasoning. It appears that the current Afghan government is encouraging capacity building by making literacy a top priority while building the workforce's capacity for more effective decision-making (Mujtaba, 2007). As a result of long-term dependence, the majority of Afghans have neglected education and innovation which has resulted in a society that has mainly embraced culture. While culture provides the foundation of a society, education provides the means to a civil society (Kaifi, 2010). In a quantitative research study by Mujtaba and Kaifi (2010), the authors were able to conclude that, "higher education among the Afghan respondents demonstrated a statistically significant and positive correlation toward ethical maturity" (p. 32).

Afghan Culture and Gender Roles

Within the Afghan culture, the roles for men, women, and children are clearly outlined (Crown, 2007). The men lead and represent the household. They are the "public face" when dealing with matters outside the home. It is expected that children will do as they are told, and follow the religious guidelines in the family along with traditional roles (Sekandari, 2007). Typically, Afghan girls are taught to be obedient daughters, brides, and daughter-in-laws, and they are also expected to not bring shame to the family (Sekandari, 2007). Therefore, women are mainly homemakers and do the child rearing (Crown, 2007; Sekandari, 2007). Fathers control the household and make all the important decisions (Emadi, 2005; Entezar, 2007). Gender roles are strictly defined and are not to be compromised. Individuals would rather act ungenuinely because of their desire to not bring shame upon themselves and their families (U.S. Army, 2004).

The Afghan culture has many strong core beliefs and values. Some of the primary values and beliefs are: pride, honor, hospitality, respect, virtue, morality, loyalty, family, reputation, religion, culture, and education. Shame also plays an important role in the Afghan culture and tradition. It is considered very shameful when an Afghan is not in touch with his or her Afghan language and culture (Sekandari, 2007). Afghan men are prideful of their families and are also responsible for the family's actions; therefore, the father makes all decisions and tries to ensure that the family members live up to his decisions in order to avoid any shame to the family. For this reason, many women are watched closely and kept close to home, because the actions of one may bring shame to a whole family and, sometimes, even the tribe (Emadi, 2005; U.S. Army, 2004).

Pride is extremely important within the culture. Standing up for one's family or tribe name is considered by Afghans to be a way of expressing pride or even patriotism (Emadi, 2005). Being Afghan and more importantly Muslim, is an unique identity of which the Afghan people are proud of (Kaifi, 2009). Men are honorable to their family and to their culture or country. There are several ways that Afghans may lose their honor; for example, one may violate a social or behavioral code, such as when a man asks about another man's wife (Crown, 2007). However, the most common way Afghans lose their honor is when they are shamed by the behavior of someone else for whom they are responsible or to whom they are related (Crown, 2007). For example, if a daughter disobeys her father, a father feels shamed at the expense of his daughter. An Afghan girl can bring shame to her family by dating, being "sexual" and even for having male friends (Sekandari, 2007).

Afghans place a lot of value on hospitality and on their guests; for example, when a guest is over one's home, the host waits to eat until the guest has begun eating (Advameg, 2011). "Afghans will carry hospitality to embarrassing extremes, but are implacable enemies" (Ewans, 2002, p. 9). Refusal to be hospitable or to accept the hospitality of others is very offensive to the Afghan people. For example, if someone offers food, tea, or gifts, it is important to accept them and not say "no." Afghans always offer food or tea to visitors, even when the host may not have enough for himself or herself (Crown, 2007).

Respect is for parents, elders, and for the self (Emadi, 2005). For example, younger individuals are to address elders by their title and not by their name (Advameg, 2011). It is a tradition to stand up to greet an individual when he or she enters the room. It is crucial to stand up and greet an individual especially when it is an elder. It is considered disrespectful and offensive to have one's back towards another, especially an elder (Crown, 2007).

Morality, doing the right thing, is especially important to the Muslim's religion, which in turn is a big part of the culture and family dynamics (Emadi, 2005; Entezar, 2007). Loyalty is to friends, family, community, and/or tribe and is a vital part of the culture (Crown, 2007; Emadi, 2005). To not be loyal typically results in "loss of honor on the part of both parties" (Crown, 2007). In regards to religion, Muslims believe that Islam is a complete way of life (Livengood & Stodolska, 2004). Culture is valued and Afghans are to follow their traditions (Emadi, 2005). Based upon Afghanistan's history, Afghan's culture and traditions come from many different tribal and religious influences (Aryan, 2010; Kaifi, 2009).

Education is very important to Afghans. Educational systems existed even before Afghanistan became a country (Aryan, 2010). Education was formally organized in Afghanistan in 1913 (Sadat, 2004). The first primary school for girls in Afghanistan was established in 1921, eighteen years after the first school for boys (Karlsson & Mansory, n.d.). Higher education was not available for girls in Afghanistan until later; some Afghan girls who were interested in higher education had to go to university in other countries, such as Turkey (Sadat, 2004). The value of education grew over the years and Afghanistan eventually had its own universities, offering higher education in many different fields for both genders (Sadat, 2004). It was not until the mid-1990's that the Taliban took over Afghanistan and shut down many of the schools, including all of the schools for girls (Sadat, 2004).

Women in Islam

According to tradition, Islam is a complete way of life (Livengood & Stodolska, 2004) that was brought to the people to support their civility because, prior to Islam, there were many unjust acts (Younos, 2002). Entezar (2007) claimed that there is a difference between traditional Islam and what now exists in the Arab nations— cultural Islam. The difference is credited to "Islamic fundamentalists," who have a strict and one-sided interpretation of Islam (Entezar, 2007). Many consider themselves Muslim, but follow an understanding of Islam that is based on what they have been taught and retained, rather than on what Islam actually is in its origins (Emadi, 2005). Younos (2002) agreed and added that it is unfortunate that many Muslims do not speak the language of the Qur'an (Arabic) and, therefore, must rely upon the interpretations of others.

According to Entezar (2007), the oppression of women and the forbiddance of their rights is part of cultural Islam. Furthermore, women in Afghanistan have had and continue to have limited access to proper translations of the Qur'an and hadiths and, as a result, believe that what is conveyed to them by Muslim clerics is the word of God or of the Prophet (Younos, 2002). Thus, the combination of lack of education for women and of the Muslim clerics spreading cultural Islam, Afghan women face oppression and many societal trials and obstacles.

Islam is considered to be a complete way of life (Livengood & Stodolska, 2004); therefore, the followers of Islam are accustomed to seeking guidance from Islamic clergy when counseling is needed. In fact, according to Gerner (2007), most U.S. Afghans do not know much about Western psychotherapy. Ali, Milstein, and Marzuk (2005) researched the role of religious leaders (Islamic clergy) attending to the counseling needs of individuals in their US communities. The researchers conducted a survey that they sent to imams throughout the US. Ali, Milstein, and Marzuk (2005) concluded that, when people came to the imams for counseling needs, the issues that they raised rarely included religious concerns; rather, they focused more on domestic and mental health issues than on issues related to social obligations and family dynamics. Johansen (2005) also stated that Muslims typically seek assistance from spiritual leaders who understand their religion. Muslims do not trust counselors who do not take Muslim religious beliefs and practices seriously. Therefore, the Islamic clergy play a central role in counseling in the U.S. because they understand religion and the cultural background of the Muslims seeking assistance.

Younos (2002) and Wadud (1999) explained that some Muslim clerics fail to note that the Qur'an uses the gender-neutral form to address both men and women. Wadud (1999) asserted: There is no distinction between the male and the female with regard to individual capacity. With regard to their potential relationship with Allah, they are the same. With regard to personal aspirations, they are also the same (pp. 34-35).

Islam, Women, and Education

Many individuals have a misguided judgment about Islam; in part, this is due to the influence of cultural Islam, and it is also due to the media, which generally shares only half of the story (Kaifi, 2009). There are many Muslim women who are educated and who did not have to fight for their right to an education (Sadat, 2004). There have been several female Muslim leaders throughout the Muslim countries; for example, Benazir Bhutto (1993-1996) was the Prime Minister of Pakistan and Sima Samar (2001-Present) is currently the chairperson of the Afghanistan Independent Human Rights Commission (AIHRC). Furthermore, Megawati Sukarnoputri (2001-2004) served as the president of Indonesia, which has the largest Muslim population in the world.

Today, however, many women in many Islamic countries are forbidden to go to school, and many Muslim women have to fight for their right to an education. In Afghanistan, parents may be reluctant to send their daughters to school. According to Emadi (2005), some Afghans condemned and strongly opposed the transformation of Afghan schools that allowed female students to attend classes, where "girls were flirts, [and] they were going everywhere, jumping like Tatar gazelles, their legs were shown above their socks [and] they had washed their hands of shame, dishonor and holy honor. And [they] shamed the Nation by their flirting" (p. 212).

Traditionally, in Afghanistan, the girls who were encouraged to go to college were allowed to obtain vocational training to become a nurse or midwife, for example, in order to better serve other women in the country (Emadi, 2005). Due to their pride and honor, Afghan men did not want their wives to be seen by a male physician without a female chaperone; therefore, female nurses were preferred, and this was an acceptable career for Afghan women (Emadi, 2005).

Therefore, it is not the religion, but cultural Islam's interpretation of the religion that has brought on the oppression of women (Entezar, 2007). Oppressing women and depriving them of human rights are not supported by the Qur'an or by Islam; as a matter of fact, Islam was one of the first religions to give equal rights to women (Emadi, 2005; Kaifi, 2009; Younos, 2002).

Furthermore, Godlas (2003) stated that the *hadiths are* the sayings and the traditions of Prophet Muhammad (PBUH) or a report from others about something the Prophet did. According to the hadiths, men and women are considered equal (Younos, 2002). Younos (2002) also claimed that, "knowledge lays the foundation of learning and education in Islam for both sexes" (p. 20). Verse 20:114 of the Qur'an reads, "Exalted is God, the true ruler. Do not rush with Recital before its revelation to you is concluded; but say, "My Lord, increase me in knowledge," (translated by Cleary, 2004, p. 20). The above quote can be interpreted to demonstrate that God asks all Muslims (men and women) to pray for knowledge. Further, Younos (2002) cited Al-Bukhari (1981) who claimed that the hadiths stated, "Seek knowledge from cradle to grave" (p. 22). This is not gender specific and is believed to speak to both men and women. Consequently, the overall message of the hadiths relating to education is that learning is an obligation for both men and women (Younos, 2002). According to Tabari (as cited in Younos, 2002), in Islam, the first object God created was the pen and the first words that were revealed to the Prophet was *iqra* (read). The Qur'an states, "Read, in the name of your Lord, who created: Read, for your Lord is most generous, the one who taught the use of the pen, taught man what he did not know" (96: 1, 3, 4, 5; translated by Cleary, 2004, p. 298). These texts imply that Islam supports learning and education equally for all men and women.

Conclusion

Education is the key to the development of a country and its capacity to develop infrastructure. As such, administrators and officials in Afghanistan must do what they can to provide an environment where people are encouraged and supported to complete their educational dreams by earning advanced degrees nationally or internationally (Mujtaba & Scharff, 2007). Educational opportunities for the local community as well as programs to encourage the return of Afghan expatriates will alleviate the brain-drain challenges facing the country. Many educated Afghan-Americans are hopeful that a stable and secure Afghanistan will emerge so they can return to Afghanistan to assist with the development process. In a qualitative research project by Kaifi (2010), the following three Afghan-American female professionals discussed the importance of education.

The Afghan female physician stated the following:

> "My grandmother was a strong woman. I'm from the mountains, she would say when questioned about her ability to remain steadfast through war in Afghanistan, refugee status in India, and poverty in America. However, I witnessed her strength falter for the first time when news arrived from Kabul announcing the death of her niece during childbirth, leaving a husband widowed and young children motherless. My grandmother quickly regained her composure, but those fleeting moments of weakness were unsettling. I would soon learn that these tragedies were not uncommon for Afghans and that, in fact, Afghanistan endured one of the highest maternal mortality rates in the world. Although I was born and raised in America, my grandmother had instilled in me the desire to help the women of Afghanistan. It was as early as the fifth grade, when I was assigned to write a career report, that I learned the vehicle by which I would reach this dream" (Kaifi, 2010, p. 98).

The Afghan female civil engineer stated the following:

> "Initially, I had entered college as a computer engineering major, but after 9/11 and the ensuing war on Afghanistan; I saw the ousting of the Taliban as a potential opportunity for a democratic Afghanistan. I

figured a time would come where there would be more stability in Afghanistan and I could go back and help re-build. I felt I would be better able to contribute to the re-building efforts in Afghanistan as a civil engineer, and so I change my major halfway through my college career to civil engineering" (Kaifi, 2010, p. 103).

The Afghan female professor stated the following:

"While I recognized that many of my Afghan peers struggled in school, earning poor grades and unable to overcome language-learning challenges, I found school to be one of the few stable and dependable areas of my life over which I had control. I dedicated hours to my homework, studying for the SAT exam and writing and re-writing my personal statements for college applications. Because of our traditional values, my parents insisted that I stay home for college, which meant I would only apply to schools within a 20-mile radius" (Kaifi, 2010, pp. 116-117).

According to Mujtaba and Kaifi (2010), "Afghanistan, however, lacks sufficient human capital that can develop the next generation of workers in a speedy manner. The Afghan workforce needs to be educated and trained so they can create a peaceful environment for themselves and effectively compete with their neighbors in the marketplace" (p. 43). High literacy rates, continuous education, vocational training, and equipping the workforce with the right skills to become industrialized are critical elements to Afghanistan's progressive development and growth (Mujtaba, 2007). Such workforce training efforts can accelerate economic development and reduce Afghanistan's heavy dependence on foreign aid. Therefore, Afghan elders and war veterans should encourage the youth to seek knowledge and to become more competitive both locally and globally. However, there might be cases when Afghan elders, as effective situational leaders, may have to humbly and voluntarily step aside to let the most knowledgeable person lead. Educational qualifications and relevant experience should be the criteria for choosing who will be best suited to make the people, the department, and the country of Afghanistan more economically competitive (Mujtaba, 2005; Mujtaba, 2007; Kaifi, 2013).

References

Advameg, Inc. (2011). Countries and their cultures: Afghanistan. Retrieved on November 14, 2013 from http://www.everyculture.com/A-Bo/Afghanistan.html#ixzz1EWqSu0ga

Ahiakpor, J. (1985). The success and failure of dependency theory: the experience in Ghana. *International Organization, 39* (3), 535-552.

Ali, O., Milstein, G. & Marzuk, P. (2005). The Imam's role in meeting the counseling needs of Muslim communities in the United States. *Psychiatric Services, 56*(2), 202-205. doi: 10.1176/appi.ps.56.2.202

Aryan, B. (2010). *From Kabul to the academy: Narratives of Afghan women's journeys to and through U.S. doctoral programs.* Morgridge College of Education, Denver, CO. Available from ProQuest Dissertations and Theses database. (UMI No. 2175611811).

Crown (2007). *Afghanistan: Cultural appreciation booklet.* Retrieved on November 14, 2013 from
http://www.mod.uk/NR/rdonlyres/DC510C8E-C58C-4DC7-B6EE-
86A69F709A12/0/afghanistan_cultural_appreciation_booklet.pdf

Dos Santos, T. (1970). The structure of dependence. *American Economic Review,* 60(2), 231-236.

Emadi, H. (2005). *Culture and customs of Afghanistan.* Westport, CT: Greenwood Press.

Entezar, M. E. (2007). *Afghanistan 101: Understanding Afghan culture.* Bloomington, IN: Xlibris.

Ewans, M. (2002). *Afghanistan: A short history of its people and politics.* NY: HarperCollins Publishers.

Frank, M. (2002). *Understanding September 11th: Answering questions about the attacks on America.*
New York: Penguin Group.

Gerner, M. (2007). *Psychotherapy in Kabul.* Retrieved on November 14, 2013 from
http://www.qantara.de/webcom/show_article.php/_c-478/_nr-562/i.html

Godlas, A. (2003). Hadith and the Prophet Muhammad. Retrieved on November 14, 2013from
http://www.uga.edu/islam/hadith.html

Hoodfar, H. (2007). Women, religion, and the Afghan education movement in Iran. *Journal of
Development Studies,* 43(2), 265-293.

Johansen, T. M. (2005). Applying Individual Psychology to work with clients of the Islamic faith.
Journal of Individual Psychology, 61(2), 174-184.

Jones, G. R., & George, J. M. (2009). *Contemporary Management.* New York: McGraw-Hill.

Kaifi, B.A. (2008). *The power of education in international economic development.* Sitara Magazine,
1(5), 16-17.

Kaifi, B.A., Mujtaba, B.G., & Xie, Y. (2009). Future Afghan-American leaders' perception of their role
in economic development in Afghanistan: A study of gender differences and willingness to
return to the motherland. *Journal of Diversity Management,* 4(3), 35-46.

Kaifi, B.A. (2009). *A critical hermeneutic approach to understanding experiences of selected Afghan-
American leaders post-9/11 in the Bay Area.* University of San Francisco, San Francisco, CA.
Available from ProQuest Dissertations and Theses database. (UMI No. 1799901131).

Kaifi, B.A. (2010). *Managing Your Future: An Educational Guide.* Davie, Florida. ILEAD Academy.
ISBN: 978-1-936237-03-6.

Kaifi, B.A. (2013). *Capitalism in a Developing, Dependent, and Divided Nation: Afghanistan's
Conundrum.* Pages 39-48. Chapter 4 in Capitalism and its Challenges across Borders. ILEAD
Academy, Davie, Florida. ISBN: 978-1-936237-08-1.

Karlsson, P. & Mansory, A. (2008). *Islamic and modern education in Afghanistan: Conflictual or
complementary?* Unpublished doctoral dissertation, Institute of International Education,
Stockholm. Retrieved on November 14, 2013 from
http://www.netreed.uio.no/articles/Papers_final/Karlsson_Mansory.pdf

Livengood, J. & Stodolska, M. (2004). The effects of discrimination and constraints negotiation on
leisure behavior of American Muslims in the post-September 11 America. *Journal of Leisure
Research, 36(2), 183-208.*

Mujtaba, B.G. (2005). Management and Leadership Developments in Afghanistan: An
Interview with Sayed Tayeb Jawad, Afghanistan's Ambassador to the United States. *Journal
of Applied Management and Entrepreneurship,* (10)4, 81-92.

Mujtaba, B. G. (2007). *The ethics of management and leadership in Afghanistan (2nd edition).* ILEAD
Academy. Davie, Florida USA.

Mujtaba, B. G. (2007). *Afghanistan: Realities of war and rebuilding (2nd edition).* ILEAD Academy,
LLC, Davie, Florida; United States.

Mujtaba, G.B. (2007). Empowering the workforce to deliver superior value through the development of a
customer-oriented culture in developing countries. In the *Global Economy: Challenges in
Developing and Transition Economies;* edited by Mina Baliamoune-Lutz, Alojzy Z. Nowak,
and Jeff Steagall; Volume 2, pages 339-372. ISBN: 978-83-89069-20-7. Warsaw-
Jacksonville, United States.

Mujtaba, B.G., & Scharff, M. M. (2007). *Earning a doctorate degree in the 21st century: Challenges and
joys.* ILEAD Academy Publications; Florida, USA.

Mujtaba, B.G., & Kaifi, B.A. (2010). Business ethics and morality in Afghanistan. *Business and
Professional Ethics Journal,* 29(1-4), 32- 63.

Mujtaba, B.G. & Kaifi, B.A. (2010). An Inquiry into Eastern Leadership Orientation of Working Adults in Afghanistan. *Journal of Leadership Studies*, 4(1), 36-46.

Munck, R. (1999). Dependency and imperialism in the new times: A Latin America perspective. *The European Journal of Development Research*, 11(1), 56-74.

Perraton, J. (2007). Evaluating Marxian contributions to development economies. *Journal of Economic Methodology*, 14(1), 27-46.

Sadat, M. H. (2004). Modern education in Afghanistan. *Lemar-Aftaab*. Retrieved on November 14, 2013 from http://afghanmagazine.com/2004_03/articles/education.shtml

Sekandari, N. (2007). *Parenting in Afghan families: The influence of war experience*. The California School of Professional Psychology, Allied International University, San Francisco, CA. Available from ProQuest Dissertations and Theses database. (UMI No. 1445058951).

Tanner, S. (2009). Indomitable Afghanistan. *Military History, August/September issue, 26 -35.*

Tapper, N. (2001). Pashtun Nomad Women in Afghanistan. *Asian Affairs*, 8, (2), 163- 170.

Tensey, R. & Hyman, M. (1994). Dependency theory and the effects on advertising by foreign-based multinational corporations in Latin America. *Journal of Advertising*, 23(1), 27-42.

Tregarthen, T., & Rittenburg, L. (2000). Economics. NY: Worth Publishers.

U.S. Army. (2004). The study of a nation. Retrieved on November 14, 2013 from http://www.atsc.army.mil/crc/iso6a10l/AfghanistanCountryStudyC.pdf

Velasco, A. (2002). Dependency theory. *Foreign Policy*, 133, 44-46.

Wadud. A. (1999). Qur'an and woman: Rereading the sacred text from a woman's perspective. NY: Oxford University Press.

Younos, F. (2002). *Gender equality in Islam*. Bloomington, IN: Authorhouse.

Chapter 5
Foreign Direct Investment (FDI) of Afghanistan

By: Danai Cheretis and Bahaudin G. Mujtaba
Nova Southeastern University

After researching and understanding the institutional and socio cultural environments of Afghanistan, it is important to also distinguish and analyze the trends of foreign direct investment. Foreign direct investments (FDI) occur when people or companies invest overseas and directly manage the firms that generate their expected financial returns (Geringer, Minor, & McNett, 2013). Unlike typical portfolio investments where investors are only interested in the profits gained and not the way the investments are operated, FDI requires the investor to understand and consider the institutional and socio cultural environments of any country being invested into in order to best operate their businesses for long-term success. Research and clarification on this topic is expected to contribute to the correlation of the underdevelopment of Afghanistan.

The chapter also provides a summary of an interview with the former Afghan ambassador to the United States about business and entrepreneurship opportunities in Afghanistan.

Foreign Direct Investment
According to the World Bank (2014), Afghanistan last reported $94,013,759 of inward foreign direct investment in 2012. This has been a huge decline since 2009 where Afghanistan boasted $213,670,260 in FDI. To put this in comparison, a developed country like Canada reported $43,085,229,811 in 2012. This huge gap and lack of FDI for Afghanistan contributes to the country's underdevelopment. There are some notable investments into Afghanistan that the industries of transport & logistics (DHL), food beverages (Coca-Cola), banking (Pakistani banks), hotels (Hyatt), and automobiles (Toyota). "The largest investor country is Turkey, with projects amounting to about $120 million, followed by Germany, India, and Pakistan. Amounting to an estimated US $180 million, the telecommunications sector has thus far attracted the most investment" (World Bank Group, 2005, p. 24).

Investment Climate of Afghanistan

"It is usually assumed strategic motives will be the driving force for decisions to invest abroad" (Geringer, Minor, & McNett, 2013, p. 43). Companies will invest where they expect to gain the most advantages relative to their industry and nature of business. Multiple factors including government policies, economic policies, economies of scale, knowledge desired, resources, technology, and other business skills are considered and vary from country to country. The generalized and assumed investment climate of Afghanistan by potential investors has hurt the country's potential for FDI that would economically and socially develop the country. After researching the factual evidence of Afghanistan's investment climate, the following strengths and weaknesses were discovered and focused on.

Strengths

Although statistical evidence shows the FDI of Afghanistan is very low and therefore unappealing to international investors, the country offers benefits that are overlooked and if emphasized could boost the amounts of direct investment into the country.

Limited Competition. Since only a few multi-national companies have invested into Afghanistan, the country offers numerous opportunities for businesses looking to dominate an industry or sector. The limited competition also means there is a high demand for quality services, products, and sources of labor. Underdeveloped countries such as Nigeria, Bangladesh, and Indonesia have all experienced growth spurts in FDI due to foreigners looking for fertile land for fresh businesses.

Strong Work Ethic. Studies show Afghanis are very high-context and family-oriented. This equates to strong, collaborative, work ethic that is highly valued in most work environments. Even by analyzing Afghans who immigrated to the United States, most have been successful and demonstrate strong entrepreneurial skills that prove they can adapt to new environments. "The Afghan community has proven to be a dynamic force with high-standards and goals. Afghans have remained successful by working hard, learning new skills, obtaining advanced professional degrees, and adapting to the American culture while keeping their own traditions" (Kaifi & Mujtaba, 2009, p.3).

Financial Profit Margins. Businesses that have opened in Afghanistan require less capital funding than doing business in other developing or developed countries. Cheap labor, cost of living, and resources allows for higher profit margins. As the country develops, these profit margins will diminish so investors who are capable should take advantage of this time-sensitive period of opportunity.

Improvements in Transportation. Although Afghanistan is far from having adequate roads and transportation infrastructure, notable improvements have been made due to the necessity the country has to upgrade its current system. The construction required means a surplus of opportunities for construction workers and the companies that will be able to grow from that success. Improved transportation framework will also allow Afghanistan to take advantage of its geographic location.

"Afghanistan is strategically located between the landlocked countries to the north—Turkmenistan, Uzbekistan, and Tajikistan—and the Iranian and Pakistani seaports to the south, as well as between potentially large trading partners such as Iran and India" (World Bank Group, 2005, p. 32).

Weaknesses
Unfortunately, regardless of the strengths the country entails that could help boost its FDI: the following weaknesses are the major inhibitors preventing it from happening. The irony behind the situation is that without the money FDI would bring into Afghanistan, these weaknesses will be very difficult to overcome and as a result will keep the country underdeveloped.

Political Instability. Western countries that could increase FDI in Afghanistan tend to stereotypically profile the country as a dangerous nation with constant warfare and terrorism. Political instability results in limited foreign investment into the country and also to increased emigration of talent and resources out of the country. "The past three decades of continuous war has left the country with a frail social, economic, and political infrastructure which has resulted in Afghans migrating to the West" (Kaifi & Mujtaba, 2009, p. 3). Potential investors that rely on the Political Risk Atlas, a reference tool that assesses the short-term and long-term political risks that impact a country's development, are likely to get automatically discouraged from investing when Afghanistan is ranked the fourth most risky country to conduct business into (PRA, 2013). Although in recent years Afghanistan has reported numerous improvements that should contribute to a better political risk assessment, "The post-Taliban Government of Afghanistan and its international partners have made great strides in spearheading reconstruction, jump-starting the economy, resettling three million refugees and internally displaced persons, and developing a policy and regulatory framework to support private investment" (World Bank Group, 2005, p. 23), these facts are having a hard time outweighing the long-term reputation Afghanistan carries.

Education Rates. As mentioned in the socio cultural analysis, Afghanistan has a very low literacy rate of about 28%. When investing overseas, the labor force of a country is analyzed to make sure they are capable of doing the work and that it can be done efficiently. Underdeveloped countries have still managed to attract FDI because they have higher literacy rates and their population is perceived to be more fitting for business development.

Infrastructure Issues. Afghanistan currently has weak infrastructure in both the government and in terms of living conditions. Poor roads, lack of common resources, limited electricity, and lack of government stability affect FDI from coming into the country.

Only about 65 percent of the main circuit of highways comprising the Afghan road network is in good condition, and the main transit road for goods to Pakistan, Afghanistan's closest trading partner, is in "disrepair" (World Bank Group, 2005). Investors would be willing to develop the infrastructure needed for businesses to prosper but they can't control the lack of government infrastructure described in the institutional component of our research. Investing in other countries with less corrupted and stable governments offers more protection and security.

Low Average Lifespan. It is also important to note the average lifespan in Afghanistan is only 50 years old, compared to the average of 72 around the world (CIA World, 2014). This is due to wars as well as the lack of necessities and infrastructure previously discussed. Unfortunately, this statistic hinders FDI and results in investors looking in other countries to start their businesses for a labor force that can be more long-term and efficient.

Interview with Former Ambassador Sayed Tayeb Jawad

Ambassador Jawad served as the President Press Secretary and Chief of Staff, as well as the Director of the Office of International Relations at the Presidential Palace. Ambassador Jawad has worked closely with President Karzai and his administration in formulating strategies, implementing policies, building national institutions and prioritizing reforms in Afghanistan. He worked with U.S. and Afghan military officials to reform the Ministry of Defense and rebuild the Afghan National Army. He was instrumental in drafting the foreign investment laws and served as President Karzai's principal liaison with the constitutional commission during the process of the drafting of the new constitution. Under his leadership, the Afghan Embassy in Washington emerged as one of the most successful missions in Washington. He also served as Afghanistan nonresident Ambassador to Mexico and Brazil, and accompanied President Karzai on most foreign trips.

Born in Kandahar, Afghanistan, Ambassador Jawad was educated at the Afghan French Lycée Istiqlal and School of Law and Political Sciences at Kabul University. Shortly after the Soviet invasion in 1980, he left Afghanistan and went into exile in Germany, where he studied law at Westfaelische Wilhelms University in Muenster. In 1986 he migrated to USA, where he received his MBA from Golden Gate University in San Francisco and worked for a number of prominent law firms.

Ambassador Jawad is a writer and commentator. He has published hundreds of articles and conducted numerous interviews with the international media throughout the world. He is fluent in English, German, and French. The following interview was conducted when he was an Afghan Ambassador to the United States (Mujtaba, 2007).

Bahaudin: Afghanistan is going through an infrastructure development process at this time. What is the status of development and progress in terms of business and management in the country thus far? What are some business opportunities for and management or entrepreneurship development? What are some of the businesses or organizations that are now doing really well in Afghanistan? What are some of the reasons for their successes?

Ambassador Jawad: Afghanistan is in a very exciting period of time. There are tremendous opportunities for visionary businesspeople to take part in its rebuilding effort. As well, the country has opened its doors for business and investment opportunities. After years of conflict and isolation, Afghanistan has re-entered the global marketplace and is effectively reintegrating. First, the people of Afghanistan adopted principles of a free market economy in the new constitution, and the Afghan government has taken steps to implement that vision. Second, the Afghan government has identified the growth of the private sector as a high priority, and reform efforts are focusing on removing obstacles to private sector development. Third, our government has expressed its intent on becoming a policymaker, not an implementer of projects, which provides companies with contracting opportunities. Thus, the efforts of the Afghan government have helped lay the foundation for successful business development. Furthermore, many international institutions involved in the reconstruction process – the United States Agency for International Development, Asian Development Bank, World Bank, IMF, and United Nations - to name a few, have their own contracting and procurement process, which present additional business development opportunities.

Since the fall of the Taliban, Afghanistan has experienced and continues to experience high rates of growth. Of course, the baseline in Afghanistan is low given the 23 year period of conflict, but one needs to keep in mind that with the destruction of infrastructure and institutions, our achievements have been remarkable, and particularly in the following areas:

Restoration of the highways has been an overriding priority of President Karzai. It is crucial to extending the influence of the new government. Many sections of Afghanistan's highway and regional road system are undergoing reconstruction. The U.S. Agency for International Development, with assistance from Japan, completed building a highway linking Kabul to the southern regional capital, Kandahar. Plans are in place to extend the road into Herat and arching it back through Mazar-e-Sharif and Kabul. This route will be referred to as the Ring Road. With its completion, all central Asian capitals will be only 32 hours from the Persian Gulf. Our next priority is to increase power generation and build water dams.

In terms of business infrastructure, there is increased access to capital. This has greatly improved in the last two years. Loans for projects in Afghanistan are available through the International Finance Corporation and the Overseas Private Investment Corporation (OPIC). Political risk insurance is available through OPIC and the Multilateral Guarantee Agency. Additionally, the first venture capital fund was announced this year, Afghanistan Capital Partners, and more venture capitalists are beginning to see the opportunities in Afghanistan.

The industrial parks offer power, water, sewer and road connections that will allow investors to establish factories, plants and offices. Thus, while the government works with donors on improving physical infrastructure countrywide, the development of industrial parks can meet most investors' business infrastructure needs.

The business environment has quickly improved in the area of banking and financial institutions. The Afghan government passed a new Banking Law in September 2003. Shortly afterward, licenses were issued. In April 2004, more than five international banks were operational in the country. This has greatly improved the country's business infrastructure since there is a mechanism to transfer and deposit funds inside Afghanistan.

Since Afghanistan has always been characterized by a strong trading tradition, there are business organizations and chambers of commerce. In 2004, the Afghanistan International Chamber of Commerce was launched, with affiliates planned in different countries. Thus, there are mechanisms in place to identify local partners if needed, facilitating business and investment.

There are also business opportunities through contracting and subcontracting with various institutions. Another major achievement for the Afghan government was the creation of the Afghanistan Reconstruction and Development Service, (ARDS), which handles procurement of Afghan government funded projects using internationally recognized procurement regulations. This open and transparent online system has made offering goods and services for Afghan government funded projects much easier.

Success stories include major companies such as DHL, Siemens, Alcatel, Hyatt and 11 foreign banks already invested in Afghanistan. Eleven private banks have received their licenses from the Central Bank in the past three years. The National Bank, Pashtani Tejarati, Standard Chartered, Pakistan National Bank and Aryan Bank are among those private banks doing well in Afghanistan. Therefore, although there are many challenges, there are also many opportunities for business managers and entrepreneurs interested in Afghanistan.

Bahaudin: How would you describe the leadership in the new government and their vision for Afghanistan? How will such new leaders and their visions change the country of Afghanistan in the next few decades?

Ambassador Jawad: The Afghan Cabinet consists of educated and qualified individuals, who are determined to establish a democratic state that will build on our rich traditions, and will make Afghanistan a long-term partner of the international community. All ministers have a higher education. It also reflects broadly the ethnic composition of the country, with Pashtuns, Tajiks, Hazaras, Uzbeks as well as Turkman and Baluch. Three women are in the cabinet including the former presidential candidate, Masuda Jalal.

Bahaudin: How would you describe the government's entrepreneurship philosophy? What are they doing to attract more international businesses and organizations to invest in Afghanistan?

Ambassador Jawad: The private sector is to serve as the engine for growth in Afghanistan. Since a new currency was successfully introduced, a stable exchange rate against international currencies has been maintained. Businesses in Afghanistan are now experiencing an inflation free environment, ensuring the autonomy of the banking sector. After enacting a new banking law, several international banks have opened branches in Kabul and we expect more.

A new investment law has also been enacted and an open trade regime has been introduced. Traders and investors are faced with limited tariffs. Border formalities are being reduced to a minimum. In addition, we have set up, with the assistance of the German government, a one-stop-shop for investors known as the Afghan Investment Support Agency. To meet international standards, a National Bureau of Standards is now being established.

Bahaudin: Is the Afghan workforce ready for the progress envisioned by the government leaders? If not, what are your recommendations? How can the international community and other expatriate professional Afghans assist in the development?

Ambassador Jawad: In general, Afghanistan lacks human capital. Our workforce needs to be educated and trained. In this regard, we strongly favor plans, such as exchange programs, that will be aimed at training our citizens to serve as a more effective work force. We need increased training and education opportunities.

Bahaudin: Afghanistan created and instituted their new Constitution just about a decade ago. Is the Constitution able to keep a balance with the culture of Afghanistan and the expectations of the international community? What are some tasks and behavioral expectations needed from all adults in Afghanistan to make sure they live according to the intentions of the Constitution?

Ambassador Jawad: Our Constitution, which was signed by President Karzai on January 4, 2004, is a balanced national charter. It provides for equal rights and full participation of women. It seeks and finds equilibrium between building a strong central executive branch (to further strengthen national unity and rebuild the national institutions) and respecting the rights and volition of the provinces to exercise more authority in managing their own local affairs. It is also a careful combination of respect for moderate and traditional values of the Afghan society and adherence to the international norms of human rights and democracy. Our constitution further reveals that our Islamic and traditional values are fully compatible and mutually reinforcing with an open democracy. The Afghan people are satisfied with their constitution as it is serving as a guideline to achieve a civil society. The people of Afghanistan have illustrated their demand for a democracy. During the Constitutional Loya Jirga in December of 2004, 502 Afghans from all walks of life and every province and community of the country gathered together, put all intricate issues on the table, and after three weeks of intense debate and emotional deliberations adopted, with near unanimous acclamation, the most progressive constitution in the region. As we will be holding our Parliamentary elections in a few months' time, we need to educate people about the culture of a Parliament and political parties.

Bahaudin: How do Afghans view the intentions of the United States of America with regards to business development in the country? Is the International Community doing what they can to assist in the speedy recovery of business infrastructure throughout Afghanistan?

Ambassador Jawad: Afghanistan's principal markets and trading partners include Pakistan, South Korea, China, Japan, India, UAE, Germany, UK, United States, and Russia. In April, Afghanistan hosted a trade and investment conference for the Economic Cooperation Organization (ECO), and Afghanistan was selected as headquarters for a two-year period by its regional member countries. Thus, Afghans are very open to business and trade from any country in the world. Most Afghans view products from the United States as representing high quality and thus welcome investments from U.S. companies. Any companies that can create jobs, help substitute for imports, and generate opportunities, are wanted. Afghanistan has a long history of working with the U.S., especially USAID, to improve infrastructure in the country. Afghans continue to welcome the U.S.'s assistance in improving the country's business infrastructure and also working with the U.S. private sector through joint ventures, contracts and other business opportunities. In terms of international assistance for infrastructure improvements, many donors, including the United States, Japan, India and others have supported the improvement of the country's road network. The Asian Development Bank and World Bank are assisting in improvements in transportation, water, power and energy. Private investment in communications and logistics has also ameliorated the business infrastructure. However, given the lack of development during the period of conflict, Afghanistan needs greater assistance from the international community in order to rehabilitate and improve the country's basic infrastructure. Improvements in this area have many positive secondary benefits. By supporting a better environment for business and trade, Afghanistan will be less dependent in the long-term on foreign aid. We hope that donors and international financial institutions will increase commitments to infrastructure improvements. It is an investment not only in Afghanistan, but also in regional stability and economic development.

Bahaudin: Are there female entrepreneurs, managers, and leaders in Afghanistan? What are some of the typical business opportunities for female leaders in Kabul? Also, based on your views, what can the government officials do to increase management and leadership opportunities for Afghan females?

Ambassador Jawad: Yes, there are many female entrepreneurs, managers and leaders in Afghanistan. However, just like other entrepreneurs in Afghanistan, they need assistance to meet their full potential. Given the lack of opportunities and education during the period of conflict, especially during the time of the Taliban, typical business opportunities for women in Kabul are in handicrafts, carpet weaving, and small-scale industry. Recently, women have entered the service industry, including operating hair salons, dress shops and guesthouses. Women who have acquired the skills are also able to engage in other sectors. For example, Cisco has sponsored a learning academy in Kabul that is training women in computer, networking and IT skills. There are already many women who were educated abroad that have brought back information technology skills that they are applying in this sector. Women who receive such training in Afghanistan will then also be able to enter jobs in this market.

Women who were educated prior to the conflict in Afghanistan or who were educated in Pakistan, Iran or other countries are able to find opportunities in the workforce and in different business areas. Many women work for UN agencies, nonprofit organizations and private companies. These women are well equipped to start or operate their own businesses if they have access to capital and are therefore poised to become our country's future business leaders. Women outside of Kabul are engaged as well in handicrafts and carpet weaving, but are also involved in the country's agricultural sector. Many women own land, farms or small-scale agricultural businesses, including milk production, dried fruits and nuts, and canning and pickling of fruits and vegetables. Given access to capital, equipment and knowledge of marketing their products, these women will be able to expand upon their entrepreneurial talents. Women's entrepreneurship has been important to the Afghan government. In 2003, the Ministry of Commerce instituted the Entrepreneurship Development for Afghan Women office (EDAW) with the assistance of USAID's Economic Governance program. EDAW provides English, computer and business training for Afghan women. Women in this program have participated in regional trade shows, and met with foreign companies interested in employing or working with Afghan women. This year, they have launched the Afghan Women's Business Association and a journal dedicated to women's business issues. The Association plans to grow to cities outside of Kabul and to strengthen Afghan women's participation in business. The Afghan government encourages donors, nonprofit organizations and private companies to support projects that provide training and tools Afghan women need to become business owners. One of these areas is access to capital. Many organizations are supporting micro-credit programs, such as CARE, FINCA, and others. The UN also designated 2005 as the Year of Micro Credit and chose Afghanistan as one of eight focus countries. In November 2004, eight Afghan entrepreneurs, including many women, were given awards for their ability to use micro finance to start or expand their businesses. These programs have greatly assisted Afghan women entrepreneurs in the past two years. Ultimately, it will be the private sector that will be the key to providing opportunities for women that are sustainable. The Afghan government will continue to work on education and training programs to benefit Afghan women and will support initiatives that build their capacity to engage in business. In order to do this, the sustained assistance of the international community is vital.

Bahaudin: What advice do you offer for Afghan professionals living outside of the country that want to help? How can they assist their motherland without leaving their current jobs?

Ambassador Jawad: Hundreds of prominent Afghan intellectuals, experts and entrepreneurs have returned to their country to assist in enhancing institutional capacity building or making major investments. Afghans who are living abroad can also play a positive role in the rebuilding effort of their country. They can organize and serve as effective advocacy groups, by actively speaking out or writing in favor of continued assistance for Afghanistan, and can also advise our government on how to implement projects.

Afghanistan is ready for international investors and has already welcomed many of them. A major achievement was the creation of the Afghan Investment Support Agency (AISA), within the framework of the Ministry of Commerce to facilitate and promote investment in Afghanistan. AISA is the "One Stop Shop for Investors" and is responsible for the registration, licensing and promotion of all new investments in Afghanistan. AISA has been able to get rid of unnecessary bureaucracy and red tape and shorten the investment registration/licensing process from several months to just five days. Thus, the process to begin an investment in Afghanistan has been streamlined. Some of the major reasons to invest in Afghanistan include:

1. One of the lowest custom tariffs in the region
2. Low tax rates
3. Low labor costs
4. A growing domestic consumer market
5. An opportunity to create employment for women
6. An eager and committed work force
7. Location and ability to reach neighboring markets
8. Freely exchangeable currency, which has experienced remarkable stability
9. Liberal investment law passed in 2002 that allows 100% foreign ownership, full transferability of profits outside the country, international dispute resolution mechanisms, and streamlined investment licensing procedures
10. Some of the key sectors for investment include:
11. Agriculture
12. Architectural, construction and engineering services
13. Building and construction materials
14. Power generation and transmission
15. Oil and gas exploration
16. Telecommunications
17. Food processing
18. Manufacturing
19. Textiles and carpets
20. Education services
21. Consumer Electronics
22. Transportation
23. Equipment and machinery sales and leasing
24. Irrigation technology
25. Leather and leather processing
26. Precious and semi-precious stones
27. Marble and other industrial stones

These are just some of the sectors available for investment. Afghanistan's abundant mineral resources and agricultural raw materials, linked with considerable potential energy resources, provide a favorable scope for industrialization efforts. In addition, Afghan carpets, dried fruits and nuts enjoyed a reputation for quality and taste in the region, and large markets are available to absorb those products again. Afghanistan is not only an emerging market, but is a gateway to investment in Central Asia. A major part of the reconstruction plan has been connecting the nation to neighboring countries to make it a key transit point in the region. With increasing stability and increasing investments in roads, railways and air routes, entrepreneurs can trade not only with Afghanistan, but also with Central and South Asia. Already, goods are flowing from Central to South Asia, from India to Iran and back. Thus, by investing in Afghanistan, you are not only accessing a market of 25 million, but a market of 150 million just in the areas immediately surrounding Afghanistan.

Bahaudin: What are some things that the international community should know about the people of Afghanistan, their hopes and their desires? What are your best memories from the past few years as you toured Afghanistan?

Visionary investors have invested in Afghanistan and are making sizable profits. The markets are less competitive right now. This provides a great opportunity for "First Movers" to make large amounts of earnings. Afghanistan is the largest market in Central Asia and can serve as a trade hub for neighboring countries. Kabul is the largest city in Central Asia in terms of population, with high demands for consumer goods. Further stabilization and reconstruction of Afghanistan will re-establish the country's role as a land bridge between Central Asia, South Asia, and Southwest Asia – a historic and growing market with a total GDP of $ 4 trillion (Mujtaba, 2007).

Summary

After reviewing the FDI trends of Afghanistan, a strong correlation can be made between the lack of foreign direct investment the country receives and its lack of development. The country obviously has low literacy rates, lack of infrastructure, and records of political instability but they are incrementally improving over recent years. These improvements will only continue and help develop the country if investments continue to grow. Donations from international organizations are not enough to contribute to the bigger picture and help Afghanistan become a thriving economy with a business sector. "It is essential that trade performance be viewed in the context of its effects on employment levels, economic growth, development, and an improvement in the overall human condition" (Geringer, Minor & McNett, 2013). Afghan-Americans can also help contribute to the development of Afghanistan by giving back to their home country and starting up businesses. Without this proper funding, the country cannot be expected to modernize.

References

Afghanistan in Brief. (2006). *The Embassy of Afghanistan, Washington, D.C..* Retrieved June 4, 2014, from http://www.embassyofafghanistan.org/page/afghanistan-in-brief

Afghanistan: The Current Situation. *United States Institute of Peace.* Retrieved June 2, 2014, from
    http://www.usip.org/afghanistan-the-current-situation
Australia and the World Bank Group: Saving lives, creating opportunity. (2011, January 1). *Australia
    and the World Bank Group: Saving lives, creating opportunity.* Retrieved June 2, 2014, from
    http://aid.dfat.gov.au/Publications/Pages/3719_4596_4159_5649_9149.aspx
Australia in a Brief, Australian Government Department of Foreign Affairs and Trade. (ed.). (2012).
    Barton : .
Bank Group (MIGA). Investment Horizons: Afghanistan. *A Study of Foreign Direct*
CIA. (2014.). World Factbook. *Central Intelligence Agency.* Retrieved June 4, 2014, from
    https://www.cia.gov/library/publications/the-world-factbook/
doi: 10.1787/9789264087255-en
Faeth, Isabel. (2006). Consequences of FDI in Australia – Causal Links between FDI, Domestic
    Investment, Economic Growth and Trade. *Department of Economics – The University of
    Melbourne.* Retrieved from http://fbe.unimelb.edu.au/__data/assets/pdf_file/
    0003/802920/977.pdf
Geringer, J. M., Minor, M. S., & McNett, J. M. (2012). *International business.* New York, NY: McGraw-
    Hill/Irwin.
IMF Program Note on the Islamic Republic of Afghanistan. (n.d.). IMF Program Note on the Islamic
    Republic of Afghanistan. Retrieved May 28, 2014, from
    http://www.imf.org/external/np/country/notes/afghanistan.htm
*Investment Costs and Conditions in Four Industries. Retrieved May 29, 2014, from
    http://www.miga.org/documents/horizon.pdf*
K. E. Meyer, S. Estrin, S. Bhaumik, and M. W. Peng (2008) Institutions, resources, and entry strategies
    in emerging economies (SMJ, forthcoming)
    http://eprints.aston.ac.uk/20355/1/Institutions_resources_and_entry_strategies.pdf
Kaifi, B., Mujtaba, B. G., and Xie, Y. (2009). The Perception of Afghan-American Leaders' Role in
    Economic Development Efforts in Afghanistan: A Study of Gender Differences and
    Repatriation to the Motherland. *Journal of Diversity Management,* 4(3), 35-46.
Kaifi, B.A. and Mujtaba, B.G. (2009). Managing diversity: An inquiry on Afghan-Muslim-American
    Professionals in the workforce. *Journal of Business Studies Quarterly,* 1(1), 1-15.
Mohmand, A. (2012, June 14). THE PROSPECTS FOR ECONOMIC DEVELOPMENT IN
    AFGHANISTAN . The Asian Foundations. Retrieved May 27, 2014, from
    http://asiafoundation.org/resources/pdfs/ProspectsofEconomicDevelopmentinAfghanistanOcc
    asionalPaperfinal.pdf
Mujtaba, B. G. (2007). *Afghanistan: Realities of war and rebuilding (2nd edition).* LEAD Academy, LLC,
    Florida; United States.
Mujtaba, B. G. (2005). Market-Based Leadership Skills for Public and Private Sector Capacity
    Development in Afghanistan. *Society of Afghan Engineers Journal,* 2(1), 01-18.
Mujtaba, B. G. and Kaifi, B. A. (2010). An Inquiry into Eastern Leadership Orientation of Working
    Adults in Afghanistan. *Journal of Leadership Studies,* 4(1), 36-46.
Mujtaba, B. G. and Kaifi, B. A. (2010). Management Skills of Afghan Respondents: A Comparison of
    Technical, Human and Conceptual Differences Based on Gender. *Journal of International
    Business and Cultural Studies,* 4(1), 01-14.
N.A. (2013). Foreign Direct Investment (FDI) in Australia. *Hellenic – Australian Business Council.*
    Retrieved from http://www.habc.gr/australia_fdi.asp
N.A. (2014). Foreign Investment – A Key Drive in Australia's Future Growth. *Pitcher Partners.*
    Retrieved from http://www.pitcher.com.au/Foreign-Investment-%E2%80%93-a-key-driver-
    in-Australia%E2%80%99s-future-growth-
N.A. (2014). Stock of Foreign Investment in Australia by Country. *NSW Government.* Retrieved from
    http://www.business.nsw.gov.au/invest-in-nsw/about-nsw/trade-and-investment/stock-of-
    foreign-direct-investment-in-australia-by-country
OECD (2010), Regional Development Policies in OECD Countries, OECD Publishing.
Overview - Australia in brief - Australian Government Department of Foreign Affairs and Trade.
    Overview - Australia in brief - Australian Government Department of Foreign Affairs and
    Trade. Retrieved May 27, 2014, from http://www.dfat.gov.au/aib/overview.html

Overview. - *Ministry of Commerce and Industries*. Retrieved June 2, 2014, from
http://moci.gov.af/en/page/8777

Palm, R. (2005). Reforming the business environment in Afghanistan . Business Environment . Retrieved
May 27, 2014, from http://www.businessenvironment.org/dyn/be/docs/74/Session2.2Palm-
FatimieDoc.pdf

People, culture and lifestyle - About Australia - Australian Government Department of Foreign Affairs
and Trade. (2012). *People, culture and lifestyle - About Australia - Australian Government
Department of Foreign Affairs and Trade*. Retrieved June 4, 2014, from
https://www.dfat.gov.au/facts/people_culture.html

Schwab, K. (2013). Global competitiveness report 2012-2013. Retrieved May 22, 2014, from
http://www3.weforum.org/docs/WEF_GlobalCompetitivenessReport_2012-13.pdf

SEPUTIENE, J. (2010). The impact of institutional environment on economic development of the
European Union countries . Retrieved May 22, 2014, from
http://www.icabr.com/fullpapers/Seputiene%20Janina.pdf - See more at:

Socio-cultural environment. BusinessDictionary.com. Retrieved June 04, 2014, from
BusinessDictionary.com website: http://www.businessdictionary.com/definition/socio-
cultural-environment.html

Taylor, Rob. (2014). Australia urged to Change Rules on Foreign Investments. *The Wall Street Journal,
May*. Retrieved from http://online.wsj.com/articles/australia-urged-to-change- rules-on-
foreign-investments-1401451517

United Nations and Afghanistan. *UN News Center*. Retrieved June 4, 2014, from
http://www.un.org/news/dh/latest/afghan/un-afghan-history.shtml

West, B. A., & Murphy, F. T. (2010). *A brief history of Australia*. New York: Facts On File.

World Bank. 2014. *Afghanistan - Country snapshot*. Washington DC ; World Bank Group.
http://documents.worldbank.org/curated/en/2014/03/19424006/afghanistan-country-snapshot

Yih Yun Yang, Jeannie., Groenewold, Nicolaas., Tcha, Moonjoong. (2007). The Determinants of Foreign
Direct Investment in Australia. *Economic Record*. Retrieved from
http://onlinelibrary.wiley.com/doi/10.1111/j.1475-4932.2000.tb00004.x/abstract

Chapter 6
Gender Inequality and Religion in Pakistan's KPK Province

By: **Farzana Rahman Safi**
University of Peshawar

In realm of collective human life, mankind has been grappling with certain problems that have plagued many civilizations and cultures. The varied response of different cultures to these problems, have been in similitude to the sings of a pendulum, trying to achieve harmony and peace among the members of society. Among such problems is the responsibilities and status of women in society. From the killing of infant females in old Arabia to the absolute freedom of modern female mankind has witnessed one failure after another in achieving an equilibrium between responsibilities and rights of two genders so that both can have rightful place in and make contribution to a society, according to and in harmony with their inherent physical and psychological natures.

Introduction

Gender! The word is quite in vogue. To understand this hippodrome of a social construction called Gender it may be undertaken that it is supposed to be different from a biological being called Sex. Gender is about the behaviors, attitudes, roles and status assigned to an individual in a social-cultural setting. The status of individuals and the power they use to rule in any society are culturally determined, as all cultures are gender sensitive.

    Gender relationship is a vital practice that influences the lives of men and women in any society. It is so important that it affects the roles we play, and the relative power we wield. It determines the opportunities and privileges we have in our societies.

    Sexism is an aspect of gender inequality that is perpetuated through gender norms. Healey explains that there are two types of sexism, hostile and benevolent. Hostile sexism includes agreement with negative stereotypes against women and "anti-minority group prejudice" whereas benevolent sexism is often "expressed as an apparently positive attitude of protection and affection" (2006:99). He asserts that both types of sexism "promote stereotypical views of women and serve to justify and rationalize their lower status" (2006:99). Gender inequality has a profound effect on women and girls everywhere as it erodes their basic rights to life, health, and security. For more than three decades, women's organizations have drawn attention to this issue and have developed a variety of strategies to delimit gender inequalities. Nevertheless, gender imbalance continues as a serious social problem. No nation has successfully eradicated it, although the incidence and types of violence differ across contexts.

Gender inequality is a serious social problem. It has an intense consequence on women and girls everywhere as it creates serious problems and violation of women basic rights across the globe and it is widespread in all countries, irrespective of social, economic, religious, or cultural group. For more than three decades, women's organizations have drawn attention to this issue and have developed a variety of strategies to delimit gender inequalities. Nevertheless, gender imbalance continues as a serious social problem. No nation has successfully eradicated it, although the incidence and types of hostility differ across the globe. Women rights and their participation in developmental activities in the Muslim world vary from place to place on account of social customs and religious interpretations.

Gender inequality, a "hot" issue, is genetically ascribed to religion, in general, and to Islam, in particular, whereas its causes are purely non-religious and largely due to misinterpretation of religious teachings. It originates from personal, political, economic, social and cultural factors. As for Islam, gender equality is part of its jurisprudence and fundamental teachings. Numerous Verses of the Qur'an and Prophetic Traditions enjoin balance in gender rights and responsibilities which categorically proves that gender inequality is not faith-based.

"O mankind! Fear your Lord Who (initiated) your creation from a single soul, then from it created its mate, and from these two spread (the creation of) countless men and women" (al-Qur'an, 4:1). The *ayat* (verse) clearly expounds that man or woman are created from a single entity and are basically equal genders. As a gender, one is not superior to the other.

Current practices of gender inequality and Islamic stance

Women role is important determinant of progress, not only because women constitute almost half of human resources, but because they have to bear the brunt of daily struggle for a graceful survival, particularly in developing economies. The women status in South Asia is sharply different from the western world.

Even though gender issues have a global phenomenon, Pakistan is the most affected. Pakistan is the second largest Muslim country after Indonesia and the number of Muslims there constitutes 11 percent of the world's Muslim population. Pakistan stands at the crossroads of geostrategic regions South Asia and Central Asia. In Pakistan generally, and Khyber Pukhtun Khwa (KPK) particularly, gender relations are dominated by the male. The gender gap favouring male has remained persistent itself in almost all factors of development in Pakistan. The status of woman is miserable in KPK province of Pakistan which is a traditional society where it is quite clear that the social position of women is expected to be inferior to that of men. This is generally true, although, as we shall see, women in this society are endowed with certain rights that assure them of some protection against the tyranny of men. The role and status of women in the KPK has been defined by centuries of cultural patterns and social restrictions and justified by unrealistic religious sanctions.

Muslim women in KPK
Interestingly, in KPK one may find a combination of practices with Muslim women who constitute more than fifty percent of local population. Female are found in a heterogeneous group wherein socioeconomic (rural/urban, educated/uneducated), ethnic and religious factors play an important role in patterning women's gendered experience. Some practices are highly recommended by Islam while others do not fit into the Islamic thought. Most people are unable to distinguish cultural practices from religiously legitimate practices. They lack a clear understanding of how Islam can be interpreted within Islam (Al-Ashmawi, 2006). In fact, Islam is seen by many scholars as a religion that consists of a set of political, economic, legal, and social doctrines that affect every facet of the social life of believers (Kurtz, 1995: 106,135; Schacht, 1982; Turner, 1974: 112; & Robertson 1970: 86).

Qur'anic teachings promote an ascetic ethic of self-control that bears on virtually all aspects of everyday activity. For Muslims, faith has not merely been a matter of private life and a personal relation with God. It has had pervasive collective and social consequences. Thus, following Stark (*et al.* 1982), it may be argued that Islam develops a strong sense of moral community, where religion is an influential social force generating social consciousness (Groves et al. 1987).

Religious equality and balance between rights and duties of men and women:
One dimension, which is particularly shaped by Islamic tenets, is the status of and relationship between men and women. Equality and justice between rights and responsibilities of both genders is a distinct goal in Islam. Contrary to commonly held belief, the Holy Quran is particularly solicitous about women's wellbeing and development. It is evident from the mention of women rights in Qur'an as detailed in Table 6.1.

However, women have been the targets of the most serious human rights violation in Muslim societies. Some Muslims of the world generally and of Pakistan particularly are engulfed in much confusion and controversy over the topic of women rights and responsibilities. They are unsuccessful in identifying and aligning the daily practices with divine sources of guidance in relation to how to treat and deal the weaker gender of society.

Table 6.1 – The Mention of Women Rights in Holy Qur'an

Women entitlement to Rights	Mention in Qur'an
Right to life	Surah Anaam, ayat 151
Right to respect	Surah Isra, ayat 70
Right to Justice	Surah Maidah, ayat 8; Surah Nisa, ayat 136; Surah Najum, ayat 38-39; Surah Hujrat, ayat 13.
Right to Freedom	Surah Imran, ayat 79; Surah Kahaf, ayat 29; Surah Baqarah, ayat 62; Surah Anaam, ayat 108
Right to Privacy	Surah Noor, ayat 27-28; Surah Ahzab,, ayat 53; Surah Hujrat, ayat 11-12; Surah Noor, ayat 16-19; Surah Nisa, ayat148-149.
Right to acquire knowledge	Surah Alaq, ayat 1-5
Right to develop aesthetic sensibilities & enjoy bounties created by Allah	Surah Aaraf, ayat 32
Right to Sustenance	Surah Hud, ayat 6
Right to work	Surah Nisa, ayat 32
Right to Marriage	Surah Nisa, ayat 4
Right to Divorce	Surah Baqarah, ayat 231 and 241

Main reasons of confusion in gender roles

The 'mental model of ignorant Muslims'
We are in agreement with Ahmad (2003) where he identified two main reasons for this confusion - mental models of ignorant Muslims and of secular minded people. The first reason is the 'ignorant Muslims' (unaware of the true message of Holy Quran and authentic sayings of the Last Prophet) have imposed their own 'self-forged model' upon the Muslim women. This model has indeed confined the Muslim woman to merely a 'beast of household burdens' and a 'sex-maid'. Such a mind-set has eradicated the women's grace, privileges and rights that she deserves in Islamic code of conduct. It is clearly held in Quran that: 'Women too have rights over men similar to the rights of men over women' (Al-Qur'an, 2:228).

This Verse denotes that rights enjoyed by men are in fact the responsibilities and duties of the women and what constitutes as the duties and responsibilities of men are in reality the rights of women. This implies a similitude and a unique balance between both genders. There is no right conferred on man that woman may be deprived of because she is a woman.

'Men, however, have an advantage over them'. (Al-Qur'an, 2:228). Here the Qur'an refers to man's superiority, but primarily, by the virtue of his greater responsibility of continuous protection and maintenance of woman, adequate provision of their needs and fulfilment of their rights. It includes provision of spiritual, moral, intellectual, psychological, economic and social support. Creator of heavens and earth has made man physically stronger, more responsible and much tolerant with reference to mundane matters of life. So man is held superior to woman in the grade of responsibility and in grade of manhood without responsibility. However, in common practice in Pakistan, men uphold their undesirable treatment of women in light of self-made impression of aforementioned *ayat* (verse). Greater portion of male population deny responsibilities and rights of women and take undue benefit from superiority.

The 'mental model of secular minded people':
Secondly, the 'secular minded' people of the society have freed woman from all family related graceful participation and has dragged her into a market of physically hard jobs, 'sex object' at work, 'beauty of office' and a 'piece of decoration and attraction'. At another extreme, this model has curbed woman into an immoral physical being that may comfort men in many ways. In general observation, the obvious consequences in most of women folk are aversion to marital responsibilities and child-bearing / rearing that has a trigger down effect in form of un-attended childhood, inadequately supervised teenage, and feebly guided life of new generation.

Role of divine guidance in a confused scenario of gender roles:
This is a scenario of two extreme mental models of mankind regarding the status, role and responsibilities of women in family and the society at large. One can easily understand the dire need of a divine guidance that may come from the Creator and Sustainer of both genders; the divine guidelines that could accurately do justice to rights and responsibilities of both males and females. Undoubtedly, whenever male segment of society attempt to allocate boundaries for gender role, the women would be the victims on the cost of maximum ease and comfort and heart-favoring of men. Whereas, the men would suffer more if women attempts to solve the disputes of gender roles because they can only see through *female lens* at male issues. It is not necessarily a deliberate and conscious attempt by both sexes but is quite a natural phenomenon wherein each gender can only apprehend, express and manage their own gender-based natural feelings, needs and expectations. That is why, men by no means can fully understand the truest feelings, natural demands and expectations of women; resulting in faulty mental models and practices as regards to women.

Chabaya (*et. al,* 2009) has argued the same and as a 'stereotypical notion of women as inadequate beings and a sex agent has gradually become well-established in the collective consciousness affecting the way in which individuals apprehend and interpret the world around them'(p. 245). An average wisdom seems to strive in knowing how actually has the gender roles been defined by the Divine

Law that unerringly knows the deepest feelings, wishes and satisfaction of both men and women.

Women in Rural KPK

The ground reality, however, is an exasperating one. The treatment of female in rural and tribal area of KPK is much different in some aspects from how she is treated in an urbanized area. In rural area women are treated as personal property. Boys are fed, dressed and dealt better than girls in a family. Boys are considered a family's pride whereas girls are more like a liability. Women are considered a source of dispute and chaos in an urban mode of life. This thought resembles the Christian's idea about Eve that she was the prime trouble maker. However, Quran holds that both Adam and Eve were equally involved and considered sinners in equal measure; and that the repentance of both was accepted.

The inferior treatment of female starts as early as her birth. The birth of daughter is not celebrated like that of boy. Guns are fired, expensive presents are exchanged among family members and an extensive meal is arranged for all relatives at birth of a boy. The expenses on girls are considered burden while on boys the money spent is an investment. By and large, a rural girl may be put in *Dini Madrassa* (religious education centres) and a boy in expensive schooling.

Women in other rural areas of Pakistan

Other provinces of Pakistan are not different in horrific behaviour to its women folk. Women, in KPK, Punjab, Sindh and Balochistan are believed to be the prime source of honour-related disputes and familial enmities. She is victim of honour killings in some parts of the country. Moreover, the practice of *Swara* had been very common in tribal and rural areas of KPK, wherein a young girl or even a child girl is handed over to an opponent family to resolve enmity between males of two families. A *Swara* girl is commonly treated inhumanly and unjustly by the family who took her. Likewise, in *Punjab* whenever a girl is claimed for immorality or adultery, she is killed under the decision of *punchayat* (a small bunch of influential local people that take up important decision of entire village or town). Whereas, it decides in some cash or other minor punishments for the boy who participated in adultery. Moreover, in *Sindh* (a province of Pakistan) young girls are married to Holy Book wherein she is not entitled to marry, to wear any wear colour than white, to enjoy get together, to inherit property, to join a job and so on. Most unfortunately! People do it with an opinion of performing a religious act. Nowhere in Islamic teachings may one find promoting such malicious practices. It is commonly held by urban male that the schooling makes a girl to transgress the boundaries of piety.

Women in urban KPK

Unfortunately, the female illiteracy rate in KPK is highest than other parts of Pakistan. In urban areas the situation is slightly better but is neither satisfactory nor aligned with the religious teachings. The female education is better than rural areas.

However, the low female literacy in urban area is due to lack of educational institutes meant exclusively for females. The gender gap in education in Pakistan suggests that the country has foregone a great opportunity by not capitalizing on the large rates of return of female schooling on economic productivity. In view of religious thought of gender segregation, most KPK families, in particular, and of Pakistan in general, prefer to abstain from admitting their daughters in schools and colleges with co-education wherein both genders work in close contact. In the point of fact, Islam talks about gender segregation in order to maintain decency, sacredness, modesty, female safety and the family unit (Wangila, 2012), it is not meant to hinder the education, progress, and development. Another aspect of urban women life is that they are treated as "second class" citizens.

Female in employment

Moreover, in KPK, one may find a different mindset altogether. Female employment and entrepreneurship here is almost non-existent. However, the rural women work much harder in agriculture than men. The unemployment rate for women is many times higher for every age group; they are last to get jobs and first to lose them. There are no laws that contain explicit provisions for equal remuneration for equal work for women, protection of labour rights for domestic workers and protection of labour rights of home based workers. Major barriers responsible for low female participation rate include inadequate recognition of their contribution, women's immobility, ignorance about opportunities, and societal perception of women as lower status dependents. To add, the female employment is commonly unwelcomed by the local people.

The misconception of confinement of women within four walls

It is based in the misinterpretation of religion in that the common thought of people is that the role of women is restricted to the boundaries of her house. Such people do not let her learn and utilize abilities and skills outside home. In Islam home is a part of female role, though, a significant role. Islam recognizes the motherhood as a role of leadership in shaping the personalities of future generations to come. The Divine message of Holy Quran signifies woman's confinement within a boundary of home only in the case of her immodest and immoral conduct; and it is not a general and constant rule but one of corrective and preventive measures in order to restore and ensure a modest way of life. Quran clearly mentions to restrict a woman of weak character until she repent and purifies herself. The misconception of the balance has drastically affected female education, employment, health, economic decisions and other developmental activities within the society. A KPK woman in such families has to stagnate and do nothing provided she may be skilful in some area. The Islamic view of education is well explained by Ngozika (2011), that education is a fundamental human right which provides knowledge and skill to both male and female. It involves the bringing up of a child in the community and constantly training him and her to adjust and fit into the changing world.

Inequalities in Female Employment

Those fewer employed among urban women are involved in jobs of different nature such as teaching, nursing, medicine, manufacturing, and small business. In an urban KPK the most educated females are working in service sector-education and health also reveals gender biasness. Women are grossly under-represented in senior posts in education and health managerial positions. However, the gap between women and men on economic participation and political empowerment remains wide (Ahmed, 2012). The gender biased attitudes towards women has made it almost impossible for women to break the 'glass ceiling' which exists within the administration (Wallin, 1999). Besides making an economic struggle these women have to adequately perform their family-related undeniable responsibilities. Compared to the rural one, such an urban female is much over-burdened with the back breaking dual responsibilities of family as well as full time job. In Country Gender Profile of Pakistan published by SDIP in 2008, it is stated that: Women are increasingly working in the labour force but their voices are often excluded from international debates.

Religious stance about female working outside home

In the point of fact Islam looks at this issue differently. Yousafzai (2006:349) mentioned the views of Khattab that "every horizon in the society is open for woman, according to Islam". She maintained Khattab's idea (p:348) wherein he put examples of Saffia bent Abdul Mutaleb and Khadija–wife of Prophet Muhammad (SAAW) and a lady arguing with *Ameerul momineen* (leader of Muslims) in a public and Hazrat Umar agreeing to her opinion. The Prophet said, 'Learn half of your religion from Ayesha'- the wife of Prophet. She was educator of Islam for both men and women. The developed economies in current century looks at legal equity in such areas as a woman's ability to register a business, own and use property while Islam has given these rights since its inception. The wife of the Prophet Mohammad, Hazrat Khadija, was a successful and famous Muslim businesswoman. Quran talks about some women, making of them examples, the wife of Pharaoh, and Maryum (Mary) daughter of Imran. Quran mentions their own merits as examples of piety and God conscious characters. Islam does not prohibit the work itself, the work may be done within its 'framework' (boundaries); Islam prohibits going beyond that 'framework' and ding the wrong things. The Quranic verse (*Sura Al Ahzab, verse 32*) indicates that women be careful while communicating and dealing to men, it states: "Hence, be not over-soft in your speech, lest any whose heart is diseased should be moved to desire you, but withal, speak in a proper way" (33:32).

The transgressing of boundaries (framework) can be abolished by bringing up human, whether male or female, to be God Conscious and God fearing; that is what Islam requires (Yusafzai, 2006: 348). A soft voice and attractive tone consequently results in a worst form of gender harassment and abuse-adultery. When parents and teachers have prepared, on basis of true Islamic thought, the woman for her role in society, only then will they have prepared a nation on solid foundations.

The crux of *Purdah*

Furthermore, the concept of *Purdah* is influenced by the same thought of placing a woman within four walls of house. It is misinterpreted in a way to discourage her lawful work and righteous mobility outside home. Islam puts the idea of *Purdah* in a cluster of practices and a code of dressing to keep women away from keeping 'unnecessary' and unwanted relation with men, and is actually designed to promote honor, modesty and dignity. The Islamic principle behind *purdah* is the prevention of *zina*-fornication and adultery (Wangila, 2012), it's not the prevention of lawful and pious activity that may benefit the society. It is rightly believed by Muslim women of KPK, that the *Purdah* –keeping body unexposed, helps protect them from the lustful temptation and potentially abusive, invasive attention from men (Shapiro 1979). That's why; the educated and urban women also prefer to cover the attractive parts of body while getting education and working in organizations of mixed gender. The educated men of KPK mostly do not hinder such practices, and education is considered most pious in Islam.

Undesirable practices related to marriage

The undesirable practices related to marriage are observable in some Muslim societies. Generally, married women are comparatively regarded more important than single women, and married women with sons are more privileged than married women without children or those with daughters. However, Quran talks about same obligation, duties and rights of both husband and wife provided making husband to take most of economic responsibility. In connection to the marriage, a young bride enters her husband's household at an extreme disadvantage as she will be subordinate not only to all men in the family but also to senior women; Indeed, a bitter rivalry between mothers and daughters-in-law and marital dispute within this household is not uncommon.

Religious obligation of inheritance and *Mehr*

The situation of gender inequality in KPK is further complicated by knowingly overlooking the women's Islamic right of property ownership, right of *Mehr* (an established and mutually agreed upon-at the time of establishing wed-lock, certain amount of money, property and gold to be given by the husband to his wife). The daughters of Pakistan are deprived of inheriting any form of their parent's property. The Holy Qur'an illustrates the law of inheritance for all family members in detail. In contrary, the most part of parent's money and property is gifted to or inherited by sons of the families. In addition, the male dominance has hindered their wives to own, supervise or sell their rightful share (inherited or *Mehr)* in form of cash and/or property and men control the overall finances (Rogers, 1983). Furthermore, if a woman may claim her share of the inheritance or *Mehr;* however, she forfeits her kin rights, and is considered insincere to her husband and earns a bad image. A consequence which Rosenfeld suggests is a great tragedy for the woman (1958). Women, therefore, are "reduced to reliance on kinship". The male-dominated inheritance and financial supervision system denies them their rights: women are forced to forfeit their share of the family inheritance as well as *Mehr* to receive life-long protection from male kin and certain rights. This is a practice contrary to what the Prophet Muhammad (SAAW) has preached and demonstrated. According to Islamic code of marriage, husband of every woman is bound by religion to pay *Mehr* and to provide means and sources of livelihood to his wife throughout her life; provided that the wife on her own will could join any job or do business that may not potentially harm her dignity, modesty and chastity. *Mehr* is an Islamic obligation on husband in addition to fulfilling all her personal and social needs according to the prevalent standards. The current anti-Islamic practice hinders the uplift of female population in all economic spheres of life affecting the overall growth and development.

Gender related practices in different regions of the world
Many countries differ in facing and combating gender inequalities. Age, class, ethnicity, caste, marital status, earning position, education, location, language and other such factors combine to make varied equations of discrimination across the world. The Gender Equality Measure (GEM) for South Asia shows lowest value (0.235) among regions of the world. The Global Gender Gap Index (GGGI) 2012 provides an overview of current performance and progress in economic participation and opportunity. Four Nordic countries- Iceland, Finland, Norway and Sweden have consistently held highest position in previous editions of GGGI, although, it states that no country has yet achieved gender equality. A global snapshot of the gender gap in the four sub-indexes shows that the 135 countries covered in the report, representing over 90 percent of the world's population, have closed almost 96 percent of the gap in health outcomes between women and men and almost 93 percent of the gap in educational attainment. According to Human Development Report 2008 mentions that Iceland, Australia, Norway, Canada, and Sweden are the highest ranked at Gender-related Development Index and Pakistan is ranked at 125 out of 157 countries. (Pakistan: Country Gender Profile, 2008).

Gender disparities in Other Countries
The constitution of Pakistan gives equal rights to both women and men. However, in practice women are rarely equal in rights to their male counterparts. Pakistani government has established processes and initiated many gender sensitive programs such as shown in Table 6.2.

However, Pakistan, in the Global Gender Gap Index (GGGI) 2012 is ranked as low as 134 (with score of 0.3103) out of 135 countries and has been placed in the poorest South Asian countries where gender based mal-practices are more common with the gender Development Index of 0.226. Unlike Western countries, in Pakistan women are considered a weaker section of society in terms of education, health, employment, business opportunities, decision making and communication. The gender-based disparities are the lowest in Iceland, Norway, Finland, Norway and Sweden. But Hausmann (*et al,* 2012) mention in the GGG Report 2012, the planet's twelve offenders are: Yemen, Chad, Pakistan, Syria, Côte d'Ivoire, Saudi Arabia, Mali, Morocco, Iran, Egypt, Oman and Turkey. Of these, eleven are Muslim states. Factors affecting Muslim women across the globe are socio-cultural influences and religious misinterpretations (Irma *et al,* 2011).

Table 6.2 - Gender Sensitive Programs in Pakistan

Program	Year of Inception
Commission on Marriages and Family Laws	1955
Women's Rights Committee	1976
Pakistan Commission on the Status of Women	1985
Commission of Inquiry for Women	1997
Ministry Of Women Development	1997
National Commission on the Status of Women	2000

Gender disparities in other countries
Some practices of gender based inequalities are common across the world. Moreover, a country may perform well in Gender Empowerment Measure, Human Development Index and Global Gender Gap Index but high level of gender inequality may still prevail. Women are globally considered as 'sex co-partners or agents' at work. The cases and frequency of sexual harassment is getting alarming day by day. The socially and morally ill-practice with female is widespread in western societies. Such as in Belgium 35% women, in Spain 90 %, in Portugal 40%, in Holland 60%, in Germany 76%, and in Japan 65% of working women are sexually harassed (Collier, 1999). Similarly, Australia, a high ranked country in the Human Development Report has alarming levels of sexual harassment; female harassment is 73% in regional Australia, while in Agriculture industry it is as high as 93% (Lucas, 2013). Though, Australia is the first country to introduce and follow Gender responsive Budgeting (GRB).

Representation of female in management and administration
The under-representation of women in management and administration is another common practice in both under- and developed economies. Most of world-class universities are headed by males. Pakistan portrays the same picture. Female participation being the lowest at educational management are not only in Pakistan but in Zimbabwe, India, China, UK and in most other countries (Coleman, 2001). In order to eradicate the inequalities between genders, some societies have made attempts to bring the women at an equal level of men. However, they have generated further harms to females. For instance, the most notorious attempt in the United Kingdom was the 1997 Ministry of Defence directive that female recruits would not be subject to the same physical tests as men. As a result, the 1998 rules applied what were called 'gender-free' selection procedures to ensure that women and men faced identical tasks. The result was a massive rise in female injuries when compared with the men (Gemmell, 2002).

Contrary to the mal-practices some countries are good players of gender equality in significant area of development. Countries like Norway and Andorra has highest female education in the world according to CIA World Fact Book 2010. Similarly, 99% of female population is educated in USA, UK, Germany, France, Canada and Australia. Moreover, in Muslim countries, like Azerbaijan, Malaysia, and Bahrain the percentage of educated female population is 99.7%, 90.7% and 91.6% respectively. However, in Pakistan only 35.4% (and in KPK only 22%) of its female population is educated and Afghanistan has as lowest as 12.6% of female population.

The economic participation of a country is judged by female employment. According to Organization of Economic Cooperation and Development (OECD) 2013 shows the highest rate of employed women as 78.5% in Iceland, 73.8% in Norway, 73.6% in Switzerland, 66.6% in Australia, 65.7% in UK and 62.2% in USA. Whereas population of female employed in different jobs in Turkey is 28.7% and a serious gender disparity in education. The Country gender Profile study of Pakistan (2008) revealed that out of 75.14 million female populations only 9.13 million are employed in different sectors.

Recommendations

Efforts are needed to change or modify the discourse through which society operates in order to promote the role and status of women in society. The following are some recommendations:

1. The *Ulima* (religious scholars) need to redefine the current practices in the light of true Islamic thought based on Quran and authentic sayings of the Prophet that could be done by using *Masjid* (mosques) as a place of accurate learning.
2. The male segment of population needs to be educated about playing a modest and pious role in society where females could work and move safely. It encompasses a true Muslim society.
3. The school and university level curriculum may be revised to include the 'true and balanced' Islamic perspective of rights and duties of both genders.
4. Media requires promoting and protecting the women status in a real Islamic perspective so that the misconceptions are corrected.
5. The female education could be improved in KPK by:
   a. Establishing schools, colleges and universities exclusively for females. It reflects the idea of turning a weakness into an opportunity aspect.
   b. Hiring more and more female teachers at all levels of education to attract more girl students.
   c. Providing more scholarships to deserving, special, and genius female students.
   d. Arrangement of skill development to female prisoners in Pakistan.
6. Women working in agriculture sector may be equipped with skills, tools and knowledge fostering their overall performance.
7. The contribution of females in agriculture needs to be acknowledged and motivated.

8. Masses could be educated about the Islamic rights of inheritance and *Mehr* in its original form in order to include females in economic activity.
9. Recruitment, training and retention of female health workers to impact general women health.
10. Establishing women centres to facilitate small scale female owned local businesses.
11. Establishment of technical skill development centre and IT training of elected female representatives.
12. The organizations should require adopting family-facilitating practices and female friendly working hours in order to foster the dignified home-making responsibilities.
13. Encouragement and facilitation of family- or home-based businesses at small, medium and large scale.
14. Men's role to be played in gender issues: to sensitize men that masculinity can be used in a healthy and positive direction instead of violence and sexual assaults, and improved relationships can be flourished based on respect for the opposite gender under God-consciousness.
15. Promotion and undertaking of research on the conditions and problems of women in Pakistan.
16. Include Gender Responsive Budgeting (GRB) in the national policy to ensure female needs fulfilment and ways in which women can contribute to society at large.

Summary
The gender inequality is a severe social problem which has extreme upshots for women and girls universally. It ends up in serious violation of women basic rights across the globe, and it is widespread in all countries, irrespective of social, economic, religious, or cultural group. In Muslim countries, the infringement of women right is mostly due to religious misinterpretation. The human society can progress smoothly if the rights and responsibilities of both genders are clearly determined and properly followed by all concerned. One should be highly careful about and attentive to the processes, tools, and practices directed towards equalizing genders; one may not transgress the natural human being in the first place. Nature is best understood by the Creator of both genders. Naturalization may not be used to justify social inequalities (Feinstein, 2010), but be considered in creating a natural and desirable balance by focusing on responsibilities of men and women first and then their rights.

References
Ahmad, A. (2012, October 25). Pakistan slides on global gender gap index. *The Dawn*. Retrieved from http://beta.dawn.com/news/759326
Ahmad, I. (2003). *Religious Obligations Of Muslim Women.*(1st ed). Lahore: Markazi Anjuman Khuddam-ul-Qur'an.
Al-Ashmawi, S. (2006). *Reforming Islam and Islamic Law*. In Donohue, John and Esposito, John (eds), Islam in Transition: Muslim Perspectives. NY: Oxford University Press.

Chabaya, O. Rembe, S., & Wadesango, N (2009). The persistence of gender inequality. in a Zimbabwe : factors that impede the advancement of women into leadership .
positions in primary schools. *South African Journal of Education,* 29 (2): 235-251. Collier, R. 1999. *Combating Sexual Harassment In The workplace.* Buckingham: Open University Press.
Coleman, M. (2001). Achievement against the Odds: the female secondary head teachers in England and Wales. Journal of School Leadership and Management, 21(3):75-100.
Gemmell, I.M.M. (2002). Injuries among female army recruits. *Journal of the RoyalSociety of Medicine,* 95(1):23-27
Groves, W.B., Newman, G., & Corrado, C. (1987). Islam, Modernization and Crime: A Test of the Religious Ecology Thesis. *Journal of Criminal Justice.* 15(6): 495–503.
Hausmann, R., Tyson, L.D., Bekhouche, Y. & Zahidi, S. (2012). *The Global Gender Gap Index,* The Global Gender Gap Report 2012. Switzerland: World Economic Forum. Retrieved fromh ttp://www3.weforum.org/docs/WEF_GenderGap_Report_2012.pdf
Healey, J.F. (2006). *Race Ethnicity, Gender and Class.* CA: Pine Forge Press.
Irma, M.B. Rattani, S., & Khan, K (2011). Women empowerment in Pakistan-Definition and enabling, disenabling factors: A secondary data analysis, *Journal of Trans-cultural Nursing,* 22(2):174-181.
Kurtz, L. R. (1995). Gods in the Global Village: The World's Religions in Sociological Perspective. Thousand Oaks. California: Pine Forge Press.
Locus, C. (2013, October, 31). Sexual Harassment levels 'alarming in rural Australia'. *The Age* Retrieved from www.theage.com.au/national/sexual-harassment-levels-alarming-in-rural-australia-20131030-2whaj.html
Ngozika, N.A., & Sunday, E.I. (2011). Gender Equity and Empowerment in Nigeria: Implications for Educational Management. *African Research Review.* 5(1): 302-312 Organization of Economic Cooperation and Development (2013). *Employment rate of women.* Retrieved from http://www.oecd-ilibrary.org/content/table/ 20752342-table5
Pakistan: Country Gender Profile Study. (2008). Islamabad: Sustainable Development Policy Institute.
Robertson, R. (1970). *The Sociological Interpretation of Religion.* Oxford: Basil Blackwell.
Rosenfeld, H. (1958). Processes of Structural Change within the Arab Village Extended Family. American Anthropologist. 60(6):1127–39.
Schacht, J. (1982). *An Introduction to Islamic Law.* UK: Oxford University Press.
Stark, R., Kent, L., & Doyle, D.P. (1982). Religion and Delinquency: The Ecology of a 'Lost' Relationship. *Journal of Research in Crime and Delinquency.* 19 (1): 4–24.
Turner, B. S. (1974). *Weber and Islam: A Critical Study.* London: Routledge & Kegan Paul.
Wallin, J. (1999). *Reflections on Anger: Women and Men in a Changing Society.* Retrieved on 3 November 2013 from University of North Carolina. Sociology Department web site: http://www.ecu.edu/soci/research.html
Wangila, M.N. (2012). Negotiating agency and human rights in Islam: A case of Muslim women in Kenya, *Contemporary Islamic Studies,* 1: 1-15
Yusafzai, N.F. (2006). *Islam: the Sermons of Imam A.M. Khattab,* (Unpublished master's thesis) Al-Azhar University, and university of Alberta.

CHAPTER 7
Gender Disparity and Economic Growth in Pakistan

By: Adiqa Kiani
Fulbright Postdoc Fellow UPENN, Philadelphia, USA.

Abstract

With the goal of achieving a better understanding of the nature and influence of gender on education of the students, this chapter focuses first on the literature related to gender disparities in the general population. The issues addressed cover both education and employment outcomes, with special attention devoted to current interventions that are designed to reduce the disparities. The chapter further examines the literature on gender and its relationship to students in education, including (a) overall gender rates at professional colleges, (b) gender disparities in education and employment outcomes associated with males and females in arts and science colleges, and (c) gender disparities at arts and science colleges. The chapter concludes by discussing implications for three different levels of education and research that can reduce the incidence of gender differences in education.

This chapter's content explores why women tend to feel a lower importance than men, and why the attention tends to be lower among the elderly than among younger people. In particular, the chapter explores the role played by education in explaining age and gender differences using three different levels. The analysis is based on data taken from various issues in Pakistan Economic Survey, WDI, and Penn World Tables for forty years during 1970-2011 for Pakistan. Implications and findings are presented.

Introduction

In this study, we have found that education accounts for some of the age and gender differences, and education also showed positive impact on GDP growth with female-male enrollment in arts and science colleges, but impact of enrollment in professional colleges and universities negatively affected the economic growth. This finding implies that education might be not up to the standard which is the high need of the hour. Female-male enrolment growth in professional colleges and universities has a positive impact on the fixed capital formation growth, while female-male enrolment growth in arts and science colleges have negative impact on the fixed capital formation growth. The reason may be that the difference between the theoretical and practical inconsistency in education. Even in practical subjects importance is given in theory and students have not given the appropriate knowledge they can make use of their theoretical knowledge. The female-male ratio and practical education may have a positive impact on the growth in fixed capital formation.

The negative impact on population growth is due to female-male enrolment in professional colleges and universities. Positive impact is due to growth in female-male enrolment in arts and science colleges on the population growth. One of the reasons may be that the culture in Pakistan is mostly headed by males. Preferences are always given to male students in science subjects but if opportunities are given to females then ultimate consequences may be unusual and much better.

The negative result is may be due to the gender discrimination in labor market and very few job opportunities available for women. The analysis of this study showed that government has not given much attention to education particularly women's education. The allocation of budget and its utilization on education is not satisfactory, it is rather poor. At all educational levels, gender gap is very high and it is getting wider. The results of our estimation illustrate that the gender gap in education is very high. In the presence of higher regional gender gap in Pakistan, especially public spending on rural areas on females education will play a remarkable role as compared to urban areas. Government should try to provide maximum education facilities to female labor force. Women may be provided with technical and vocational education so that they are furnished with skills.

Gender discrimination or less fundamental human rights of women is a key issue of our study. Females frequently have fewer rights than males, whether it is official appreciation and defense, or entry to community information and knowledge, and very low administrative authority both inside and external issues. This efficient inequality decrease community contribution of women, frequently enhances their defenselessness to poor life style and consequences are that the females standing for an unbalanced proportion of the deprived residence of the planet.

Basically, there are four special measurements of gender discrimination {i) admission and accomplishment in education, {ii} development in physical condition, {iii} indexes of authorized trade and industry, {iv} equal opportunity of women in culture and marriage which determines the empowerment of women. In Pakistan, the gender discrepancy in education is extremely high. From the last few years, male literacy rate increased from 58% to 65% while the female literacy rate increased from 32% to 42%. The gap is still 23% in male-female literacy ratio. In 2008, literacy rate of males was 68.2 % and of females was 43.6%. In Pakistan gender discrimination is a major problem, but few activists such as the National Plan of Action for Women (NPAW) and All-Pakistan Women's Association (APWA) emphasized on gender parity and is still struggling hard to attain gender equality. It's not easy to attain equal rights for women without reconstructing the whole culture that the nation is based on which is Hinduism; Pakistan is one of the more progressive Muslim states regarding women's rights.

In Pakistan, social actives strive for women to get equal opportunity in education and employment. These types of actions as well give confidence to females, mostly in countryside regions of Pakistan. It is very difficult for females to get their equal rights in such an established culture. The social inequality and feudalistic system further boost the gender inequality.

In Pakistan, the rural areas have a high rate of poverty and very low literacy rates. In 2002 it was verified that 81.5% of the 15-19 years old female from cohort group of rich families were present at school compared to 22.3% of females from poor families. In contrast, it was confirmed that 96.6 % of males aged 15–19 years taking admission from rich families compare to 66.1% of 15-19 years old males from poor families who had been admitted in school. [HIES, 2002] Females living in the rural areas were not encouraged to obtain education and were forced to work at home. The majority of rural areas only has primary schools and still do not have secondary school for girls. Girls are forced to get married and usually do household work.

Gender disparity in education leads towards the gender disparity in employment. In Pakistan during 2008, only 21.8 % of women had opportunities to participate in the labor force although 82.7 % of males were engaged in employment. According to the labor force survey, only 6.5 % of 47 million employed females which become 9 million women out of whom, 70 % (6.3 million) were employed in agriculture. The earnings of Pakistani females in the labor force are usually less than that of males, because of their lower education and skills [PSLM, 2008]

Female-male ratio at arts and science colleges is showing continuously increasing over time, while trends of female-male ratio at professional colleges indicates the gradual increase till 1992-93, and after 1993 continuous decrease, and drastic decline after 2004-05. Moreover, female-male ratio at university level shows fluctuating trends having only nominal increase in 1990-91 and 2004-05. Now the scenario is clearer after 2004-05, indicating clear trends for all three educational levels i.e. gradual increase in ASCF, sharp increase in UNIF and sharp decline in PCF respectively. We can easily conclude that it this need of the hour to study the issues of these trends and its impact on economic growth for Pakistan as female are contributing more over time through their higher education and through their better services too.

The purpose of the study is to highlight not just the direct effect of education and gender bias in education on economic growth but also to explore the indirect effect of education and gender bias in education on economic growth.

Literature Review
Burkey (1996) discussed the major structural weaknesses in Pakistan. He stressed upon the poor human capital. He found that due to poor human capital, physical capital too was poorly utilized and education was becoming polarized. Human

capital was also of poor quality because women were not treated equal to men. He found that there were some improvements in infant mortality rate, increase in life expectancy but fertility rate was still high. He suggested that the right type of education and population control was necessary for economic growth.

Hamid and Siddiqui (2001) indicated gender differences in demand for schooling in three industrialized cities of Pakistan during April-June 2000. Dependent variables were demand for schooling and discontinuity of education while independent variables included income, assets, parental characteristic, family characteristics and community characteristic. They found that mother's education, mother's work status, and the income of household had greater impact on female demand for school. Abbas (2001) analyzed the importance of human capital embodied labour input on the economic growth. He used panel data for both the countries like Pakistan and Sri Lanka using OLS technique to estimate the perpetual rate of growth during (1970-94). He took GDP as dependent variable and human capital and physical capital as independent variables.

Moheyuddin (2005) analyzed gender inequality in education and its impact on income, growth, and development. Gender inequality in education is independent variable explained by religious preference, regional factors, and civil freedom. He found that low investment in women's human capital was not simply an efficient economic choice for developing countries. He also found that promoting gender equality in education and employment may be one of those few policies that had been termed 'win-win' strategies.[3] He suggested that an exogenous increase in girls' access to education will create a better environment for economic growth and particularly strong for middle income groups.

Ahmed and Bukhari (2007) analyzed trade liberalization on gender inequalities in Pakistan during 1973 to 2005. The overall gender inequality was based on three variables, including labor market, education and health facilities. Exports and imports to Gross Domestic Product (GDP) ratio, per capita GDP, and number of girl schools to number of boy schools ratio were identified as important determinants of overall gender inequality in Pakistan and especially in the labor market. Gender inequality in education attainment was explained by per capita GDP, number of girl schools to number of boy schools ratio and number of female teachers per school.

Chaudhry and Rahman (2009) estimated the impact of gender inequality in education on rural poverty in Pakistan. They used primary survey based data collected from the villages of Muzaffar Garh district of Punjab for the months of November-December, 2008. They applied Logit regression model using poverty as a dependent variable and education was one of the independent variables. The main findings of the empirical analysis were that gender inequality in education had significant impact on rural poverty. Female-male enrollment ratio, female male literacy ratio, female-male ratio of total years of schooling of population, education of household head, female-male ratio of earners, age of household head, asset

---

[3] That creates benefits for all and to avoid conflicts.

holding and land holding were significant variables having negative impact on the probability of being poor at the rural level.

Barro (1991) analyzed a gender-neutral growth model for 98 developed and developing countries. He used time series data during 1960-1985. Annual average growth rate of per capita real GDP was dependent variable while the independent variables included real GDP per capita, secondary and primary school enrolment rate, consumption to real GDP ratio, revolution per year. He used OLS estimation technique. He found that the growth rate was positively related to the initial level of human capital. So, poor countries had to catch up with rich countries if the poor countries had high human capital per person.

Hill and Kings (1993-1995) examined the growth recursive model. They used OLS estimation for 127 countries during the period of (1975-1985). Dependent variable was GNP and independent variables included female/male enrolment ratio, female secondary enrolment rate, and logarithm of capital stock, interaction of capital stock and enrolment, labour force, interaction of labour force and enrolment. They found that the level of education had positive effect on GNP. They also found that the larger the gender inequality in education the more GNP was reduced.

Durham (1999) analyzed the growth model for 105 developed and developing countries for the period of (1960-1989). In this study, dependent variable was growth rate of real per capita GDP and independent variables included log of initial GDP, investment to GDP ratio , male and female education rate, openness to trade, government spending to GDP ratio and continental dummies. He used generalized least square (GLS) random effects analysis. He found that male educational rate is positively related and female education rate is negatively related to economic growth, but both human capital measures showed insignificant impact.

Kambhampati and Pal (2001) analyzed that the child school enrollment rate and primary level of attainment in West Bengal during (1987-89). Girls' enrolment rate was less due to cultural constraints, greater distance from school, opportunity cost and the benefits of the girls' education. Father's education had a significant impact on both boys and girls enrolment rate. They found that females headed households not only increased the enrollment rate of their daughters but also their achievement level which had no impact on their son's education. They suggested that if women increase collective household welfare rather than perpetuate discriminatory practices it would be better for their households.

Breierova and Duflo (2002) analyzed the impact of massive school construction program called Sekolah Daser INPRES[4] program by the Indonesian Government during 1973-1979 on the women's fertility. They have used OLS, 2SLS and instrumental technique to estimate the impact of education (both male and female) fertility, child mortality, difference in education (between husband and

---

[4] The program was designed explicitly to target children who had not previously been enrolled in school. The general allocation rule was that the number of schools constructed in each district was proportional to the number of children of primary school age not enrolled in school in 1972. There is thus a negative correlation between the number of schools per capita constructed in each region and enrolment rate in before the program.

wife) and average education. They found that the age of marriage was associated more with woman's education than with man's education. Their findings suggested that even average education in the household had an effect on reducing child mortality.

Klasen and Lamanna (2003) analyzed gender inequality and economic growth in the Middle East and North Africa (MENA). They used panel data during (1960-2000). Regional education, employment and GDP growth were dependent variables and explanatory variables included the annual population growth, annual labor force growth, initial GDP/capita (log), openness, average investment rate, initial years of schooling for males, the initial female-male ratio of years of schooling, and various indicators of initial gender gaps in employment. Gender inequality in education and employment had a significant negative impact on growth.

Teal and Soderbom (2003) analyzed relationship among openness to trade, human capital and productivity. They used panel data for 93 developing countries during (1970-2000). They found that openness to trade and higher level of human capital increased productivity. They viewed that doubling the openness would increase the technical progress by 0.8 percent per annum but this would possible only with increased skilled labour force.

Clark (2003) examined a relationship among female literacy, information technology, and democracy. She thought that there was a theoretical background among female literacy rates, information technology and democracy. She took data from the World Bank and the United States Central Intelligence Agency for 149 countries during the year 2000. Her hypothesis was that the female literacy rate would be an important factor in the technology in a country. Female literacy rate was taken as dependent variable while independent variables include female primary school enrolment, aid per capita (country ability to increase their communication index store), percentage of GDP, GDP per capita and urban population.

Narrayan and Smyth (2004) estimated causal relationship between real income, export and human capital in China. They used error correction and co integration model for the period of (1960-99). They found that real export, human capital, and real income were co-integrated when real exports was a dependent variable but not co-integrated when human capital was dependent variable.

Chen (2004) highlighted the effects of the level of information and communication technologies (ICT) infrastructure on gender inequality in education and in employment. He used as instrumental variable (IV) while applying panel regressions for data of 209 countries during the period of 43 years (1960-2002). He found that the level of ICT infrastructure had a positive effect on gender equality in education in order to enhance long-term economic growth. This study showed that reducing gender inequality in education also reduced gender inequality in employment. He suggested that the level of education among the common population was important for the improvement of gender equality in schooling and gender equality in the labor market.

Coulombe and Jean-François (2004) examined the impact of human capital on economic growth. They used a two-way error correction panel data approach for 14 OECD countries during 1960-95. They found that the human capital indicators had a positive and significant impact on the permanent growth path, long run levels of GDP per capita and labor productivity. They suggested that the distribution of human capital investment might be important for long run standards of living. They also suggested that the investment in the human capital of women had a much stronger impact on growth than the investment in the human capital of men.

Denis (2005) estimated the cost and benefits of obtaining education. He believed that the one of schooling does affect the wage level but wage also affected by number of years of experience, race, sex and marital status. He computed the rate of return on education. His results showed if there was an increase in one year of schooling then on average wage would gone up by $0.583. Female education was significant at the 1% significance level. It showed that rate of returns on female education were high.

Baliamoune (2007) analyzed long-run relationship and short-run dynamics between gender inequality and openness to international trade in Morocco. She used time series data over the period 1970-2002 and applied vector error-correction model (VECM). She found that there was a stable long-run relationship between gender equality and openness to trade. In the short-run, openness did the adjustment to the long-run equilibrium. Gender inequality had increased in the second half of the 1980s and the first half of the 1990s, a period during which Morocco had implemented several trade and financial reforms, which implies that whenever the gender inequality and openness start to diverge, trade openness played a vital role to correct this divergence.

Methodology

Measurement of gender discrimination is not an effortless assignment due to more than a few reasons. Primarily it lacks disaggregated information through gender at the same time as present significant development on gender-disaggregated information on education and employment, currently small equivalent data of adequate aspect on gender inequality in right to use of knowledge, property, and dynamic capital. Therefore, several social movements that make an effort in the direction of connect gender disparity with economic development will suffer from this shortcoming. In Pakistan female working age population is equal to that of their male counterparts but only a few women work in the formal labour force. It is due to the gender differential in human capital level. In Pakistan, females constitute 52% of population but majority does not work in the labour market[5].

---

[5] Seguino (1999) who argues that gender discrimination in the labour market will favour growth, as it will lead to lower female wages in export-intensive sectors. The argument advanced differs from this by focusing on access to employment rather than wages

Data and Variables Construction

In this study we have used the annual data from 1970-71 to 2008-09 taken from Pakistan Economic Survey (various issues) and Labour Force Survey (various issues). We have used number of variables that influence economic growth i.e. population, labour force, human capital, investment, imports and exports. In this study we have analyzed the long-run economic growth changes. We have taken all the variables in growth form as this reduces the skewness of the data and data becomes stationary at levels.

Variables construction:

The following variables are used in this study.

(i)   *Measure of Output/Growth*

If the amount of output is continuously increasing, it shows that the country is progressing. Different proxies are used for economic growth such as GNP, real GDP, and GDP per capita. It is said that GNP is a broad measure of output growth but not an appropriate measure of output growth due to high variation in foreign earnings. As Pakistan real GDP is continuously changing but the real per capita income is not increasing faster. Most of the studies use GDP as a dependent variable. We have also used GDP growth as a dependent variable in our analysis.

(ii)   *Human Capital*

Human capital is an important variable for the development of an economy. For instance Romer (1990) argues that with higher rate of human capital, economic growth tends to increase faster. The enrolment rate can be calculated by a number of students of the same age group enrolled in the selected class from total population. In Pakistan fundamental time-series data are not readily available. For human capital the proxies usually used are the school enrolment rate, mature literacy rate and education and health investment. In this study, we also used different levels of education e.g. enrolment of professional colleges, art and science colleges and universities as a proxy for human capital.

(iii)   *Trade*

Through trade, countries can have access to larger markets, obtain optimistic externalities and exchange rate constraints. In our study, we used the data of import and export for the openness of an economy. Iqbal and Zahid (1998) found that increased openness of an economy promote faster economic growth.

(iv)   *Population*

Population growth also has a vital impact on economic growth; and through human capital formation it may control economic growth. A productive population would be helpful to enhance economic growth. If a country has a large population along with increased dependency burden then it reduces the per capita income. Also the two major source of economic development, such as physical capital and human capital, remained poor in that country like Pakistan. We have used growth in labour force in our study both as a dependent and independent variable.

(v) **Labour Force**
Labour force can be defined through the people who are officially worked or worked in labor market. Typically, working age people above 14 years age and below 60 years are considered to be in the labour force. Different proxies are used for labour force such as labour force contribution activities and employed work force. We have used civilian labour force 15 years and above working in different areas of the economy.

(vi) **Physical Capital**
Different proxies are used for physical capital that is gross household investment, real physical investment as a proportion to real GDP, real physical capital stock as a ratio to GDP. In this study we have also used gross fixed capital formation as a proxy for physical capital.

Results and Discussion
For the estimation purpose, we have analyzed the gender differential between education and employment and their impact on fixed capital formation, growths of population and labor force and overall GDP growth.

Before estimation we have applied the stationarity test. We have applied ADF test for stationarity. To analyze the effects of gender inequality in education in three different institutions including Arts and Science Colleges, Professional Colleges and Universities, and their overall impact on economic growth, we have applied simultaneous equation system. These are gender differential in education and in employment has a i)- negative impact on GDP growth, ii)- negative impact on growth of fixed capital formation, iii)- negative impact on population growth and iv)- negative impact on labour force growth also.

Table 7.1: Stationary Check: Unit Root Test

Variables	Level		
	Lags	Intercept	Trend & intercept
GGDP	0	-2.9399 (-5.830704)	-3.5312 (-5.870612)
GGFCF	1	-2.9422 (-5.233412)	-3.5348 (-5.319862)
GPOP	0	-2.9399 (-4.518686)	-3.5312 (-6.549280)
GLF	1	-2.9422 (-3.820167)	-3.5348 (-3.885311)
GX	1	-2.9422 (-4.275413)	-3.5348 (-4.720319)
GIM	0	-2.9399 (-5.752791)	-3.5312 (-6.064994)
GPCF	0	-2.9399 (-4.530893)	-3.5312 (-6.102305)
GASCF	0	-2.9399(-6.759642)	-3.5312(-6.680078)
GUNIF	1	-2.9422 (-4.108974)	-3.5348 (-4.229513)
GIR	1	-2.9422 (-3.520774)	-3.5348 (-3.852908)

Note: Values in the parenthesis denote Mackinnon critical values for the rejection of null hypothesis at 5% level of significance

Table 7.1 reveals that all the variables are stationary at level, since the tabulated values are less than calculated values, so the null hypothesis is rejected. The series is stationary at lag 0 and 1. After stationarity check, simultaneous equation model is used for consisting of four equations, which includes growth of GDP (GGDP), growth of fixed capital formation (GGFCF), growth of population (GPOP), and growth of labor force (GLF). For estimation purpose GDP growth rate is taken as dependent variable in first equation while in other three it is treated as explanatory variable.

Dollar and Gatti (1999) viewed that countries which have low female educational attainment tends to promote economic growth; while the countries which have highly educated females education levels, would be significantly positively affect economic growth. Reason may be that educated females further promote education to the large extent.

Estimated Model:

Table 7.2: Results of Simultaneous Equation Model for Enrolment at Professional Colleges Using GMM

Dependent Variables	GGDP	GGFCF	GPOP	GLF
Constant	7.83855	-3.864	9.33236	-3.7378
	(3.837)	(-4.5178)	(5.34696)	(-4.1716)
GGDP		0.43815	-1.63754	0.71332
		(3.82240)	(-3.29133)	(3.22391)
GGFCF	0.52810		-2.20961	0.089063
	(3.712)		(-5.10786)	(0.96325)
GPOP	-1.72740			
	(-3.281)			
GLF	0.54133	0.8102		
	(5.124)	(4.31816)		
GPCF	-0.42737	0.1679	-0.18824	0.187473
	(-2.386)	(2.29578)	(-1.3528)	(1.58942)
GX				-0.06605
				(-0.74581)
GIM			0.18177	
			(1.3911)	
GIR		-0.6327		
		(-5.21816)		
Wald test χ^2	0.000000	0.000000	0.000000	0.000000

Results showed in Table 7.2 that impact of GGFCF is positive and significant on GDP growth as its coefficient is (0.5281). The result is consistent with few studies including Stephen Klasen (1999) Iqbal and Zahid (1998). They also viewed that economic growth is increased with allocation of high rate of physical capital. Also the impact of GLF is positive and significant because its coefficient is (0.54133) showed positive and significant impact on growth of GDP. It may be due to the increase in population rate tends to increase growth of GDP as much as people involved in labor market. GPCF has negative impact on the GDP growth. The professional colleges in Pakistan may not provide the education up to the international standard because of the financial constraints. In our analysis, significance of all variables reflects the importance for the enhancement of GDP growth rate. Along with the academic institutions, professional colleges play vital role to increase GDP growth rate and standard of these institution may also be increased and improvement in the standard of these institutions probably up to international level further increase the GDP growth. In Column 2 Growth of fixed capital formation (GGFCF) is taken as dependent variable while growth of GDP, labor force growth (GLF), female-male growth ratio in professional colleges (GPCF), and growth in interest rate (GIR) are used as independent variables, coefficient of growth in GDP is (0.43815) indicating significant positive impact on growth of GFCF. This may be due to when public and government have enough resources then the use of machinery may increase in a country which further increases the GDP. Further the coefficient of GLF is (0.8102) indicating increase in labor force participation may further increase the growth of capital formation. The coefficient of GPCF is (0.1679) having positive significant impact on growth of GFCF showing that the professional play important role as human capital to enhance physical capital formation. Clark (2003) provided the empirical evidence that increase in female enrolment in professional institutions further increases the use of modern technology. The coefficient of GIR is (-0.6327) having significant impact on growth of GFCF and consistent with the theory showing negative relationship between interest rate and investment.

In column labor force (GLF) is taken as dependent variable while the independent variables include growth of GDP, growth of fixed capital formation (GGFCF), female-male growth ratio in professional colleges (GPCF), and growth of exports (GX). Impact of GGDP on GLF is positive and significant as the coefficient of GGDP is (0.71332). It may be due to when the GDP increases the more employment opportunities increases in the society or the demand for labor increases. As the demand for labor increases the people who are working increase their working hours because of high wages. The impact of GGFCF on GLF is positive and insignificant. The reason may be that labor demand increases due to increase in GGFCF. Growth of exports is negative but insignificant impact on GLF. Which indicates that with more and more population needs of the people increase and exports may be reduced.

In column 1 of Table 7.3, GDP growth (GGDP) is taken as dependent variable and it depends on growth of POP (GPOP), growth of capital formation (GGFCF), growth of labor force (GLF), and female-male growth ratio in arts and science colleges (GASCF). The GPOP has negative and significant impact on GGDP. But GGFCF is (1.2001) positive and significant impact on growth of GDP. Sandarajan and Thakur (1980) also viewed that GDP growth increases with an increase of physical capital. Likewise, the coefficient of GLF has positively significant impact on GGDP Impact of GASCF on growth of GDP is positive and significant as its coefficient is (0.06430) though to small. The reason may be that the demand for getting education in arts and science colleges is increasing over time in this changed era of science and technology. This is also the need of how to provide more and more facilities to the young people to learn and also motivate them.

Table 7.3: Results of Simultaneous Equation Model for Enrolment at Arts and Science Colleges Using GMM Technique

Dependent Variables	GGDP	GGFCF	GPOP	GLF
Constant	4.80473	-7.7725	3.63301	-2.873
	(6.5610)	(-0.0998)	(9.8603)	(-2.232)
GGDP		0.79518	-1.63754	0.61462
		4.4432)	(-3.29133)	(2.4751)
GGFCF	1.2001		-0.0849	0.0546
	(-3.5809)		(-0.6578)	(1.9512)
GPOP	-0.567			
	(3.1486)			
GLF	0.24328	0.4223		
	(3.56445)	(3.2884)		
GASCF	0.06430	-0.13867	0.08544	-0.237
	(0.13005)	(-1.6031)	(0.7247)	(-1.736)
GX				-0.0052
				(-0.769)
GIM			0.0177	
			(1.1943)	
GIR		-0.06781		
		(-1.7801)		
Wald test χ^2	0.000000	0.000000	0.000000	0.000000

In column 2, the dependent variable is growth of fixed capital formation (GGFCF) while the independent variables include growth rates of GDP, growth of labour force (GLF), growth of interest rate (GIR), and female-male growth ratio in arts and science colleges (GASCF). Results indicate that the coefficient of GGDP is (0.79518) having a positively significant impact on GGFCF. Further the coefficient of GLF is (0.4223) positive and significant impact on GGFCF. Klasen (2000) , Lorgelly (1999) estimated if female health improved then labour productivity will increase. Impact of GIR and GASCF are negative and insignificant on growth of GGFCF as coefficients of both are (-0.06781) and (-0.13867). This negative impact is due to wider gap between male and female education attainment. There may be many reasons of having this gap, i.e. unequal distribution of income in hands, less expenses, poor infrastructure, less motivation, and traditional system of societies which may create the hurdles in the way of women to get education.

In column 3, growth of POP depends on growth of GDP, growth of fixed capital formation, female-male growth ratio in arts and science colleges (GASCF), and growth of imports. Results of this equation indicate that GGDP is (-1.4882) indicating negatively significant impact on POP growth. Barro (1998) suggested that if female education increased then fertility rate decreased. The coefficient of GGFCF is (-0.0849) negative and significant impact on GPOP. Highly educated women have more awareness and they emphasis on high standard of living and small family sizes. And the coefficients of GASCF and GIM are (0.08544) (0.0177) positive and insignificant impact on growth of POP. In Pakistan majority of the families are headed by male, women's role is minimal. Also the result of female-male enrolment has positive impact on the population growth. In column 4, the labor force growth (GLF) is dependent variable while the independent variables include growth of GDP (GGDP), growth of capital formation (GGFCF), and female-male growth ratio in arts and science colleges (GASCF) and growth of exports (GX). The coefficient of GGDP is (0.61462) having a positively significant impact on GLF. Whenever GDP increases then demand for labor also increases. Also the coefficient of GGFCF is (0.0546) showing positive and insignificant impact on GLF. Coefficient of GASCF is (-0.237) which has a negative and insignificant impact on GLF. People want to get more education so they do not enter in labor market. And the coefficient of GX is (-0.0052) showing negative but insignificant impact on GLF.

Table 7.4: Results of Simultaneous Equation Model for Enrolment at University level of Education Using GMM Technique

Dependent Variables	GGDP	GGFCF	GPOP	GLF
Constant	2.3025	-5.3081	7.99004	-6.7245
	(2.1915)	(-4.3291)	(1.5825)	(-5.815)
GGDP		0.6832	-1.0065	0.8029
		(1.0639)	(-1.2731)	(3.8131)
GGFCF	0.898		-0.0764	0.1035
	(2.995)		(-1.408)	(2.9287)
GPOP	0.6443			
	(3.9659)			
GLF	1.2238	1.3877		
	(5.1366)	(8.1912)		
GUNIF	-0.0319	0.08715	-0.05672	0.0737
	(-0.379)	(1.9397)	(-0.929)	(2.5413)
GX				-0.0085
				(-0.6698)
GIM			0.01889	
			(1.0162)	
GIR		-0.026		
		(-0.4163)		
Wald test χ^2	0.000000	0.000000	0.000000	0.000000

In column 1 of Table 7.4, the growth of GDP growth is dependent variable (GGDP) and the growth of population (GPOP), growth of capital formation (GGFCF), growth of labor force (GLF), and female-male growth ratio in universities (GUNIF) are independent variables. Results showed that growth of POP growth of GFCF and growth LF have positive and significant impact on growth on GDP as their coefficients are (0.6443) (0.898) and (1.2238). And the coefficient of GUNIF is (-0.0319) having a negative and insignificant impact on economic growth. If more females enrolled in the university then this may become positive and significant. According to Stephen Klasen (1999) God has gifted all the men and women equal innate ability. In column 2, the growth of capital formation (GGFCF) depends on growth of GDP (GGDP), growth of labor force (GLF), growth of interest rate (GIR), and female-male growth ratio in universities (GUNIF). The coefficients of GGDP GLF and GUNIF are (0.6832) (1.3877) and (0.08715). GGDP having positively insignificant impact on GGFCF but GLF and GUNIF have positive and significant impact on growth of GFCF. Rate of return on female education is high (Khan, 1985; Schultz, 1993; Blau and Kahn, 1997), these also highlighted the importance of female education. If more female educated then the use of modern technology increases and the capital intensive industries expand. Ultimately may the import reduces and export increases which reduce the trade deficit. It also shows that the female education has direct and indirect both impacts on the economy. And the coefficient of GIR is (-0.026) which has negative and insignificant impact on GGFCF. In column 3, shows the dependent variable is growth of POP (GPOP) while independent variables include growth of GDP (GGDP), growth of fixed capital formation (GGFCF), female-male growth ratio in universities (GUNIF), and growth of growth of imports (GIM). The coefficients of GGDP, GGFCF and GUNIF are (-1.0065), (-0.0764) and (-0.05672) having negative and insignificant impact on growth of POP. And the coefficient of GM is (0.01889) which has positively insignificant impact on POP growth. The reason may be that when population increases then more goods required in country then imports increase. In column 4, the dependent variable is growth of LF (GLF) while the independent variables include growth of GDP (GGDP), growth of capital formation (GGFCF), female-male growth ratio in universities (GUNIF), and growth of exports (GX). The coefficients of GGDP, GGFCF and GUNIF are (0.8029), (0.1035) and (0.0737) all these variables have positive impact on LF growth. And the GX has negative and insignificant impact on growth of LF as its coefficient is (-0.0085). All these levels of education are important for women.

The results show that gender inequality in education and employment is not a small issue, but it is a growth issue. Increasing female education reduces fertility, decreased child mortality, and increases the education opportunities for their children. As we know, gender gap in education results in gender gap in employment. Gender equality increases human capital in a country.

Conclusion

Economists have always been interested to examine the factors which are responsible for higher economic growth. In Cobb-Douglas production function, physical capital and labor force always remain most important factors of production. After the introduction of technology, it remains an important factor for many years. Some developing countries grow rapidly with same technology. After that emphasis was given on embodied labor force through training and education. The countries emphasizing on fundamental education, developed fast relative to other countries; one of the reasons may be the alteration of new skills. Therefore, we can say the education remains a significant issue for fast growing economies.

In this study, we highlighted the direct and indirect effect of education on economic development. The indirect effect of education is measured with growth in fixed capital formation, population growth and growth rate of labor force. Simultaneous equation model is used for estimation purpose. We have summarized the effect of gender inequality growth in education on the GDP growth, growth in fixed capital formation, population growth, and labor force growth.

We have estimated four equations model using GMM model. Starting from equation 1, in which GDP was taken as dependent variable. Results showed positive impact on GDP growth with female-male enrolment in arts and science colleges, but impact of enrolment in professional colleges and universities have negative. Likewise, the other three equations are estimated. The overall results indicated that female-male ratio is low in professional colleges and more in arts and science colleges, while capital formation effected positively to GDP and population growth significantly but negatively as expected. All results are robust and consistent with the theories.

Policy Implication

Analysis of our study showed that the government has not given much attention to education particularly women's education. The allocation of budget and its utilization on education is not satisfactory. The results of our estimation illustrates that the gender gap in education is very high leading towards the conservative society. Following policies may also be applied:

1. If government policies reduce financial cost and social cost, it will help to increase female-male enrolment ratio and improve female efficiency.
2. With the increase in investment on human capital, economic growth may increase. There should be better infrastructure and organizational facilities for female to grow.
3. In the presence of higher regional gender gap in Pakistan, public spending on rural areas on female education will play a remarkable role as compared to urban areas.
4. Usually women take less interest in corruption practices, so they should be encouraged in government services, which will definitely have better impact on economic growth.

5. Government should also provide maximum education facilities particularly technical and vocational education to women, so that they are endowed with skills, which not only help them to increase the GDP growth, but also the standard of their own living may improve.

References

- Abbas, Qaisar 2001 Endogenous Growth and Human Capital: A Comparative Study of Pakistan and Sri Lanka. *The Pakistan Development Review* 40: 4 Part II (Winter 2001) pp. 987-1007.
- Ahmed, N. and S. Bukhari 2007. Gender Inequality and Trade Liberalization: A Case Study of Pakistan. *Research Report : 67*
- Barro, R. 1991. Economic Growth in a Cross-Section of Countries. *Quarterly Journal of Economics* 106: 407-443.
- Baliamoune, M. 2007. Trade and Gender Inequality in Morocco. *ASBBS E-Journal 3: 1*
- Baliamoune, M. and M. McGillivray 2007. Gender inequality and growth, evidence from Sub-Saharan Africa and Arab countries. *African Development Review, 21 (2): 224-242, 2000.*
- Breierova, Lucia and Duflo, Esther (2003). The impact of Education on Fertility and Child Mortality: Do Fathers Really Matter less than Mothers. Massachusetts Institute of Technology DEV/DOC 15.
- Burki, Shahid. Javed 1996 Pakistan: Growths Set by Structural Rigidities. *The Pakistan Development Review* 35: 4 Part I (Winter 1996) pp. 315-342.
- Chaudhry, I. and S. Rahman, 2009. The Impact of Gender Inequality in Education on Rural Poverty in Pakistan. European Journal of Economics, Finance and Administrative Sciences. *ISSN 1450-2887.*
- Chen, D. 2004.Gender Equality and Economic Development, the Role for Information and Communication Technologies. *World Bank Policy Research Working Paper 328.*
- Clark A., Rebecca 2003 Female Literacy Rates, Information Technology and Democracy.
- Coulombe, Serge and Jean-Francois, Tremblay 2004 Literacy, Human Capital and Growth. University of Ottawa.
- Dougherty Christopher 2003 Why is the Rate of Return to Schooling Higher for Women than for Men? ISBN 0753016427.
- Ferrant, G. 2009 Gender inequality and growth, a new way to think the measure and the relationship. *Preliminary version: October, 2009.*
- Hamid, Shahnaz and Siddiqui, Rehana 2001 Gender Differences in Demand for Schooling. *The Pakistan Development Review* 40: 4 Part II (Winter 2001) pp. 1077-1092.
- Jacobs, J. 1996. Gender inequality and higher education. *Annual. Review. Sociology (1996). 22:153–85*
- Kambhmpati S. Uma and Pal, Sarmistha (2001) Role of Parental Literacy in Explaining Gender Differences: Evidence from Child Schooling in India. *The European Journal of Development Research* 13: 2 (December 2001) pp. 97-119.
- King, E. and A. Hill. 1995. *Women's Education in Development Countries.* Baltimore: Johns Hopkins Press.
- Klasen, S and F. Lamanna 2003. The Impact of Gender Inequality in Education and Employment on Economic Growth in the Middle East and North Africa.
- Klasen, S. 2006. Pro Poor Growth and Gender Inequality.
- Moheyuddin, G. 2005 Gender inequality in education, impact on income growth and development. *Essay: 2nd Session WBI's E-Course: Gender, Economic Development and Poverty Reduction.*
- Narayan and Smyth (2004) Temporal Causality and Dynamics of Exports, Human Capital and Real Income in China. *International Journal of Applied Economics,* 1: 1(Winter 2004) pp. 24-45.
- Pelletier, Denis 2005 Introduction to Econometrics: SAS and Multiple Regression. North Carolina State University EC451.

- Sabir Mohammad (2002) Gender and Public Spending on Education in Pakistan: A case Study of Disaggregated Benefit Incidence. *The Pakistan Development Review* 41: 4 Part II (Winter 2002) pp. 477-403.
- Soderbom, Mans and Teal Francis (2003) Openness and Human Capital as Sources of Productivity Growth: An Empirical Investigation. C

Chapter 8
Women Managers in Universities of Pakistan

By: Qudsia Batool
AJ&K

Universities all over the world are facing vital challenges and some appealing opportunities in a progressively competitive global context. Women as managers and their roles in management has become a focus of special attention and has become more important in this era. Career advancement of women managers, in recent years, has emerged as an important area of research in the field of gender and management. Little research is available on this issue of women in management and leadership in Pakistan specifically with reference to universities. Women are rare in top management positions in all sectors including universities when women cannot reach at professoriate level at the same rate as males. It has been realized that gender equality is necessary for the meaningful economic, political, and social development of any society.

This chapter discusses gender representation in the public sector general universities of Pakistan and factors that undermine women's representation.

Introduction
In Pakistan, women are more than 50% of the population but their representation in the top management position is rare. A number of studies have been conducted to examine the factors affecting women's advancement in management careers, these studies provide a useful insight into the phenomenon of scarcity of women in top management, and they are narrow in nature and are restricted in focus. These studies are largely based on the experiences of women managers in the western and industrialized countries. It is clear that women all over the world are underrepresented in upper management, and generally they face discrimination and marginalization on the basis of their gender. The promotion of gender equality and women empowerment is one of the eight millennium development goals. The percentage of women faculty in the universities has increased over the past few years, but they remain underrepresented at professorial and senior management levels. There are so many factors that cause the underrepresentation of women in

top management positions such as organizational, socio-cultural and individual. Due to patriarchal social system women cannot easily get opportunities to reach top management positions. Although women are 53% of population and still long way away from participating in the same footing as their male counterparts. Top management and leadership positions are still the domain of men. According to literature, the "think manager think male" mindset seems to be prevalent. Gender stereotypes are deeply entrenched in our society. Men don't want to hand over their birthright to this new breed of women in the platter of gold. Society is patriarchal. People in the organization are a part of a society and their attitudes towards women are not encouraging. Organization culture is shaped by men because men are in the decision-making positions.

The continuous underrepresentation of women at more high-ranking and management echelons of the global higher education sector is being given attention with the recognition that universities as well as countries cannot afford to neglect women's management capabilities as well as their leadership potential (Ramsay, 2000).

Gender imbalance in universities seems to be a global phenomenon (Benschop & Brounds, 2003 & Foster, 2001). Women are new-comers to administrative positions in all organizations as well universities. Women have accomplished specialized and administrative decision making positions at lower and middle levels of organizational ladder. It is still challenging for women to get executive positions in the universities (Denton & Zeytinoglu, 1993). Management and leadership positions have traditionally been predominantly male domain. Over the previous three decades, the international community has assured to encourage gender equivalence and eradicating inequalities against women (www.un.org), through the convention on the elimination of all forms of discrimination against women (CEDAW).

The Beijing declaration and platform for action (1995), world conference on Higher Education Report of 1998 (Morley, 2005) held in Paris focused on the importance of enhancing "participation and promotion of women" particularly their active involvement in decision-making". The millennium summit (2000) focused on the gender equality and equity. In the 2005 world summit, member states guaranteed to achieve the internationally decided development goals (www.un.org). International community focused on the gender equality and equity (www.un.org) "Gender mentions to the social difference and relationships between males and females who learned from societies and cultures and change with the passage of time. 'Gender roles are cultured behavior in a particular society or a community (www.un.org).

Different approaches, such as WID (Women in Development), WAD (women and development), have introduced for gender equality and equity all over the world. Gender and Development (GAD) finds to assimilate awareness about gender and ability into mainstream progress (UNESCO, 2000) and emphasize to apply suitable gender planning in order to guarantee that consequential situations and outcomes are fair to women and men (UNESCO, commonwealth, 1995).

There is a big difference between the status of women and men in Pakistan. But these differences remain without any major change. According to global gender gap report (UNESCO, 2011), Pakistan is ranked 134 out of 135 in the economic opportunities participation and 127 in educational attainments. The Beijing report also noted that Pakistani women continue to face patriarchal structure.

Gender Representation in public sector universities of Pakistan
In Pakistan, the percentage of women in ministerial position is 6% and 94% men. The percentage of women in labor force is 34% and 80% of men. The percentage of women legislators, senior officials and legislators is 2% and percentage of men is 98%. The percentage of women as professional and technical workers is 26% and men are 74% and women bear 70% of poverty burden (Baig & Jabeen, 2011). According to AEPM (2010), there are an estimated 7000 female teachers while 19000 male teachers in public sector universities of Pakistan. Although women are 53% of the population,

* In the public sector general universities of Pakistan, there are 3 vice chancellor, 14 deans, and 8 directors.
* 45.31% men are lecturers while 54.69% women are lecturers (2012, universities website).
* 55.46% men are assistant professors, while 44.54% women are Assistant professors
* 59.73% associate professors are men while 40.27% women
* 65.68% professors are men while 34.32% women.

At entry level proportion of women is higher than men but as they moved up the occupational ladder their proportion is going to be slow down. In the study sample of 412 women, 180 women were master's degree, 172 were MPhil and only 60 women were PhD. Women are in low numbers in research degree.

Amondi (2011) indicated that organizational and socio-cultural barriers limit women's access to top management positions in universities. According to Hadrian & Terry (2007), promotion criteria, lack of education, and experience cause the underrepresentation of women in top management in academia. White (2008) indicated that lack of family support and domestic responsibilities limits women's access to top management positions. Flechl (2009) identified how women manage their work-life balance; the findings indicated that there are some historical and cultural issues as well as individual conditions, which make it hard to combine work and life.

The ILO (2004) found that obstacles are originated by discriminatory behavior towards women managers and this focused a key element in the prevailing position of women in management across the globe. Moreover gender stereotyping is reluctant to bring reform. Negative stereotyping by others is a substantial hurdle to the job progression of women in management. Such attitudes are prevalent and severely rooted and carry on to effect on women's job progression in the role of administrators. Djajadikert and Trireksani (2007) identified that human capital (research productivity, level of education and year of experience) are the key elements that positively affect the career progression of female academics in Australia.

Measures taken by other countries for Gender Equality

The underrepresentation of women in top management position is a global phenomenon. But some countries have made progress due to international commitments, such as Finland which reserves quota for women in top management positions to fill gender gap in management and leadership positions. In Sweden, the proportion of women in management and leadership position is higher as compared to other parts of world.

According to global gender gap report 2012, Sweden is named as a world leader in equality. In Australia, lot of efforts were made to bring women in management and leadership positions. They introduced affirmative action plan, EEO as well as WEXDEV model etc. to bring diversity in management and leadership positions. Improvement has been made after such efforts but still women are behind their male counterparts. In Canada and Australia, the situation of women in management and leadership position is encouraging, 27% women professors in Turkey is highest percentage in all over the Europe.

According to global gender gap report (UNESCO,(2012), women have been the principal beneficiaries of HE expansion phenomenon in all regions. Women's participation increased from 8 to 28% while men's participation from 11 to 26%. Literature shows that in Turkey women do not apply for top management positions due to their domestic responsibilities. Although after the implementation of international commitments, the situation and position of women has improved but still need improvement in top management positions until gender gap fills. There is a need for diversity in management and leadership positions.

Factors that undermine the women's representation

Organizational Factors:

These are also called organizational barriers. Organizational culture seems to be a change–resistant element that promotes an environment dominated by male values and justifies most women's self-exclusion from university administration (Thomas, et al. 2009). Women continue to be underprivileged by deeply entrenched organizational and societal obstacles and by progression system that largely depend on the publication of candidates (Foster, 2001). The aim of the gender equality is to treat both men and women equally and create equal opportunities by eliminating structural and procedural barriers to women's success (Meyerson & Kolb, 2000). Selection and promotion practices are negatively associated with the advancement of women in Pakistan.

The study showed that recruitment and selection practices are discriminatory such as interviewing committees mostly consists of men. Monitoring and practice of selection and promotion policy is discouraging. Women in spite of fulfilling criteria are not being promoted.

Socio-cultural Factors:
Women reported that family consideration affects their career such as women do not apply for senior management positions. The women reported that they have to sacrifice their personal and social time due to their dual responsibilities. The women reported that they have support from their spouse and family for the job. Women have to undertake many roles and responsibilities in their life which undermines their career progression. The concepts of women being not suitable for management positions weaken the women's ability to be promoted to top management positions. Due to domestic responsibilities, women are reluctant to apply for top management positions and refuse to relocate to get promotion.

Recommendations for Gender Equality
* Develop a data base that show the position of women in leadership positions
* Need to re-shape the organization's culture
* Family friendly policies by universities
* Introduce formal mentoring, networking, quota for women (top management positions), scholarships for research degree
* Gender sensitized programs
* Awareness campaigns
* Year wise Gender analysis(selection of candidates) of selection boards
* Encourage women in research and development
* Representation of women in selection boards and decision-making bodies
* Leadership courses/trainings

Summary
The study reveals that structural and socio-cultural factors cause the underrepresentation of women in top management positions in almost all spheres of life. The study has shown that women do not progress to the top management positions, even the rank of professor, as quickly as men. The result showed that women are underrepresented due to gender inequity in universities and gender inequity relates to the socio-cultural barriers. Masculine organization culture generates inequity such as women have lack of network, mentoring and career progression. Encouraging women for higher ranks is the final equity goal. Women are under-represented in executive positions due to continuous systemic and cultural barriers.

The study found that overall socio-cultural barriers (Domestic responsibilities, stereotypes) are the leading factors that undermine the women's representation at top management positions/career progression. Child care, career and family, gender discrimination, and stereotype are the barriers for women that undermine their competitiveness in promotion and slow down their career. The study shows that women can effectively manage career and family. Women generally feel obligated to assume more family responsibilities than men. Women in spite of doing jobs have to do lot of work at home. So work and family remains a challenge for women. "Glass ceiling" restricts the women's rise to top management positions. These barriers are invisible. When a glass ceiling exists, men occupy high percentage of higher ranks and women tend to be underrepresented in higher positions. "Glass ceiling" exists in its strongest forms restricting the women's opportunities for getting top management positions. The problem of female underrepresentation in top management position in higher education management is not attributable to one factor, but also cycle of discrimination at all levels.

The lack of diversity in management has negative implications for universities' future capacity to respond to change. All these barriers are interrelated and having correlation among each other. All these factors hinder women's representation at top management positions. The main reason of this bias against women is the society because individual and organizations are a part of a society.

References

Amondi, O. (2011). Representation of women in top educational management and leadership positions in Kenya. *Journal of advancing women in leadership*, 31, 57-68.

Bagilhole, B. (2002). Academia and the reproduction of unequal opportunities for women. *Journal of science studies*, 15(1), 46-60.

Benschop,Y & Brounds, M. (2003). Crumbling ivory towards: Academic organizing and its gender effects. Gender, work and organization, 10(2), 194-212.

Brown, M. (2006). Barriers to women manager's advancement in education in Uganda. *Journal of education management*, 10(6), 18-23.

Bain, O., & Cummings ,W. (2000). Academe's glass ceilings: societal, professional, organizational and institutional barriers to the career advancement of Academe women. *journal of comparative education* , 44(4), 493-514.

Beninger, A. (2010). *Women Academia: A cross cultural perspectives on work-life balance*.PS433, Research report 2010.

Bonawitz, M., & Andel, N. (2009). *The Glass ceiling is made of concrete: The Barriers to promotion and Tenure of Women In American Academia*. Published By Forum On Public Policy Pennsylvania State University.

Bingham, & Nix. (2010). *Women faculty in higher education: A case study on Gender Bias*. Forum On Public policy, west Texas A&M University.

Benschop,Y.,& Janson,W. (2010). Transparency in Academic Recruitment: A problemetic Tool for Gender equality. *Journal of Organizational studies*, 30(12), 1-25 ISSN 0179-8406. www.sagepub.co.uk.

Baig, M. & Jabeen, N.(2011). Gender stereotypes and women in management-The case of banking sector of Pakistan. *Journal of south Asian studies*, 26(2), 259-284.

Denton,M.,&Zeytinoglue,I. (1993) .perceived participation in decision-making in a university setting:The impact of gender. *Journal of industrial and labor Relations* , 46(2) ,329-331.

CEDAW. (1995). *UN treaty Series* vol. 12 (49), p. 13.

Foster, N. (2001). A case study of women academics views on equal opportunities, career prospects and work family conflicts in UK university. *journal of career development international*, 6, 28-38.

Morley, L. (2005). Gender equity in commonwealth higher education. *journal of women studies international forum*, 28 ,209-221.

Ramsay, E. (2000). *Women And leadership in higher education: Facing international challenges and maxmising opportunities*. Keynote address: University of South Australia.

UNESCO.(2000). Gender equality & Equity. Review of UNESCO's accomplishments since 1995. UNESCO.

UNESCO(2012). Global Gender Atlas 2012

White, K. (2001). Women In the professoriate in Australian. *International journal of organizational behavior* . 3(2), 64-76.

Wallace, M. (2006).The Paradox and the price: A case study of female academic managers in an Australian regional university. *Advancing women in leadership journal*, 21.

Winkler, J. (2000). Faculty reappointment, tenure and promotion barriers. *professional Geographer.* 52(4), 737-750.

Chapter 9
Emotional Intelligence and Women in Pakistan

By: Razia Begum
College of Home Economics, University of Peshawar

Pakistan is a South Asian country of strategic significance, bordered with Afghanistan, Iran and China, endowed with tremendous resources. Capable manpower is the only resource which could give competitive edge to a country in a global market. Pakistan in this case is very rich as its population is hardworking, dedicated and ambitious. Particularly female population, despite of many socio-cultural, economic and educational barriers, still their labor force participation is significant in almost every sphere of economy ranging from manual field work to office jobs in organizations.

However, brought up in collectivist cultural norms, Pakistani females are equipped with immense emotional intelligent skills; therefore they are comparatively better able to deal stringent work situation. This chapter focuses on identifying the emotional qualities of Pakistani females. Finding their skills use in organizations for creating an inspirational workplace, managing turbulent and stressful job situations.

Introduction
Organizations have vividly changed in the last few decades, bringing more flat structure, empowerment, and autonomy even at the lower levels, to reap the benefits of individual talent. Jobs are now more customer-focused, thus, necessitating the presence of emotionally competent employees to deal with stakeholders in an astute way. Thus, emotional intelligence (EI) has become a critical success factor for organizations today. The awakened interest of prominent global organizations like, FedEx, HSBC, and the International Finance Corporation in emotional intelligence have compelled others to consider it too in their managerial scheme (Freedman, 2010; Jain, 2013; Serrat, 2009).

As a concept Emotional Intelligence has become the matter of interest for academicians, business community as well as the general public, convinced with the fact of its significance even more than the conventionally-defined intellectual abilities (Ahmad et al., 2009). Previously, the Intelligence Quotient (IQ) – set of standardized tests to measure intelligence – is used to evaluate intelligence of a person but the supporters of EQ argue that having high score on IQ test does not guarantee superior performance at work. As IQ denotes cognitive abilities which help to predict the technical expertise of a person, ensures whether s/he will be able to handle any job well. However, handling a job well does not guarantee the achievement of pinnacle of one's position in organization in future (Cherniss and Goleman, 2001). Daniel Goleman asserts that up until 90% of the abilities possessed by top performers fall in the realm of EI. Despite of the significance of IQ, EQ is equally needed for finest performance, thus, one could confidently claims that EQ helps to predict performance much better than merely by IQ (Freedman, 2010)

Emotional intelligence is defined as a multi-faceted phenomenon, and it acts as a bridge between emotions and cognition to strengthen human relations at work (Naseer et al., 2011; Jain, 2013). Thus, it serves as a core of effective organizational human interactions and relationships arise out of it (Cherniss and Goleman, 2001).

Evolution of EI
Although the explicit work on emotional intelligence started in 1980s, the core concept of it could be traced in the early researches of Robert Thorndike work on social intelligence in late 30's; David Wechsler (1958) who identified EI as "the global capacity of the individual to deal effectively with his environment"; Ohio State Leadership Studies (1940's) identified 'consideration' as vital for effective leadership; Howard Gardner (1983) signified multiple intelligence, incorporating interpersonal and intra personal intelligence, as important as the typical IQ previously been taken as the only intelligence standard and which helps to understand and control oneself and others for better work atmosphere (Cherniss, 2000; Cavallo and Brienza, 2001).

Initially the term "Emotional Intelligence" was coined by Salovey and Mayer in 1990s (Naseer et al., 2011). Based on their work on non-cognitive aspects of intelligence, described it as a type of social intelligence of a person, helps in understanding, differentiating and controlling one's own emotions and of others. Thus, they defined it as "the compilation of four kinds of skills: perceiving and expressing emotions, understanding emotions, using emotions, and managing emotions". The concept of EI flooded academia and research after the famous writing of Daniel Goleman (1995) *"Emotional Intelligence: Why It Can Matter More Than IQ"* (Serrat, 2009). Therefore, the term 'Emotional Quotient (EQ)' came to surface and is defined as a "set of competencies demonstrating the ability one has to recognize his or her behaviors, moods, impulses, and to manage them best according to the situation" (Poskey, 2013). Furthermore, Goleman expanded Salovey and Mayer's four skills model into five categories of Self-Awareness, Self-Regulation, Motivation, Empathy, and People Skills (Simmons, 2001).

In the course of evolution of EI, it has been defined in many ways but the basic theme remained the same that emotionally intelligent people are very much aware of their own self and others. EI describes the self-perceived ability to identify, evaluate and mange emotions of one's own self and others. People of high EI are better self-aware and work to be attuned to others' emotions as well (Ashraf, 2013). They are more flexible, positive thinkers and are inclined to make accurate decisions and bring creative solutions. On the other hand, people of low EI are rigid and less capable of coping with organizational changes and uncertainties (Ladd and Chan, 2004).

Managing Emotions at work with Emotional Intelligence

Emotional intelligence interplay with organizational effectiveness begins from the very early process of recruitment of human force till their final deliverance of products and services to ultimate consumers (Cherniss and Goleman, 2001). In the context of organization, emotions are those high-intensity feelings employees experience which affect cognitive processes and behaviors at work (Ashraf, 2013; George, 2000). Human emotions are exhibited in many verbal and non-verbal forms. The knowledge and understanding of such contextual signs helps to judge self and people's reaction better (Chaudhry et al., 2013). It plays a powerful role in affecting one's performance, which in turn affects the work of organization. Thus, the increasing complexities of organizational processes necessitate identifying and managing employee's emotions wisely (Jain, 2013).

Emotional intelligence is one among the numerous capabilities of a human being; the intelligent use of which is needed for one's physical and psychological adaptation (Batool and Khalid, 2009), because in organizations, it is all about the management of emotions for the sake of desired results (Naeem et al., 2008). EQ defines the self-concept (Ashraf, 2013), self-awareness and understanding of strengths and foibles of self and others (Cavallo and Brienza, 2001). EI equips a person to perform well in problem situations, uncertainties, have active participation in decision making and own the consequences of their decisions later on (Kiyani et al., 2011; Ladd1 and Chan, 2004). As EQ has a substantial relevance with work-related issues. It helps to access the management styles, polices, employees' potentials in a unique way. Therefore, its significance could not be denied in dealing with human resource management, relationships, and customer's service management (Serrat, 2009; Jain, 2013).

Why we need emotionally intelligent employees?

Employees are defined as people working for private and public employer (s), resultantly rewarded in financial and nonfinancial form (World Bank, 2013). Present day demands have shifted organization's style and criteria of superior performance. Employee's productivity is not only measured by academic achievements and trainings but on how well they get along with others in individual as well as in team performance (Freedman, 2010; Chang et al., 2012; Jorfi et al., 2011). It needs the personal qualities of self-confidence, emotional stability, and considerate attitude of employees. Therefore, vigilant organizations are now focusing on training and improving the social, emotional, and interpersonal skills of their employees to promote better workforce and leadership (Serrat, 2009; Weiss, 2000; Jain, 2013). Goleman's writings suggest that people of high EI reach to the top of organization in their career ladder. He labeled such people as "star" employees who differentiate themselves from "average" employees on the basis of more interpersonal and emotional skills (Haver et al., 2013). Those 'star' employees participate in decision making, utilizing their talent for the achievement of personal and organizational goals (Kiyani et al., 2011). Research conducted on finding any personal competencies which could differentiate between high performers and average ones, on 358 managers of the Johnson & Johnson Consumer & Personal Care Group (JJC&PC Group) across the globe found that highest performers have more emotional competence than others. Moreover they identified the competencies of high performers as: Self-Confidence, Achievement Orientation, Initiative, Leadership, Influence and Change Catalyst which possessed by superior performers (Cavallo and Brienza, 2001). Therefore, EI is not only helpful in identifying employee's current competencies but could also be used to predict and prepare them for future organizational leadership (Ghani, 2012; Dulewicz and Higgs, 2003; Mir and Abbasi 2012).

Up until now, organizations HR and training polices were focused on enhancing hard skills i.e. technical, analytical skills of the employees. But in the long run these skills alone cannot earn success and rapport for organization. Consequently, organizations turned to teach soft skills (relationship management, interpersonal skills) to their employees (Poskey, 2013; Sigmar et al., 2012; Goleman, 1998), inspired by the fact that emotional intelligence could be learned and enhanced with practice and experiences, which opens up an opportunity for organizational training of employees to capitalize on their talent (Weiss, 2000; Jain, 2013).

Striving for promoting emotionally intelligent workplace supports organization to prevent itself from numerous problems. As problems in workforce EI hinders organizational affectivity as a whole but is extremely challenging for managers, who are supposed to design team performance (Simmons, 2001; Freedman, 2010; Chang et al., 2012). Employees of low EI is found significantly correlated with thefts, frauds, and getting injuries in physical work (Poskey, 2013). A study conducted in Lahore – the second largest city of Pakistan population wise – linked low EI with poor mental health and depression, thus, signified EI important for mental health (Batool and Khalid, 2009; Ashraf, 2013). When researches were carried to identify work place issues, up to 76% were related to people and relational aspects, followed by 24% of technical and financial nature (Freedman, 2010; Goleman, 1998). Moreover, self-awareness is a powerful indicator of mental health of employees; those having high self-awareness are in a better position to get hold of their moods. Conversely, low self-aware people experience more dissatisfaction and failures at work (Batool and Khalid, 2009). Therefore we need to design and promote such workplace where emotional intelligence has been taken care of as a valuable asset and considered it to be the driver of growth and productivity. Cherniss and Goleman (2001) model of "Intelligence and

Organizational Effectiveness" (Figure 9.1), for promoting emotionally intelligent workplace would serve as a benchmark in this regard.

Figure 9.1 - Model of Intelligence and Organizational Effectiveness

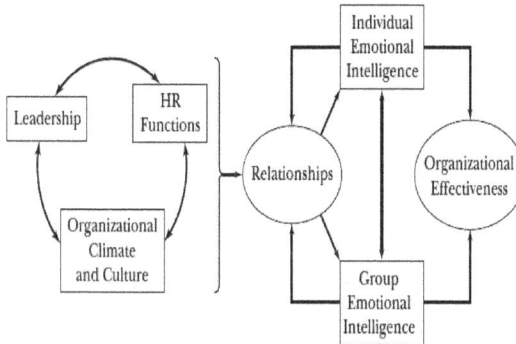

Source: Cherniss and Goleman (2001). The Emotionally Intelligent Workplace

Relation of Emotional Intelligence with Gender

Research on relationship of emotional intelligence and gender are still inconclusive (Chaudhry et al., 2013). However, the conventional-notion of relating women with emotionality based on gender, goes into her advantage when it comes to emotional intelligence. Her strength of emotional intelligence and emotional stability – which helps to define self-concept of a person – has become the powerful indicator of 21st century organization's growth (Ashraf, 2013; Jorfi et al., 2011). Females have significantly high self-regard score than males, lack of which is proved to be the major predictor of depression (Batool and Khalid, 2009). The study conducted on managers of Johnson & Johnson Consumer & Personal Care Group found women high in adaptability and service orientation, while men were good in competency and change promoters (Cavallo and Brienza, 2001).

Likewise, numerous studies confirm that generally women are more aware of their emotions, good in interpersonal relations, team building, displaying empathy and tolerance (Simmons, 2001), have the ability to motivate, and inspire which are needed for leading towards a common vision (Marre, 2013). Women leadership has been found to be more of a participative nature, characterized by empowerment, delegation, consensual decision making (Ashraf, 2013), they are high in emotional abilities when their performance is peer-evaluated in organization (Cavallo and Brienza, 2001). Resultantly, women are bringing more innovations in top-board decisions which affect the whole staff and organizational performance afterwards (Nash, 2013).

If we look at the global statistics to find out the female labor force participation in various fields, we can see that women involvement in employment and economic activities has considerably grown (Mehra and Gammage, 1999) in the last ten years (1993-1994) to utilize her potential and gaining economic independence. But issues of balance in compensation and gender still needs to be addressed (ILO, 2004).

Women's Emotional Intelligence in Pakistan

Factors like trade expansions, economic integrations, technological advancements, shift from agriculture to industry and then to service activities have altered the face of global business operations, as well as the employment patterns. South Asian countries are striving to increase employment and country workforce. Likewise, Pakistan is also struggling to enhance citizen's employability, especially of females, through skills enhancements, uplifting literacy, and providing more job opportunities to them.

Hitherto, the reported literature asserts Pakistani women to be very high or very good in emotional intelligence and self-esteem, which organizations could capitalize on. But before affirming something about the emotional intelligence and capabilities of Pakistani females, we need to understand the female position in the context of culture, economy and other relevant variables prevailing in Pakistan.

Pakistan's total population is reported to be 180 million in 2014, with the Gross Domestic Product (GDP) of 3.59 percent in the fiscal year 2012-13 and Annual Growth Rate averaged 4.94 Percent. The aggregate literacy ratio is 58 % in the year 2010-11, with prominent disparities among genders, rural / urban areas and provinces. Among provinces Punjab leads with 60% literacy rate followed by Sindh, Khyber Pakhtunkhwa, and Balochistan with 59%, 50% and 41% respectively (Pakistan Economic Survey, 2011-12).

Among the sectorial economic contribution services are on the top which accounts for 53 percent of total GDP (prominent sub-service sectors are: public administration and defense 18 percent; wholesale and retail trade 17 percent; and transportation 10 percent). On the other hand Industry contributes 25 percent; agriculture and its allied activities contribute 22 percent of the total of GDP (World Bank, 2013). Despite of tough efforts on the part of working population, the country labour force lags behind in productivity and efficiency as compared to the South Asian countries due to illiteracy, lack of skills, training, capital, and limited market opportunities. Resultantly, Pakistan is ranked 136 out of 142 countries in labor market efficiency in the World Economic Forum's Global Competitiveness Report 2011-12 (Ameen, 2012). Although, policy makers are struggling to uplift the labour force participation rate in the country. As the Labour Policy of Pakistan 2010 has the objective of promoting labour participation based on merit and striving for elimination of gender discrimination in jobs (Pakistan Economic Survey 2011-12)
Female Labor Force Participation

A country's population provides labor power which plays vital role in the socio- economic uplift of a country (Pakistan Economic Survey 2011-12). As a whole Pakistan labour participation rate is very low (approximately 33 %, year 2011) which is very low as compared to the other South Asian countries labour force participation of 45 percent (Ameen, 2012). The total labour force participation (Table 9.1) on the basis of Crude Activity Rate (CAR) and Refined Activity Rate (RAR) is given between year 2008-09 and 2010-11. Among these two, the CAR shows the overall participation rate, while RAR give much improved picture as it depicts labour force of 10 years of age and above.

If we consider RAR female labour force values only, we could see that overall female participation rate is 21.7% (augmented 37.4%). But their participation disparity is greater in urban areas i.e. 55.7% (10.7% female, 66.4% male) in the year 2010-11 as compared to the rural areas disparity of 42.45% (female 27.6%, to male 70.0 %) in participation in year 2010-11.

Females' economic participation depends upon age, education, family norms, marital status, access to economic and productive facilities, etc. (Ejaz, 2011). It shows that females of rural areas participate much more in labour activities generated in rural areas. But those activities are mainly of unskilled and semi-skilled nature which requires a lot of physical labour and efforts on the part of her in addition to her numerous household responsibilities (Kazi and Raza 1991). On the other hand, female participation in rural as well as urban areas shows an increasing rate today as compared to previous years which is a promising indicator of her improved socio-economic status and productive involvement in the country (Pakistan Economic Survey 2011-12; Ejaz, 2011). However, her participation is still lowest in South Asia where it is 44 percent on average (Ameen, 2012).

Table – 9.1 Pakistan's Labor Force Participation Rates

Indicators	2008-09	2009-10	2010-11	Indicators	2008-09	2009-10	2010-11
Crude Activity (Participation) Rates (%)				Refined Activity (Participation) Rates (%)			
Pakistan				Pakistan			
Total	32.8	33.0	32.8	Total	45.7	45.9	45.7
Male	49.6	49.5	49.3	Male	69.3	68.8	68.7
Female	14.9	15.5	15.6	Female	20.7	21.5	21.7
Augmented				Augmented			
Total	38.8	38.8	38.4	Total	53.9	53.9	53.5
Female	27.0	27.2	27.0	Female	37.5	37.9	37.4
Rural				Rural			
Total	34.3	34.5	34.3	Total	49.2	49.4	49.1
Male	49.2	49.0	48.6	Male	71.0	70.2	70.0
Female	18.5	19.3	19.4	Female	26.4	27.6	27.6
Augmented				Augmented			
Total	42.7	42.6	42.2	Total	61.2	61.0	60.4
Female	35.6	35.8	35.4	Female	50.7	51.2	50.3
Urban				Urban			
Total	29.9	30.0	30.0	Total	39.3	39.5	39.5
Male	50.4	50.6	50.6	Male	66.3	66.4	66.4
Female	7.6	7.8	8.1	Female	10.1	10.3	10.7
Augmented				Augmented			
Total	31.0	31.1	31.0	Total	40.8	41.0	10.8
Female	9.9	10.1	10.1	Female	13.1	13.3	13.3

Source: Labour Force Survey 2010-11

The sectorial female labor force participation (Table 9.2) shows that majority (75% female vs 36.2% males; year 2010-11) of females are engaged in agriculture and its allied activities followed by community, personal services (11.5 %) and manufacturing sector (10.9%). The rest of the sectors have her minimum participation. The common fact among all the sectors, that female work is mainly of manual nature, lengthy working time and extensive physical excretion. In agriculture too, she works and assists men; thus, she hardly ever earn personal income for her own efforts. Improvements in female employment if any, are assessed as her shift from agriculture to manufacturing and from low wage to higher wage level which is again far behind the global development tendencies. Pakistani female economic participation is also affected by her demographic factors like age, level of education, and marital status, family and home responsibilities.

Table 9.2 - Pakistan's Labor Force Share by Major Industries

Employment Share by Industry (%)									
		2008-09			2009-10			2010-11		
Major Industry Divisions		Total	Male	Female	Total	Male	Female	Total	Male	Female
Total		100	100	100	100	100	100	100	100	100
Agriculture/forestry etc.		45.1	37.3	74.0	45.0	36.6	74.9	45.1	36.2	75.4
Manufacturing		13.0	13.3	11.9	13.2	13.9	11.0	13.7	14.5	10.9
Construction		6.6	8.3	0.4	6.7	8.5	0.3	7.0	8.9	0.2
Whole sale and retail trade		16.5	20.5	1.6	16.3	20.2	2.1	16.2	20.4	1.6
Transport/storage and communication		5.2	6.6	0.2	5.2	6.6	0.3	5.1	6.6	0.1
Community/social personal services		11.2	11.1	11.6	11.2	11.2	11.2	10.8	10.8	11. 5
*Others		2.4	2.9	0.3	2.4	3.0	0.2	2.1	2.6	0.3

Source: Pakistan Bureau of Statistics, Labour Force Survey 2010-11

Pakistan's Bureau of Statistics reports an increase in female participation as a workforce from time to time since last decade. However, to become an active and strong workforce she still needs to travel a long road of struggle, to overcome her economic problems comes in a way of her productive participation in a country development.

Socio-Cultural Dimensions
Gender socialization and role identities are formed in a culture, which determine roles expectations for both genders in family, community and in workplace. Values vary in every culture; however it helps to define the EI of any society. Being male or female affects how one should act in a given culture. It's a common notion of eastern cultures that women are supposed to be emotional, caring and more attentive to the other's emotions as well, while men are socialized to have control over their

emotions. Likewise, gender based differentiation or inequality is a global phenomenon which prevails in almost every culture. South Asian societies – developing countries – are not an exception, where gender stereotypes founded separate working spheres for society. Bread earning and dealing with outside world as "men's work" while rearing children and household responsibilities as "women work".

Gender disparities do not prevails uniformly across the region/country due to differences in political, economic, social, and cultural factors. In Pakistan gender discrimination is more prominent in rural areas, especially where there is lack of education, infrastructure and awareness. A study carried in rural areas of District Mardan (Khyber Pakhtun khwa (KPK) Province) on identifying the socio-economic and cultural constraints of women found females in poor socioeconomic status; illiterate, unskilled and low in general awareness, which hinders her economic participation. However, older females have been consulted in decisions and other family matters. On the contrary, where literacy is high coupled with other socio economic developments, gender discriminations are less obvious and families desire to educate their females (Din and Khan, 2008).

Generally, Pakistan is a patriarchal society where discretionary powers lie in the hands of men. As gender separates life spheres for men and women, thus, intelligence develops on different information which brings differences in EI of men and women. Pakistani females have more pressures from family and society which attunes her more to the society norms and expectations. On the other hand, they are full of potential, dedication, and growth drive. Time has proved that whenever any women came forward in education and any economic activity afterwards, it has been proved as really successful and inspirational move.

Emotional Intelligence at Work: Empirical Evidences

Gender debate continues to exist, albeit social science experts and researchers believe that men and women have different styles of communication, interpersonal relations, decision making and problem solving styles in organizations. Goleman's research signify that female brain has more neurons which works on feelings, which makes the female respond immediately to others problems and trying to solve it. This makes a female a better customer- responsive employee (Marre, 2013). Studies on thousands of male-female EI confirm that, on average, females have more self-awareness, empathy, skilled in interpersonal relations. Conversely, men are more self-confident, optimistic, and flexible (Simmons, 2001).

As emotional intelligence deals with context-suitable expression of emotions, the question now arise that how those women act in organizations in the course of her roles and duties, who have been brought-up in a Pakistani (Eastern) culture. The process of socialization also bring differences in EI based on gender, where females are encouraged to express more care, affection while men are expected to have control over their emotions. As culture and family trains her to be emotionally positive, this pays her in the effective emotional management, conflict handling, and stress management in organization. Thus, women are found to be friendlier and cooperative in workplace. Field researches on Pakistani females working in rural areas identified extra efforts on her part, where they struggle to confirm to her gender role expectations of the society, as well as striving to continue her formal employment.

In the subsequent section we will look at women's various roles in organizations mediated by her emotional intelligence for enhancing organizational productivity.

Leadership Role
Undoubtedly, stakeholders look at top management to understand the organizational style of operations. Leadership skills have been recognized as the most significant asset of organizational success, among which EI has appeared as one of the important factors in determining leader's effectiveness (Ghani, 2012; Dulewicz and Higgs, 2003; Harms and Credé, 2010; Haver et al., 2013; George, 2000; Mir and Abbasi 2012). People were convinced by the conventional thought that men would be effective leaders. However, recent work patterns changed people perceptions, as now women as a leader could also be equally effective due to her unique abilities. For Pakistani women having leadership role in organization is still developing but still studies conducted on Pakistani female in leadership role, found positive relationship between her EI, self-esteem and leadership style (Ashraf, 2013). As business are getting complex day by day, need for vigilant and emotionally intelligent leaders are arising which brings an opportunity for women in leadership positions. Subsequently, female participation in top management decisions is more appreciated by the staff and female motivation induces employees for better performance (Ghani, 2012).

Entrepreneurial role
Promoting and developing entrepreneurship is 21st century notion of modern business world (Scott, 1986). Entrepreneurship is needed to increase employment opportunities, and utilize diverse talent. Females are specially benefiting from it because of multi-faceted challenges in other jobs, and role expectations of family and society (Kalim, 2012). Particularly, females of rural population are equipped with many skills but due to lack of mobility, education, and capital they cannot always enter into professional jobs. On the other hand, if they are trained and facilitated to start small home-based businesses, that will be helpful for their economic gain as well as for country employment generation.

Although in Pakistan women participation is only 2% in trade unions (ILO, 2013). But those self-employed women by any small scale businesses, and entrepreneurial activities exhibit responsible attitude by making on-time debt payment to the financing agencies better than their male counterparts (Haq, 2011). Entrepreneurial activities gave self-confidence to the females of Pakistan, enable them to assist in family incomes, and developed respectable living standard. However, government should help them in providing credit facilities, skills training, marketing their goods and services and also to develop business linkages locally and globally (Shah, 2002). At present, components of emotional intelligence of females and her entrepreneurial orientation have been identified as a valuable addition in their work (Pradhan and Nath, 2012).

Role in Service organizations

Women are good in adaptability, stress management, relational skills, and have the capacity to cover up negative emotions better than their male colleagues (Ashraf, 2013). All these are highly required skills in successful service sector jobs where she has a direct contact with customers of numerous demands. Employees in a banking services, telecom services needs skills which could be best described by 'Emotional intelligence,' by learning and practicing EI skills employees learn to better understand customer needs and demands, thus, become able to align the services to satisfy consumers. Habib Bank, first commercial bank in Pakistan established in 1947, is of the opinion that hiring female employees gives them benefit of improved customer services. They are better able to satisfy customer queries; male customers don't behave rudely with women on the desk in bank. The same EI skills practice stands true for private/foreign banks working in Pakistan. A CEO of Unilever Pakistan Foods remarked that female seller have the benefit of convincing public effectively because they themselves are the consumers and have the ability to appeal to customers demand in appropriate way (Haq, 2011; Naeem et al., 2008).

Service sector jobs are characterized by issues of stress and conflicts, especially, this is more prominent in nursing profession. Therefore it necessitates the need for learning and practicing EI skills to encounter the stress and conflicts in their stressful jobs. Annually, Pakistan is producing 13,132 female nurses among the four provinces, but in comparison to the patients, one nurse is for 3,175 patients (Manzoor et al., 2010), which is extremely low. The government could work on it to improve the human resource dedicated to healthcare, particularly females who are excellent in dealing with human needs.

Future Prospects of Female Participation

Pakistani female workforce is improving day by day seeking numerous jobs in public and private sectors, serving on various positions from first-line to top-level management, and from armed forces to manufacturing, bureaucratic, entrepreneurial, civil, services industry to multi-national corporations. Her journey of advancement in gaining position in economic spheres is surely backed up by her efforts in gaining required education. According to Higher Education Commission of Pakistan (HEC), among the 1.1 million university students 47% are females. In the job market females make up approximately half employees among the MBA graduates hired by Habib Bank of Pakistan (Haq, 2011). Researches proved that when opportunities of access to education, resources, and skills acquisition are being provided, females have contributed superbly in poverty alleviation, and economic growth (ILO, 2011). Recently, customer friendly bank polices, trade department policies, government focus on establishing small scale businesses gave momentum to female entrepreneurship. Females with superior social and interactional skills, and better awareness of customer demands are joining this field successfully. This way they are not only increasing their own income level but also generate further employment for other females of their community.

Summary

This chapter analyzed diverse literature on the current environmental uncertainties, every day increasing customer demands and competitive pressures that organizations are confronted with. It identified human resource as a single asset that could help to gain competitive edge in the market. As far as the composition of abilities and skills of human resource is concerned, merely cognitive abilities are not required for success. In fact, the present turbulent times require such people who are not only good in cognitive abilities, but also equipped with appropriate socio-emotional skills and its management so as to adapt to the situational demands of any job.

Emotional Intelligence at workplace is defined as the awareness, management, and use of emotions of self and others in such an intelligent way as to produce better working relationships. Emotionally intelligent employees are better able to cope with job stress, conflicts, and create an atmosphere of relations based on trust and mutual cooperation.

Pakistan, being a South Asian country, held potentially significant position in trade and other economic activities. It has approximate population of 17 million, but unfortunately the labor force participation is very low, i.e. 45%. The female labour force rate is even more low, 22% only, of the total labour force. The potential reasons responsible for this problem is socio-political and economic constrains, low concern for female education, lack of awareness, gender stereotypes, cultural norms, and conventionally- bounded notions of female labour force participation.

Conversely, if we consider the competencies of female labour force serving at various positions in organizations, we find that Pakistani females are well-equipped with the potential competencies and social skills needed for productivity. Despite of the numerous constrains and demands on her role, the female still proved to be emotionally intelligent and competent in social sector jobs as of education, health, finance, and entrepreneurship; other than her traditional participation in agriculture and industry. In the workplace, the female is more considerate to human needs, has an optimistic attitude, and is concerned for positive interactions.

If we take a futuristic view of the females of Pakistan, we would see that female literacy and cultural perceptions of gender roles are improving which further paves way for her productive economic participation. This trend will help to reduce gender disparities, facilitate gender empowerment and social equality in the region. But still overall efforts of stakeholders are needed to bring change in the general attitude towards female education, employment, access to facilities, and economic participation.

Bibliography

Abbas, I., and Haq, J. (2011). A Relationship between Emotional Intelligence and Self Esteem: study in universities of Pakistan. Arts and Design Studies, 1:10-15.

Ahmad, S., Bangash, H., and Khan, S. A. (2009).Emotional Intelligence and Gender Differences. Sarhad Journal of Agriculture, 25(1):127-130.

Ashraf, H. (2013). Emotional Intelligence and Self Esteem as Determinants of Transformational Leadership Style: Pakistani Women Leaders in Focus. The International Journal of Social Sciences, 13(1):51-65.

Batool, S. S., and Khalid, R. (2009). Low Emotional Intelligence: A Risk Factor for Depression. Journal of Pakistan Psychiatric Society, 6(2):65.

Chaudhry, A. A., Jan, F. A., Sajjad, M., Ali, S. (2013). Emotional Intelligence and Students: A Pakistani Perspective. World Applied Science Journal, 22(3):319-325.

Cavallo, K., and Brienza, D. (2001). Emotional Competence and Leadership Excellence at Johnson & Johnson: The Emotional Intelligence and Leadership Study. Consortium of Research on Emotional Intelligence in Organizations. Retrieved on 08-22-2013, from http://www.eiconsortium.org.

Chang, J. W., Sy, T., Choi, J. N. (2012). Team Emotional Intelligence and Performance: Interactive Dynamics between Leaders and Members. Small Group Research, 43(1):75-104. doi: 10.1177/1046496411415692.

Cherniss, C. (2000). Emotional Intelligence: What it is and why it Matters. Paper presented at the Annual Meeting of the Society for Industrial and Organizational Psychology, New Orleans, LA:pp.1-14.

Cherniss, C., and Goleman, D. (Eds.). (2001).The Emotionally Intelligent Workplace: How to Select For, Measure, and Improve Emotional Intelligence in Individuals, Groups, and Organizations. San Francisco: Jossey-Bass: A Wiley Company.

Chaudhry, A. A., Jan, F. A., Sajjad, M., Ali, S. (2013). Emotional Intelligence and Students: A Pakistani Perspective. World Applied Science Journal, 22(3):319-325.

Din, M. J., and Khan, M. (2008). Socio-Economic and Cultural Constraints of Women in Pakistan with Special Reference to Mardan District, NWFP Province. Sarhad Journal of Agriculture, 24(3):485-493.

Dulewicz, V., Higgs, M. (2003). Leadership at the Top: The Need for Emotional Intelligence in Organizations. International Journal of Organizational Analysis, 11(3):193 – 210.

Ejaz, M. (2011).The Determinants of Female Labor Force Participation in Pakistan: An Instrumental Variable Approach. Centre for Research in Economics and Business, Lahore School of Economics – Pakistan: pp 1-54.

Freedman, J. (2012). Women's leadership Edge: Global Research on Emotional Intelligence, Gender, and Job Level. Retrieved on 08-21-2013, from http://www.6seconds.org/category/eq-business/.

Freedman, J. (2010). The Business Case for Emotional Intelligence. White Paper. Retrieved on 08-21-2013, from http://www.6seconds.org/, pp 1-41.

George, J. M. (2000). Emotions and Leadership: The Role of Emotional Intelligence. Human Relations, 53(8):1027-1055.

Ghani, N. B. A. (2012). The Role of Leader's Emotional Intelligence towards the Performance of Organizations. International Business School, University Technology Malaysia; pp 2-19.

Government of Pakistan, Finance Division (2012). Pakistan Economic Survey 2011-12.

Goleman, D. (1998). Working With Emotional Intelligence. Retrieved on 08-22-2013, from http://www.nytimes.com/books/

Harms, P.D. and Credé, M. (2010). Emotional Intelligence and Transformational and Transactional Leadership: A Meta-Analysis. Journal of Leadership & Organizational Studies, 17(1):5-17. doi: 10.1177/1548051809350894.

Haver, A., Akerjordet, K., Furunes, T. (2013). Emotion Regulation and Its Implications for Leadership: An Integrative Review and Future Research Agenda. Journal of Leadership & Organizational Studies, 20(3):287-303. doi: 10.1177/1548051813485438.

Haq, R. (2011). Working Women Seeding a Silent Social Revolution in Pakistan. Retrieved on 08-21-2013, from http://www.riazhaq.com/

International labor Organization (2004). Global Employment Trends for Women, pp 1-17.

International Labour Organization (2011). Gendered Review of SME Policy: Towards Gender Parity in Pakistan (TPG) Project, pp 1-87.

International Labour Organization: Pakistan (2013).Bi-Annual Newsletter, Issue III:1-12

Jain, D. (2013). Implication of Emotional Intelligence in Contemporary Organizations: An Empirical Study. International Journal of Applied Research and Studies, 2(4):1-8.

Jorfi, H., Yaccob, H. F., Shah, I. M. (2011). The Relationship between Demographics Variables, Emotional Intelligence, Communication Effectiveness, Motivation, and Job Satisfaction. International Journal of Academic Research in Business and Social Sciences, 1(1).

Kazi, S., and Raza, B. (1991). Duality of Female Employment in Pakistan. The Pakistan Development Review, 30 (4, part II):733-743.

Kalim, A. (2012) Women Entrepreneurship the Emerging Workforce in 21st Century: Turning Challenges into Opportunities. Proceedings of 2nd International Conference on Business Management, Lahore Pakistan.

Kiyani, A., Haroon, M., Liaqat, A. S., Khattak, M. A., Bukhari, S. J. A., and Asad, R. (2011). Emotional Intelligence and Employee Participation in Decision-Making. African Journal of Business Management, 5(12):4775-4781. DOI: 10.5897/AJBM10.808

Ladd, B. S., and Chan, C.C.A. (2004). Emotional intelligence and Participation in Decision-Making: Strategies for Promoting Organizational Learning and Change. Strategic Change, 13: 95–105.

Manzoor, I., Daud, S., Hashmi, N. R., Khan, M., Zafar, J., Babar, S., Zafar, M. (2012). Reasons for Selection of Nursing Profession in Pakistan. Professional Medical Journal, 17(4):728-734.

Marre, W. (2013). Why We Need Women Leaders. Retrieved on 08-21-2013, from http://willmarre.com/blog/.

Mehra, R., and Gammage, S. (1999).Trends Countertrends and Gaps in Women's Employment. World Development, 27 (3):533- 550.

Mir, G. M., and Abbasi, A.S. (2012). Role of Emotional Intelligence in Developing Transformational Leadership in Higher Education Sector of Pakistan. Middle-East Journal of Scientific Research, 12 (4):563-571.

Naeem, H., Saif, M. I., Khalil, W. (2008). Emotional Intelligence and Its Impact on Service Quality – Empirical Evidence from the Pakistani Banking Sector. International Business & Economics Research Journal, 7(1):55-62.

Nash, H. (2013). Report Shows Women Bring Much-Needed Emotional Intelligence to the Boardroom. Retrieved on 08-22-2013, from www.harveynash.com.

Naseer, Z., Chishti, S. H., Rahman, F. and Jumani, N.B. (2011). Impact of Emotional Intelligence on Team Performance in Higher Education Institutes. International Online Journal of Educational Sciences, 3(1):30-46.

Pakistan Economic Survey (2012). Population labor force and employment 2011-12:pp 161-175.

Poskey, M. (2013). The Importance of Emotional Intelligence in the Workplace: Why It Matters More than Personality. Retrieved on 08-20-2013, from http://www.zeroriskhr.com.

Pradhan, R. K., and Nath, P. (2012). Perception of Entrepreneurial Orientation and Emotional Intelligence: A Study on India's Future Techno-Managers. Global Business Review, 13(1):89-108. doi: 10.1177/097215091101300106

Serrat, O. (2009). Understanding and Developing Emotional Intelligence. Asian Development Bank.

Shahzad, K., Sarmad, M., Abbas, M. and Khan, M. A. (2011). Impact of Emotional Intelligence (EI) on Employee's Performance in Telecom Sector of Pakistan. African Journal of Business Management, 5(4):1225-1231.

Shah, N. A. (2002). Changing Role of Women in Pakistan: A Study of Social and Economic Activities of Women Entrepreneurs. University of Karachi. Retrieved On 09-09-2013, from http://eprints.hec.gov.pk/.

Siddiqui, S. (2013). Challenges for Working Women in Pakistan. The DAWN National Weekend Advertiser. Retrieved on 08-22-2013, from http://dawnadvertiser.wordpress.com/category/careers/

Sigmar, L. S., Hynes, G. E., Hill K. L. (2012). Strategies for Teaching Social and Emotional Intelligence in Business Communication. Business Communication Quarterly, 75(3):301-317.doi: 10.1177/1080569912450312

Simmons, K. (2001).Emotional Intelligence: What Smart Managers Know. Retrieved on 08-21-2013, from http://www.asaecenter.org/index.cfm.

Weiss, R. P. (2000). Promoting Emotional Intelligence in Organizations: Making Training in Emotional Intelligence Effective. Retrieved on 26-08-2013, from http://www.workplacecoachinstitute.com/.

World Bank (2013). Pakistan: Economic Indicators. Retrieved on 08-22-2013, from http://www.tradingeconomics.com/countries.

CHAPTER 10
Micro-finance to Empower Women in Pakistan

By: Ayesha Zahid, Sumaira Rehman and Ch. Abdul Rehman
Superior University, Lahore, Pakistan

Women constitute an integral part of any society and are a source of untapped opportunity. Their contribution to economy is hampered by the limited availability of credit, that too at high interest rates. Empowerment of women can create positive change in their families in particular and society in general. Islamic microfinance is established to facilitate the development of micro and medium entrepreneurs by providing them interest free loans. Empowering women with the interest free Islamic microloans can create a positive change in the society. This study aims to explore the role of Islamic microfinance in the empowerment of women entrepreneurs in Pakistan.

Based on interpretive phenomenological approach, this study explores the role of Islamic microloans on the social, personal and economic empowerment of women entrepreneurs. Semi structured interviews from women entrepreneurs using a purposive sampling technique were conducted to collect the data. Thematic analysis technique is used for data analysis to gain in-depth understanding of the phenomenon.

The findings of the study revealed that there is a significant contribution of easy availability of the Islamic interest free loans on the lives of poor women. The access to easy interest free Islamic finance creates a significant increase in the economic, social, personal, and family empowerment of women entrepreneurs.

Introduction

Women constitutes an integral part of any society but their importance is undermined due to gender discriminatory policies set by the government and norms by societies in both developing and developed worlds. Women constitute a major share of the population, but still experience status disparity in developing and developed nations (Rehman and Naoroze, 2007). This untapped market is currently the target of international organizations like United Nation which are using women empowerment as a strategy to reduce poverty and population growth rate (Kabeer,

2001). Hisrich (1984) argues that the financial community rates women as a second class citizen. Financial markets have been showing gender discrimination and possess a certain bias towards women entrepreneurs' and had been a major obstacle in their efforts to start up a new business or strengthening their position (Thabethe, 2006). Furthermore as per Khan and Noreen (2012), 70 % of world poor are women who are rarely financially independent due to hurdles in accessing credit and financial services. This makes them most vulnerable members of the society. In order to overcome this financial, social, and economic instability, microfinance can be considered an important tool to improve the situation. Littlefield, Murduch, and Hashemi (2004) argue that microfinance can be used as a developmental tool to create emancipation and women empowerment. The role of microfinance is considered significant by many researches (e.g. Mayoux, 2001 and Guérin, 2006 for the African context; Mahmud, 2003; Holvoet, 2005 and Moodie, 2008 in Asia; Velasco and Marconi, 2004 in Latin America).

Researchers from different parts of the world agree that women empowerment is created by microcredit if microcredit program is structured according to social and economic context of women (Hartungi, 2007; Holvoet, 2005; Guérin, 2006). The studies are mainly conducted to study the impact of conventional microcredit and women empowerment in developing country context. Conventional microcredit is interest based which is forbidden in Islam. Islamic finance is a solution to this faith based conflict in financing decisions (Saqib, 2006). Many writers such as El-Gamal (2006), Ahmed (2001) and others believe in the great potential of Islamic banking to be involved in microfinance programs to cater for the needs of the poor who usually fall outside the formal banking sector. The existing studies on Islamic microfinance are mainly done in Malaysia, Bangladesh, Indonesia and Egypt. There is little literature available on role of Islamic microfinance in women empowerment in the developed world as well as developing countries in general and Pakistan in specific. The above mentioned studies mainly explore or describe the nature of Islamic microfinance products and their respective mechanisms. Little research is done in gauging their impact on women empowerment.

There are very limited offerings of Islamic microfinance products in Pakistan. Therefore, majority of Muslims are forced to use interest based products or exploitive informal money lender. Only two institutions Akhuwat foundation and Wasil foundation are offering limited Islamic microfinance products to both men and women. No exclusive offerings are designed for women. The importance of women empowerment through micro credit and possible bridging of gap that exists between religious beliefs and practice demands a study to explore the role that Islamic microfinance can play in the empowerment of women. The aim of this research is to explore the role of Islamic Microfinance products in the empowerment of women entrepreneurs in the light of social and financial structures in Pakistan. The study focuses on the women entrepreneurs from Lahore District that are using Islamic Microfinance products to reveal their rich experiences and role played by Islamic Microcredit in empowering their lives.

Context

Women possess a disadvantaged position in developed and developing countries. This can be tracked from studying history starting from post-world war II period. Cheston and Kuhn (2002) argue that women hold low paid jobs mostly in informal sector in most economies of the world. Pakistan being the 6th largest country in terms of population where 23% of people live below poverty line (Economic Survey of Pakistan, 2009-10) among this 55.8% are women (Alkire and Santos, 2010). According to Khilji (1999), the socio cultural values prevailing in Pakistani society are embedded in the rich history of the area which had been influenced by Muslim emperors, British colonial rule, as well as by Indian and American cultures. Every era had left a mark on the society, which resulted in a blend of conservative and liberal norms of society.

Pakistan is an Islamic state where religion is one of the factors that affect the socio cultural strata of society. Ali argues that religious leaders have portrayed selective teachings of Islam that creates patriarchy in the Pakistani Society and has negatively affected the well-being of women. This is further enhanced by the work of Maqsood (2004) that women hold a respectable status in Islam and religion does not discriminate between men and women. It is clearly stated in Quran that both men and women are equal. The Quran states:

> *"Every soul will be (held) in pledge for its deeds."* (Qur'an, 74:38)
> *"Whoever performs good deeds, whether male or female and is a believer, we shall surely make him live a good life and we will certainly reward them for the best of what they did"* (Qur'an, 16:97).
>
> *"For men who submit [to God] and for women who submit [to God], for believing men and believing women, for devout men and devout women, for truthful men and truthful women, for steadfast men and steadfast women, for humble men and humble women, for charitable men and charitable women, for men who fast and women who fast, for men who guard their chastity and women who guard, for men who remember God much and for women who remember -for them God has prepared forgiveness and a mighty reward"* (Qur'an, 33: 35).

The above verses of Quran provide clear evidence on the equal status of women in terms of their creation, deeds and rewards but the patriarchal practices are the reason behind low status of women in Pakistani society. This is being supported by the work of Karmi (1996). These findings are further supported by the work of Hassan (2002); Hibri (2004) and Wadud (2007). Pakistani culture is dominated by hierarchical relation where the male member of the family has more influence on the other members. Moreover, the women do not possess the rights to property in many parts of Pakistan (Blood, 1995; Black, 2003). Patriarchy, socio-cultural, and religious norms prevailing in the society is the major obstacles faced by women in encountering poverty trap (Essers, 2007; Jamali, 2009; Rehman and Roomi, 2012;

Ufuk and Ogzen, 2001). Empowerment of women by entrepreneurial activities is one way of reducing poverty and creating economic development of this marginalized community.

A study by World Bank (2002) highlights that woman entrepreneurial activities with easy access to finance creates empowerment and subsequently contributes to the development of economy. Women entrepreneurs experience problems in accessing the finance, obtaining credit and face discriminatory behavior of financial institutions (Nayyar, 2007). According to Niethammer, et al. (2007) women entrepreneurs have limited access to institutional credit because of less knowledge of how to access formal finance and having no ownership or control of land or property that could be used as collateral. Consequently, anecdotal evidence suggests this is a particular issue for women in Pakistan. To enable access of finance to poor and vulnerable women Islamic microfinance can be considered an effective alternative that needs to be researches. State bank of Pakistan has made a 5 year strategic plan to increase the outreach of micro finance and Islamic microfinance. Little attention is given to study the role of Islamic products in the empowerment of women entrepreneurs in Pakistan as well as in developing countries. That shows a gap to induce a research study to explore the impact of these Islamic microfinance products on women entrepreneurs.

Women Empowerment
Kabeer (2001) defines empowerment as a capacity to make right decisions. Narayan (2002) defines empowerment as the freedom to make choices and take actions. Empowerment is defined by Mayoux (2000) as multidimensional changes in the power relations. The power structures directly affect the lives of women by influencing their choices to make right decisions (Mayoux, 2001: 18). This is in concordance with Bali and Swain (2006) who argues that in feminist paradigm empowerment hold more strategic orientation of women needs than mere economic and social wellbeing. The multidimensional nature of empowerment (Malhotra, Schuler and Boender, 2002) gives a holistic view of the subdomains like psychological socio cultural, economic, familial, political and legal where women can make choices. United nation (2001) provides further support by defining women empowerment as a set of processes that help women expand their choices and subsequently take control and ownership of their lives. Kabeer (2001) explains choices as strategic life choices that can change the lives of people. He argues the role of agency, awareness about power structures and self-esteem are the fundamental pillars of women empowerment. He further proposed that empowerment can be measured by examining three dimensions that are resources (women must have access to resources in order to make choices), agency (the decision making in setting their own goals and ways to accomplish them) and achievement (the outcomes resulted in betterment of their lives as result of the previous two factors).

Women Empowerment and Microfinance

Women empowerment and microfinance is an emerging phenomenon. Previous studies conducted in Africa, Europe, India, Bangladesh, Malaysia, and Indonesia reveal the significant role of microcredit in the empowerment of women entrepreneurs. The policy development circles around the globe are considering women empowerment in the context of microfinance to alleviate poverty (DFID, 2006: 1). Women economic empowerment is considered to be the tool to solve social and economic problems; an empowered women work for the betterment of their family and community (Cornwall and Edward, 2010). The access to credit and economic resources make women independent and exercise agency. The financial independence is translated into better bargaining power in household and community affairs. This subsequently results in increased self-respect and esteem. Therefore, microfinance has the potential to empower women.

Kabeer (1998) reveals that Bangladeshi women contribution to household wellbeing due to access to micro credit reduced domestic abuse shows the importance and relevance of micro credit with the empowerment of women. Joloshev (2010) argues that microfinance provides an empowering sustainable path for women entrepreneurs. Mahmood (2013) investigates the role of microfinance in women's economic empowerment, well-being of the family and lack of access to finance from commercial banks due to non-availability of track-record and collateral. The results show a positive impact of microfinance on family wellbeing.

Pakistan microfinance sector is comprised of 6 micro finance banks, 10 micro fiancé institutions and 4 rural support programs. This sector in Pakistan lacks operational effectiveness due to high fixed cost. Therefore, the primary objective of social support is ignored by these institutions. The operation inefficiencies lead to high interest rates for borrowers (Rauf and Mahmood, 2009). Madiha (2007) studied ethnographic and discourse analytical methods to investigate the socio-cultural settings of microfinance and ROSCAs (Rotating Savings and Credit Associations) in Pakistan. The study's focus was community not women. Asim (2008) found insignificant effect of microcredit on family wellbeing and other empowerment indicators on the females of Lahore district. On the contrary the study conducted by Chaudary and Nosheen (2009) on the rural, urban and tribal areas of southern Punjab reflect a positive significant relationship between the access to microcredit and empowerment of women entrepreneurs. A study of Bahawalpur district by Noreen (2011) indicates that provision of collateral free micro loan to rural women enhance their income generating abilities thus leading to their economic and social empowerment. The above studies deal with conventional microcredit; and there is a dearth of literature on Islamic Micro finance and women empowerment.

Islamic Micro finance

The inherent problem with the conventional microfinance products are high interest rates. The core principle of Islamic finance is the prohibition of Riba. Interest or Riba is forbidden in Islam. Therefore, the conventional microfinance products create a conflict in one's religious belief system and the practical needs. Akhter (2009) conducted a study on Islamic microfinance in Pakistan proposed the use of Zakat, Waqaf and Takaful to increase Islamic microfinance products contribution to entrepreneurship. The most commonly used Islamic products in Pakistan are Murabaha 40% and then Ijara 30% (New Horizon, 2007: 42). Ahmed (2009) argues that customer satisfaction and service quality has weak influence on the performance of Islamic banks in Pakistan.

Only two institutions Akhuwat foundation and Wasil Foundation are offering limited Islamic microfinance products to both men and women. Akhuwat is using self-Help group lending and individual / household lending (male and female). Individual lending requires two personal guarantors from outside the family as collateral. They do not consider women as their target market (Akhuwat, n.d.). According to Harper (2007), contracts are cosigned by male and female members of the family to avoid duplication and conflicts. The above overview of the literature reflects that studies are done on role of micro finance and women empowerment but there is no study found that directly address the role of Islamic microfinance in the empowerment of women. The existing literature on Islamic microfinance is mainly focused on the nature of the products and their differences with conventional finance. Women are not considered a target market of Islamic microfinance (Ahmad, 2002); therefore, this topic did not get the attention of researchers yet. Not only this area is under-researched the majority of studies are done in Africa, and with developing countries perspective. There is a need to study the growing phenomenon of Islamic microfinance and women empowerment in Pakistani Context.

Methodology
4.1 Preconception
Preconceptions are the theoretical knowledge that the researcher possesses on the particular subject and practical experiences in the field of interest (Lindfors, 1993). In a qualitative study the understanding of preconceptions and perspective is important.

4.2 Perspectives
Perspectives are ideas and conceptions of the researcher to collect and analyze data (Hantaris and Mangen, 1996). The researcher approach or perspective act as a lens that helps in scrutinizing concepts, reality and relevance of information that need to be reported (Lundahl, et al. 1999). The interpretation of the study may also reflect the perspective of researcher. This study will identify the role of Islamic micro finance products in the lives of women entrepreneurs in Pakistan.

4.3 Research paradigms
Women entrepreneurs have different contextual backgrounds and look at things from different perspectives and qualitative study is required to develop this understanding about their individual, subjective perspectives. This gets support

from the work of Leedy and Ormrod (2005:133). The ontology assumption of this research is that the social world dealing between Islamic microfinance and women's entrepreneurship and economic empowerment is a single hard fact. However, the social and cultural context allows people to have their own beliefs, so a single fact has many realities (Saunders, et al., 2003; Gill and Johnson, 2002). Therefore, social and cultural factors are indirectly taken into consideration in this research.

The perception of women about the Islamic microfinance products is a social phenomenon and contextual factors are needed to be incorporated in generation of knowledge. Therefore, this study is based on epistemological assumption of interpretivisim as fundamental to the exploration of the role of Islamic microfinance product on women entrepreneurs.

4.4 Data Collection Methods
Semi structured interviews of women entrepreneurs using Islamic micro loans were conducted to collect the data. This is supported by the work of Weiss (1995) that supports the use of participants narratives obtained by face to face qualitative interviews to get understanding of a phenomenon through rich data.

4.5 Sampling Strategy
Purposive sampling is a way to discover the multiple realities (Lincoln and Guba, 1985). Therefore, in this study the purposeful sampling method will be employed to conduct semi structured interviews. Moreover, due to cost, time, and access limitation this method of sampling is considered to be suitable. As per Roger and Nall (2003), small sample size is appropriate for semi structured interviews. This size also has the rationale from the research of Miles and Huberman (1994) that suggest a small sample size that can provide rich thick descriptions are appropriate for understanding of the phenomenon, which is in line with the interpretivisim paradigm followed in this study

Women who have been running their businesses for last two years using Islamic micro finance products are selected from Lahore district to collect the data.

Based on the intensive literature review an interview schedule was prepared to explore the impact Islamic microfinance product on empowerment, by understanding the changes in personal, social, family and institutional life of a women entrepreneur. For this study, a total of 15 women were interviewed. The interview was conducted in Urdu at the site of the respondent's work. The rapport was established by explaining the purpose of research and seeking their permission to use the data for sharing and publication. With the permission of respondents, interviews were recorded. The transcriptions were sent to each person for checking to ensure the quality and authenticity of research (Guba and Linchon, 1998). Adopted from the work of Stirling and Attride (2001), thematic analysis was performed to identify the emerging themes, thereby organizing it for further qualitative analysis.

Patton (1990) contends that a constant comparison, repeated coding, grouping, generating concepts, drawing networks, and representing the author's conceptualization is need to perform qualitative data analysis. This study employed the above guidelines in four steps. Initially MS excel was used to create a framework matrix with columns representing key themes and cases were mentioned in rows. The raw data was pasted into the matrix. Then in the second step the data was summarized in each cell by creating sub-columns to signify subthemes. This was followed by grouping together of similar cases to create a map and interpret the similarities. Finally, results were narrated with the help of quotes form the matrix to support the arguments. This process is done repeatedly to ensure the fact that analysis is comprehensive and encompasses the meanings of data.

Demographic Profile of the women Entrepreneurs
All the respondents are aged between 30-45 years. There are three respondents living in a joint family system, the rest are living in an independent set up. It appears that women started their business by taking loans in a mature age. The maturity in terms of age seems to have influenced their decision to start their own venture. In terms of education they are not highly educated (5 out of 15) never went to school, 6 of them have done high school and only two went to college. The respondents belong to very poor class, where women are not sent to school due to poor financial conditions and discrimination in allocation of resources on gender bases. The education does not seem to play any significant role in the business initiative taken by women.

Most of the women (13 out of 15) did not have any prior business experience. Their narratives explain that life course events have motivated them to take a loan and start their own business. The number of children is more as we can see except for one person who is a widow the number of children are more. The more children mean more financial responsibilities. The women are the main bread winners of the house as their husbands either does not have a job or work on a very low salary therefore the main responsibility rests on the shoulder of women of the house. The majority of the women belongs to very poor class and started their business with a very small amount between Rs. 8000-15000 (5 out of 10). 60% of the women only source of capital was the Islamic micro loan, the rest 40% had their saving and loan in the initial capital to start the venture. All the women are involved in providing different types of services like beauty, stitching, and retailing. This shows that they found it convenient to offer services with a small investment and without any prior business experience. The primary role of women in a Pakistani society is a care giver (Ahl, 2006) and the men hold the main responsibility of but in this sample the women are assuming the role of main breadwinner and hold the responsibility to earn a respectable living for the family. The respondents are running small scale enterprises which are mainly sole proprietorship. The respondents are active users of the loan and regularly take credit ever since the inception of their business. They have to repay the loan in 10 equal installments.

The sample does not represent the population; yet it satisfies our study objective to explore and understand the role of Interest free small Islamic micro loan on the lives of women entrepreneurs in Pakistan. The data is deliberately collected from respondents of different sectors to bring out diverse experiences of the women entrepreneurs.

The findings of the study are divided into different sections pertaining to the dimensions used to understand the empowerment of women due to the access to the easy Islamic micro credit. The role of interest free Islamic micro loan is identified by understanding its impact on the family, gender roles, self and enterprise level. The reasons for using Islamic loan are also discussed to understand the role of religion in the decision to take micro loans.

Women empowerment and the wellbeing of the family
Empowerment has multiple facets. One perspective of empowerment is the role of women in the wellbeing of the family. Different researchers are of the opinion that when compared to men, women spend more on the wellbeing of family when they have control of the family income (John Hoddinott and Lawrence Haddad 1995; Linda Mayoux 1995; T. Paul Schultz 1995). Families play an integral role in the lives of women in developing countries. One of the reasons stated by all the women entrepreneurs to take the loan and start the business is the wellbeing of the family. The statements of the women mentioned below are conforming to the studies mentioned above.

One of the participants Shahida shared her reasons for starting the job as follows:

> *"It was difficult for me to meet the both ends. Now I have started earning. My husband earning had a minor contribution to house and it was insufficient to fulfill the needs of our house. Now our food has improved and kids also got admission in the school and are able to continue their education."*

Similarly Iram stated that:

> *"A gap came when my husband fall sick. The whole family was disturbed that what will happen now. We were not able to send our kids to school. They would look at the food in other houses. Then I thought that I am educated why not use this and started working. Then I started doing efforts."*

These women were forced to start their work due to insufficient income and circumstances of their respective household. The income generated by these women is used to provide provisions to their families. Safia in her account explained the impact of her work on family in the following way:

> *"My household got very good. The basic necessities of life improved like our eating habits. Children got better clothes to wear. They started going to good schools. There is not betterment more like this"*

Saira shared her experience below:

> *"Where we eat once in a day Alhamdulillah now we eat thrice a day. There was irregularity in the studies of children due to non-availability of the money to pay the fee. But now they are going regularly. My two elder daughters are also going to academies as well"*

Another account describes the impact and reasons for stating up the venture in the following words:

> *"Sometimes there was something to eat, but at times we didn't have anything to eat. This is the true reality that there were times we had nothing to eat. But now thanks to Allah everything has become okay after starting this business."(Haleema)*

In case of Iram and all other entrepreneurs the primary reason to take loan and initiate their business was to take care of their children and family. In majority of the cases the husband is either not working or his salary is very low to meet the expenses of the family; so women took the initiative to support the family. The positive aspect is that they received the support of their husband and in-laws in managing the business and house. This is in concordance with the studies by Amin et al. (1994), Naveed (1994), Hashemi et al. (1996), Osmani (1998) etc. which had shown that empowerment of women through microfinance loans create improvement in the well-being of their families. Cagatay (1998) added the health and education as non-monetary indicators of well-being. The finding of the current study confirmed the previous findings.

Micro Finance, Women Empowerment and Economic Development
The literature on gender signifies the contribution of economic outcomes on the improved status of women in household that is reflected in their participation in decision making (Rakowski 1995). Most of the accounts highlight the way in which the micro loans helped in improving their income, status, and participation in decision-making, thus contributing positively to socio economic development. Many women stated that:

> *"I have to beg the money from my husband's younger brothers. Some of them gave and someone refused to give. But now, sometime they take/beg from me. If I have, then I definitely give them. I was also not feeling well and unable to get the medicine. Now it becomes possible for me to take medicines timely and everything is fine now. It has increased respect level in family. Relatives feel that now as we have everything so they give more respect. That's all. The circumstances become better." (Razia)*

"My family members like my brothers, my sisters and my in laws all of them who left me and have started giving me respect now. Everybody closed their doors on me. Now everybody respects me. They started giving me honor which they have never given me before. Everyone try to invite me at their place. For now I am doing efforts for the bright future of my kids." (Saira)

"Thanks to Almighty Allah, I have a lot of respect. I did not have a fridge since I have started to earn I have my own fridge, television, my own plot. I am thankful to Allah that I found good livelihood, my children are well off, I am well off, and we have a lot of respect in our neighborhood as well as family." (Haleema).

For these women, there is a change in their socio economic position and status in the family due to access to easy Islamic micro finance. The narratives of other women entrepreneurs also reflects that they experience a positive change in their family status. In Pakistani society income disparity creates social distance among the family members. The access to interest free Islamic loans helps the entrepreneurs in income generation in a respectable manner. The family members and in-laws who were reluctant to meet these respondents now give respect to them and seek their advice in making decisions. Irem stated that her relatives got motivated seeing her performing a good job and took the initiatives and started their own work.

Research studies (Hashemi et al. 1996; Hirschland 2003) done to evaluate the role of microcredit on creation of women employment shows that women can earn more and get economically independent. In agreement to this most of the account of women entrepreneur's highlights that access to the Islamic micro loans increased their propensity to earn and subsequently helped them in exercising agency. A study on developing countries by Fidler and Webster (1996) stated that women easy access to financial services resulted in improvement in their social status and income. These findings of the current study confirm the work of previous researchers in the Pakistani perspective.

Islamic Micro Finance, Empowerment through Self Development
Empowerment has a collective and individual effect on the lives of women which are intrinsically interlinked with each other. Empowerment relates to having an agency, autonomy to make a choice, generating self-confidence at individual level, and also creates mobilization of women at collective level (Sen, 1990). The extent of empowerment on the individual personality is reflected in the person's ability to make choices and make decisions, and change in the self-confidence and self-esteem. The role of availability of credit in gaining personal empowerment is explored by asking probing questions to determine change in the self-confidence and decision making capabilities of women entrepreneurs. The findings are reflected in the accounts of women given below:

"I felt too much improvement in my decision making ability. When you take decision in your life, you have to face enormous difficulties. Now, I don't feel any difficulty. I meet with the people of Akhuwat, and others talking with them and...I become very confident. If you ask me to speak in front of 10,000 people. I can easily speak" (Shagufta).

"Before starting the business I wasn't confident whether I would be able to do something. I always thought that probably I wouldn't be able to do it. But when a person has power of money then automatically a person gets confidence and motivated to do something and says yes I can do it."(Irem)

"I am a bit more mature, now I understand people, I understand things and take every decision with a cool head. I have changed a bit, first of all other's daughters come to me they learn this work and then earn by themselves. Some are elder to me some are younger and when they start earning by themselves due to the work which they have learnt from me so it always give me happiness and confidence." (Nagina)

The above excerpts show that the entrepreneurial activity has created self-confidence and increased the self-esteem of the women. Similar to the above narratives all the respondents experience increased self-confidence and improved ability to make decisions. They attributed this change to the availability of loan which enables them to start their own venture.

Islamic Micro Finance, Empowerment and Enterprise Development
The women entrepreneurs are running micro enterprises in service, retail and manufacturing. In services they are providing beauty, and stitching of clothes, in retailing they are involved in buying and selling of clothes and karyana shop. All the women are actively involved in the management of their business. The majority of the women do the purchasing of material themselves; in some cases their husbands help in purchasing, cutting (stitching services) and selling of goods. Their business are mostly home based like beauty salons, sewing, and stitching, even they are selling clothes at home without the involvement of men. These findings are similar to the results reported by Roomi (2005) that in Pakistan women entrepreneurs prefer to work with women. These enterprises were set up by women and managed by them. The women approached the microcredit providers with the idea to start up a business and receive loans in their names. All the respondents have received the loan for the startup of the venture.

The easy availability of the loan creates a positive impact on the women. Haleema shared her development as: *"Thanks to Allah they (Akhuwat) gave the entire help. I started my business from a loan Rs.10,000.00 and now my turn over is Rs.150,000.00."* Similarly Safia shared that: *"The important thing is that I have*

expanded a lot. First I used to work at home only. And now I give work to others too. First if I had 3 women working for me, I gradually had 5, then 10, 20, 25 30. "
  Saira articulates her experiences as: *"I started with one chair now I have two chairs in my salon and two girls are working with me as student. The loan taken from Akuwat has helped me in expanding my business and up gradation of the infrastructure. "* Nagina shares her growth in the following words:

> *"I came to know about Akhuwat, someone told me about them I contacted them and applied for a loan. They were very nice in their dealings. I got some loan from them and invested it in my parlor, I spent that money on its maintenance. Then I increased my chairs. I stayed in touch with Akhuwat and went on taking some loan year by year. And by the grace of ALLAH Almighty now I am having my own 6 chairs. "*

The above contextual accounts highlights that the loan has helped the poor women to become entrepreneurs and create jobs for themselves and others in the community. The similar experiences are shared by other women entrepreneurs'. They are enjoying growth in their business due to the availability of easy credit to them.

Why Islamic Microfinance?
Interest (or Riba) is forbidden in Islam. Therefore, the conventional microfinance products create a conflict in one's religious belief system and the practical needs. Islamic Micro finance products are interest free and focus on the empowerment of poor. The majority of the respondents have never used conventional loan. Only 2 out of 15 had used conventional micro loans but they are not satisfied with them due to their high interest rates which are against the beliefs of Islam. The respondents have strong faith in God (Allah). Their beliefs are reflected in their excerpts given below:

> *"I took loan before starting this business. But that's not mine. I took that loan from Kashaf for the sake of my husband's business. That loan became the reason of my illness. But I researched and found that actually I was misguided by them (Kashaf). They told me that this amount is not the interest. This is our commission and salaries of employees. But I was not satisfied. I took that amount of loan. Then I beg the forgiveness from Allah and never took again the amount of loan with interest. "(Shagufta)*

> *"I took this loan because it was interest free interest is prohibited in Islam. Being a Muslim that wasn't good and there is no blessings in such money which is linked with interest so that's why I choose it*

although it is small in amount but it does have its own blessings"
(Rubina)

"Interest is prohibited in Islam. And Allah dislikes the person who
gives or takes interest so if we do not follow the rules of Islam then we
can't get success." (Iram)

"See the money without interest is halal. The money which involves
interest is haram" (Safia)

The above narratives highlight the stance of women entrepreneurs on the kind of loan they want to take and the reason behind it. While looking at the demographic profiles of the respondents of the study, it is revealed that they are not highly educated but they have clarity on the saying of Quran about business and the use of interest in the business. Similar reasons were given by the other women entrepreneurs that income is halal and it has the element of 'Barkat' in it if it is earned without the use of interest. A study by Chaudary and Nosheen (2009) on the rural, urban and tribal areas of southern Punjab highlighted the demographic factors like age, marital status and women inclined towards Islam have significant impact on women empowerment and use of micro credit. The above findings are in alignment with that study.

Discussion
While going through the accounts of the women entrepreneurs with an aim to identify the role of Islamic microfinance on the empowerment of women entrepreneurs, three themes were identified along with a number of subthemes. These are related to the family wellbeing, socio economic empowerment and the role of religious beliefs in the lives of the women. Drawing upon these themes as a lens to understand the role of Islamic micro finance on the lives of women entrepreneurs, it is evident that empowerment is a multidimensional concept (Tripathy and Jain, 2010).

The women entrepreneurs interviewed in the study shed light on the extent of their economic empowerment due to the availability of easy credit facilities. The earnings from the venture were on their discretion and they exercise agency in making decisions pertaining to enterprise development and use of their earnings. This is in concordance with the previous studies that define different dimensions of empowerment as control of resources and exercise agency to make decisions (Roy and Narayanasamy, 2000, Kumar et al., 2008). The entrepreneurial ventures undertaken by these poor women are the result of their desire to develop economic empowerment, thereby creating a better environment for their family and themselves.

The primary motive shared by all the women behind their initiative to take loan and start an entrepreneurial venture is the wellbeing of their family in the wake of difficult economic circumstances bored by them. Their inability to feed their children with adequate food and to provide education had led them to think about doing something to change the worse situation in their favor. The availability of easy interest free credit triggered their desire to be in control and contribute towards the betterment of the household. Different researchers are of the opinion that when compared to men, women spend more on the wellbeing of family when they have control of the family income (John Hoddinott and Lawrence Haddad 1995; Linda Mayoux 1995; T. Paul Schultz 1995). The findings of the study also reveal that the income generated by the women entrepreneurs is spent on the food, health and education of the children and other family members and this conforms to the studies noted above.

Religion as part of the context had a significant effect on the women belief about their income. The demographic profile reflect low literacy rate in a majority of the cases but the participants have a clear understanding of ***Halal Rizaq*** and the prohibition of ***Riba*** in Islam. In this study the internalization of religious values is observed in the participant behaviors. They are not ready to take loans from other institutions even at a lower rate due to their religious beliefs. The participants are of the opinion that the income earned by using interest is not Hilal and lacks the element of Barkat in it. The following verses of the Holy Quran clearly reflects the instructions regarding Riba.

> *"That which ye given in Riba in order that it may increase on (other) people's property hath no increase with Allah; but that which ye give in charity; seeking Allah's countenance, hath increase manifold" (30:39).*

> *"That they took Riba, though they were forbidden; and that they devoured men's substance wrongfully. We have prepared for those among them who reject faith, a grievous punishment" (4:161).*
> *"O ye who believe! Devour not riba, doubled and multiplied; but fear Allah; that ye may (really) prosper". "Fear the fire, which is prepared for those who reject faith". And obey Allah and the Messenger; that ye may obtain mercy" (3:130-2).*

The teachings of Islam evident from these verses of Holy Quran explain that God has declared interest an unwanted activity. As a Muslim living in a Muslim society, it is important to note that people will have mixed belief systems, some strongly follow the path defined by God, and others reflect a mixed behavior. The women entrepreneurs in this study clearly followed the teaching of Islam and they appear to be strong believers of Islamic values. This resonates with the work of Black (2003) in that Pakistani society religion affects the personal and public lives of people. This is further supported by the work of Malik (2006) that suggests collective nature of Islam shapes the pluralistic culture prevailing in Pakistan. He further asserts that Islamic values dominate the regional identities in Pakistan.

Drawings from the above arguments together in the Islamic context we found that the easy access of interest free Islamic finance clearly contributes to the empowerment of women entrepreneurs. This is in support of the work by Littlefield, Murduch, and Hashemi (2004) that consider microfinance as a useful developmental tool to create emancipation and women empowerment.

The availability of credit helped women in creating employment for themselves and in some cases for others as well. The income generated was used for the well-being of family. Women used their agency to make decisions which reflect their personal empowerment. Moreover, there is some indication that access to Islamic microfinance helped in creating economic and personal empowerment of women entrepreneurs in Pakistani Society. This is supported by the work of Holvoet (2005), which suggests that only platform can encourage women's social, economic and political empowerment in the wake of skeptical financial instruments is microfinance

The findings of the study did not indicate any patriarchal practices experienced by women during their discourse which is in contrary to the studies by Roomi and Harrison (2010) which states that women feel restricted in going out and exercising their agency. The current study is based on the experiences of women who belong to very poor class where male members are either not working at all or their contribution is minimal to the household expenses. The male members are involved in the business and cooperated with the females. This is supported by the work of Shaheed (2010) that highlights the heterogeneity in behaviors of women belonging to different classes.

Conclusion

This chapter has explored the role of Islamic microfinance in the empowerment of women entrepreneurs in Pakistan. Of particular interest here is that the finding of the study reveals that women entrepreneurs exercise agency and experience socio economic empowerment as a result of easy access to Islamic microcredit. The women entrepreneurs despite low literacy rates are the firm believers of Islamic values and prefer Islamic mode of finance on the conventional finance. The study supports the view of Rahim and Rehman (2007) that Islamic microfinance interest free nature helps in the socio economic development of poor and small (micro) entrepreneurs. The study supports the findings of many researchers (e.g. Mayoux, 2001 and Guérin, 2006 for the African context; Mahmud, 2003; Holvoet, 2005 and Moodie, 2008 in Asia; Velasco and Marconi, 2004 in Latin America) that consider the role of microcredit significant in the empowerment of women. This is a pioneering study in exploring the role of Islamic Microfinance in the empowerment of women entrepreneurs. This study has important implications for the policy makers in that they consider the women conditions and perspectives when designing Islamic microcredit products. Furthermore, religious beliefs need to be clearly articulated in designing the credit programs.

References
❖ Akhter, W., Akhter, N. and Jaffri, K. A. (2009). 'Islamic micro-finance and poverty alleviation: a case of Pakistan'. Presented at CBRC, Lahore.
❖ Akhuwat (2007b). Retrieved on 3rd Oct 2013 from URL: http://www.akhuwat.org.pk.

❖ Ali, S. S. (1997). 'A Critical Review of Family Laws in Pakistan: A Woman's Perspective'. In Shaheed, F. and Mehdi, R. (ed.), Women's Law in Legal Education and Practice in Pakistan: North South Cooperation, 198-223.

❖ Badran, M. (2009). 'Feminism in Islam: Secular and religious convergences'. One world Publications.

❖ Bali-Swain, R. (2006). 'Microfinance and women's empowerment'. SIDA Working Paper, Stockholm: Division of Market Development, Swedish International Development Cooperation Agency.

❖ Black, C. (2003). 'Pakistan: The culture. New York: Crabtree Publishing Company'. Badran, M. Islamic Feminism: "What's in a Name"? Retrieved on 28th December, 2005 http: //weekly. ahram. Org. eg/2002/569/cul. htm.

❖ Blood, P. R. (1995). 'Pakistan: A country study'. Library of Congress: Federal Research Division.

❖ Chaudary, I. and Nosheen, S. (2009). 'The Determinants of Women Empowerment in Southern Punjab, Pakistan: An Empirical Analysis'. European Journal of Social Sciences, 10(2), 13-29.

❖ Cheston, S. and Kuhn, R. (2002). 'ARDCI: Empowering Women through Microfinance: ARDCI's Experience by Noni Ayo, 2-13.

❖ Cornwall, A. and Edwards, J. (2010). 'Introduction: Negotiating empowerment'. IDS Bulletin, 41 (2), 1-9.

❖ Creswell, J. W. (2012). 'Qualitative inquiry and research design: choosing among five approaches'. (3rd Ed) Sage Publication, New Delhi.

❖ Denzin, N. K. and Lincoln, Y. S. (2003). 'Introduction. The discipline and practice of Qualitative Research'. In Denzin, N. K. and Lincoln, Y. S. (Eds.), the landscape of Qualitative Research: theories and issues, Sage Publications: California, 1-45.

❖ DIFD (2006). 'Poverty and Social Impact Assessment: Pakistan Microfinance Policy'. Oxford Policy Management: UK.

❖ Economic Survey of Pakistan (2009-10). 'Finance Division (Economic Advisory Wing)'. Government of Pakistan.

❖ Essers, C. (2007). 'Entrepreneurship in public private divides: Business women of Turkish and Moroccan descent playing family ties'. Paper presented at reconnecting diversity to critical organization and gender studies, Critical management studies conference, 11-13

❖ GEM (2010). Retrieved from http://www.gemconsortium.org/docs/266/gem-2010-global-report.

❖ Guba, E. G. and Lincoln, Y. S. (1998). 'Competing paradigms in qualitative research in Denzin, N. S. and Lincoln, Y. S. (eds.), The Landscape of Qualitative Research, Theories and Issues'. Sage Publications, London.

❖ Guerin, I. (2006). 'Women and money lessons from Sengal'. Journal of Development and change, 37(3), 549-570.

❖ Hammersley, M. (1992). 'On Feminist Methodology'. Sociology, 26 (2), 187 -206.

❖ Hantrais, L. and Mangen, S. (1996). 'Cross-National Research Methods in the Social Sciences: A Cassell, Imprint Wellington House'. London: UK

❖ Hartungi, R. (2007). 'Understanding the success factors of Micro-finance institution in a developing country'. International Journal of Social Economics, 34(6), 388 – 401.

❖ Hashemi, S., Sidney, M., Schuler, R. and Riley, A. P. (1996). 'Rural Credit Programs and Women Empowerment in Bangladesh'. World Development, 24 (4). 635-653.

❖ Hassan, K. and Alamgir, D. (2002). 'Micro financial Services and Poverty Alleviation in Bangladesh: A Comparative Analysis of Secular and Islamic NGOs in Islamic Economic Institutions and the elimination of Poverty, ed. Munawar Iqbal'. 113-186. Leicester: The Islamic Foundation.

❖ Hassan, R. (2002). 'Is Islam a help or hindrance to women's development? in Meuleman, J. editor Islam in the era of globalization: Muslim attitudes towards modernity and identity'. Routledge, 189–209.

❖ Hisrich, R. D. and Brush, C. (1984). 'The woman entrepreneur: Management skills and business problems'. Journal of Small Business Management, 22(1), 30-37.

❖ Holvoet, N. (2005). 'The impact of microfinance on decision making agency: Evidence from south India'. Journal of Development and change, 36(1), 75-102.

❖ Hossain, T. B. M., Siwar, C. and Mubarak, T. (2008). 'Determination of the effective ways if microfinance for Islamic Banksto Eliminate Poverty: an empirical Investigation. Prosiding Perkem III, JILID 1, 822 – 832.

❖ IFAD (2009). 'Rural finance policy'. Rome.

❖ Islam, N. (2009). 'Can microfinance reduce economic insecurity and poverty? By how much and how?'. DESA Working paper No. 82, United Nations Department of Economic and Social Affairs.

❖ Kabeer, N. (1998). 'Money can't buy me love? Re-evaluating gender, credit and empowerment in rural Bangladesh'. IDS Discussion Paper 363. Brighton, Institute of Development Studies, University of Sussex: UK.

❖ Kabeer, N. (1999). 'The conditions and consequences of choice: Reflections on the measurement of women's empowerment'. UNRISD Discussion Paper No. 108. Geneva United Nations Research Institute for Social Development.

❖ Kabeer, N. (2001). 'Reflection on the measurement of women's empowerment. In discussion women's empowerment theory and practice'. Sida studies No. 3: Novum Grafishka A. B. Stockholm.

❖ Karmi, G. (1996). 'Women, Islam and Patriarchalism in Yamani, M. (eds.) Feminism and Islam: Legal and Literary Perspectives'. New York University Press: New York.

❖ Khan, A. M. and Rehman, A. M. (2007). 'Impact of Microfinance on living standards, Empowerment and Poverty Alleviation of Poor People: A case study on Microfinance in Chittagong District of Bangladesh'. Business Administration Master Thesis: Umea School of Business, Retrieved on October 1, 2013.

❖ Khan, M. (2012). 'ROSCAs and Microfinance in Pakistan: Community and Culture'. PhD Thesis: University of Leicester, Retrieved on October1, 2013.

❖ Khan, R. E. A. and Noreen, S. (2012). 'Microfinance and women empowerment: A case study of District Bahawalpur (Pakistan)'. African Journal of Business Management, 6(12), 4514–4521.

❖ Khilji, S. E. (1999). 'Management in Pakistan in Warner, M. (ed.) international encyclopedia of Business and Management'. International Thomson Press: London.

❖ Kossmann, K. H. (2008). 'Micro Finance and empowerment from a woman's perspective- The effect of Micro-Finance on the empowerment of women in Bangladesh'. Master Thesis: Copenhagen Business School Retrieved on October 1, 2013.

❖ Ledgerwood, J. (1999). 'Sustainable banking with the poor, Microfinance handbook: An Institutional and financial perspective'. The World Bank: Washington.

❖ Leedy, D. and Ormrod, E. (2005). 'Practical research'. Merrill Prentice Hall and Pearson: New York.

❖ Littlefield, E. and Rosenberg, R. (2004). 'Microfinance and the Poor; Breaking down walls between microfinance and formal finance'. Finance and Development, 41(2), 132-144.

❖ Lorber, J. (2000). 'Using Gender to Undo Gender: A Feminist Degendering Movement'. Sage: London.

❖ Lundahl, U. and Skärvad, P. (1999). 'Utredningsmetodik för samhälsvetare och ekonomer'. Studentlitteratur, Lund, 62(3), 71-73.

❖ Mahmood, A. G. (2006). 'A simple Fiqh-and Economic Rationale for mutualization in Islamic Financial Intermediation'. Rice University.

❖ Mahmood, S. (2013). 'Access to Finance and the Role of Microfinance for Women Entrepreneurs in Pakistan'. PhD Thesis: Birmingham City University, Retrieved on October 1, 2013.

❖ Mahmud, S. (2003). 'Actually how empowering is microcredit?'. Journal of development and change, 34(4), 577-605.

❖ Maj-Britt, J. and Lindfors, I. (1993). 'Att Utveckla kunska – Om metodologiska och andra vägval vid samhällsvetenskaplig kunskapsbildning'. studentlitteratur,: Lund, 76-77.

❖ Malik, I. H. (2006). 'Culture and customs of Pakistan'. Connecticut Greenwood press: Westport.

❖ Maqsood, R. (2004). 'An article on the role of women in trade Unions and struggle of the PTUDC in Lahore.' Journal of Entrepreneurship, 13(9), 28-52.

❖ Mayoux, L. (1998a). 'Women's Empowerment and Micro-finance programmes: Approaches, Evidence and Ways Forward'. The Open University Working Paper No 41.

❖ Mayoux, L. (1998b). 'Participatory programme learning for women's empowerment in micro-finance programmes: negotiating complexity, conflict and change'. IDS Bulletin, 29(2), 39-50.

❖ Mayoux, L. (1999). 'Questioning Virtuous Spirals: micro-finance and women's empowerment in Africa'. Journal of International Development, 11, 957-984.
❖ Mayoux, L. (2000). 'A forthcoming. Selected Programme Case Studies: SHDF, Zambuko Trust, SEF, CGT and SCF'. Vietnam Programme, ILO: UK.
❖ Mayoux, L. (2001). 'Tackling the down side: Social capital, women's empowerment and micro-finance in Cameroon'. Development and Change, 32(1), 435-464.
❖ Mayoux, L. and Hartl, M. (2009). 'Gender and rural microfinance: Reaching and empowering women – a guide for practitioners'. IFAD report, International Fund for Agricultural Development: Rome.
❖ McNeil, P. and Chapman, S. (2005). 'Research Methods'. (3rd ed.), Routledge: London.
❖ Moodie, M. (2008). 'Enter microcredit: A new culture of women's Empowerment in Rajistan?'. Journal of American Etnologist, 5(3), 454-465.
❖ Morduch, J. (1998). 'Does microfinance really help the poor? New evidence from flagship programs in Bangladesh'. Working Paper No. 198. Stanford CA: Hoover Institution: Stanford University.
❖ Morduch, J. (1998). 'Does Microfinance Really Help the Poor? New Evidence from Flagship Programs in Bangladesh'. New York University: New York.
❖ Mustafa, Z. and Ismailov, N. (2008). 'Entrepreneurship and Microfinance-A tool for empowerment of poor- Case of Akhuwat-Pakistan'. Master Thesis: Malardalen University, Retrieved on October1, 2013.
❖ Nayyar, P., Sharma, A., Kishtwaria, J., Rana A. and Vyas, N. (2007). 'Causes and Constraints Faced by Women Entrepreneurs in Entrepreneurial Process'. Journal of Social Sciences, 14(2), 99-102.
❖ Niethammer, C., Saeed, T., Mohamed, S. S. and Charafi, Y. (2007). 'Women entrepreneurs and access to finance in Pakistan'. Women Policy Journal, 4, 1-12.
❖ Patton, M. Q. (1990). 'Qualitative Evaluation and Research Methods'. (2nd Ed.) Newbury Park, CA: Sage Publications Inc.
❖ Pease, A. and Pease, B. (2001). 'Why Men do not Listen and Women cannot Read Maps'. Orion: London.
❖ Petersen, P. M. and Hogh, E. L. (2009). 'Small loan Big expectations-a thesis on microfinance to women as a development Strategy'. Master Thesis: Copenhagen University, Retrieved on October 1, 2013.
❖ Rahman, M. H. and Naoroze, K. (2007). 'Women empowerment through participation in an aquaculture experience of a large scale technology demonstration project in Bangladesh'. Journal of Social Sciences, 3(4), 164-171.
❖ Rauf, A. S. and Mahhood, T. (2009). 'Growth and performance of microfinance in Pakistan.' Pakistan Economic and Social Review, 47 (1), 99-122.
❖ Rehman, S. A. and Roomi, M. A. (2012). 'Gender and work life balance: A phenomenological study of entrepreneurs in Pakistan'. Journal of small business and enterprise development, 14(2), 1325-2300.
❖ Remenyi, D., Williams, B., Money, A. and Swartz, E. (1998). 'Doing Research in Business and Management: An Introduction to Process and Method'. SAGE Publications Limited: London UK.
❖ Ritchie, J. and Lewis, J. (2003). 'Qualitative Research Practice'. Sage Publications Ltd: London.
❖ Roger, A., Rennekamp, R. and Martha, A. (2003). 'Using Focus Groups in Program Development and Evaluation'. University of Kentucky: London.
❖ Saqib, S. and Amjad, R. (2006). 'Diversity of Providers in mf is both desirable and likely in future'. Retrieved at 2nd October 2013 from URL:www.pmn.org.pk/downloads/start.download.dramjadsaqib.
❖ Saunders, M., Lewis, P. and Tronhill, A. (2007). 'Research Methods for Business Students'. (4th Ed.), Pearson Education Ltd.
❖ Sen, A. K. (1990). 'Gender and co-operative conflict in Tinker, I. ed. Persistent inequalities'. Oxford University Press: New Delhi.
❖ Sen, A. K. (1993). 'Capability and well-being in Nussbaum and Sen, eds. The quality of life. Helsinki'. World Institute of Development Economics Research.
❖ Sen, A. K. (1999). 'Development as freedom'. Knopf: New York.

❖ Smolo, E. and Ismail, A. G. (2011). 'A theory and contractual framework of Islamic micro-financial institutions.' Operations Journal of Financial Services Marketing, 15(2), 287-310.

❖ Stirling, A. and Attride, J. (2001). 'Thematic networks: An analytical tool for qualitative research'. Qualitative Research, 1(2), 385–405.

❖ Ufuk, H. and Ozgen, O. (2001). 'Interaction between the business and family lives of women entrepreneurs in Turkey'. Journal of Business ethics, 31(6), 95-106.

❖ UNIFEM (2000). 'Progress of the world's women'. United Nations Development Fund for Women: New York.

❖ United Nations (2005). 'UN millennium development goals. New York: United Nations'. Retrieved on 4th October 2013 from http://www.un.org/millenniumgoals.

❖ Velasco, C. and Marconi, R. (2004). 'Group Dynamics, gender and microfinance in Bolivia'. Journal of International Development, 16(3), 519-528.

❖ Wadud, A. (2007). 'Inside the gender jihad: Women's reform in Islam'. One World Publications.

❖ Welter, F. (2011). 'Contextualizing entrepreneurship – conceptual challenges and ways forward'. Entrepreneurship theory and practice, 35(1), 165-184.

❖ World Bank (2001). 'Engendering development: Through gender equality in rights, resources, and voice – summary'. DC: Washington.

Chapter 11
Leadership and Employee Motivation

By: Memoona Zareen[6] and Kiran Razzaq
Superior University, Lahore, Pakistan

"Where ever you go, no matter what the weather, always bring your own sunshine"
(Anthony J. D'Angelo). The saying by Anthony J. D'Angelo is very true equally for
both male and female leaders as they have skills and abilities of leadership and
keep on influencing their followers in their specific leadership styles according to
the need and requirements of the followers for their motivation and development
regardless of the constraints and problems. Employee motivation is vital as
motivated workers become a competitive advantage of any organization with high
degree of job involvement and dedication towards accomplishment of
organizational as well as individual goals. This competitive advantage can be
sustained with continuous coaching and mentoring of employees for their learning
and development with effective leadership skills. In this way, manager-employee
relationships become important for achieving organizational goals and
commitments.

Introduction
Managers vary in their values, attitudes, and behaviors, and in the way they lead
their followers; hence, they apply different leadership styles and strategies
according to situations and circumstances. In performance management practices,
three main leadership styles are widely used based upon leader-follower
relationship, their characteristics, and organizational environment: transactional,
transformational and laissez-faire leadership styles. Studies have revealed that all
leadership styles become effective in various situations and prove effective for
engagement and involvement of employees. As such, when used effectively, all
leadership styles can have significant positive impact on employee engagement and
motivation. Transactional leadership style has the highest impact on employee
motivation in the banking sector and transformational leadership style has lowest

---

[6] National College of Business Administration & Economics, Lahore, Pakistan.

impact, while the Laissez-faire leadership style has an intermediate impact on employee motivation. Further it has been seen that in different organizations different leadership styles prove to be more effective according to leader follower relationship, and nature of tasks and assignments.

Employee motivation is based on values, behaviors, and the way managers lead. Motivated employees become more involved and committed to their tasks and assignments and work hard for the achievement of organizational goals. They see themselves as more valuable for the organization and that this is a place for learning and development of their capabilities. Such employees remain loyal with organizations for longer times and eventually become an irreplaceable competitive advantage by being more experienced and committed. When organizations facilitate a culture in which organizational values, norms, vision, mission, and objectives are shared with the employees, their motivation and involvement can be achieved more easily. Leader-follower interaction is very important in any organization for effective communication and coordination with employees about organizational goals and objectives and to accomplish them within deadlines.

According to Werbel and Gilliland (1999), coordination and collaboration between employees and organizational values is the reflection of employee involvement and its turnover towards the organization. The employees' personality, prior experience (Roberts, 1991 and Rothwell, 1992), behavior (Williams, 2004), dedication for learning and development (Hadijimanolis, 2000), and leader's influence (Hage and Dewar, 1973) are factors that affect an employee's desires, needs, satisfaction, and motivation for work. This leads management intellectuals and scholars towards the development of leadership styles for manager-employee interaction based on mutual values, behaviors and attitudes. Supervisory behaviors vary significantly even in the same job in various situations especially when encouraging and motivating other employees by helping them in difficult tasks. Previous research on leadership styles, work values and attitudes have focused on finding specific behaviors and attitudes which produce the strongest impact on employee motivation. Based on these behaviors of leaders, three important leadership styles emerged: transactional, laissez-faire and transformational leadership[7] styles (Zareen, Razzaq and Mujtaba, 2014).

Transformational leadership style mainly focuses on transformation of values and beliefs of followers by inspiring them (Johnson and Dipboye, 2008). In laissez-faire leadership style leaders delegate full decision-making authority to followers by giving them guidance and related support to make them more involved in the tasks and motivate them for organizational performance. While in transactional style of leadership, leaders closely monitor their followers and motivate them with rewards on good performance as a result some employees

---

[7] The academic research on the three leadership styles from the authors was published at the journal of *Public Organization Review* as follows:

- Zareen, M., Razzaq, K., and Mujtaba, B. G. (2014). Impact of Transactional, Transformational and Laissez-faire Leadership Styles on Motivation: a Quantitative study of Banking Employees in Pakistan. *Public Organization Review*, Online First. DOI: 10.1007/s11115-014-0287-6.

perform with their hand, head and heart to achieve assigned goals (Mujtaba, 2014; Ashforth & Humphrey, 1995). Managers and leaders on daily basis perform variety of tasks, requiring various types of leadership styles according to situations and nature of the decisions (Griffin, 1999), in order to achieve maximum employee work performance. Importance of leadership cannot be ignored for the performance maximization, motivation of employees and to facilitate them in adoptability of organizational culture and their engagement in organizational goals through coaching and mentoring.

Evolution of Leadership in Organizational Culture
Literature on leadership has shown a progressive pattern, which starts from focusing on the attributes and characteristics of a leader, then concentrates on behavior and afterward emphasizes the contextualized nature of the leadership with describing the outcomes of leadership and terms of effects on followers.

The main cause of competitive advantage for any kind of organization is effective leadership (Zhu, Riggio, Avolio 2005; Avolio, 1999; Lado, Boyed and Wright, 1992; Rowe, 2001). Riaz and Haider (2010) state that effective leadership always plays an important role in the growth and better performance of the organization. Research has shown that as compared to career satisfaction, job success is more dependent on leadership styles. Leaders confer the chance to lead, not because they are appointed by senior management but because they are perceived and accepted by followers as leaders (Boseman, 2008).

The idea of leadership started with the unique focus on the theory of "Great Man." The proponents of the great man theory assume that leaders are born and have innate qualities; therefore, leaders cannot be made. The word "man" was intentionally used to indicate the role of males only. Originally, leaders were thought to be those having success stories which were largely linked with military men (Bolden, 2004). Even in the present times some management researchers and organizational psychologists believe in the great man concept (Organ, 1996). Existing literature on leadership styles has further elaborated the common characteristics of leaders which distinguish them from followers. The underlined philosophy pertains that if anyone has qualities such as adaptive, receptive, motivated, achievement-orientated, self-assured, crucial, energetic, persistent, self-confident, etc., then s/he is a leader or potential leader (Stogdill, 1974; McCall, 1983). Later on, theories presented about leadership were more focused on behaviors of leaders exhibited in the past so the people can be trained as effective leaders (Robbins and Coulter, 2002).

The other school of thought came with the idea of situational theories with the assumptions that appropriate leaders' behaviors vary according to undergoing situations as the most effective leadership behavior is the one which is most inclined towards the situational variables (Griffin, 1999). Related theories were presented later on with similar focus such as contingency theory which was related to environmental variables to figure out the leadership style concerned with a situation. No specific leadership style is the best fit for all situations as it depends on the characteristics of leaders, and capabilities of the followers, and the most important is the complexities of the situations and problems on hand and the role of issues in overall organizational success (Hicks and Gullett, 1987; Griffin, 1999).

Leadership Styles

Much of the literature on leadership styles mainly focuses on the two main scopes of leadership i.e. transactional and transformational leadership (Zareen, Razzaq and Mujtaba, 2014). Transactional and transformational leadership have been of great interest to many researchers in the modern age. Adopting either transformational or transactional leadership behavior helps in the success of the organization (Laohavichien, Freedendall and Cantrell, 2009). This might be the reason that different authors of the recent past considered transactional and transformational leadership as predicating variables and investigated their relatedness with other principle variables. Both transformational leadership and transactional leadership helped in predicting subordinates' satisfaction with their leaders (Bennett, 2009). However, in some situations both cannot provide the ultimate satisfaction to their subordinate and partially contribute as illustrative variables. A study of Chen, Beck and Amos (2005) found that followers were satisfied with the contingent reward dimension of transactional leaders and individualized reflection of transformational leaders. In this way a third leadership style evolved as laissez-faire leadership style to contribute in job satisfaction and employee engagement to optimize organizational performance by employee motivation.

Transactional Leadership

Transactional leadership has been centered on leader-follower exchanges. Followers perform according to the will and direction of the leaders and leaders positively reward the efforts. The baseline is reward system which can be negative like disciplinary action, if follower fails to obey; it can be positive like praise and appreciation, if subordinates meet the terms and conditions directed by leaders to achieve the assigned goals. Research has proposed three characteristics of transactional leadership which are contingent rewards, active management by exception and passive management by exception.

Transactional leaders communicate with their followers 'what they should do' and 'how they should do it' and then monitor them closely; followers perform tasks and obtain contingent rewards upon satisfactory performance and get punished on non-satisfactory performance (Zhu, John, Riggio and Yang, 2012; Gilani, Cavico, and Mujtaba, 2014). Transactional leaders observe performance on the basis of their predetermined parameters and take actions to change follower's behaviors so they perform as directed(Sosik and Jung, 2010).According to Epitropaki and Martin (2005), transactional leadership encourages followers' organizational identification by triggering followers' self-categorization processes. When leaders offer rewards and observe performance for corrective actions this leads towards a relationship between leader and follower for continuous learning and better understanding of their role in the organization. Such employees feel more committed towards organizational goals (Zhu, et al., 2011).

Transformational Leadership

Transformational leaders facilitate new understandings by increasing or altering awareness of issues. As a result, they foster inspiration and anticipation to put extra labor to achieve common goals. Transformational leadership is another extreme as these leaders influence the attitudes and beliefs of followers and motivate them according to their own interest for the betterment of the organization (Burns, 1998). According to Burns (1998), transformational leadership is based on four dimensions such as personality, communication, rational stimulation, and individualized thought. Some researchers interchangeably use transformational leadership as charismatic leadership.

According to McLaurin and Al-Amri (2008), "personality" is one among the many "qualities" of a transformational leader than the only "element". Transformational leadership is believed to be more widespread at upper levels of management than at lower levels (Tichy and Uhich, 1984).

Transformational leadership style is entirely different from transactional leadership style. Transformational leaders try to develop the followers' full potential (Bass, 1985; Johnson and Dipboye, 2008) by influencing and engaging them. Followers feel more transformed and developed and organizational commitment achieved by internal satisfaction and motivation as employees find organizational environment beneficial for their development.

Transformational leadership adds value to transactional leadership as it emphasizes on followers' personality, attitude and beliefs on performance outcomes and results in "augmentation effect" (Bass, 2008; Yukl, 2010). The main foundation of the transformational leadership style is the leader's ability to motivate the follower to accomplish more than what the follower planned to accomplish (Krishnan, 2005). Burns (1998) proposed that transformational leaders go in a relationship with the followers in that they motivate each other to higher level which results in value system congruence between the both.

Laissez-Fair Leadership

A third dimension of leadership acknowledged by experts is laissez-faire. Laissez-faire leadership style is the one in which a leader delegates all the decision-making powers to followers. Bradford and Lippitt (1945) described laissez-faire leadership as a leader's disregard of supervisory duties and lack of guidance to subordinates. Laissez-faire leaders offer little support to their subordinates and are careless to productivity or the necessary completion of duties (Lewin, Lippitt, and White, 1939). Such leaders give complete freedom to their followers to make decision by providing them all necessary tools and resources. In this case expectations from followers become very high to solve their own problems but when they go through the process and ultimately make a decision the whole process becomes a good learning opportunity to develop and to know about necessary organizational tools

(Eagly, Mary, Schmidt and Engen, 2003). Laissez-faire leadership style becomes more effective in situations when followers are highly skilled, motivated, capable, and willing to doing things by their own (Chaudhry and Javed, 2012).

Laissez-faire leadership style also best fits in the situations when there are large numbers of decisions, where decision making is easy, and followers have to perform routine tasks with fewer complexities and less demanding criteria or when rules and regulations are pre-determined for more intended strategies and decisions. This leadership style is inappropriate when followers lack in knowledge, experience and expertise or when they tend to be un-willing or unable to make decisions by their own. People vary in nature and the way they respond and behave in different situations, some of them lack the ability to set deadlines or managing their projects independently by solving problems or aligning their objectives with the organizational goals (Eagly, et al. 2003). Such employees require high relationship orientation with their managers and leaders; in these circumstances laissez-faire leadership style fails, resulting in poor performance of employees in the form of off-track efforts and missed deadlines.

Modern employees are more aware of and concerned with their expertise and competency development and their role in organizational success. They feel motivated and involved when allowed to make decisions and highly satisfied to see the positive outcomes of their decision. All the employees cannot be motivated by financial rewards and fringe benefits as they want to utilize their knowledge for effective decision making to be a part of the organization's success (Zareen, Razzaq and Ramzan, 2013). According to Werbel and Gilliland (1999), coordination between employee and organizational values is the reflection of employee involvement and motivation and can be achieved by follower-leader relationship.

Laissez-faire leaders give their followers a full chance to use their capabilities to understand the ongoing problems by facilitating them with necessary resources and guidance and then offer them the liberty to make decisions accordingly (Chaudhry, and Javed, 2012). This process ends up on feedback from the leaders if they find it necessary, but it gives follower the feeling of empowerment and involvement in success of the organization. Employees' intention to remain a part of the organization and to continue the job, positively associates with perception of correspondence towards organizational values (Aryee, Luk, and stone, 1998; Mitchel, 2001; Spector, 1997).

Role of Employee Motivation in Organizational Performance

Motivation is defined as forces that determine the direction of a person's behavior, a person's level of effort and the level of persistence (Mujtaba, 2014). As a hypothetical construct, motivation usually stands for that which energizes, directs and sustains behavior. It also explains the degree and type of effort that an individual exhibits in a behavioral situation. Similarly employee motivation predicts behaviors towards job responsibilities, tasks and assignments and their needs. These needs of individuals become associated with their internal satisfaction and motivation. Leader-follower relationship becomes an important element of employee satisfaction and engagement in the organizational environment. Many theories and literature have proved that well satisfied and motivated employees become more involved in their work and exert all their energies to perform their job, tasks and assignments (Khan, 1990) with higher job satisfaction (Zareen, Razzaq and Mujtaba, 2013). On the other hand leaders make certain contracts with their followers for continuous learning, which results in their development and improvement in capabilities and competencies. Studies have revealed that employee motivation, work satisfaction, and job involvement are interrelated and results in organizational commitment and loyalty. Such employees remain with the organizations for longer run and perform their duties deliberately and dedicatedly for their learning, training and development.

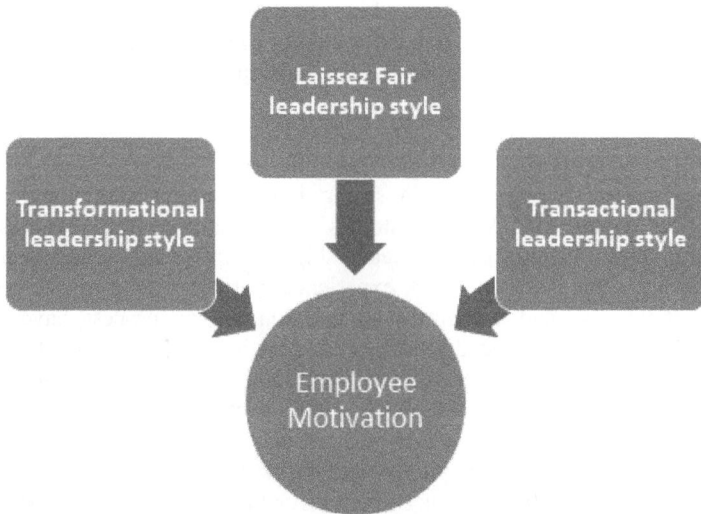

Figure 11.1- Theoretical Framework for Motivation
(Zareen, Razzaq and Mujtaba, 2014)

Transformational leaders strive to deal with greater need of following individuals by influencing them (Judge and Piccolo, 2004). Transformational leaders, by definition, seek to transform (Lowe, Kroeck and Sivasubramaniam, 1996). When the organization does not facilitate them with such an environment or if the followers become unwilling for transformation by being happy with what they are and how they perform, such leaders and managers become frustrated (Judge and Piccolo, 2004). Employees become more committed to organizational goals when they are considering them valuable and may remain with the organization for longer times (Zareen,et al., 2013). Transformational leaders undergo a tacit commitment with their followers that they will be developed in a positive way and in response followers become a product of transformation (Zhu, et al., 2011). Transactional leaders engage their followers in work with positive and negative reward system for their motivation and commitment. As a result followers perform their tasks and responsibilities in an attempt to achieve the rewards and to avoid punishments.

A third leadership dimension was eventually acknowledged by experts - the laissez-faire leaders. This type of leadership style allows for complete tolerance, and the groups often lacks in direction because the leader does not help in making decisions but supports followers by guiding how they go through the decision making process. While dealing with laissez-faire leadership style, leader gives followers many opportunities to make decisions, to utilize their competencies, develop their capabilities, and to learn from their own mistakes. This leadership style is effective with decisions which are not very crucial for the organization and cannot be allowed for an extended period of time so the organization does not lose its direction. Figure 1 shows the relationship of various leadership styles with employee motivation.

Effect of Demographics on Leadership Styles
Demographic variables have a strong impact on leadership styles and leader-follower interaction. Various studies have analyzed the relationship between demographic differences and leadership practices and concluded that gender differences, age, years of work experience, period of time in one organization or current position and organizational decision-making process have an impact on leadership styles and leader-follower interaction. Effect of gender differences is more apparent on leadership styles (Eagly and Johnson, 1990). Gender differences emerge in terms of use of power and supervisory actions, male leaders prefer to go along with transactional leadership styles and masculine personality traits whereas female leaders choose to pursue transformational leadership styles (Rozier and Hersh-Cochran, 1996), being more relationship oriented and apply more individualized consideration (Bass, Avolio and Atwater, 1996, Styfla (2008). Personality traits and decision-making also goes side by side in organizations. Female leaders tend to be more conscious about their followers and the groups they lead and make decision by avoiding risky situations while male leaders make more decisions at times with higher risks for themselves and their groups (Ertac and Yigit 2010).

With the growing age leaders usually follow the transformational leadership style while the followers with growing age become less responsive towards their leader's behavior and rely more on their own past work experience, knowledge and understanding. In few organizations more aged employees do not like their young bosses and managers and become more resistant to changes implemented by them. Followers with many years of working experience show similar behaviors, they feel comfortable with their old styles of doing things and thus might be more reluctant to new information and mechanisms (Katz, 1982).

When employees spend long time with one organization they set specific patterns of doing things and resist change (Katz (1982). In organizational culture, whenever policies implemented with advance technologies highest resistance comes from employees working with the organization from longer time being unwilling to learn about innovation, rules, and policies. These employees when lead by their leaders and managers become unresponsive towards transformational process and can be controlled through transactional styles of leadership (Ali and Ali, 2011).

Leadership by Women and for Women

Leadership is more about personality attributes; and a leader is the one who has the ability to influence follower behaviors through personality development. Leadership is the skill to make others do the thing in the leader's way and the outcome should remain visible in the absence of leaders. Gender has a strong impact on behavioral concerns, relationship orientation, decision making styles and behavior towards leaders and leadership. Women usually tend to be more relationship oriented, work better with personality influences, and have proven to be risk averse in decision making for themselves and their following individuals or groups. In this sense female leaders pursue more transformational leadership style and influence their followers for transformation of their personality with the development of their capabilities and competencies and to motivate them for better performance.

Leader-follower relationship and the willingness of both is crucial for effective guidance, learning and development. Followers should be mentally and physically willing and comfortable to follow the instructions and decision made by the leader.

As discussed earlier in this chapter, the concept of leadership was originated by Great Man theory and the idea was related to men. Only men were considered to be potential or actual leaders to lead their followers without any involvement of women in this role. Male gender by nature is more dominating and men feel uncomfortable in following women being more resistant and unwilling. Now in our advanced world many females are working in organizations on various levels. One way they are leading the nations by being a part of the politics and holding top positions. Elsewhere they are on top management, middle management and at times supervisory positions leadings teams and groups performing better than their male counterpart in certain departments. All these positions give them authority and responsibility to lead their subordinates either males or females, while the male dominancy concept is not fully over yet, which results in dissonance at workplace. In this regard male followers become resistant or unresponsive towards leadership process and raise conflict and anarchy, which results in failure of transformational style of leadership due to unwillingness of follower to follow female boss. In these situations, transactional and laissez-faire leadership styles work better with favorable leader-follower work performance.

Another aspect of transformational leadership is proven more effective with female followers. They learn and perform well when transformational leadership style is adopted and becomes comparatively less productive with transactional or Laissez-fair leadership styles. While male leaders prefer to go along with transactional style of leadership so this type of leader follower interaction becomes less effective in terms of performance when male leaders apply transactional leadership style to female followers. This leadership style conflicts and gender disparity issue can be resolved better by understanding the needs of followers, nature of work and requirements or organization and one best style can be adopted according to that or the leaders may fluctuate between transformational and transactional leadership styles accordingly.

Leadership to enhance employee work motivation in Banking Sector
The banking sector of Pakistan is well established and still growing with large number of private banks and financial institutions working side by side with government banks on national, international and multinational levels. Large number of males and females are working in more than 30,000 branches nationwide with a huge ratio of women on managerial levels. Many bank branches are fully managed and lead by female managers. Banking jobs are considered tough and highly demanding with many expectations from employees as they face continuous customer interaction with ongoing internal operations side by side. Managing banking activities on day-to-day basis and for achievement of long term goals leader-follower interaction becomes more important because of close interaction, diversity in nature of decisions, and sensitivity and significance of decisions. Many studies have revealed that for banking sector especially dealing with branch banking activities transactional leadership style has proven more successful for the motivation and involvement of banking employees as compared to other leadership styles.

Effective leadership is considered to be the main cause of competitive advantage and the reason of success for any kind of organization (Zhu et al., 2005; Avolio, 1999; Lado et al., 1992; Rowe, 2001). Managers in the banking sector tend to be more inclined towards exercising transactional leadership as compared to transformational leadership style. They share an exchange relationship with their employees using rewards and punishments as tools to positively and negatively influence employees (Zhu et. al., 2012) to meet their targets. Since the transactional leadership is based on contingent reward and punishment behavior, managers positively reward individuals with praise or recognition when they perform at or above expectations. Similarly, negative rewarding approach is also used in the form of correction, coercion, criticism, and/or other forms of punishment, when performance is below the expected standard (Janseen, 2000).

Transactional leadership style is found to be positively and significantly related to employee's motivation as compared to transformational and laissez-faire leadership styles in banking sector (Epitropaki and Martin 2005), which pertains to the provision of either positive rewards in case of meeting established goals or negative rewards when the performer fails to achieve the desired objectives (Khan, 1992). Further non-managerial employees in banks with comparatively lower educational level prefer to perform task and responsibilities according to instructions and directions of managers and feel reluctant to take decisions by their own. They feel more relaxed with close monitoring of their bosses to avoid risk of making wrong decisions (Zareen, Razzaq and Mujtaba, 2014). This leads managers to use more transactional leadership style to get work done through their employees with close monitoring and comparatively more vertical structure for effective job involvement and work motivation of employees. While laissez-faire and transformational style of leadership seem to be comparatively less effective to engage and motivate banking employees, yet it is positively associated with few departments like advances where employees want to be more involved in decision making on the basis of their knowledge and understanding for the evaluation of creditor, calculation of applicable interest rate based on evaluation report and the assessments of amounts which can be sanctioned.

Summary
This chapter concludes that all three leadership styles (transactional, transformational, and laissez-faire), have a strong and positive impact on employee motivation and involvement. Transactional leadership style has the strongest impact on employees with lower educational level and lesser experience and when they want to be closely monitored by their leaders and managers, and when they are unable or unwilling to make decisions by their own and want to perform task as directed. While laissez-faire leadership style becomes effective in the situations of more certainty with comparatively less risky decisions and when followers are well aware of nature and requirements of decision and able to make decisions accordingly. To enhance employee motivation and involvement, managers and leaders should provide regular feedback on decisions made by followers. Transformational style of leadership works well with employees if followers are willing and keen to learn for the transformation of their personality and development of their capabilities. Transformational leaders become more like role models for their followers and influence them in a unique way. Most important factor for leadership is that managers and leaders should adopt the appropriate style according to undergoing situation and values and attributes of the followers to make them motivated and committed to organizational goals for the optimum performance of organization.

Employee motivation is crucial to make workers more committed towards the job, tasks and assignments by emphasizing on manager-employee relationship. Employees who are not motivated may be more likely to put less effort at the workplace as compared to the employees with the high-level motivation. Managers and leaders should come up with the policies amd leadership styles that would enable them to attract and retain their employees at their respective institutions. Thus, identifying leadership styles that tend to enhance motivation of employees would be a significant benefit for the management of various organizations.

References

Aryee, S., Luk, V., and Stone, R. (1998). Family-Responsive Variables and Retention-Relevant Outcomes among Employed Parents. *Human Relations*, 51(1),73–87.

Ashforth, B. E. and Humphrey, R. H. (1995). Emotion in the Workplace: A Reappraisal. *Human Relations*, 48(2), 97- 125.

Avolio, B. (1999). Full leadership development: building the vital forces in organizations. Sage Publications, Thousand Oaks, CA.

Bass, B. M. (1985). Leadership and Performance Beyond Expectations. New York: Academic Press.

Bass, B. M. (2008). The Bass handbook of leadership: Theory, research and managerial applications (4th ed.). New York, NY: Free Press.

Bass, B. M., Avolio, B. J. and Atwater, L. (1996), The Transformational and Transactional Leadership of Men and Women. *Applied Psychology: An International Review*, 45, 5-34.

Bennett, T. M. (2009). *The relationship between the subordinate's perception of the leadership style of IT managers and the subordinate's perceptions of IT manager's ability to inspire extra effort, to be effective, and to enhance satisfaction with management.* Dissertation at Nova Southeastern University.

Bolden, R. (2004). What is leadership?, Research Report 1, Leadership South West. Centre for Leadership Studies, University of Exeter.

Boseman, G. (2008). Effective leadership in a changing world. *Journal of Financial Service Professionals*, 62(3), 36-38.

Bradford, L. P., and Lippitt, R. (1945). Building a democratic work group. *Personnel*, 22, 1–12.

Burns, J. (1998). The Empowering Leader: Unrealized Opportunities, in Hickman, R. G. (ed).Leading Organizations: Perspectives for a New Era. Sage: London

Chaudhry, A. Q., Javed, H. (2012). Impact of Transactional and Laissez-Faire Leadership Style on Motivation: *International Journal of Business and Social Science*. 3(7), 258-264.

Chen, H., Beck, S., and Amos, L. (2005). Leadership styles and nursing faculty job satisfaction in Taiwan. *Journal of Nursing Scholarship*, 4(37), 374-380.

Eagly A. H., Mary C., J. Schmidt and van Engen, M. L. (2003). Transformational, Transactional, and Laissez-Faire Leadership Styles: A Meta-Analysis Comparing Women and Men. *Psychological Bulletin*, 129(4), 569–591.

Eagly, A.H. and Johnson, B.T. (1990). Gender and Leadership styles: A Meta analysis, *Psychological Bulletin*, 168, 233-256.

Epitropaki, O., and Martin, T. (2005). The moderating role of individual differences in the relation between transformational/transactional leadership perceptions and organizational identification. *The Leadership Quarterly*, 16(4), 569-589.

Ertac, S., and Yigit, G.M., (2010). Deciding to decide: gender, leadership and risk-taking in groups, TÜSİAD-Koç University *Economic Research Forum working paper series*, 1028.

Francis, R. and J. Krishnan, J., (2002). Evidence on Auditor Risk-Management Strategies Before and After the Private Securities Litigation Reform Act of 1995. *Asia Pacific Journal of Accounting and Economics*, 9 (2), 135-158.

Griffin, R., (1999). Management (5th Edition) Houghton Mifflin Company. Evaluations, and Career Outcomes. *The Academy of Management Journal*, 33, 64-86.

Gilani, S. R. S., Cavico, F. J. and Mujtaba, B. G. (March 2014). Harassment at the Workplace: A Practical Review of the Laws in the United Kingdom and the United States of America. *Public Organization Review*, 14(1), 01-18.

Hadjimanolis, A., (2000). An Investigation of Innovation Antecedents in Small Firms in the Context of a Small Developing Country. *R&D Management*, 30(3), 235-245.

Hage, J., and Dewar, R. (1973). Elite Values Versus Organizational Structure in Predicting Innovation. *Administrative Science Quarterly*, 18(3), 279-290.

Hicks, H. and Gullett, C., (1987). *Management* (4th Edition), International Student Edition. McGraw-Hill, Inc.

Ali, H., & Ali, H. (2011). Demographics and Spiritual Leadership: Empirical Evidence from Pakistan, *Business & Management Review*, 1(10), 36-42.

Janssen, O. (2000). Job Demands, Perceptions of Effort- Reward Fairness and Innovative Work Behavior. *Journal of Occupational and Organizational Psychology*, 73(3), 287-302.

Johnson, S. K. and Dipboye, R. L., (2008). Effects of charismatic content and delivery on follower task performance. *Group & Organization Management,* 33(1), 77-106.

Judge, T. A. and Piccolo, R. F., (2004). Transformational and Transactional Leadership: A Meta-Analytic Test of Their Relative Validity. *Journal of Applied Psychology,* 89(5), 755–768.

Kahn, W., (1990). Psychological conditions of personal engagement and disengagement at work. *Academy of Management Journal,* 33, 692-724.

Kahn, W. (1992). To be fully there: Psychological presence at work. *Human Relations,* 45, 321-349.

Katz, R. (1982). The effect of group longevity on project communication and performance, *Administrative Science Quarterly,* 27 (1), 81-104.

Krishnan, J., and Zhang. Y. (2005). Why Some Firms Solicit Shareholders' Voting on Auditor Selection. *Accounting Horizons,* 19 (4), 237-254.

Krishnan, V.R., (2005). Transformational leadership and outcomes: role of relationship duration. *Leadership and Organization Development Journal,* 26(6), 442-457.

Lado, A., Boyd, N. and Wright, P., (1992). A competency-based model of sustainable competitive advantage: Towards a conceptual integration. *Journal of Management,* 18, 77-91.

Laohavichien, T., Fredendall, L., and Cantrell, R., (2009). The effects of transformational and transactional leadership on quality improvement. *The Quality Management Journal,* 16(2), 7-24.

Lewin, K., Lippitt, R. and White, R. K. (1939). Patterns of aggressive behavior in experimentally created "social climates. *Journal of Social Psychology,* 10, 271-299.

Lowe, K. B., Kroeck, G. K., and Sivasubramaniam, N. (1996). Effectiveness correlates of transformational and transactional leadership: A meta-analytic review of the MLQ literature. *The Leadership Quarterly,* 7, 385-425.

McCall, M. and Lombardo, M., (1983). *Off the track: Why and how successful executives get derailed.* Greenboro, NC: Centre for Creative Leadership.

McLaurin, J. and Al-Amri, M., (2008). Developing an understanding of charismatic and transformational leadership. *Proceedings of the Academy of Organizational Culture, Communications and Conflict,* 13(2), p. 15

Mujtaba, B. G. (2014). *Managerial Skills and Practices for Global Leadership.* ILEAD Academy: Florida.

Organ, D., (1996). Leadership: The great man theory revisited. *Business Horizons,* 39(3), 1-4.

Podsakoff, P., Moorman, R. and Fetter, R., (1990). Transformational leader behaviors and their effects on followers' trustin leader, satisfaction, and organizational citizenship behaviors. *Leadership Quarterly,* 1(2) 107-142.

Riaz, A., and Haider, M.H. (2010). Role of transformational and transactional leadership on job satisfaction and career satisfaction. *Business and Economic Horizons,* 1(1), 29-38.

Robbins S.P. and Coulter M. (2002). *Management* (7th Edition). Prentice Hall Inc., New Jersey.

Roberts, E.B. (1991). *Entrepreneurs in High Technology: Lessons from MIT and Beyond,* New York: Oxford University Press.

Rothwell, R., (1992). Successful Industrial Innovation: Critical Factors for the 1990s. *R&D Management,* 22(3), 221-239.

Rowe, W., (2001). Creating wealth in organizations: The role of strategic leadership. *Academy of Management Executive,* 15, 81-94.

Rozier, C.H. and Herch-Cochran, M.S. (1996). Gender differences in managerial characteristics in a female-dominated health profession, *Health Care Supervision,* 14 (4), 57-70.

Sosik, J. J., and Jung, D. I., (2010). *Full range leadership development: Pathways for people, profit and planet.* Rutledge, New York, NY.

Spector, P. E. (1997). *Job Satisfaction.* Thousand Oaks, Calif.: Sage.

Stogdill, R. (1974). *Handbook of Leadership* (1st Edition). New York: Free Press.

Stafyla, A. (2008). Gender and leadership in Greek enterprises, 4th European Conference on Management, Leadership and Governance, Ryeson University, Toronto, Canada.

Tichy, N. and Uhich, D. (1984). The leadership challenge: A call for the transformational leader. *Sloan Management Review,* 26, 59-68.

Turner, A. N. and Lawrence, P. R. (1965). *Industrial jobs and the worker.* Harvard University Press, Boston.

Werbel, J. D., and Gilliland, S. W. (1999). Person-Environment Fit in the Selection Process. *Research in Personnel and Human Resources Management, 17,* 209–243.

Williams, S.D. (2004). Personality, Attitude, and Leader Influences on Divergent Thinking and Creativity in Organizations. *European Journal of Innovation Management,* 7(3), 187-204.

Yukl, G., (2010). *Leadership in organizations* (7th edition). Upper Saddle River, NJ: Prentice Hall.

Zareen, M., Razzaq, K., and Mujtaba, B. G. (2014). Impact of Transactional, Transformational and Laissez-faire Leadership Styles on Motivation: a Quantitative study of Banking Employees in Pakistan. *Public Organization Review,* Online First. DOI: 10.1007/s11115-014-0287-6. Website link for Online First: http://link.springer.com/article/10.1007/s11115-014-0287-6?sa_campaign=email/event/articleAuthor/onlineFirst

Zareen, M., Razzaq, K. and Mujtaba, B. G. (2013). Job Design and Employee Performance: the Moderating Role of Employee Psychological Perception. *European Journal of Business and Management,* 5(5), 46-55.

Zareen, M., Razzaq, K. and Ramzan, M. (2013). Impact of Employee Retention on Performance: the Moderating Role of Employee Psychological Perception towards Retention Plan. *International journal of contemporary research in Business* 4(10), 822-833.

Zhu, W., Riggio, R., Avolio, B. J., and Sosik, J. J. (2011). The effect of leadership on follower moral identity: Does transformational/transactional style make a difference? *Journal of Leadership and Organizational Studies, 18*(2), 150 – 163.

Zhu. W., John J. S., Riggio R. E., and Yang B., (2012). Relationships between Transformational and Active Transactional Leadership and Followers' Organizational Identification: The Role of Psychological Empowerment. *Institute of Behavioral and Applied Management,* 13(3),186-212.

Chapter 12

CORPORATE SOCIAL RESPONSIBILITY IN CENTRAL AND SOUTH ASIA

By: Maike Emmi Lina Koehler
Ramkhamhaeng University

In today's world, many companies are dealing with Corporate Social Responsibility or simply CSR. However what exactly is CSR? So far it has not been clearly defined and narrowed. There are various definitions and philosophies about Corporate Social Responsibility. Many companies also talk about sustainability or just social responsibility but what they mean intends the same: It always deals with the company's responsibility on a social, economic, and ecological basis. This chapter explores CSR and how it is being viewed from a corporate perspective.

This chapter discusses the child labor situation in Asia, more precisely in Pakistan, India and Uzbekistan on the basis of the international companies IKEA, Nike and H&M and how they are trying to improve these situations with the help of education in the form of Corporate Social Responsibility programs.

Introduction

Although the term Corporate Social Responsibility is relatively new, the idea of this concept has been around much longer. Even in ancient times there were responsible corporate actions in the form of charges of food and money from the wealthy Greeks to help the most vulnerable. Likewise, in the 19th century, there were many companies that distributed donations to social organizations or demonstrated local commitment.

Nevertheless, the actual concept of Corporate Social Responsibility comes from the 20th century. The first contact with it was approximately in the United States in the 1950s when Howard R. Bowen wrote: "It refers to the obligations of businessmen to pursue those policies, to make those decisions, or to follow those lines of action which are desirable in terms of objectives and values of our society."

In the 1960s Keith Davis wrote "social responsibilities of businessmen have to be commensurate with their social power" which also means that social responsibility might either end in a positive and a negative way. Moreover at that time many companies began to release public company reports for the first time in order to demonstrate their social responsibility.

From the 1970s on, many approaches have been made to define Corporate Social Responsibility. A more precise definition of Corporate Social Responsibility has succeeded by Archie B. Carroll, who talks about the concept of 'giving back to society' as essential idea and that it should definitely focus on voluntariness! "In summary, the total corporate social responsibility of business entails the simultaneous fulfillment of the firm's economic, legal, ethical and philanthropic responsibilities."

CSR in Pakistan, India and Uzbekistan

The three countries of Pakistan, India and Uzbekistan are located in Central and South Asia and cover an area of about 3,288,917,654 km², wherein India is the biggest with 3,287,590 km². Pakistan covers 880,254 km² and Uzbekistan 447,400 km².

In India, the population has grown rapidly in the last years up to 1,239,260,000 in 2013 from 1,076,250,000 in 2003. In 2013 the density in India was 376.9 per km² and in Pakistan it was 234.4 per km² whereas in comparison the density in the Uzbekistan was only 61.4 per km², which is still double of USA with 34.2 per km². However in India the density in fertile areas goes up to 800 – 1000 per km². Both Pakistan's and Uzbekistan's populations count more than 90% Muslims whereas in India Islam is practiced by about 13%.

All three countries suffer from different problems that make child labor arise and even attractive to execute. About 1/3 of India's population is under 15 years which brings the median age to 27 years in 2014, compared to this Pakistan is a very young country with a median age of 22 years and more than 100 million people under 30.

Although economists expect Pakistan to be the 18th largest economy in the world with a GDP of US$ 3.33 trillion by 2050 more than 20% of the population suffer from poverty below the international poverty line of US $1.25 a day and roughly ¾ of those are living in rural areas.

About 15 million people are working in the textile sector, which is highly positioned in the exports of Pakistan. With contribution of 9.5% to the GDP the textile sector makes Pakistan the 8th largest exporter of textile products among Asian countries. Especially soccer balls from Pakistan are well known. About 70 percent of all global hand-stitched soccer balls are produced here.

Similar to Pakistan, Uzbekistan also plays a leading role in the textile sector however especially in production and export of cotton. The country with a median age of 27.1 years is independent from Soviet Union since 1991 and since then ruled by Islam Karimov who was elected as the first president. Although the country actively demonstrates the importance of human rights, several human rights watchdogs criticize it as "an authoritarian state with limited civil rights" and "wide-scale violation of virtually all basic human rights".

In 2013, Uzbekistan was number six of the world's largest producers of cotton and number two in export of cotton. More than one million people are employed in the cotton sector, including children.

The difference between the demonstration of human rights in Uzbekistan and the actual situation how it really is, is clearly shown when it comes to cotton picking children. Children are forced to pick what Uzbeks refer to as "white gold" as it is essential to the national economy. The youngest children employed by the Uzbekistani government are about 9 years old. Since their early childhood they are told to look forward when the time comes for them to harvest. This time is called "pahta" and children are inculcated by the government to consider it as "opportunity for them to contribute to their nation's prosperity".

India has rapidly grown during the last years and thus poverty here is widespread as well. About 12% in 2014 are living under the international poverty line, although the number is declining. However according to UNICEF 1/3 malnourished children worldwide are living in India, and about 42% of Indian children under the age of five suffer from underweight.

The country is facing various problems in their public health sector. The World Health Organization reports that each year about 900,000 Indians die from drinking contaminated water or from breathing polluted air.

India, Pakistan, and Uzbekistan face several challenges. Many companies are producing in low cost countries to stay competitive and increase their profit. This in turn makes those countries hire children, as they are even cheaper and most likely faster in manufacturing with their smaller hands. Thus it can be challenging for companies to balance and draw a line where profitability ends and unacceptable exploitation of people, especially children starts. IKEA, Nike, and H&M belong to those companies.

IKEA

IKEA is a furniture company that was founded in 1943 by Ingvar Kamprad. The name comes from the initials of the founder, Ingvar Kamprad, and combines it with the first letters of the farm Elmtaryd in the municipality Agunnaryd in southern Sweden, where he grew up. Ingvar Kamprad was just 17 years old when he registered the name IKEA. IKEA originally sold pens, wallets, picture frames, table runners, watches, jewelries and nylon stockings and covered so the needs of the people to buy products at reduced prices. From 1948, the company then sold furniture produced by local manufacturers in the forests close to Ingvar Kamprad's residence. The demand grew strongly and subsequently this division expanded continuously.

In 1992 a Swedish documentary film was released and brought IKEA in connection with child labor. The 47-minute film called '*The Carpet Slaves: Stolen Children of India*', was produced by Kate Blewett and Brian Woods. It represented the child slavery in North India and declared that IKEA is one of the clients of this factory. The documentary shows about 300,000 young children held as slaves in an unhygienic and dangerous factory. Their task was to work on looms and produce the popular rugs that are exported in many cases. Some of the young children were even chained to their looms.

After the accusations of being involved in child labor, IKEA responded promptly and ended the business relationship to the factory in Pakistan immediately. They also added a condition to all contracts with suppliers that child labor is strictly prohibited. This clause is based on a United Nations Convention on the Rights of the Child of 1989. To personally convince herself, Ikea's Business Manager Marianne Barner traveled to Pakistan, India, and Nepal to assure that suppliers do not operate child labor.

Moreover Vandana Verma, who acts as an ombudsman for IKEA South Asia in the context of child labor, visits Uttat Pradesh frequently. This Indian state is one of the poorest, densely populated, and least developed. About 150,000 - 175,000 looms are estimated in the area of Uttar Pradesh in Northern India, in total about 450,000 - 525,000 weavers.

In the following years Ikea has had to deal with child labor more often and was tired of constant confrontation with it as this has both a strong negative PR effect and results in loss of revenue; they therefore decided to break new ground. IKEA wants to avoid child labor before it arises at all. They came to this realization with the help of UNICEF and a meeting with them. Vandana Verma already pointed to the lack of education, which now constitutes the central point for IKEAs Corporate Social Responsibility regarding child labor. IKEA donated half a million dollars to start a project that is against child labor. The company built educational institutions, especially for women and children in 500 villages that gave opportunity for an estimated 54,000 children benefiting directly.

The project is a three-year child rights project in the carpet belt of Uttar Pradesh. By establishing self-help groups IKEA wants to help reducing the dept-burden, which is one of the main reasons why families make their children work. Moreover women do also get the chance to learn writing and reading and are taught basics in health, nutrition and children's rights.

Despite the success of the project with more than 24,000 children attending school in 2000 child labor still exists in India, Pakistan and many other countries.

However especially for those two countries IKEA has instructed companies for regular monitoring and unannounced checks. In India they have hired KPMG and PricewaterhouseCoopers and in Pakistan Inspectorates Corporation International (ICIL) to fight the war against child labor.

Moreover, IKEA believes that they can accomplish much more on social and environmental improvements when they work with experienced partners. Among many others their partners are WWF, Save the Children and UNICEF.

The partnership with UNICEF is widespread in its cooperation. IKEA has donated over $200 million in cash as well as in in-kind donations. In addition, IKEA plays a major role when it comes to philanthropic donations, selling of Greeting Cards and marketing and promotion activities around the world. However UNICEF describes IKEA as a true partner as they are truly committed to social responsibility, especially concerning children.

The partnership of IKEA and UNICEF is particularly strong in India. They estimated to have helped over 74 million children in India by 2012 to get better possibilities in the future not only for themselves but also for their families. With the help of IKEA children's rights concerning education and protection are promoted; furthermore the company makes a contribution to the improvement of child survival. They try to improve water and sanitation conditions and avoid malnutrition. By offering millions of children the chance for education IKEA has improved their families' lives.

NIKE

In 1964, Bill Bowerman and Phil Knight founded the American company Nike. At that time, the sporting goods supplier still had the name Blue Ribbon Sports, which was later changed to Nike coming from the Greek winged goddess of victory. Back then, the German brand Adidas was very strong and the business idea from Nike was to dominate the U.S. market by importing low-cost high-tech sport shoes from Japan. Adidas produced its shoes in Germany and the U.S., which was quite expensive; therefore, it was attractive for Phil Knight to outsource the production to lower-cost locations.

Then, in 1996, Nike suffered a stroke of fate when Life magazine featured the company on its cover showing a 12-year old child stitching a NIKE football, thus accusing the company of child labor. "On the Playground of America, Every Kid's Goal Is to Score: In Pakistan, Where Children Stitch Soccer Balls for Six Cents an Hour, Their Goal Is To Survive".

About 70% of all soccer balls are stitched in Pakistan. Since the publishing of this article, Nike has become a kind of poster image regarding unethical use of offshore workers in the poorer regions of the world. Nevertheless, the article still initiated public acts of demonstrations and boycotts. For example, students demanded to the administration and athletic directors at their universities to ban the products of Nike. In addition, Nike has often suffered accusations of exploiting its employees by not paying the required minimum wage. Nike has all the allegations initially ignored and tried to distract. The company said that the factories do not belong to the company, but this did not stop the press to continue reporting about the poor working condition.

In 2002, there were reports about a factory in Vietnam in which accidents happened regularly because of the dangerous environment. This includes the use of chemical products, such as adhesives and solvents. These chemicals are an extreme cause for disease. After these allegations and an immense media attention, the company decided to take action. It was initiated by organizations such as Vietnam Labor Watch. They declared that Nike was responsible for the problems in the factories.

Thus Nike decided to create a code of conduct and implemented it in the cooperation with its factories. The company has increased from three in 1996 to eighty-six compliance officers in 2003. They used to monitor plant operations, working conditions and ensure the maintenance of code of conduct all over the world.

In addition, Nike donated a lot of money, such as 2004 for tsunami relief. The Nike Foundation is a nonprofit organization solely supported by Nike. It is an active supporter of the Millennium Development Goals that are specially focusing on education against child labor especially about caring for girls in developing countries. The intention is to get better health, education, and economic opportunities.

Nike still has to challenge the allegation that they are only interested in profitability. In order to face those allegations, Nike states on their website that The Nike Foundation is not "a social issue; it is smart economics". According to Nike India loses about $10 billion each year due to adolescent girls who become mothers each year. That's the reason why Nike founded Girl Hub in collaboration with the U.K. Department for International Development (DFID). Girl Hub aims to improve lives of adolescent girls who are living in poverty. This program, where girls are encouraged to actively participate is established worldwide and helps girls in family planning, direct assets and resource creation.

However, Girl Hub is only one part of the movement that Nike calls "the girl effect". The girl effect is not only active in India but all over the world. Nike states that girls are "the most powerful force for change on the planet". By educating and explaining basic understanding to girls of how to prevent issues as child marriage, pregnancy, and HIV/AIDS they will be an important part to fight poverty. Nike's website mentions that "When you improve a girl's life through education, health, safety and economic opportunity, these changes have a positive ripple effect on their families, communities and nations. Our work aims to shift the social norms that hold girls back, and drive better investments that directly benefit girls."

H&M
In 1947, the fashion empire H&M was founded in Sweden by businessperson Erling Persson. H&M stands for Hennes and Mauritz. The word Hennes is Swedish and means for her, whereas Mauritz comes from the hunting and gun store Mauritz Widforss, which was bought in 1968. Within the last years, H&M has grown into an international fashion empire that employs more than 73,000 people in 1800 stores in 34 countries. The philosophy of H&M 'Fashion and quality at the best price' means that they want to offer the latest fashion for the best price and the cheapest price respectively, which naturally leads to a purchase of raw materials as low as possible.

Similar to IKEA, there was also a documentary shown on television regarding allegations of being involved in child labor. The Swedish TV report accused H&M of benefiting from child labor.

In the case of H&M, it was not the same as with a direct supplier to IKEA, however, the sewing bought cotton picked by children in Uzbekistan. In the Central

Asian state, the children do not work willingly but then abused as cheap workers by the authoritarian regime. H&M responded promptly in order not to compromise the credibility of the company. The representative of the company Katarina Kempe admitted that the mentioned sewing works for H&M, but also added that the company does not own any factories, and thus has no business relations with the cotton suppliers or knowledge where the cotton comes from. Such a contract would be required to be able to make demands.

Uzbekistan is the largest exporter of cotton in Asia, the probability of use of cotton from this country is correspondingly large. H&M tried to improve the social situation of cotton farmers around the world. They participated in projects, such as Better Cotton Initiative, whose goal it is to make the world's cotton cultivation ecological, economic, and sustainable. Since early 2007 H&M sells its own organic collection in its German stores. The raw materials are exclusively from controlled cultivation in Turkey. H&M explains that the demand for sustainably harvested raw materials has increased, but the share of the world market is only 0.1 percent so far. The mission of Better Cotton Initiative on the website says:

> *BCI exists to make global cotton production better for the people who produce it, better for the environment it grows in and better for the sector's future. BCI works with a diverse range of stakeholders to promote measurable and continuing improvements for the environment, farming communities and the economies of cotton-producing areas. BCI aims to transform cotton production worldwide by developing better cotton as a sustainable mainstream commodity (Better Cotton Initiative, 2012, para 1).*

By having a partnership with Better Cotton Initiative H&M wants to contribute in creating better lives for farmers and their families. Better Cotton has been successful in Pakistan, India and many other countries. They report about "Better Farm Management in Pakistan," "Better Use of Water in Pakistan," "Farmers learning from each other in Pakistan," "Better Child Rights in India," "Women Leading the Way for Better Cotton in India" and many other stories.

However, the situation in Uzbekistan has not changed much, what made H&M make a major decision. Since 2013, direct suppliers have to sign a commitment that states that they are not using Uzbek cotton. Furthermore their 300 most important fabric suppliers have to stop sourcing Uzbek cotton and the company itself makes no business with direct suppliers and strategic fabric mills still using Uzbek cotton. To ensure this H&M has planned to conduct random checks.

Furthermore, since 2004 H&M is also in a partnership with UNICEF and has several projects running to avoid child labor and strive for education of children.

In 2009, H&M started the "All for Children" initiative that focuses on the rights of children in South India, this initiative helps prevent child labor and improves access to health and nutrition care services. This program runs until 2014 and appeals to child protection policies and structures, education, community mobilization, social protection and health and nutrition services.

In February, 2014, H&M started 3 global programs with UNICEF, WaterAid and CARE, that will go on for a period of three years. H&M will support these programs with about $27 million and will help making improvements in education, clean water and strengthening women.

H&M believes that children's early education and development is the best start in life so they can achieve their full developmental potential. That is the reason why they aim for more than 73,000 children attend preschool by 2017.

A partnership with WaterAid will ensure that more than 250,000 children will have access to clean water, sanitation and hygiene at their schools. This will help them to develop in a safe and healthy environment. Moreover a partnership with CARE aims to strengthen women and focuses on inspiring and offering advice to women in economically poor communities. Women should be given the opportunity to start their own small enterprises; thus H&M aims to get them access to tools, knowledge, skills or seed capital that will enable them.

Summary

This chapter provided a brief introduction to the working situation in Central and South Asia and many other countries as well. Low cost countries are used to keeping cost of production low and to increase profits, although exactly this had led to working and living situations where people, especially children are being exploited and are kept away from the classroom. Very often they have no chance of education or not even access to a healthy and safe environment. Children suffer from malnutrition and other diseases.

For a few decades, companies are more aware of the terrible working conditions many employees are exposed to and are trying to contribute to an improvement of their lives. Companies have formed several programs under the concept of corporate social responsibility. In this chapter, the focus lied on three companies: IKEA, Nike and H&M, which had to face accusations of child labor and mistreat of their employees. All three companies have either formed their own programs or are active in a partnership with another company like UNICEF. With the help of their CSR programs and initiative, they have been able to offer millions of boys and girls an education and thus creating a better future.

Bibliography

Books:
Beer, L. & Carey, W.P. (2012) *International Management, Culture, Strategy and Behavior* McGraw-Hill Irwin, New York
Carroll, A.B. & Buchholtz, A.K. (2009) *Business & Society : Ethics & Stakeholder Management* , Cengage Learning , Stamford, Connecticut
Schreck, P. (2009) *The Business Case for Corporate Social Responsibility: Understanding and Measuring Economic Impacts of Corporate Social Performanc e*. Physica Verlag, Heidelberg
Zerfass, A., Van Ruler, B., & Sriramesh, K. (Eds.) (2008). Public Relations Research. European and International Perspectives and Innovations. VS Verlag für Sozialwissenschaften, Wiesbaden

Internet:

Better Cotton Initiative (2012) about BCI BCI's continuing mission; available at:
    http://bettercotton.org/about-bci/#contentBox (04.2014)

Carroll, A.B. (1999) *Corporate Social Responsibility Evolution of a Definitional Construct*, BUSINESS
    & SOCIETY, Sage Publications, available at:
    http://www.academia.edu/419517/Corporate_Social_Responsibility_Evolution_of_a_Definiti
    onal_Construct (04.2014)

Hall, P. (2001). *The Carpet Slaves: Stolen Children of India.* available at:
    http://www.filmthreat.com/Reviews.asp?Id=1810 (04.2014)

IKEA (2000) *History of IKEA since 2000* available at:
    http://www.ikea.com/ms/de_DE/about_ikea/the_ikea_way/history/2000.html (05.2014)

IKEA (2003) *Social and Environmental Responsibility* available at: http://www.ikea-
    group.ikea.com/corporate/PDF/IKEA%20Report2003.pdf (04.2014)

Pientka, C. (2007) Online Newspaper Article *Baumwolle gepflückt von Kinderhand* available at:
    http://www.stern.de/lifestyle/mode/hm-produktebaumwolle-gepflueckt-von-kinderhand-
    603979.html (04.2014)

The Nike Foundation. *The Girl Effect: Adolescent girls are the most powerful force for change on the
    planet* available at http://girleffect.org (04.2014)

US Department of State (2005) Bureau of Democracy, Human Rights, and Labor *Uzbekistan* available at:
    http://www.state.gov/j/drl/rls/hrrpt/2004/41717.htm (05.2014)

Chapter 13
Value Alignment and Conflict Management

By: Daria Prause, Jatuporn Sungkhawan, Tipakorn Seanatip, and Bahaudin
G. Mujtaba

*During 2013 and 2014 years, many countries (Afghanistan, Pakistan, Thailand,
Nigeria, Syria, Iraq, Ukraine, etc.) have been experiencing protests at a scale which
we have not seen that often around the globe. Currently, thousands of people in
Pakistan have been protesting as they want their prime minister to step down. For
another example, during early 2014, a peaceful country such as Thailand was
trapped by the cycle of hurting itself as the opposing protesters planned to destroy
each other due to political differences. Similar to Pakistanis, Thais were protesting
as they were not happy with their elected prime minister. Between the supporters
and opponents of the previous Prime Minister Thaksin Shinawatra (red shirts and
yellow shirts), the protesting in Thailand became a prolonged crisis and chronic
economic pain on ordinary citizens until the Thai military stepped in to stop the
economic devastation on Thai people. Similarly, young girls going to school have
often become victims as means to an end for various political parties (often in
Afghanistan, Pakistan, Nigeria, and other locations). Unfortunately, such tragic
situations are likely to happen when people's values are not aligned with those of
the government's. As such, this chapter discusses value alignment as an important
ingredient for the education of all citizens and professionals in a country. Specific
cultural challenges facing females in some parts of Afghanistan and Pakistan are
presented as well. Finally, conflict management styles and skills are presented.*

Protests in Thailand[8]
At the beginning, many individuals in Thailand believed that the protests will not
last too long; however, the government tried to solve it, but their strategies seem to
have further prolonged the protests. The people of Thailand opposed the new
elections even before reformation took place in the last few months of 2013 and

---

[8] Contributed by Tipakorn Seanatip, Institute of International Studies; Ramkhamhaeng Univeristy.

initial months of 2014. Now, at the end of 2014, the military has taken over and is in charge of the government.

The effects of these protest for Thailand's economy is not too severe yet, when it is compared with other problems which exist in the country. For example, the flooding challenges in Bangkok a few years ago, the protesting of rubber gardeners in the southern part of Thailand, and the pledging rice project seem to have had a bigger impact on the foreign investor sentiment than ongoing political protests over the past year. However, based on what we see, the street protests remained active for many months in 2014, but the situation was not terrifying or dangerous when it is compared with other countries' protests which are a times very violent.

Thailand's anti-government protest leader Suthep Thaugsuban mobilized people to join the Bangkok shutdown by focusing on seven major spots in the capital, including the Government complex, but they did not block the airport and public transportation services as was done several years ago by the protestors. However, these protests did bring about a serious impact for tourism business which generates much revenue for the local economy and creates more than 1 million positions for Thai workers. Due to the protests, leaders in many countries warned tourists to avoid going to Thailand. Moreover, AIS Company, which is in the telecommunication and cell phone connection business, has experienced the impact of these protests as some customers have canceled their phone service because they believe that the previous Prime Minister's, Mr. Taksin Shinawatra, clan still has a relationship with this company. Many foreign investors do not dare to invest in the country as they would not be sure about the ending of these protests in Thailand. Consequently, prolonged protests could harm the economic growth of the country and decrease the quality of life for Thai citizens. Many are of the opinion now that changing the Prime Minister through prolonged protests and violence can delay the development of the economy, and growth would be much slower than neighboring countries such as Malaysia, Singapore, Vietnam, and the Philippines. Therefore, Thailand must remain politically stable in order to not lose the advantages being offered with the ASEAN Community trade agreement which will start in 2015.

The protestors not only ousted Yingluk Shinawatra from the position of Prime Minister, but they also would like to get rid of the Taksin regime and maintain the royal institution. Even though the previous Prime Minister Taksin lives aboard, he still has much influence in Thai politics through his sister and colleagues. Mr. Taksin's sister was the first female Prime Minister of Thailand, but many believed that her administration is a puppet of her brother who is still in charge of running the party. Moreover, many believed that the controversial legislation amnesty bill for the deposed former Prime Minister Thaksin Shinawatra to allow him to return from the self-imposed exile is the main issue of protesting. Many of the opposing people disapproved of this legislation. Furthermore, people want to discredit her government for failing to properly handle the crisis, which ended up expanding to various cities around Thailand. Nonetheless, having a female prime minister elected through a democratic process speaks volumes about the opportunities available to women in Thailand. Perhaps Thailand can serve as a good example of male-female equality through a democratic process.

The subsequent political and economic crisis is not inclusive of the 2 trillion bath loan project for the high speed train which has become a draining challenge for the people of Thailand. It is estimated that these challenges will bring about a large amount of public debt for more than 50 years on Thai people. Therefore, it is not a reasonable investment as only a selective group of people can reap the benefits of the high speed train project. The government should concern itself with how to thoroughly develop the country's infrastructure, how to solve the poverty problems, and how to effectively deal with the rising prices of various goods. As such, the people of Thailand need a leader who has such diverse abilities and knowledge to proactively and reactively cope with these problems and lift the Thai economy to a higher level while enhancing quality of life for the majority of its citizens. Perhaps the key to a peaceful country is to make sure the values of a country's citizens and their political leaders are aligned. The same is true for employees and their organizations.

Leading Common Value: Aligning You and Organization[9]
Recently, a colleague sent a complaint message through social media that "I am very bored now; I could not be patient anymore, my team is not listening to my teachings, my boss also assigns a lot of work to me only, it is not fair to me. I am very stressed and work unhappily. I would like to resign next year but I need to find out a new job first. Do you have any new job opportunities to recommend to me?" The key question is: why do we as workers sometimes lack motivation and engagement in dealing with a tough situation in a positive manner?

This is a tough question with many possibilities and reasons. One possible reason might be "comfort zone" that make people afraid and fearful to work beyond their scope. As such, they are scared of doing something more or differently from what they have been conditioned or socialized with during their orientation. Another possible reason might be that the attitude is an answer; but what kind of attitude would keep people motivated and engaged in a positive manner with their workplace? Regardless of the reason or answers, the challenge is to figure out how to move them from the feeling of comfort or secure area of life to the uncomfortable and more challenging areas of personal and work life. In other words, they have to be engaged in doing things differently but must align their personal and professional goals to have high levels of motivation for the achievement of high performance.

From years of consulting and executive coaching experiences, we have found that most such cases come from the lacking of alignment for the need between the organization and the employee. The organization needs to achieve the financial stability, higher market share, more customer satisfaction, internal process improvement, and they need capable and engaged employees. The employee needs life security, taking care of family, to be an entrepreneur, social recognition,

---

[9] Contributed by Jatuporn Sungkhawan, International Advisory Associates; Bangkok, Thailand.

freedom or autonomy to think and act based on his/her learning and experience. Without an aligning of both organization and individual needs, it is difficult to achieve both goals. In order to create self-engagement and sustain motivation you need to consider the following alignment approach.

Vision aligning

Most organizations have a vision and mission which are supported by strategic goals around financial, customer retention, internal process efficiency, and human capital in order to provide direction and drive the organization and their workforce. However, many of us cannot see the relationship to self, and, furthermore, it should be noted that some employees are highly satisfied with their jobs and are at a comfort zone; therefore, they do not have a personal vision and goal for any further professional achievements.

Why do we need to think about our vision and goal?

This is a question that some employees and managers never think about. Same as the organization we also need to set our direction as a vision and individual strategic goals around career, growth, wealth, health, family, etc. These goals keep us motivated, and we know what we live for; then we can spend time and energy toward the right destination and on the most important things which would achieve our individual strategic goals.

How to align our individual vision and organizational vision

Many of us have recognized both organizational strategic goals and individual strategic goals but cannot always align them. For example your personal goal is to achieve the family happiness and growth without thinking about the organizational strategic goals. You might concentrate time and energy on the family issues more than work. You may not want to transfer or move from the family, and there might be a lack of motivation and engagement to achieve the organization vision and goals. But you need to think of the other side of coin and work hard with intrinsic motivation and be fully accountable to achieve the organization's vision and strategic goals. The consequences of this aligning action are to strengthen personal competency and to get promotion and to earn more money and reputation. These will contribute to personal goals by adding more value to the family such as being a role model for the kids, being able to support them in term of financial and higher level of networking, and being able to coach with different more innovative perspective

The self-alignment model is presented to include more than vision aligning, it also explains how to develop and align the transferable competencies that include knowledge, skills, values, and behaviors to achieve your personal goals.

IAA Self Alignment Model

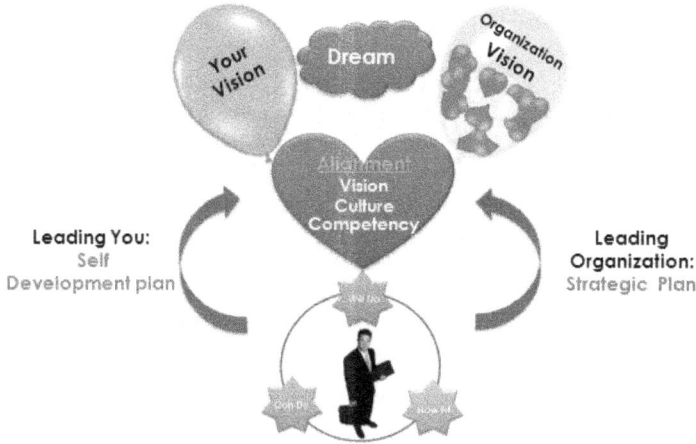

Figure 13.1- IAA Self Alignment Model
©International Advisory Associates Co., Ltd.

Table 13.1 – Application of the Alignment Model in a Hotel

| | Vision | Values and Culture | Competency | |
			Skills	Knowledge
Hotel	Be a five star hotel that delighting the stakeholder	• Work as a team • Customer focus • Continuous development	• Customer service • Emphatic communication	• Food and beverages • Customer behavior • Charming Personality
Alignment	Delighting customer	• Customer service • Team work	• Service expertise	• Customer behavior • Personality
Employee	Dream to be the owner of beauty Salon that be the first choice of customer	• Service mind • Customer first • Collaboration	• Service ability • Beauty salon	• Hair style design • Customer profile • Personality

From Table 13.1 model, we can see that while the employee works at the hotel he or she has to motivate and engage himself or herself to develop and always practice the required kills of good customer service; the consequence of doing this can cause the customer to be very satisfied with his/her stay at the hotel. At the same time the employee is practicing good customer service with a great smile to eventually achieve his/her own dream goals.

So let us align the self and organization for more productivity, and to work more happily. By aligning between self and the organization, we can avoid getting in working trap of feeling like we are the victim. We can get out from victim mode and be the victor of our own life. This victory model and attitude should be taught to both male and female professionals so they can serve their society to the best of their abilities.

Gender Alignment Challenges in some South Asian Countries

Cultural values must also align with religious values to make sure both males and females are treated with respect and dignity; otherwise, conflicts will continue to exist. While Islam has provided clear guidelines for both men and women, there are some cultural practices in Afghanistan and Pakistan that have created challenges for the growth or education of women. While the number of young girls going to school in Afghanistan and Pakistan has increased in the last few decades, there are still a minority of individuals in society who believe their daughters should not be educated. This view is partially culture-based and to some extent due to the insecurity of political climate which is still present at times in Afghanistan and Pakistan, as well as some other countries. In the rural cities, due to dangers faced by young girls like that which was endured by the 2014 Nobel Prize winner Mallala Yusefzia and others, some girls are less interested in schooling because of their families' reluctance to have them educated and/or the shortage of schools in their villages (Mujtaba, 2007). The government officials, and many of the local school administrators, have launched a promotion to entice children to attend school despite the fact that they face some parents who do not want to send their daughters to be educated mostly due to safety concerns in the environment. In some cases, young kids (both boys and girls) do not go to school because of rules and policies that require certain books and uniforms. For example, a ten-year-old girl, Nahida, stopped going to school and said: "My father died last year and the teacher told me to wear a black uniform, but we could not afford it." There are nearly millions of Afghan boys and girls attending school, and out of these 30 percent are girls. However, approximately one million Afghan girls, in the seven to thirteen age ranges, have been deprived of an education for various reasons. Yet, since late 2001, the number of Afghan girls and boys going to school has quadrupled. One of main reasons for girls not attending school is because they have no sufficient and well-equipped school facilities. It is very difficult for young boys and girls to study under torn tents in the freezing cold weather. Many officials believe the reason more girls do not come to school is because of the weak economy, insecurity and the lack of investment in the schooling system.

Another major problem facing young women that get married is the fact that they are often alone for many years with their in-laws without much support from the husband. For example, Fatima's husband has been working abroad for nearly eight years to support their family and four children. Fatima only sees her husband every two years. Added to this challenge of having a distant husband is the fact that women have to defend themselves in the family disputes and quarrels. Fatima says: "I am harassed by my in-laws when my husband is abroad...My husband is like a protector and a guardian and when this protection is not there I become vulnerable" (Babukarkhail, 2004...as cited in Mujtaba, 2007). It has been a tradition for many Afghans to travel to far away countries in search of earning money and economic stability. Some leave their wives at home to take care of the kids and stay away for years to be able to send money home to their families. Yes, some travel abroad to earn money for their dowry, which is a gift of money or valuables given by the groom's family to the bride before the wedding can take place. Dowry is a cultural tradition that is still being practiced by some families. Hopefully this practice, in its current format, will hopefully soon disappear in all areas of the country. Sometimes, young males get into debt after having to pay out huge amounts towards their dowry, as requested by the bride's family.

Unfortunately, the necessity to work abroad in order to save money for a dowry has created huge social pressures for family life, especially for some young men and women. Some men are stressed because they often have to earn large amounts of money before they can get married, and women face other challenges as a result of such practices. Of course, most women would feel unhappy when their husbands leave them for long periods of time to work in foreign countries. This loneliness and separation can lead a young person to depression. The other sad element is that some in-laws may treat the new brides as domestic servants which can be a huge blow to one's self-confidence...further leading to worse cases of depression. There have been reports of newly married women trying to kill themselves by taking poison or trying to shoot themselves. Sadly, a newly-married girl's life gets worse when she has to live with her in-laws, under such bad conditions, without her husband. So, Afghan and Pakistani males have to be careful, and plan accordingly to not leave their wives by themselves in a bad environment when possible. While some women may complain to the family elders or to the government officials, there are perhaps thousands of women who are in the same situation as Fatima, but only a handful are courageous enough to come forward and talk about their situation. Many young people today disagree with the dowry system, and believe the tradition was imposed many centuries ago by "other" foreign cultures. Many say that they are unhappy about the "bride price" imposed by some elders. Many young men tend to say that "The bride price is too high in our area so we are forced to go abroad to work." Some believe that the custom of demanding a "high" dowry for women is rooted in values of an uneducated society: "In comparison to most of our women the men are ignorant and they impose such strict values in the name of religion" (Mujtaba, 2007, p. 175).

Reports, according to some relief workers, confirm that the number of Afghan women committing suicide and setting fire to themselves because they cannot bear their lives has risen dramatically in the last decade. Furthermore, it is estimated that more than 50% of all marriages in Afghanistan are now "arranged." The term "arranged marriages," for adult males and females, usually implies that the male's family or representative initiates or makes a request (the occasion is known as khaustgaurrie) to the female's father, mother or other family members for her hand in a marriage to the designated "boy" or "groom to be." Once the request has been made, then the girl's family is supposed to speak with her to see if she wishes to be married at this time and whether she wants to marry this "boy" or not. If she agrees, then, and only then, the girl's family will give candy to the boy's family, implying that they can be engaged to be married. Depending on how well the two families know each other this process might take from a few weeks to several months before the girl's family says "yes" or "no" to the request. If the girl wants to marry someone else or is expecting another family to make a request for her hand in marriage to their son, then she will respectfully decline the request by saying "no" or the fact that she is not ready to get married at this time as she wants to continue her education or take care of her mom, dad or an elderly grandparent. In areas where educational facilities and opportunities are not available, most girls tend to get married at a younger age, provided that they are healthy. In many cases, girls are engaged and married off around the age of 18, some older and some younger. Unfortunately, in some cases, a good number of the "arranged marriages," that are not to the satisfaction of the girl or bride are to settle debts or feuds between family members or even tribes. Despite the fact that this is not a cultural or religious intention, such acts cause "women" to be regarded as commodities rather than wives, sisters, and mothers. Due to such perceptions, conditioning and a few abusive men, some women are treated like slave workers by their families and husbands. Since many are not able to attend schools, they remain uneducated and their only options are limited to bearing children, taking care of the children, and/or doing house chores. While household chores or taking care of children are good tasks for both males and females, what makes women stressed and depressed is the manner in which some males treat them. The fact is that over 300 Afghan schools were burnt down in 2006 or simply closed after threats from opposition groups, leaving hundreds and thousands of students nowhere to go for an education. Such insecurity is not limited to children and girls as adult women are also negatively impacted. Due to security reasons, the overwhelming majority of women in Afghanistan and Pakistan are still encouraged to cover their entire bodies and faces. As a matter-of-fact, even the United Nations personnel had supposedly circulated a memo to all their staff in Afghanistan, advising women to cover their heads in Kabul (most likely for security reasons).

In a male-dominated society with difficult conditions present, professional women are against a "tide" that will require major forces to block and overcome as officials search for equality and synergy. Many professionals are often shocked by the lack of basic development when visiting Afghanistan or some Pakistani schools. Even the universities and ministerial offices are not up to par, lacking basic necessities. According to some experts, there is a huge gap between the reality on the ground and the "remarkable progress" claimed by most western diplomats who sit in fortified compounds behind guards and concrete blocks. So there has to be a passionate and consistent effort on the part of all leaders in countries such as

Afghanistan and Pakistan to align current practices with true religious and international human rights for the education of both male and female candidates in all areas around the country.

Conflict Management Skills for a Diverse Workplace[10]

The goal of this section is to look into conflict management practices and strategies for a diverse workplace. Diversity of the workforce, especially females in the workplace working alongside men, is a reality of life in almost all countries nowadays. Even in South Asia's Afghanistan and Pakistan, globalization has led to many males and females migrating to countries all over the world to seek personal development, better market opportunities and new challenges. Today's workplace is a melting pot of diverse individuals and it has increased the requirements of conflict management skills training. We discuss conflict management for effectively solving personal and organizational conflicts.

In classical approach to conflict, it was believed that any conflict was about negotiable interests only. According to this point of view, an individual should be socialized to resolve the conflict and might as well be punished for the lack of socialization or negotiation on the problem. While using the above stated approach, people came to realize that basic human needs cannot be negotiated as they provide security, personal identity and physiological satisfaction which in their turn depend on the socio-economic, gender, nationality, and other traits (Birkhoff, 1998, para. 4).

It has been said that "Organizations are collections of people who work together and coordinate their actions to achieve a wide variety of goals or desired future outcomes" (Jones and George, 2014, p. 5). A good manager should provide possibilities for his/her employees to coordinate and cooperate within the organization, regardless of gender or cultural differences. It means that they need to plan, organize, lead and control of human and other resources to achieve organizational goals effectively and efficiently without the dysfunctional conflicts or the "glass ceilings" obstacles. Conflict management begins with the understanding that people see things differently and might not be equipped with the same information about the situation or issue (Weiner, 2011). Of course, being trusted and transparent in conflicts is vital in achieving high organizational performance. Today's managers know that cultural awareness in a key component to effectively managing work tension and bring the efficiency of human resources up. On the organizational stage, the manager ought to establish good relationships that allow people to work together without causing any tension or dysfunctional conflicts. It includes the tasks of leading, motivating, and coordinating team members to work together and understand each other.

---

[10] Contributed by Daria Prause, Nova Southeastern University.

Conflict Types

Some people consider conflict as fighting, although it is important to realize that there are other sides to conflict. Oxford Dictionary (2010) sees conflict as conditions in which one or more persons might experience a clash of opposing wishes or needs. In conflict, we can see that the main idea is the opposing opinion or concern of one person towards the actions, thoughts or words within his or her circle.

Conflict is the struggle that results when two or more individuals perceive a difference or incompatibility in their interests, values, or goals (Mujtaba, 2014, p. 244). Conflicts can arise from ambiguous roles and goals, stereotypes, biases, different procedures, distribution of resources, irreconcilable differences, perception of information and personalities, and the structures in place. In a diverse workplace, every interaction has a potential for conflict. Some conflict is good for team performance. Too much conflict causes team leaders to spend much time responding to it. *Conflict management* is the process of dealing with conflict in an effective manner. Positive conflict (conflict that is managed effectively) is great for team performance, and negative conflict can be very hurtful.

Conflict can consist of many components (Behrman, 2012, para. 2; Mujtaba, 2014, p. 245). Number one is disagreement or differences in the position of the parties participating in the conflict. For the issue to emerge, a misunderstanding or discrepancy in the opinions or needs would take place. When two or more people have diverse opinions of one scenario the disagreement appears. A vivid example of disagreement can be points of view on job responsibilities from the employee's and supervisor's points of view. Sometimes managers can ask for additional tasks to be done as a part of organizational team performance which might be considered as inappropriate or out of line. For the disagreement to arise parties take different sides according to their beliefs, values and needs. Parties are the second component of any conflict, be it at a workplace or in social settings. It is important to recognize all the parties in order to successfully solve the conflicting issue. Third constituent of any conflict is the needs, beliefs, interests and concerns of the parties. According to Maslow's pyramid of needs, each human being possesses basic or physiological need such as breathing, eating and sleeping, which influences one's behaviors in life. The basic needs are accompanied by safety, love or belonging, esteem and self-actualization (Maslow, 1943, pp. 81-86) which are required to be met for a human being to feel integrity and safety. The fourth component is perceived threat which determines people's actions and their position in the conflict. In reality, perceived threat might not be the same as the real threats they confront; thus people's behavior could be modified inappropriately (Behrman, 2012, para. 3).

A low level of emotional intelligence, which is "ability to understand and manage one's own moods and emotions and the moods and emotions of other people" (Jones and George, 2014, p. 82), might worsen the conflict as people express thoughts they never wished to be revealed or when someone acts "in a fit of temper" by threatening to take some action.

Here, the main focus is on the conflict at a diverse workplace or organizational conflict. Organizational conflict is "the discord that arises when the goals, interests or values of different individuals or groups are incompatible and those individuals or groups block or thwart one another's attempts to achieve their objectives" (Jones and George, 2014, p. 532). Organizational conflicts are at times due to diversity of workers and their views.

We can define diversity as "acknowledging, understanding, accepting, valuing, and celebrating differences among people with respect to age, class, ethnicity, gender, physical and mental ability, race, sexual orientation, spiritual practice, and public assistance status" (Green, López, Wysocki, Kepner, 2002, para. 4). Workplace diversity implies focusing on the dissimilarities of people at a workplace. If well managed and organized, a diverse workplace can be a good force and provide an organization with productive partnership, creativity, wider possibility for recruitment and increased productivity. "Diversity is often interpreted to include dimensions which influence the identities and perspectives that people bring, such as profession, education, parental status and geographic location" (Woods, Borman, 2010, para. 1). Some team members can be focused on their children's education; others draw more attention to their cultural site, thus managers should motivate and organize their teams accordingly. Getting people of diverse cultures to work together as a productive team is extremely difficult as it can cause fraction and collision of cultures (Scrumpeter's notebook about Chua's paper, 2014, para. 5). On the other hand, others state that "well mitigated differences can actually strengthen team cohesion" (Lundrigan, Tangsuvanich, Yu, Wu and Mujtaba, 2012, p. 2).

Well-resolved conflict can give the organization benefits that were not expected, including an increased understanding among colleagues due to the discussion needed to resolve the conflict. The discussion could expand people's awareness on how to achieve goals and understanding without "undermining those of other people" (Mankletow, Carlson, 2005, para. 5). Another outcome of effective conflict resolution is increased group cohesion with mutual respect and "renewed faith in their ability to work together" (Mankletow and Carlson, 2005, para. 6) as well as improved self-knowledge and understanding the values of their own.

The supervisors' and managers' personal characteristics play an important role in the group cohesion and understanding. Attraction-Selection-Attrition (ASA) framework "explains how personalities may influence organizational culture" as managers or founders "hire employees…whose personalities are similar to their own" (Jones and George, 2014, p. 85); this forms a special team cohesion and shared values, and may cause to outcast the employees who are different in age, gender, origin or socio-economic factors.

Managers of a diverse workplace where a conflict is taking place need to recognize the need for decision in effectively resolving this dilemma by generating relevant alternatives and choosing a strategy for conflict management. Managers can then assess the alternatives to recognize the advantages and disadvantages of each of them and choose the best alternative to deal with the situation. After implementing the alternative it is always important to collect feedback to evaluate the outcomes of chosen alternatives. Management commitment is important in tracing any conflicts or discrimination on diversity. "Top managers need to develop ethical values and performance or business oriented attitudes" to make the use of their human resources (Jones and George, 2014, p. 153). Accuracy of perception and diversity awareness give individuals opportunity to modify behavior and attitudes which leads to increase diversity skills, better interaction and healthier work environment.

Conflict Management Strategies

Historically, conflict management strategies evaluated from a basic face-negotiation theory by Ting-Toomey (1988) and competing theory among team members to manage intergroup conflict by Cohen and Ledford (1994) to the well-known Thomas and Killman's 5 model strategy (1974). Thomas and Kilmann defined five modes for responding to conflict situations which are used by managers in decision making process (Mujtaba, 2014, p. 246).

1. *Competing* is when an individual pursues his/her own concerns at the other person's expense (Kilman, 2007, para. 5). This mode can be described as forcing and using a formal authority or power one possesses to satisfy their own wishes and desires. A party should act in a very assertive way without any cooperation which might be necessary for emergency or time sensitive situations. Ethical dilemma is likely to occur in this type of conflict strategy as one of the parties could find it difficult to act in a way that helps the organization or others as it goes against his or her principles and interests.

2. *Accommodating* is when the individual neglects his/her own concerns in favor of some other person. This type of conflict solving technique appears when parties cooperate very well and one of the members is an expert in the given situation, thus is able to provide a better solution even if it works against somebody else's goals and desired outcomes.

3. *Avoiding* is when the person neither pursues his/her own concerns nor those of the other individual (Kilman, 2007, para. 8). This type of situation takes place when one of the parties doesn't want to participate in the conflict and pays no attention to it. It might happen when one of the parties has no interest in the conflict, doesn't wish to win the argument or emotionally unwilling to create any tension, hoping that the situation would pass by.

4. *Compromising* resolves the conflict with partial satisfaction of both parties. Sadly, neither party gets all of what he or she wants but they settle in the middle through compromise in order to move on.

5. *Collaborating* implies working together to find a solution that satisfies parties. The definition of collaboration in many dictionaries can be summed up as cooperation with the other party to express and hear concerns in the effort to find a mutually satisfactory outcome. It is also

called a "win-win" scenario which is possible when one takes in to the consideration wishes of all parties, broadens the frames of usual solutions, and analyses all of the ideas to create absolutely new and fresh outcome.

These conflict tactics can also be classified into three general groups: "integration (working with people), distributive (working against people), and avoidance (working away from other people)" (Cupach and Canary, 1997). The ultimate goals of any conflict managing technique are to create a positive and conflict free atmosphere at the work place, find a better solution to a problem, and provide long life for the organization and teams in it.

Quickly and effectively resolving such conflicts can speed up the team's progress toward achieving its purpose (performance challenge). When dealing with day-to-day conflicts, misconducts, and disagreements, remember to use the 4-F model by emphasizing the facts, feelings, future expectations, and following up (Mujtaba, 2014, p. 247).

➢ *Facts*. Stick with the facts and describe the behavior that is creating the problem or conflict. Avoid attacking the other person. Avoid using "you" statements.

➢ *Feelings*. State the impact of the problem or conflict, your feelings, the feelings of team members, and how the problem makes the team suffer. Use "I" statements by mentioning how the above mentioned problem or fact impacts you or your employees and colleagues.

➢ *Future expectations*. Clearly describe future expectations, norms, and rules of conduct.

➢ *Following up*. Managers should follow up with the parties involved to make sure employees are meeting the expected standards as agreed. If they are, then the manager has an opportunity to reinforce this good behavior. Otherwise, the manager will have another opportunity to start the process again (or take drastic actions as appropriate).

When conflicts exist, all team members must persist on behavior change until it is changed so the team can effectively proceed with its objective. In most organizations, it clearly becomes imperative for managers to be able to address and effectively resolve conflicts. Also, when confronted with an ethical conflict in a culturally diverse organization, it is important for a manager to be capable of recognizing the key factors in order to determine the most appropriate strategy.

Summary
This chapter emphasized that employees and managers must focus on the alignment of their values with the organizations where they work. If employees are not happy, they are not going to be motivated to work as best as they can. Similar value alignments must be made by politicians if they are truly working for the people who

voted them into leading positions. As such, value alignment becomes important for the proper functioning of an organization and society.

Notwithstanding 21st century society advances and huge number of different researches on conflict management and legal codes that promote healthy work environment at diverse workplaces, our society still faces significant challenges in managing diverse work environments, especially gender conflicts. Diversity education, conflict management training, and development of creative thinking and open mind can benefit modern companies in their fierce competition in the market and be the crucial step in creating competitive firms with a strong human resources component.

References

Avrich K., Mitchel C. (2013). *Conflict Resolution and Human Need: Linking Theory and Practice.* Routledge.

Behrman H.W. (2012). *Confronting and Conflict Resolution.* Office of Quality Improvement and HR Development in University of Wisconsin-Madison. Retrieved on August 17, from http://www.ohrd.wisc.edu/onlinetraining/resolution/aboutwhatisit.htm.

Birkhoff J. E. (1998). *The Conflict Resolution Syllabi Sampler.* Wine State University and William Waters. Retrieved August 24, from http://www.campus-adr.org/Classroom_Building/content/brief_history_of_cr_studies/.

Birkhoff J.E. (2001). *Gender, Conflict and Conflict Resolution.* Mediate Co. Retrieved on September 11, 2014, from http://www.mediate.com/articles/birkhoff.cfm.

Carter S. B. (2011). *Gender Wars Not Only Create Conflict Among Women, They Create Significant Workplace Stress.* Phycology Today. High Octane Women (11, 2011), p. 15. Retrieved on September 11, 2014, from http://www.psychologytoday.com/blog/high-octane-women/201111/gender-wars-not-only-create-conflict-among-women-they-create-significa.

Double-Bind Dilemma for Women in Leadership: Damned if You Do, Doomed if You Don't. (2007). Catalyst. New York.

Citation [Def. 1] in Oxford Dictionary online. Retrieved August 9, 2014, from http://www.oxforddictionaries.com/us/definition/american_english/conflict.

Citation [Def. 2] in Wikipedia. Retrieved September 8, 2014, from http://en.wikipedia.org/wiki/Gender_role.

Cupach, W. R., Canary, D. J., & Spitzberg, B. H. (2010). *Competence in interpersonal conflict* (2nd ed.). Long Grove, IL: Waveland.

Dickinson J.B. (2013). *An examination of multi-dimensional channel conflict: a proposed experimental approach.* Journal of Behavioral Studies in Business, vol. 6. Retrieved August 26, 2014, from http://www.aabri.com/manuscripts/121244.pdf.

Eisenhardt K., Kahwajy J., Bourgeois L.J. III (1997). *How Management Teams Can Have a Good Fight.* Harvard Business Review Blog. Retrieved August 17, 2014, from http://hbr.org/1997/07/how-management-teams-can-have-a-good-fight/ar/1.

Green K. A., López M., Wysocki A., Kepner K. (2002). *Diversity in the Workplace: Benefits, Challenges, and the Required Managerial Tools.* University of Florida, HR# 022. Retrieved on August 26, 2014, from http://edis.ifas.ufl.edu/hr022.

Genovese F. Interview from August 20, 2014.

Holt, J.L. and DeVore, C. J. (2005). Culture, gender, organizational role, and styles of conflict resolution: A meta-analysis. *International Journal of Intercultural Relations*, 29(2), pp. 165-196.

Jones G. R., George J. M. (2014). *Contemporary Management, 8th edition.* McGraw Hill, New York.

Lundrigan M., Tangsuvanich V., Yu L., Wu S. and Mujtaba B. (2012). Coaching a Diverse Workforce: The Impact of Changing Demographics for Modern Leaders. *International Journal of Humanities and Social Science,* 2(3), pp. 2. Retrieved August 18, 2014, from http://www.ijhssnet.com/journals/Vol_2_No_3_February_2012/6.pdf.

*Man*kletow J., Carlson A. (2005). *Conflict Resolution. Resolving Conflict Rationally and Effectively.* Retrieved August 27, 2014, from http://www.mindtools.com/pages/article/newLDR_81.htm.

Maslow, A. H. (1943) *Conflict, frustration, and the theory of threat. Journal of Abnormal and Social Psychology*, 38, pp. 81-86.

Michelman P., Corkindale G. (2007). *How to manage conflict.* Harvard Business Review Blog. HBR IdeaCast. Retrieved August 17, 2014, from http://blogs.hbr.org/2007/11/harvard-business-ideacast-71-h/.

Mitchel R., Rosemoor D. (2001). Why Good Leaders Can't Use Good Advice. *Journal of Leadership Studies*, 8(2), pp.79-105.

Mujtaba, B. G. (2014). *Managerial Skills and Practices for Global Leadership.* ILEAD Academy: Florida.

Mujtaba B. G. (2007). *The ethics of management and leadership in Afghanistan* (2nd ed.). ILEAD Academy: Florida.

Mujtaba, B. G. (2007a). *Afghanistan: Realities of war and rebuilding (2nd edition).* LEAD Academy, LLC, Florida; United States.

Pay Equity and Discrimination. (2013) Institute for Women's Policy Research. Retrieved on September 8, 2014, from http://www.iwpr.org/initiatives/pay-equity-and-discrimination.

Pohlman, Randolph A. & Gardiner, Gareth S. (2000). Value-Driven Management: How to Create and Maximize Value over Time for Organizational Success. New York: American Management Association.

Thomas K. W., Kilmann R. H. (1974, 2007). *Thomas-Kilmann Conflict Mode Instrument.* Mountain View, CA: CPP Inc, Partly retrieved on August 18, 2014, from http://www.kilmanndiagnostics.com/overview-thomas-kilmann-conflict-mode-instrument-tki.

Thomas K.W. (2006). *Making conflict management a strategic advantage.* Retrieved August 20, 2014, from http://www.psychometrics.com/docs/conflictwhitepaper_psychometrics.pdf.

Thomas K. W., Thomas G. F. (2008). Conflict styles of men and women at 6 organizational levels. *International Journal of Conflict Management*, 14(2), 01-12.

Scrumpeter's notebook (2014). *Downside of Diversity.* [Review of the article The Costs of Ambient Cultural Disharmony: Indirect Intercultural Conflict in Social Environment Undermine Creativity by Chua R. Y. J.]. Retrieved on August 16, 2014, from http://www.economist.com/blogs/schumpeter/2014/01/schumpeters-notebook.

Weiner J. (2011). *Conflict Resolution.* Wall Street Journal Interview. Retrieved August 16, 2014, from http://live.wsj.com/video/linkedin-ceo-on-conflict-resolution/D5B8A41F-D492-47C9-A110-4BB1F24366AC.html#!D5B8A41F-D492-47C9-A110-4BB1F24366AC

Woods. S, Borman T., Schmidle D. (2010) *Workplace Diversity.* Cornel University, ILR School. Retrieved August 20, 2014 from http://www.ilr.cornell.edu/library/research/subjectguides/workplacediversity.html.

Chapter 14
Dynasties and the Iranian Culture

By: Navid Reza Ahadi[11] and Bahaudin G. Mujtaba

This chapter is a short review of the Iranian culture as well as historical changes and development in Iran. The chapter provides a discussion of industrialization in Iran after medieval age. The section also includes how males and females have played an important role in shaping the Iranian culture and the process of modernization. Discussions include improvements of the education system in the country from Safavid Dynasty period. Safavid Dynasty ruled Iran from 1501 to 1736 all the way to the last monarchy (Pahlavi dynasty) until establishment of Islamic Republic of Iran in 1979.

Introduction
Iran is a country that has gone through major changes as most countries in the region to adopt international culture and suit the society in such a way to be part of cultural exchanges and globalization. People want to improve and experience modernization as well as the process of adopting modern education system for both genders. As discussed in this chapter, Iran has gone through at least 600 years of history after medieval age; and this chapter shows how it struggled to integrate culturally all the way to the last monarchy of Iran where women have had good opportunities for education.

The culture of Iran is made up diverse traditions and practices. Today, Iranian workers are made up of younger and older individuals, men and women, as well as professionals with some and many years of management experience (Tajaddini, Mujtaba and Bandenezhad, 2009). Iran was formerly known as Persia until 1935 and it is home to one of the world's oldest continuous major civilizations. Culturally speaking, based on Hofstede's 1980 findings, Iran is classified in near

---

[11] King Mongkut's Institute of Technology – Latrabang. Some of this content was originally published as follows and integrated here with the permission of the author: Ahadi, N. R. (2014). The Rules of Dynasties to Shape Iranian Culture, Society Education System and People's Struggle to Integrate with International Culture after Medieval Age. *International Journal of Technical Research and Applications*, 2(1), 41-44.

Eastern cluster, including Turkey and Greece. However, in a more recent research conducted through GLOBE project, Iran is considered to be part of the South Asian cultural cluster consisting of such countries as Afghanistan, Pakistan, India, Thailand and Malaysia. These findings may seem very different from the image of Iran as a predominant Islamic/Middle-Eastern country which is often confused with its neighbors. Iran has many commonalities with neighboring Muslim countries; however, due to its unique historical, linguistic, and racial identities it has a different and unique culture.

The nationalist aspect of Iranian culture is related to Ancient Persian civilization and Zoroastrianism heritage which date 3000-2000 BC and are still prevalent in the society. On the other hand, Islamic traditions also continue to play to their significant role in the Iranian society. Iran has the largest population in, and is one of the largest countries of, the Middle East. As a result of the 1979 Islamic revolution, Iran went from being perceived as one of the most modern and Westernized countries of the Middle East, to being regarded as a fundamentalist Islamic country. Before the 1979 revolution, Iran underwent modernization as a direct consequence of the former Iranian monarch's policies. The ensuing Islamic revolution overthrew a 2,500-year-old history of monarchy and replaced it with an Islamic Republic. This revolution changed the entire structure of the country as well as that of workforces. Technocrats were replaced by ideologists, and a competent and skilled workforce was replaced with a loyal workforce.

In 1980, the Iraqi invasion of Iran led to a devastating eight-year war between the two countries. After the war, in the 1990s, Iran started an era of reconstruction, trying to move beyond a war economy and opening its doors to a market economy. From the 1990s to the present day, Iran's political and economic environment evidenced the struggle to maintain a balance between religious ideology and economic prosperity. One growing challenge is the demography of Iran. Approximately 70 percent of Iran's population is under the age of 30, thus putting great pressure on the country to provide education and employment opportunities in order to maintain social stability. This also leads to a high rate of unemployment, which stands nearly at 11 percent, although unofficially the figure is estimated at roughly 20 percent. Moreover, the brain drain is another factor which restricts economic development of the country.

The Iranian culture is deep rooted in traditions with a strong emphasis on cultural institutions, such as religion and family. In-group orientation is one of the distinguishing features of the Iranian culture, which suggests loyalty and cohesiveness towards small groups such as family and close friends. For example, this influence of local culture on personnel practices, with its focus on pre-existing relationships and nepotism that take precedence over skills and competencies, can be seen especially in recruitment and selection, performance management and compensation. Under some circumstances, favoritism may be regarded even as a positive or humane act toward friends, family and acquaintance.

Iran is considered as a collectivist country and, as a result, communication is implicit and high-context. Persian language and literature are full of nuance and metaphors which should be interpreted in their context and cannot be taken at face value.

Today, Iranian women are in the forefront of many changes in their country. The majority of Iranian women are primarily responsible for domestic tasks. Although the status of women at home depends on their social class, the majority of Iranian women are responsible for housekeeping, childcare, and all other aspects of running a home. Thus, employed women must bear much pressure from home and work responsibilities. Despite the existing role pressures that women confront in Iran, the number of women participating in the workplace is increasing steadily (Tajaddini, Mujtaba and Bandenezhad, 2009). The increase in women's economic activity in recent decades is related to the growing number of educated women, along with financial pressures and the increasing need for women's income-generating activities. Nowadays, Iranian women participate in most fields of work and education. In addition, many women are determined to realize their talents and capabilities in line with new ideas of gender equality and women's rights. Nevertheless, there are still debates in Iran about the probable conflicts between women's traditional and modern roles and their consequences. Women's lives in Iran are still highly influenced by the behavior and attitudes of the men around them, like their fathers or husbands. Furthermore, there are additional difficulties and barriers in the labor market at the wider societal level, such as employers' preferences for male employees and formal or informal job-segregation policies, which practically limit women's employment participation. It is anticipated that only 20–25% of Iranian college-educated women join the labor force and their participation at the managerial level is just 13% (Jamali and Nejati, 2009).

On the other hand, various surprising transformations are undergoing in the Iranian society. Nowadays, the structure of 'the family' has changed radically in Iran. The men are not the only "breadwinners" anymore, and women share the procurement of livelihood. This means that women actively pursue further education to lead to better career prospects. Furthermore, similar to many developed nations, Iranian women make up more than 60 percent of university entrants. All these changes have led women to participate more in the public domain and progress into the managerial ranks. Nowadays, it is easy to find city and town councilwomen, even in the country's rural areas. Several members of parliament are selected among women and recently, a 50 year old gynecologist became Iran's first woman cabinet member since the Islamic revolution, as the health minister (Tajaddini, Mujtaba and Bandenezhad, 2009). While the Persian culture has a rich history of literature and poetry, we will explore some of the dynasties which have influenced the Iranian culture of the past several centuries.

Safavid Dynasty

A pivotal point in the creation of modern Iranian national identity and culture was the Safavid dynasty. After a Moghul invasion, Iran was divided into few smaller countries, each of these ruling a part of Iran, but it wasn't until the Safavid dynasty, under the leadership of Shah Ismail, when all of these smaller territories united under the national identity of Iran. At the same time, Shah Ismail declared himself "king of kings" of the newly formed Iranian country, thus creating the environment from which most of the cultural developments of the modern Iranian identity stem from.

The Safavid dynasty heavily influenced the character and identity of the Iranian culture, affecting everything from the religious to the social aspects of the country. Not long after the establishment of the Safavid Empire, under the rule of Shah Ismail the 1st period of deep social and religious changes began which had far reaching consequences extending beyond the physical borders of the newly established country. One of the most influential steps taken by the dynasty, was the official decision to make Shia the state religion of Iran, a defiant move to the growing regional geopolitical and military influence of the Ottoman empire, who by this point in history had conquered the rest of the middle east, leaving Iran as the last eastern power (in the area) with the power to stop their implacable advance. This religious declaration was not only viewed as a way to clearly differentiate themselves from the Sunni Ottomans. It was also the perfect opportunity to gain support and influence from a vast area of surrounding territories, which also refused to be engulfed by the Ottoman Empire. Communities from Anatolia (supporting alawit and shiaghezelbash which supported Safavid dynasty), Iraq, Caucuses and Kurdistan all quickly identified themselves with Iran's movement before the impending advance of the Ottomans, leading to a more unified front of Shia resistance.

There was another very important aspect which the new Safavid dynasty understood was of uttermost importance before they could truly stand up the Ottoman's power, they had to modernize their military power. In order to solve this, it was decided stronger ties with western powers, especially England and Spain, was the best way to obtain greater military knowledge. Both Spain and England also feared the growing Ottoman influence in the Middle East, specially their powerful and growing armies, it made a lot of sense to support Iran in the face of a common enemy. Through these ties, which were pursued by many kings, such as Shah Abbas, Iran achieved impressive military feats, including the recovery of many islands and ports across the Persian Gulf from Portuguese occupation. Furthermore, through the increased interaction with the international community, Iran managed to attract the opening of many embassies, business from around the globe started to flow into the country as nations across Europe (and as far east as India) started to gain great interest in Iran's resources and the fact it could act as a very effective bridge between central Asia and the middle east.

Apart from helping to modernize their military, the capital investment was put into developing the country's infrastructure, it went into building roads, buildings, with the main focus into art and education development, it wasn't a coincidence that during this time Iran became an undisputed leader in architectural developments, some of the structures built during this period still, to this day, remain some of Iran's most impressive tourist attractions. The far reaching consequences of Iran's opening to outside nations didn't stop there, another interesting result of this international interaction was the cultural exchange that took place between Iran and it's architecture flourished during these times. However, all this started to fall as it gets to the end of Safavid dynasty; they paid great attention into building roads, securing the roads, modernization of military, art, and architecture. Some of the places that remain today from that time are considered to be the finest Islamic arts, places such as mosques and palaces. Also as Moghul rulers of India had Persian culture and used Persian language as the official languages of the royal family, Iran exported its culture furthermore and influence at central Asia.

Afsharid Dynasty
Though there were some conflicts that occurred during this dynasty, such as the sporadic wars that were fought with the Uzbeks from central Asia and greater Khorasan and Ottoman from Anatolia, the main force that brought down the Safavid dynasty came from within. Lack of discipline, mismanagement and a serious case of state corruption forced a decline that came to a conclusive end in 1736 by Nader Shah Afshar which established Afsharid dynasty. That said there was a short period of partial development, though it didn't include much art and culture, instead in the military aspect of the country he spent most of his time to reclaim and securing Iran's borders and lands leading Iran for the opportunity of becoming an empire once again. Nader Shah during his short rule had great military and defeated the Moghul Empire and captured Delhi. After the occupation he brought back thousands of elephants, camels, gold and jewelry which till this day some of them are considered to be Iran's most valuable jewelries. All of this was achieved under the leadership of Nader and in the name of the newly formed Afshared dynasty. Nader was assassinated by one of his generals, bringing this time in Iranian history to an abrupt end, though a lot was achieved in the name of bringing the entire country united under "one flag".

Zand Dynasty
Shortly after the death of Nader Shah, Karim Khan Zand established the Zand dynasty. This period of time was marked by few wars outside of the countries', which wasn't a bad thing since during this period a lot of developing went into the road structure of the territories. Technology was provided to increment the facilities in agriculture, the economy as a whole became stronger and wealthier. The fact that many bazaars opened countrywide during this time reflect the thriving conditions people found themselves living in this period in history. No better example exists of the prosperity during the Zand dynasty than the Zand Palaces, which to this day stand the test of time.

Qajar Dynasty
As the end approached for the rather peaceful and prolific Zand dynasty by the death of Karim khan, the power of Agha Mohammad Khan increased exponentially until the Qajar dynasty was formed under his control. This time in history marks a

very contrasting stage of development between Iran and the European Nations, while most of Europe saw a rapid increase in wealth through their plans of world colonization, efficient economies, fast developing technology and very solid educational systems, Iran suffered under a leadership more interested in turning society into a consumer's society than developing the economy and education. It was a common sight to see the Qajar Shah during this period spend long period of time traveling through Europe not caring about much else than their hedonistic tendencies. All while the economy of their country slowly suffered under the pressure of a poor education system and an aging approach to technology. Overall, there was an increase in the amount of exchange that existed between Iran and Europe, goods were imported back and forth and many higher class Iranians travelled through the European nations. These encounters failed to bring the industrial and technological growth the Iranian stagnating economy needed, they did influence certain positive changes. Western schools started opening during this period, thus offering a more updated way of looking at education than the traditional schools in Iran offered the youth at the time. Books (though a very limited number of them) were translated into Farsi allowing for a new source of modern knowledge.

Modernization of Education and Cultural Integration

In general terms, this dynasty was not particularly marked by peaceful and prosperous times, yet another layer of chaos during this period was brought along by a lack of central government. This weakening political instability was brought along, in part after Safavid dynasty increased wave of Turkish immigrant tribes who introduced a federalist type of government, called Ilati. It focused control and decision making upon tribe leaders and this result into an issue because of the lack of strong central government, corruption, miss-management and to some stage wars between clans surprisingly enough, this type of governance did spread enough to directly affect the internal stability of the country. Even worse, through an open support of a consumer's society and a disregard for technological advance, education and infrastructure investment, the country entered a period that turned Iran into a relatively poor country.

Even though it can be argued that through the increased interaction of the traveling higher classes of Iran across Europe, a lot of European culture and resources, such as books, where firstly introduced into the Iranian society, it wasn't until Abbas Mirza (crown prince of fathali shah) that real cultural exchange started happening. His trip to Europe and education there opened his eyes to countries weaknesses. He ensured the brightest students in Iran had the chance to pursue higher learning in many universities in countries like France and England. He even managed to put the focus back into the education system, and the intense need of one in order to achieve some sustained level of economic, academic and cultural development. He understood deeply that if Iran was to turn into a modern country it needed its people to know and understand the emerging technologic revolution, at the same time they embraced an open mind towards education and the need to innovate.

It was depressing for Iran that from 16th to 19th centuries European countries developed very fast by relying on human resources, education, and cultural development and was on its way to industrialization. Soon European countries were ahead of the world with new invention and technology and later on established their colonies across the world. In the 19th century, Iran like many other Asian countries, suffered in economy, government, and from lack of modernization. The more educated people start realizing the gap between Iran and Western countries. They began to seek reform and development which unfortunately wasn't very effective in Qajar period, for the reform many of Iranian educated they were inspired by France revolution and other external factors in the beginning of Qajar dynasty. We see chaos across the country as after Safavid dynasty, many Turks tribes migrated to Iran and they brought State federalism. By early 18 century, we see rise of European empires and their interference in Iran those empire were sometimes friend or enemy of Iran and sometimes a model or symbol of development and modernization, some of these empire were British Empire, French Empire (later republic), Russian Empire, Ottoman Empire, as all the above empires were looking for their own political, economic and cultural interest at the same time. It created a situation where Iranian government couldn't create a good definition of Iranian culture which resulted in even more influence for foreign powers.

By the end of Zand dynasty and rise of Agha Mohammad Khan, which established Qajar dynasty, Iran started a new chapter on its history, during this sensitive time as Europe was developing very fast with many colonies across the world, inventing new technology, modern military and education system, and efficient economy. At the same time, lack of Eastern countries, miss management corruption lead most middle eastern countries slowly into depression , and Iran was one of these countries toward end of the Qajar dynasty

When Mozafaredin Shah declared himself king at the age of 43, unfortunately he didn't do much to continue education development. He cut the funds of teachers and students family, His weaknesses in politics and cultural stability encouraged people to start standing for their rights; for example women started standing for equal education as men. Until that time most middle class girls were tutored at school by private teachers. When Safiyehyazdi started opening the first women school a new chapter for justice and equality began in Iran and the surrounding countries. She invited women to join the school and enjoy the same right of studying as men and they even established a freedom organization to defend women's right in 1868.

In 19th century, Iran was struggling between its traditional culture and the need to adapt to Western culture in order to turn the country into a modern and educated society and each of these had its own followers and supporters. In some way, the 19th century was a cultural revolution in Iran struggling to convert from the traditional culture into a modern culture with keeping the traditional element in it.

Pahlavi Dynasty

By the end of Qajar dynasty and beginning of Pahlavi dynasty, Reza Khan was an officer in Iran's military. He later used his troops for the coup and to end Qajar dynasty. During Reza Shah Rule, he started a new development for the country; his modernization in Iranian history is remarkable although there are critics in his rule but no one would deny certain industrialization, cultural and education development during his time. He established national public education system, built a strong centralized government. He improved health care and built hospitals across the country. He also managed to send his son and many scientists and students for higher education in Europe with the hope that one day they could come back with knowledge to develop the country. Reza Shah's form of dictatorship did cause some problems especially with religious leaders. He also changed Iran's international name (Persia) to its local name Iran to be used officially and interchangeably. As Reza Shah understood, in order to move toward a modern country, he banned hijab for Iranian women and tried to push Iranians in the direction of a western society.

Both Qajar and Pahlavi dynasties had a number of reasons that facilitate ending their dynasties which include corruption, dictatorship, and mismanagement, but the key fact was that they tried to westernize Iranian culture rather than modernizing it. This missed integration toward international culture was the main reason they fell, a rich culture with thousands of years of history and national identity with strong religious society has the potential to integrate and share common values with western cultures to some degree. Rather than irritating to force Western culture to substitute rich Iranian culture, a modern society is achievable with fundamental infrastructure in culture and education system to be able to communicate and integrate to international values.

Summary

Iran is a country with a large population the Middle East environment and similar to its South Asian counterparts, they demonstrate a collective nature and orientation. This chapter reviewed the process of Iran's modern day cultural creation from a historical point of view. It also explored the establishment of Iran's modern education system, adoption of Western style of school, the integration of Iranian culture to the Western culture and Iran after medieval age.

References

Ahadi, N. R. (2014). The Rules of Dynasties to Shape Iranian Culture, Society Education System and People's Struggle to Integrate with International Culture after Medieval Age. *International Journal of Technical Research and Applications*, 2(1), 41-44.

Axworthy, M. 2007. Empire of the mind. London: Hurst.

BBC News. 2014. Iran profile. [online] Available at: http://www.bbc.co.uk/news/world-middle-east-14542438 [Accessed: 26 Feb 2014].

Fis-iran.org. 2014. Civil Society in Iran: The Case of the Tribes | Foundation for Iranian Studies. [online] Available at: http://fis-iran.org/en/irannameh/volxiii/civil-society-tribes [Accessed: 26 Feb 2014].

Iranchamber.com. 2014. History of Iran: Safavid Empire 1502 - 1736. [online] Available at: http://www.iranchamber.com/history/safavids/safavids.php [Accessed: 26 Feb 2014].

Koutlaki, S. A. 2010. Among the Iranians. Boston: Intercultural Press.

Nyu.edu. 2014. Brief History. [online] Available at:
  http://www.nyu.edu/greyart/exhibits/iran/briefhistory/ [Accessed: 26 Feb 2014].
Tajaddini, R., Mujtaba, B. G., and Bandenezhad, M. (2009). Management Skills of Iranians: a
  Comparison of Technical, Human and Conceptual Differences based on Gender, Age and
  Longevity in Management Ranks. *Labour and Management in Development*, 10(1), 1-18.

Chapter 15

WOMEN, SOCIAL MEDIA, AND IMPLICATIONS FOR EMPLOYMENT

By: Janice M. Karlen
City University of New York - LaGuardia

As technology and social media platforms evolved and became part of everyday life, individuals need to consider their impact in a constantly changing environment vastly different from the past. Information that was closely held by friends and family is now available to millions of people around the globe, including potential and current employers. Since women comprise the majority of users of most social media sites, they are most vulnerable from repercussions involving the various types of information made publicly available as well as the failure to appropriately manage privacy in technological forums.

This chapter discusses the differences in usage of social media by men and women, employers accessing information as part of the recruitment process that applicants make publicly available and monitoring practices and policies affecting employees in the workplace.

Introduction

The ongoing growth in digital media reflects general trends towards the emergence of a more connected world where people can share and find information more readily and conveniently. Social media technologies in particular facilitate access to intimate knowledge about individuals that is increasingly used by managers and agencies for marketing, surveillance and recruitment purposes. Social media has aided individuals in following their family, friends, celebrities, and random others. Businesses can delve further into the privacy areas of potential and current employees than ever before. This is primarily because people use social media to announce what they are doing, who they are communicating with, where they are and a myriad of other details regarding their personal lives. They blog about their opinions and openly publicize their plans. At the same time, many individuals voice concerns over issues of identity theft and inappropriate use of their personal information, but often lack the knowledge necessary to manage their public persona.

Social Media Utilization in General

According to "*Worldwide Social Network Users: 2013 Forecast and Comparative Estimates*," nearly one in four people worldwide used social networks in 2013 ("Social Networking Reaches", 2013). The Pew Research Center's Internet & American Life Project reports that as of May 2013, about 72% of online adults in the United States use social networking sites, and 18% use Twitter (Brenner & Smith, 2013). In addition to personal usage, more businesses are taking advantage of the benefits that social media sites offer. In a study by global management consulting firms Booz & Company and Buddy Media, it was found that 96% of companies surveyed plan on increasing their investments in social media. Advertising and promotions, public relations, and customer services were listed as the main uses or benefits though other uses such as market research and recruitment were reported.

Microsoft Trustworthy Computing division released data in 2012 from a survey of 5,000 people whose online behaviors and attitudes varied widely about how their actions impacted their overall online profiles and reputations. Fourteen percent of people believed they have been negatively impacted by the online activities of others, even unintentionally so. Of those, 21% believed it led to being terminated from a job, 16% being refused health care, 16% being turned down for a job, and 15% being turned down for a mortgage (Lynch, 2012).

Gender Differences in Use of Social Media

Men and women have been known to react and behave differently when it comes to their use of communication media, but of recent interest is the manner they differ in their use of social media. There is an average gap of 8% between the proportion of men and women who use social media, with women outperforming men in social media use. This has been a historical trend that has consistently shown in numerous surveys conducted since 2008. Currently, three-quarters (74%) of online women use social networking sites. Women are significantly more likely than men to use Facebook, Pinterest, and Instagram, while they are about at par with men in using Twitter and Tumblr (Duggan & Brenner, 2013; Hashtags Staff, 2013; Roy, 2014). Conversely, 63% of LinkedIn users are men (Duggan & Brenner, 2013). Women also spend more time texting than men even as they spend more time on social networks (Clipson, et al., 2012).

Aside from their frequency of use of the different media sites, the two genders also differ in the manner by which they relate to them. Pettit (2013) determined in an empirical study that women exhibit more positive sentiments in social media, both in what they communicate and how they respond to what is communicated to them. Women also have a wider range of community interest in social media, including social, spiritual, and relationship aspects (Clipson, et al., 2012).

Social Media and Recruitment

According to Watt (2013), companies increasingly use social media not only to attract employees, but also to screen them. Specifically, recruiters will seek to access social media profiles as a means of understanding the attitude, appearance, behavior, and professionalism of potential recruits, while screening out individuals who do not appear to fit the company's preferred employee profile. Ideally human resource professionals want this method to be a force for "good" not only in the more obvious areas of recruitment and selection but also within areas such as motivation and team-building (Alastair, 2013). This creates conflicts because women tend to create more intimate social media profiles and share more personal aspects of their private lives without giving sufficient thought to how potential employers may view their information. This is an area in which "candidates need to be increasingly aware that unless they have their privacy setting correctly adjusted, potential employers can see a good deal of what they are up to" (Watt, 2013). It is significantly ambiguous within the law, with employment groups arguing that employers could potentially face lawsuits for discrimination if they reject individuals purely based on their social media profile. However, in modern recruiting with huge numbers of candidates and criteria, it is often very difficult to determine or prove the precise reason why a qualified candidate was rejected, unless he or she were applying for a very specific job from a narrow pool of applicants.

A more worrying trend is the issue of companies' demands for access to the Facebook and other social media accounts of applicants, despite this being a violation of Facebook's own policies (Horn, 2012). In theory, women have the right to refuse to hand over their password. However, in practice many of them expect that this will result in their no longer being considered for the position, and thus they tend to comply (Del Riego et al, 2012). Individuals who refuse and then are not selected also face similar issues to those discussed in the previous paragraph, namely being unable to prove that their rejection was due to their refusal to hand over their log in details. This represents an area in which expectations are clearly not in line with practice, as women who are technologically savvy may set their privacy settings to prevent potential employers from accessing their social media profile, only to find they have to grant access anyway. Fortunately, from a privacy standpoint, legislation in this area is beginning to be tightened. For example, the states of California, Utah, New Mexico and Arkansas have passed laws that prohibit employers from requesting access to job applicants' social media profiles.

Despite the progress made in this area, there are still over forty U.S. states in which potential employers have the ability to demand access to social media sites, even those protected by passwords or privacy settings, as part of the recruitment process. However, as women become more aware of these types of screening techniques, they are becoming better able to counter these measures. For example, women have increasingly begun to create multiple social media profiles on sites such as Facebook. Some of these profiles are kept private and completely hidden from the view of all but the individual's friends, while others are 'sanitized,' or even enhanced through the addition of information designed to increase the apparent attractiveness of the candidate. This has resulted in prospective employers being more aware of the advantages and disadvantages of using social media information for applicant screening. As such, this is an area in which the users of social media sites are potentially able to protect their privacy, provided they are cognizant of management's practices.

Social Media and the Employment Relationship

During the employment relationship, the issue of privacy is one that consists of laws which are vague and not commonly known. The implication is that privacy issues are relegated to employer discretion that is guided by modest legal requirements. In an article by Sprague (2008) he makes the statement that "Employees have virtually no privacy." In the workplace, most firms keep database records of computer keystroke activity, internet addresses visited and phone numbers dialed. Other practices include video monitoring in the workspace, using GPS to track company vehicles, reading emails originating from company computers, whether or not they are from company or personal accounts, and reviewing employee postings on social media sites. Many women are unaware of these practices and may engage in social media activities during the workday, using company devices without realizing the potential consequences.

While the social media activities of the public are potentially used by companies and managers for external marketing and business reasons, there is also a growing trend for social media usage to affect the employee and employer relationship. This is increasingly the case as the use of social media in the United States and other developed nations' workplaces is on the rise, with people using social networks to discuss employment related issues, and companies monitoring the use of the internet by their employees (Mello, 2012). In general, the vast majority of modern businesses have policies regarding how employees can use social media in the context of their work, and what an employee can divulge about the company online. However, at the same time, Sánchez Abril et al (2012) argue that "despite granting employers access to information about their private lives by participating online, respondents expect that work life and private life should be generally segregated—and that actions in one domain should not affect the other." This raises an obvious conflict over the extent to which the ability of employers to access and control employees' activities on social media is in line with employee expectations of their right to privacy.

In general, many issues in this area can be addressed by ensuring that employees are informed about the company's policies on using social media, and that these policies are reasonable. For example "it is unlawful if a manager inquires about personal information displayed on social sites in the workplace"; however, "an employer has the right to search the cell phone of an employee if there is notice in its policies that employees have no expectation of privacy for information" (Barron, 2012).

At the same time there are potential conflicts of interest between employers and employees regarding the use of social media in a non-official capacity.

According to Hunt and Kessler (2013), lifestyle discrimination statutes protect an employee's right to use Facebook and other social media sites to pursue their private lives in any way they wish, so long as this does not interfere with their ability to do their job. When their personal activity relates to their work then the borders can become more blurred. In some cases, such as the BBC, social media policies quite clearly distinguish between personal activity which is not done in the name of the BBC, official BBC activity, and personal activity which relates to the BBC. It is the last of these categories that is the most divisive, due to the potential reflections on the organization.

There is obviously an argument here that an employee has the right to blog in a personal capacity regardless of their expertise, and the right to do so is legally protected unless it has an obvious negative impact on their employer. However, as IBM notes, its employees should "be aware of your association with IBM in online social networks. If you identify yourself as an IBMer, ensure your profile and related content is consistent with how you wish to present yourself with colleagues and clients" (IBM, 2013). This shows perhaps the most challenging aspect of personal social media usage. If a woman uses a public social media site to present herself as having certain views or opinions differing from her employer, colleagues and clients can easily access these opinions and may form judgments which may influence the woman's career.

Another important issue in this area is the extent to which employees are protected from retribution when they share thoughts and opinions about job conditions with coworkers. While many companies try to prevent their employees from doing this, Gross (2012) notes that employees do have the right to complain about their job if their complaint is intended to address a specific issue. However, "whining about them to anyone who will listen can still get you fired, especially when it happens on a platform that can spread those complaints all over the world in seconds" (Gross, 2012). Company policies are generally falling in line with these requirements, with Wal-Mart's policy only acting to prevent "inappropriate postings that may include discriminatory remarks, harassment and threats of violence or similar inappropriate or unlawful conduct" (Greenhouse, 2013). However, in the case of General Motors, the company's social media policy contains instructions that "offensive, demeaning, abusive or inappropriate remarks are as out of place online as they are offline" (Greenhouse, 2013). This may be seen as an example of a bad policy as it attempts to prevent employees from voicing protected criticisms of labor policies or the treatment of employees. Furthermore, it is important to note that if these comments are made on a public site then the employee cannot expect privacy-- while risking possible retaliation from colleagues and management viewing these comments--even though legal action is not permissible.

Cautioning employees that all corporate-owned equipment and technology will be monitored is a beneficial first step, to be followed by forewarning and training about such behavior as posting comments that disparage other employees or leaking confidential organizational information. Business leaders need to understand that claims of defamation, discrimination or creation of a hostile work environment may emanate from poorly understood requirements and inadequately trained staff.

Implications, Recommendations and Suggestions

It is demonstrated how the increased use of social media has had significant impacts on the privacy of individuals. However, expectations of privacy have been relatively slow to catch up with these impacts. In particular, many women continue to expect that the information they place on social media websites will be private, and not exploited by companies or employers, either actually or potentially. The evidence from this study has indicated that this is not the case, and despite the existence of laws designed to prevent abuse, this information is widely accessed and used by companies for a wide range of purposes. The solution to this issue is for women to become more aware of the potential "publicness" of their personal information and to moderate their expectations of privacy in universal media. Women need to take responsibility for knowing how to keep their private information truly private, and not rely upon external organizations to protect them. In particular, they need to ensure that they regularly check their privacy settings to ensure their chosen level of privacy matches their expectations, and they are not implying any consent by their actions, as well as regularly managing their accounts to prevent potential employers from viewing private information. Privacy expectations and the actions taken to guarantee privacy in social media usage will change as individuals become more informed and knowledgeable regarding the privacy impacts of social media use.

From the corporate perspective, companies failing to provide employees with a widely communicated and lawful allowable-use social media policy are risking legal and ethical complications, according to Millennials, Social Media, and Employee Usage, a white paper from Corpedia Inc., a Phoenix-based governance, risk control, education, and consulting firm (Steffee, 2012). Furthermore, inappropriate use of social media in the employment process and without sufficient procedure and controls may leave an organization open to complaints of discrimination. While difficult to prove, such allegations are damaging to the organization and may be expensive to defend.

The situation is not all negative, however. Women's greater use of social media may be an advantage in the workplace. Women are better able to communicate with clients and promote work-related collaboration than their male colleagues. In a study commissioned by Microsoft, women were found to more likely use social media in four of the top five implementations, namely to communicate with colleagues, to share/review documents, to communicate with clients, and to promote a work-related initiative (Proffitt, 2013). These are positive ways in which social media can help women be more effective in the workplace and on which they can build for their future success.

References

Alastair. (2013, October 11). How is Social Media Impacting Your Role in Human Resources? [Web log comment]. Retrieved from http://employee-relations.hr.toolbox.com/groups/strategy-administration/employee-relations/how-is-social-media-impacting-your-role-in-human-resources-5282898?reftrk=no&trdref=4e6577736c6574746572.

Barron, D. (2012) *Social Media: Frontier for Employee Disputes.* Baseline. 114, 14.

Brenner, J, & Smith, A. 72% of "Online Adults are Social Networking Site Users" August 5, 2013 Retrieved from http://pewinternet.org/Reports/2013/social-networking-sites.aspx.

Del Riego, A. Abril, P. and Levin, A. (2012) *Your Password Or Your Paycheck?: A Job Applicant's Murky Right To Social Media Privacy.* Journal of Internet Law. 16(3) 1-26.

Clipson, T.W.; Wilson, S.A.; & DuFrene, D.D. (2012) The Social Networking Arena: Battle of the Sexes. *Business Communication Quarterly*, 75(1): 64-67

Duggan, M & Brenner, J (2013, Feb 14) The Demographics of Social Media Users – 2012. Pew Research Center. Retrieved 4 April 2014 from http://www.pewinternet.org/files/old-media/Files/Reports/2013/PIP_SocialMediaUsers.pdf

eMarketer June 18, 2013 Social Networking Reaches Nearly One in Four Around the World Retreived from http://www.emarketer.com/Article/Social-Networking-Reaches-Nearly-One-Four-Around-World/1009976#2SSIdHZRSxQXVme1.99.

Greenhouse, S. (2013) http://www.nytimes.com/2013/01/22/technology/employers-social-media-policies-come-under-regulatory-scrutiny.html?pagewanted=all&_r=0 Accessed 14th October 2013.

Gross (2012) http://edition.cnn.com/2012/02/07/tech/social-media/companies-social-media/index.html Accessed 14th October 2013.

Hashtags Staff (2013, Aug 6) Gender and Social Media: How Men and Women Differ. Hashtags.org. Retrieved 4 April 2014 from http://www.hashtags.org/business/management/gender-and-social-media-how-men-and-women-differ/

Horn, L. (2012) *Facebook Condemns Those Requesting Passwords of Interviewees, Employees.* PC Magazine. 1.

Hunt, R. and Kessler, L. (2013) *Wanna Be Friends? The Potential Impact Of Lifestyle Discrimination Statutes On Employer Facebook Policies.* Journal of Legal Studies in Business. 18, 45-68.

IBM (2013) http://www.ibm.com/blogs/zz/en/guidelines.html Accessed 14th October 2013.

Lynch. (2012, January 24). Microsoft & Data Privacy Day: Put Your Best Digital Foot Forward [Web log post]. Retrieved from https://blogs.technet.com/b/microsoft_blog/archive/2012/01/24/microsoft-amp-data-privacy-day-put-your-best-digital-foot-forward.aspx?Redirected=true.

Mello, J. (2012) *Social Media, Employee Privacy And Concerted Activity: Brave New World Or Big Brother?* Labor Law Journal. 63(3) 165-173.

Pettit, A. (2013). Identifying the real differences of opinion in social media sentiment. *International Journal Of Market Research*, 55(6), 757-767. doi:10.2501/IJMR-2013-065

Proffitt, B. (2013, May 28) Women Collaborating with Social Media More Than Men. *ReadWrite.com.* Retrieved 4 April 2014 from http://readwrite.com/2013/05/28/women-collaborating-with-social-media-more-than-men-infographic#awesm=~oAQbPIwxwi4D3B

Roy, J. (2014). How Men and Women Use Social Media Differently in One Graphic. *Time.Com*, 1.

Sánchez Abril, P. Levin, A. and Del Riego, A. (2012) *Blurred Boundaries: Social Media Privacy and the Twenty-First-Century Employee.* American Business Law Journal. 49(1) 63-124.

Sprague, R. (2008) Orwell Was An Optimist: The Evolution of Privacy in the United States and Its De-evolution for American Employees. *John Marshall Law Review.* 42 (2008): 83-134.

Steffee, S. Avoiding Social Media Catch 22s. *Internal Auditor*, 69 (5), 13-15.

Watt, G. (2013) *Recruitment profiling by social media.* Money Marketing. 3/21/2013, 54.

Chapter 16

Communicating as a Woman in the IT World[12]

Effective communication can be a challenge for any individual in a homogenous workplace, and it is especially more difficult when there is diversity of gender, age, ethnicity, language, culture, and other such dimensions. With increased diversity of gender in the modern workplace, communication lines may get crossed causing miscommunications between the two sexes. These differences create biases that affect the way women are seen and perceived in the industry. The comments of Microsoft CEO on October 2014, which was discussed in chapter one of this book, regarding females not asking for a raise being "good karma" is one example that our leaders can use awareness of the challenges women face in the workplace. As such, this chapter focuses on the status of women in the information technology (IT) industry in the United States by providing the latest statistics, discussing some of the existing challenges, and offering recommendations for professionals in this industry. Having a diverse workforce can provide a competitive advantage for firms, and having women at all levels of the hierarchy in the workplace can attract more diverse professionals. Suggestions and recommendations for the creation of a fair and diverse workplace for IT firms are provided.

Introduction

Books like *"Men Are from Mars, Women Are from Venus"* by John Gray and *"You Just Don't Understand"* by Deborah Tannen are just two examples of top selling publications that discuss the mystery of the communication gap between men and women. This topic has been a mystery for decades. It has been scientifically proven that men and women communicate differently, causing friction between the two groups. This pop culture trend has prompted many people to constantly analyze the two groups in hopes to better understand the differences, and to attempt to adapt to

---

[12] Published in the *International Journal of Gender and Women's Studies* and reprinted with the permission of the authors.

- Wee-Ellis, O., Dorsett, A., Montfort, C., Valdes, N. and Mujtaba, B. G. (2014). Communicating as a Woman in the Information Technology (IT) World. *International Journal of Gender and Women's Studies*, 2(2), 61-74.

those differences so that life can be a little more harmonious amongst men and women.

During this research we aimed to not only discover why men and women have a difficult time communicating, but specifically why this is so within the Information Technology industry, and the effects that follow due to lack of communication. We also took it several steps further to question a few other debates that pertained to this theme. The first question pertained to the breakdown of the major differences between men and women that have been hypothesized over many years, and what did these components translate to mean. The next area we decided to touch on involved the issue of women being outnumbered in the workplace. Is this outnumbering due to lack of communication, or are there underlying issues that cause women to be looked at differently in the workplace.

We further discuss common stereotypes that hinder the performance and the growth of women across all industries. Some of these stereotypes are looked at as factual behaviors that are used to characterize women as a whole. Finally, we felt the need to tie everything together by bringing attention to where these differences end up leading, and that is the topic of discrimination. Although both men and women groups can be the face of discrimination, our focus remained on what women in the Information Technical industry have to endure, along with other findings we found were important to mention.

Men and Women Communication Differences

One would think by the way that men and women differ, that the two come from two different planets. This is actually the running theme that people tend to use when making jokes pertaining to the battle of the two sexes. The two speak different languages. Is there a science to this? There actually is. Over 30 years of research has shown that although the two do not speak a different language, but that the way they view particular situations differs because of their sex, and many other factors (Cameron, 2007; Mujtaba, 2010).

According to researchers, diversity plays a major factor in the differences in men and women, and how their actions are affected in the workplace because of it (Cameron, 2007). Cameron brought up the issue of men being looked over for call center jobs because of stereotypes on how they may talk to customers, or if they may have a difficult time building rapport and connecting emotionally with customers (Cameron, 2007). Authors like Simon Baron-Cohen, author of *"The Essential Difference,"* believe that men and women are suited for particular jobs. Simon Baron-Cohen believes that the female brain helps them be the most wonderful counsellors, primary school teachers, nurses, caretakers, therapists, social workers, mediators, while the male brain makes men the most wonderful scientists, engineers, mechanics, technicians, musicians, architects, and electricians because females tend to be more empathetic, while males tend to be better with analytical situations (Cameron, 2007).

Many agree that these stereotypes are formed from patterns that are noticed and displayed by women (Leigh, 2010). A common assumption that we found was that many of these authors believed that these gender differences begin very early in life, and that even if the two sexes grow together within the same culture, they still are affected by gender differences within that culture (Leigh, 2010). Deborah Tanen's book, "*You Just Don't Understand,*" is mentioned in more than one article we researched. Tanen believes that this gender separation can begin as early as three years of age, and progresses depending on how the child is raised (Leigh, 2010).

An actual geneticist and author, Anne Moir, and her co-author Daniel Jessel, both agree that men and women process information differently, and in detail discuss this topic in their book called "*Brain Sex*" (Leigh, 2010). There were many examples of gender communication characteristics that were given that we will now review. One characteristic was women for the most part focus on building and maintaining relationships, while men tend to focus on power, rank, and status. Women speak to gain information/insight and build rapport, while men speak to report to persons or only give information. Another characteristic was that men focus on facts and logistics, and women focus on feelings, senses, and meanings (Leigh, 2010).

Over the past three decades this controversial topic has raised questions on whether this is sexism, or is it science (Cameron, 2007). Just like in Leigh's article, Cameron touches on common characteristics that are observed between men and women that separate the two when it comes to communication. For example the point made about men being more focused on the facts and trying to find logic in something, while women will go off of their feelings and find relationships to be very important. If these differences are not managed properly, or are overlooked and ignored, then miscommunication is naturally to follow. So how is this managed? The goal is not to continue this battle between the two sexes, but to embrace the two communication differences, and use these differences as an advantage to create synergy (Leigh, 2010). If men seek information, then women can attempt to provide information upfront to avoid potential friction. If metaphors are being used, the two can try to find neutral ones that pertain to movies or nature, instead of sports or home-life (Leigh, 2010). Finally, in a business setting getting to the point is always a great idea, because time is money. So with that said, women can gear towards sticking to the facts, and do research so that if there are follow-up questions, they are already prepared. If women use the knowledge they have about the opposite sex in their back pocket, they have a better fighting chance of surviving and successfully thriving in male-dominated industries.

Women Outnumbered

The tech world has been a male dominated field for a long time. Although women have been able to make their presence known in other traditionally male dominated fields, making that same imprint in the Information Technology (IT) industry has been a little more challenging. IT is still a field in which women are outnumbered (Mujtaba and McFarlane, 2011). Information technology is a field where men hold 75 percent of all jobs, and nearly 90 percent of the executive positions at Fortune 500 companies (Humphrey 2013). There has been a decrease in degrees awarded to women in computer science in the past few decades. This industry has a "masculine feel" notwithstanding successes by other women in this field, for instance Marissa Mayer CEO of Yahoo (Humphrey 2013). According to the founder of a nonprofit tech company and whom also is a veteran of tech careers, "there's no reason it can't be changed" (Humphrey 2013). The annual conference which commenced at the beginning of October of 2013, the Grace Hopper Celebration of Women in Computing in Minneapolis, and it was named after United States Naval Rear Admiral Grace Hopper, one of the pioneering women in computer science. The message being transmitted during this conference was "women belong" (Humphrey 2013).

Even though the number of jobs requiring high-tech skills has grown within the past few decades, the percentage of undergraduate degrees given to women in both computing and information sciences has fallen. According to the National Center for Women and Information Technology in 1985, statistics showed that 37 percent of IT degrees went to women while only 18 percent in 2009. At the University of Minnesota Professor Maria Gini was the only woman in the department faculty for many years and stated that this year 3 out of 38 are women pursuing majors in computer science. There are women in the field who say that the disparity in this field is due to the misperception that tech workers are antisocial, and stare at computers all day. These stereotypes might also lead to such perceptions that women must look a certain way to partake in a particular profession. For instance, Liz Lupper, a project manager at Clockwork Active Media Systems from Minneapolis, said, "If people think about the stereotypes of someone who works in software or hardware development they don't think of someone who looks like me, I wear a lot of dresses. I go to rock shows" (Humphrey 2013, para. 3). This image that has been created is one of the biggest problems. There is not a visible role model in this field for women to look up to. Many women have admitted to stumbling into the field, and that it was not an intentional career path.

Many issues can arise since IT is a male dominated field and, at times, it can be uncomfortable moments for women. There was a presentation made by two men at TechCrunch Disrupt Hackathon presenting an app called Titstare in a pitch that was inappropriately containing jokes with regard to women's breasts. At another conference there was a women experiencing an uncomfortable moment when she overheard men making sexual jokes about her while she sat in front of them. Out of frustration, she took pictures of them and made a tweet with regard to her disapproval, and in turn lost her job, along with one of the men (Humphrey 2013). Needless to say, these scenarios happen in all male dominated fields, and sexual harassment trainings can aid to create a greater awareness of such challenges. Women in the IT field find the Grace Hopper Celebration to be a moment to unite and create this awareness. According to Kate Agnew, who works for Target and also leads the Twin Cities chapter of Girls in Tech a networking and advocacy group, "there's still a stigma against women in technology, but there is a shift happening." Girls in Tech hosted an event regarding developing applications for Google; there are other projects on the way including all girls CoderDojo, which has an agenda of teaching programming. In addition to projects like CoderDojo there is a contest hosted by Technovation Challenge, which is a contest for teens seeking to develop apps. This is also a great way to allure young women into the field.

Today, more than half of all PhDs in life sciences are awarded to women compared to a 13 percent back in 1970, yet there is still a significant absence of women in math-intensive fields (Yoshida, 2011). Against the thought that this absence could be due to discrimination against women, according to a review written by Stephen Ceci and Wendy Williams of Cornell University, there is little evidence for sex discrimination in some fields and concluded that the cause is not directly related to such discrimination (Yoshida, 2011). In the same review written by Stephen Ceci and Wendy Williams, there was no evidence found of sex discrimination in regards to research being published. On the other hand it was noted that the lack of women being published was due to a lack of resources. Such explanation provided was due to women holding teaching positions which did not allow them to dedicate the time nor effort into preparing as often nor as high quality research for publication as males (Yoshida, 2011).

Another concern which arose was women being at a disadvantage when it came to obtaining funding for their work. There is a 1997 Nature publication by Wenneras and Wold, which found that women needed to be "2.5 times more productive" than the male to be funded by the Swedish Medical Research Council in 1995 (Yoshida, 2011). But this study was questioned on methodological and conceptual issues and in 1996 a study of females funded by a UK panel found that they have published 11.2 papers on average while males had published an average of 13.8 papers (Yoshida, 2011). Research does suggest that prior to the 1980s it was even more difficult for females to be receiving grants than males.

Diversity is a great competitive advantage, and having both men and women working in the IT field will be of a great benefit for its growth (Mujtaba, 2010). Like most fields the innovations and or thoughts that women, men, and individuals from different races and cultures can provide such diversity (Mujtaba, 2007). As stated by Schlosser from Thomson Reuters, the company makes a point of building diverse teams through referrals and outreach. Tech-related job postings are examined for balance between seemingly masculine words (string, assertive) and those that may appeal to women (collaboration, problem solving). Having a diverse group is important to all professions. Nancy Lyons, the president and CEO of Clockwork, said "women often bring an emotional intelligence to hard-to-understand technology."

Common Stereotypes

Even though some might argue that men and women are the same, the two will clearly always have their differences. Women have to fight harder to be noticed over the male competition. Women in the workplace are often wrongly and stereotypically viewed as less decisive, slower to make decisions or even naïve at time (Mujtaba, 2010). It might not be close to accurate for all women, but the stereotype of their work ethics does affect them whether they realize it or not.

Women and minorities in the information technology world as well as most other fields often work twice as hard and twice as long to be viewed equally to men in the workforce (Nieves and Mujtaba, 2006; Mujtaba, Cai, Lian, and Ping, 2013; Hussain and Mujtaba, 2013; Jones and Mujtaba, 2006; Mujtaba and McFarlane, 2011 and 2005; and Mujtaba, Griffin and Oskal, 2004).

Emotion is a big part of why women are seen to have a tough time communicating in a male driven industry. Women tend to be more compassionate, caring, and more careful with decisions versus men. Emotion can affect the business interests if women do not want to "step on anyone's toes." Men are known to be goal focused and tend to have the mindset to not let anything get in the way of what they want. It is hard to tell women not to show any emotion, but it is a good suggestion to learn the right time to display them. For example, when a business is in the middle of a negotiation, women will tend to give more of an apologetic tone that could end up working against them. Even if the women don't necessarily agree with what is being presented, women should keep a straight face as men do and be professional at all times.

Women should realize that sometimes risk can work in their favor. Men learn to compete at a young age where they learn how far they can push a situation. Many entrepreneurs are known for being successful by taking risks (i.e. Mark Zuckerberg). Most women are afraid of rejection, and of possible negative outcome on projects. If women do not take risks, how are they going to know what is going to work or not? Men will take whatever risks are necessary to get to the top, and that is what women should also be doing in a professional and ethical manner. By putting their emotions aside and simply doing what they feel is the right move, this stereotype will affect them less. Women should see taking risks as a positive thing. If the end results are not what they expected, something can still be learned from that particular situation, and can be used in the future. People who tend to take risks are often more respected.

A great tool that works for men is networking. Women tend to shy behind their desk and projects. Even though they might be working hard, it does not necessarily put them in the limelight. Networking allows employees to stand out, especially when competition is high. Women should understand that not every relationship is going to turn into a friendship. Sometimes in the business world it is whom you know that can help you get to the top. Without putting oneself out there, one is putting himself or herself into potential risk of not being noticed for their efforts and the promotion opportunity might go unnoticed. Women should put themselves out there professionally, and let others know what they are capable of doing and achieving.

Criticism and denial is never a fun thing to deal with. Women tend to not handle them as well as men do. When a man is criticized, he likely will not take it to heart and just deal with it. Women might take criticism more personal than what it actually is, resulting in excuses or tears. If women want to be considered at the same level as men in the workplace, they should learn how to interpret criticism when given and realize that denial is not a bad thing. When something is denied, it should be seen as an opportunity on how we can make it better. Women should be worried of their credibility in the workplace and avoid any emotional breakdowns.

Confidence can take an individual a long way. Whether it is verbally shown or physically shown, confidence makes the person appear to be knowledgeable and creditable. If someone is standing in front of a meeting during a presentation with no confidence, individuals present during the meeting will lose interest and think the person does not know what they are talking about. Men are more comfortable with themselves so that if they need to lie about something, it can go unnoticed because they presented themselves with enough confidence for the individual to not even question it. Woman should step out of their bubble, even if they are not comfortable with doing so. This will make less people question what they are saying. If a woman believes she deserve a raise, she should speak with the head manager and express it with confidence. However, perhaps one should keep expectations down so that if there is ever denial, at least it was expected.

Discrimination, Recommendations, and Other Findings
Women and minorities are facing discrimination in the workplace for varying reasons. According to the author of *"Workforce Diversity Management,"* in its simplest form, discrimination means treating people differently, which is not necessarily unfair or illegal (Mujtaba, (2010). Additionally, discrimination is illegal and unlawful when protected classes of people are treated adversely from others who fit into the mold of the norm. Illegal discrimination is unlawful, and when this is proven in the court system, the perpetrators and their organizations will be assessed fines inclusive of penalties, judgments, and damages. These organizations will also have the burden of paying attorney costs and fees plus the stigma that will be associated with these results. Now let's look at diversity a bit further in the IT industry.

According to experts like Valentino Lucio (2012), the writer of the article *"The IT industry is begging for women workers,"* women workers in the IT field are very scarce and hard to find. This is so because men predominantly dominate the IT field and there are stigmas associated with women performing certain jobs. Because of this, diversity is hindered and the workforce will not be conducive for inclusiveness. The percentage of females entering the information technology fields is significantly disproportionate in comparison to their male counterparts. The trend doesn't look good because these entrants keep getting smaller, and when you look at the mid-management and upper levels it is even worse. Because few women are employed in this sector, most women aren't inclined and are unmotivated to pursue academics related to this industry. It is becoming worrisome for employers because they would like to hire more females to work for their companies but this isn't the case. Women aren't seeking careers in this sector so employers have no choice but to hire males. The reasons women aren't employed in this industry may be cultural and stereotypes (Lucio, 2013). This may have to do with how kids are differentiated and treated differently. Jenny Slade, who is the communications director for the National Center for Women and Information Technology, emphasized that unconscious bias is the reason women aren't attracted to the information technology field. Boys are given toys that facilitate putting things together and then taking them apart whilst girls are given dolls to play with which encourages teamwork. Because of such conditioning, boys and girls will be more inclined and persuaded to pursue vocations that they have been exposed to or learned.

To engender women in the IT field, organizations are going into their local communities setting up outreach programs to allow middle grade kids to get acquainted with the STEM subjects. The STEM subjects are science, technology, engineering, and mathematics. Doing this will enhance girls and other minorities' abilities and confidence in pursuing careers in this sector. From this article, it is evident that racial and gender bias is prevalent in this occupation group. The reasons for these findings are that women comprised 25 percent of the workforce, and other minority women inclusive of Asians, African Americans and Hispanics are grossly disproportionately represented. There are more women working in other capacities in these firms other than in IT positions. According to Slade, the technology field is predominantly represented by Caucasian males therefore heterogeneousness is hindered. Slade exclaimed that in 1985 approximately 37 percent students earning computer science degree in the US were women. In 2010 this figure dramatically fell to 18 percent. She also inferred that during the early years the high percentage was due to the newness of the industry, and the latter was when women realized gender stereotype became very prominent.

To enhance inclusiveness in the information technology field companies and organizations are formulating ways to attract and retain women. They are working hard to achieve this, and a company based in San Antonio named Rackspace Hosting Inc. is doing this. Rackspace has instituted a diversity program that includes mentorship programs and networking events that will facilitate interest in the IT field.

In another article on FoxNews.com dated October 14th 2013, it was echoed, affirmed, and reinforced again that women undoubtedly are an endangered species in Silicon Valley. Vivek Wadhwa is an outspoken advocate for women in corporate boardrooms. Recently she had heated exchange of words with Twitter CEO Dick Costolo when they conferred about diversity issues in Silicon Valley. It is evidenced by the dialogue in this report that board members and the companies refrain from promoting women to the upper echelons of these corporations, because of the potential for conflicts. Mr. Rick Divine exclaimed that CEOs stay far away from these perceived issues. Mr. Devine additionally emphasized that few women are starting technology firms and they're not many women founding information technology companies.

Based on the literature presented in this paper, it is the decision of the authors that overwhelming information has been presented that has substantiated and predicated that discrimination, biases, stereotypes, and other indifferent attributes are used when promoting workers in the information technology industry. Because of this plethora of evidence, the information technology sector of our economy isn't heterogeneous hence diversification is hindered. Additionally, since this is a proven fact, people who are affected by discrimination in this realm tend to take flight instead of standing their ground and fight. The articles also stated that women are hired in these firms but not in the information technology capacities. Instead, they are gainfully employed in other administrative functions which are indeed necessary for all businesses to operate successfully.

According to one of these articles, it was reiterated that its Caucasian men first and utmost then the other classifications of society afterwards. Also, another executive inferred that there was widespread fear of promoting women to middle and senior managerial roles in these companies because of the fear of conflict. The authors construed that men in the upper echelon of these companies refuse and deliberately bar women from entering their all boys club, because they don't want to breakdown and change the status quo. Because those who are at the helm of these corporations refuse to allow female and other minorities to assume top managerial positions the status quo remain intact. If the status quo is changed in this employment sector of the society, women will be more inclined and motivated to prepare themselves to work in the information technology field of study.

To enhance and drive diversity in the information technology industry companies in this sphere have to first change their organizational culture. Organizational culture change should be done in small steps so that the workforce doesn't get overwhelmed. Additionally, each small step is a victory and this should be celebrated. By changing this, diversity initiatives and goals should be instituted so that it is deeply embedded and is evidenced throughout these organizations by having a heterogeneous workforce. These businesses also have to formulate diversity initiatives so that inclusiveness will be initiated, embraced, facilitated, and enhanced. Corporations in the IT field have to educate their workforce on the benefits of a heterogeneous workforce. They will also have to have mentoring programs to educate, train, and alleviate the issues related to a diversified workforce. When these corporations have fully formulated their diversity management plan, top managers will have to institute the plan. It is imperative that senior management assume the role of diversity champions in these companies, because when they do their followers are more apt to follow. Last but not least, executives at these information technology corporations should do a diversity audit at least once annually to ensure that diversity is maintained throughout their workforce.

Summary
In closing, it is easy to see that men and women differ in many different ways. With differences like the ones we have discussed, communication lines are liable to get crossed and can cause a number of issues between the two sexes. These differences create biases that affect the way that women are looked at in the workplace. Their competence is constantly questioned, and they are being measured against men that may evidently be less qualified, but men may still get promoted before these women are given such opportunities.

These stereotypes discourage some women from entering fields like Information Technology because men are constantly being praised and told that they are better for the job than women, and are more qualified for jobs that require analytical thinking or logistics. A common characteristic that is mentioned when women are brought up in the discussion of the "battle of sexes" is emotion. It is spoken about in a negative connotation, and looked down upon, but in fact is sometimes needed in many workplaces found today. Although some of these patterns of characteristics can be found, nothing is ever true for all and it must be understood that there are several variations of all types of people. Having a diverse workplace is important for countless reasons, competitive advantage being the number one reason. Having women in the workplace brings a great balance that creates a diverse environment that will benefit any company. The characteristics that women will "bring to the table" will fill the gap of whatever the men are lacking, bringing the company to a "full circle."

References

Cameron, Deborah (09/30/07). *Do men and women speak the same language?* The Guardian Retrieved 10/18/2013 from: http://www.theguardian.com/world/2007/oct/01/gender.books

Humphrey, Katie *(10/01/2013). Male Dominated Field.* StarTribune Lifestyle Section. Retrieved 10/18/2013 from: http://www.startribune.com/lifestyle/225855931.html

Hussain, R. I. and Mujtaba, B. G. (2012). The Relationship between Work-Life Conflict and Employee Performance: A Study of National Database and Registration Authority Workers in Pakistan. *Journal of Knowledge Management, Economics and Information Technology*, 2(6), 84-94.

Jones, C. and Mujtaba, B. G. (2006). Is Your Information At Risk? Information Technology Leaders' Thoughts about the Impact of Cybercrime on Competitive Advantage. *Review of Business Information Systems*, 10(2), 7-20.

Leigh, Edward (n.d.). *Men and women communicating in the workplace.* The Center Healthcare Communication. Retrieved 10/18/2013 from: http://www.communicatingwithpatients.com/articles/male_female_communication.html

Lucio Valentino (08/11/2012). *The IT Industry is begging for women workers.* My SA Home Page. Retrieved 10/16/2013 from: http://www.mysanantonio.com/news/local_news/article/The-IT-industry-is-begging-for-women-workers-3781840.php

Mujtaba, B. G. (2007). *Mentoring Diverse Professionals.* (2nd edition) Llumina Press: Florida.

_____, (2010). *Workforce Diversity Management: Challenges*, Competencies and Strategies. (2nd edition). ILEAD Academy: Florida

_____, Cai, Hongman, Lian, Y., and Ping, H. (2013). Task and relationship orientation of Chinese students and managers in the automotive industry. *Journal of Technology Management in China*, 8(3), 142 – 154.

_____ and McFarlane, D. A. (2011). Virtual Performance Management and Information Technology in the Twenty-First Century Workplace. Pages 147-164. Part III, Chapter 9 in *Modern Competitiveness in the Twenty-First Century: Global Experiences.* Edited by Jessica M. Bailey, Claudette Chin-Loy, Nikolaos Karagiannis, and Zagros Madjd-Sadjadi. Lexington Books: New York. ISBN: 978-0-7391-6628-4.

_____ and McFarlane, A.D. (2005). Traditional and Virtual Performance Management Functions in the Age of Information Technology. *The Review of Business Information Systems*, 9(3), 53-64.

_____; Griffin, C.; and Oskal, C., (2004). Emerging Ethical Issues in Technology and Countermeasures for Management and Leadership Consideration. *Journal of Applied Management and Entrepreneurship (JAME)*, 9(3), 1-10.

Nieves, R. and Mujtaba, B. G. (2006). The Effect of Cultural Values, Professional Engineering Cultures, and Technology on International Joint Ventures in Mexico and the United States. *International Business and Economics Research Journal,* 5(6), 1-10.

Twitter (and the Tech Industry) has a woman problem. (10/14/2013). Fox News. Retrieved 10/16/2013 from: http://www.foxnews.com/tech/2013/10/14/twitter-and-tech-industry-has-female-problem/

Yoshida, K.S. *(02/14/2011). Keeping Women Down.* ARS Technica. Retrieved 10/18/2013 from: http://arstechnica.com/science/2011/02/does-sex-discrimination-in-science-keep-women-down/

Chapter 17
Distributive and Procedural Justice

By: Ikwukananne Udechukwu
Columbia Southern University

Fairness and equality are important concepts for all men and women in every workplace. As such this chapter explores the concepts of fairness and justice. The literature on Organizational Justice (OJ) is replete with several attempts and suggestions to either integrate or leave independent, distributive justice and procedural justice. This debate, mostly through methodology, has gone on for many years without any conclusive solutions. In fact, that debate, currently, is almost silent.

This chapter attempts to resurrect that debate, while proffering an alternative thought to the unresolved intellectual quandary of OJ. We begin its discovery, using semantics as a tool, to make the case for a different way of thinking about organization justice. Finally, we provide several proposals and constructs that should guide researchers and practitioners in retooling our current knowledge about what is fair and what is just in the context of distributive justice and procedural justice.

Introduction
The semantics of "fairness" and "justice" has been little explored both colloquially and academically particularly with rapid changes occurring in the business landscape. The synonymous and interchangeable use of both words in current research in Organizational Justice (OJ), "fair" and "just", and the tacit acceptance of their interchangeability, remains an academic mystery. Greenberg (1990) called for a deeper understanding and resolution of this issue. Martin and Fellenz (2008) were harsh in their criticism of OJ research, by stating unequivocally, "Despite the high levels of activity in the field, justice researchers have rarely asked moral questions or critical questions regarding the implications of fairness considerations on organizational reality" (p. 415). Such moral questions would include, is being "fair" the same thing as being "just"? Tomlin (2012) raises somewhat similar questions by asking "But what is it for something to be fair or unfair – what is our best

understanding of the concept?" (p. 200). In turn we ask the question, what does it mean to be "just" or "unjust"?

Both terms, "fairness" and "justice", have generally been studied conceptually under the umbrella of OJ, where distributive justice and procedural justice have remained prominent fixtures of that framework. For example, Skarlicki and Folger (1997) suggested that "scholars have argued that if organizational decisions and managerial actions are deemed unfair or unjust, the affected employees experience feelings of anger, outrage, and resentment" (p. 434). The implication of this statement made in that research study of OJ, where distributive and procedural justice were partly a focus, suggests the deliberate interchangeability of both terms, "fair" or "just", within the context of OJ research. "OJ deals with the role of fairness as a consideration in the workplace" (Greenberg, 1990, p. 400; Fortin & Fellenz, 2008, p. 416). So, is OJ really measuring "fairness" or is it measuring "justice"? Research is silent on this matter even though, and colloquially, it has managed to convince us that it does both. This isomorphic confusion was highlighted by Greenberg (1990) who saw the distinction between distributive justice and procedural justice as one of content approach versus process approach, though this chapter takes the position and approach that the distinction is one of semantics.

Bos, et al. (1997), Hartman, et al. (1999), and Hauenstein, et al (2001), as with many other well-meaning researchers, have argued extensively on whether procedural justice and distributive justice should be treated as two distinct concepts or if they should be conceptually combined together. Bos, et al. (1997) opined that "it is now time to integrate the procedural and distributive justice domains" (p. 96). At the heart of the endless debates on these theoretical concepts are semantic indiscretions of what it means to be "fair" versus what it means to be "just", which has not yet been clearly and fully addressed in the OJ literature, and for which Fortin and Fellenz (2008) had considered the "black box" of OJ research. In fact, both authors stated, ""While outcomes and antecedents of perceived (un-)fair treatment, or reactive justice, have been the focus of a larger body of research in organizations, the proactive creation of fairness or unfairness (proactive fairness) has received little attention in field research up to date. The unfolding of justice or injustice in organizations remains largely a black box" (Fortin & Fellenz, 2008, p. 415). Thus, can "fairness" and "justice" be theoretically conceptualized in the same frame work if we are to arrive at a more informed conceptualization of "fairness" and "justice" since this inevitably impacts how both distributive and procedural justice are conceptualized? What are the outcomes of being "fair" or being "just"--- equality or equity? How "fair" and just" is defined in the future should have profound future implications for OJ research.

According to Hauenstein, et al (2001), "Distributive justice refers to the perceived fairness of the distribution of outcomes whereas procedural justice is defined as the perceived fairness of procedures used in decision making about the distribution of outcomes" (p. 39). Notable is the term "justice" which is used within the distributive register, while the description of the register is simultaneously emblazoned with the term "fairness". Again, this could be another implicit isomorphic confusion and perpetuation of the interchangeability in usage of "fairness" and "justice", supported by the proposition that "fairness" or "justice" both lead to some outcomes. What these outcomes should look like in both cases or what inspires such outcomes is often less clear or discussed in the literature of distributive and procedural justice. Again, the Fortin and Fellenz (2008) "blackbox" in OJ research, once again, becomes self-evident. What is consistent in OJ research is the longstanding investment in the idea that what is "fair" must also be simultaneously and semantically be the same as being "just." This problem of semantics is believed by this researcher to be at the heart of the conceptual and isomorphic confusion that bedevils the debate on whether distributive justice should be treated differently from procedural justice or whether distributive justice should be integrated with procedural justice.

What is fair and what is just?
While "fairness" has often been discussed in terms of various aspects of OJ to include, distributive justice, procedural justice, and interactional justice, "fairness" may be semantically different from "justice". What we consider "just" may not necessarily be "fair" and what is considered "fair" may not necessarily be "just". Fairness has also been studied in terms of equity theory where we measure one's input relative to their outcomes, when compared against another's input relative to their outcomes. Tomlin (2008) using Broome's Theory of Fairness, highlights the fact that "Fairness is a pro tanto value – fairness is not everything, and we should not always do what is fair; the importance of fairness varies with context; fairness is a strictly comparative concept" (p. 201). The implication of these statements is that when fairness is not achieved through comparisons as equity theory might suggest, and within specific contexts, then, only unfairness is evident and possible. MacCoun (2005) notes that "fair procedures produce fair outcomes" (p. 185). In line with the same logic, when justice is not achieved through comparisons as equity theory suggests, and within specific contexts, then, only injustice is evident and possible. Thus, the direct association between "fairness" and "justice" in studies of OJ evidence by the definitions of distributive justice and procedural justice, based on this logic, at best, is tenuous and questionable. Thus, the mechanisms that directly link "fairness" to "justice" has to be further explored, and this unfortunately, has to be reflected in future OJ studies since we know that fairness can only lead to unfairness and justice can only lead to injustice. It would be illogical to bring both terms within the same semantic experience and domain even though they share the same constructs. Yet, one cannot ignore the sameness of the constructs deployed in the definition of "fair" and "just" even though both are semantically dissimilar.

For illustrative purposes, assume we have three individuals with increasing level of skills, abilities, and predispositions: person 1 has skill set 1, person 2 has skill set 2, person 3 has skill set 3. Also, assume we have 60 oranges to share among the three individuals for their inputs to work relative to their skill sets. These oranges are the resources and opportunities to be distributed among the varying skill set and capabilities available. In a fair system, regardless of increasing skill level denoted by the numbers, we assign 20 oranges to each individual. In a just system, we can assign 10, 20, and 30 oranges respectively, with individuals having higher skills, denoted with increasing numbers, receiving higher number of oranges. In either scenario, you still have the same outcome or 60 oranges in total. The issue really becomes about how the pie is shared---do you do so "fairly" or do you do so "justly"? On what basis should the decision to be either "fair" or "just" supposed to be built on? This question may suggest that distributive justice and procedural justice may be constructs that exist in either situations of "fairness" or "justice" and not just in one concept as depicted in current OJ research.

Within each of the illustrations in either "fairness" or "justice", is equally the perception of the distribution and the corresponding procedures used in allocating opportunities and resources, "matched" or "aligned" with the existing skill sets and competencies, so that "fairness" in itself as with "justice", requires the same technical application of distributions and procedures within its own domain. The significance of these distinctions occurs every day in the lives of individuals, organizations, and nations as each struggle to decide if being "fair" is the right course of action than being just, or vice versa, particularly when decisions regarding the allocation of resources arises. Within political, ethical, and social realms, these illustrations provided also reflect the outcomes of being "fair" or just" which can either be equality or equity. Tomlin (2012) summarizes these perspectives noted by stating, "Fairness is a concept that pervades our moral and political discourse" (p. 200).

Thus, the issue of "fairness" or "justice" appears more likely than not to be about "matching" or "aligning" or "allocating" existing resources, capabilities, and opportunities against/to existing competencies and skill sets, within context, in order to achieve either an outcome of equality or equity. Within the *Fairness domain*, you can only achieve being "fair" or "unfair" since "fair procedures produce fair outcomes" (MacCoun, 2005, p. 185). And, within the *Justice domain*, you can only achieve being "just" or "unjust." Through distributive justice and procedural justice, OJ studies have attempted, albeit unsuccessfully, to house "fairness" and justice" under the same domain. Hence, the continuing debates about either the mutual exclusivity or commonality of distributive justice and procedural justice in OJ research.

In addition to this, the idea of "fairness" or "justice" is not entirely about distribution of resources nor is it entirely about the procedures employed in the distribution of resources nor its consequent outcomes. Tomlin (2012) notes, "fairness is not everything" (p. 201). While maintaining their importance, the key to the distinctions between "fairness" and justice" exists in the "alignment" and/or "matching" activity with the intended outcome of achieving either equality of equity. Thus, both concepts are contextual and comparative. Equity theory is instructive because it reflects this "matching" and "alignment" activity missing in OJ research, as it tries to match one entity's inputs relative to their outcome, with the input and outcomes of another entity. So, while equity theory lacks the conceptual power and sophistication of OJ, OJ in turn lacks the "alignment" and "matching" capacity of equity theory. Hence, another contributory reason for the extended confusion and endless debates about the convergence or divergence of distributive justice and procedural justice in OJ research.

This then raises the ultimate question, should we then focus study on a new concept called Organizational Fairness (OF) independent of Organizational Justice (OJ), since both appear to be drawn from the same constructs but may ultimately arrive at two distinct and different outcomes---equality or equity, each with its own sets of potential peculiarities, challenges, and complexities? Should we also focus on these two new concepts since what is considered "fair" may not necessarily be "just", and vice versa? As a result, distributive fairness and procedural fairness should emerge and become functions of activities within the fairness domain while distributive justice and procedural justice should also emerge as functions of the justice domain.

Nonetheless, the interchangeability of the semantics of "fairness" and "justice" in OJ research, should remain a great concern to researchers because of the unintended and harmful impact such interchangeability could have on broader theoretical conceptualizations underpinning existing and future OJ research. This could also have huge implications for individuals, organizations, and nations. For example, suppose an organization intends to achieve an equal outcome which is drawn from being fair, how does Organizational Justice address "fairness" when the terminology itself is embedded in the activity of "justice"? This isomorphic confusion is clearly reflected in figure 3 above which depicts concerns with the existing conceptualizations in OJ research. This problem arises out of little understood semantics of "fair" and just" than it does from any obvious errors in the existing conceptualization of OJ.

These sorts of semantic distinctions between "fairness" and "justice" could help reduce the debates on distributive justice and procedural justice, and whether both should either be distinct concepts or if they should be combined. In addition, "The face of justice research was changed by the arising focus on procedural justice, or the perceived fairness of the procedures used to determine an outcome" (Fortin & Fellenz, 2008, p. 417; Thibaut & Walker, 1975). Nonetheless, "Similar to distributive justice research, the choice of criteria for procedural fairness has been found to be context dependent, but the rationale behind choosing particular criteria of procedural fairness over others has not been the focus of investigations, and ethical implications have not been considered." (Fortin & Fellenz, 2008, p. 417; McFarlin & Sweeney, 2001). The illustrations above clearly show that both concepts, "fairness" and "justice", share several commonalities that lead to different outcomes---equality or equity. These general outcomes can be the basis for the criteria in deciding if "fair" actions/decisions should be taken or if "just" actions/decisions should be implemented. This could imply that the outcome that is sought should drive the framework (Tornblom & Vermunt, 2007) on whether actions or decisions should be "fair" or "just", since OJ studies, through distributive justice and procedural justice has failed to effectively capture both outcomes---

equality and equity, either conceptually, contextually or comparatively, at the same time, and under the same domain. Thus, what these concepts mean should be as distinct as what they do.

Proposal 1: Organizational fairness should be researched in terms of distributive fairness and procedural fairness within the fairness domain.

Proposal 2: Organizational justice should be researched in terms of distributive justice and procedural justice within the justice domain.

Proposal 3: Global Justice (GJ) is a combination of both Organizational Fairness (OF) and Organizational Justice (OJ).

Global Justice (GJ) = Organizational Fairness (OF) + Organizational Justice (OJ)
Where GJ =< 1.0

These proposals allow for "fairness" and "justice" to stand independently and yet accommodate their integration since being "fair" appears to be distinct from being "just" even though both share similar characteristics. Global Justice (GJ) is a term that can integrate OF with OJ and yet allow OF and OJ to remain mutually exclusive concepts. GF is not possible without data from OF and OJ, and GJ should be less than or equal to 1.0. The gymnastics of trying to keep these variables separate and yet integrated, has failed in many research attempts mostly because of the flaw in the semantics of "fair" and "just" in each of those research.

Why Semantics and Meaning matter in Research?

Readers may wonder why the meaning of words and semantics matter. They matter because the semantics of both "fair" and "just" are covert aspects of the theoretical framework of OJ research, even if not overtly and consciously obvious or acknowledged. "Research usually starts with the definition of the core concept addressed in the study in order to identify the territory and the boundaries of its conceptual content (Dano, et al., 2006, p. 46; Bringberg & Hirschman, 1986). In OJ studies, the semantics of "fair" and "just" has not been clearly outlined or identified, and as previously stated elsewhere in the paper, this may be contributing to the confusion associated with the possible integration or independence of distributive justice and procedural justice.

However, "Revealing these roots does not expose the correct meaning of a word, but can often allow it to be seen in new light, in which figure, ground, and shadow shift, enabling the exploration of connections and associations obscured by the dully overfamiliar" (French, 1999, p. 258). Wright (1997) further added that "A form of words maybe perfectly clear when taken in isolation but may become ambiguous – or even take on quite different meaning – when other factors are introduced" (p. 44). Thus, making a case for the review of OJ variables using the tools of semantics may be as valuable as the methodological approaches which have repeatedly been applied, albeit unsuccessfully, to the same problem, thus, the endless debates about the convergence or divergence of distributive and procedural justice in OJ research. This choice in the use of semantics is deliberate and is designed to showcase its power in identifying problems traditional methodologies may sometimes miss.

Managerial Implications

The implications of this chapter is that it will increasingly become untenable to suggest that being "fair" automatically implies being "just," or that being "just" implies being "fair," even if research in OJ appears to sufficiently adopt this questionable semantic inadequacy. The implications of this emphasis should reverberate at the individual, organizational, and global levels. The value of semantics is that it informs the quality and focus of theoretical conceptualizations. And, we argue that in some research, addressing such semantic imperatives should be of utmost importance, when issues such as face and nomological validity are to be achieved.

The other implication, particularly in practice, is that employers must now decide if they intend to be "fair" or "just" with their employees. To assume that an employee who has been treated "fairly" must also feel that "justice" has been achieved seems to be a questionable leap of the imagination. And in turn, to assume that an employee who has experienced "justice" may feel "fairness" has been adequately applied, again, may be unrealistic. These are questionable assumptions that are already built into OJ research. For example, a high performing employee recently promoted to the executive ranks may feel "justice" has been served because promotion was incumbent on their exceptional performance. But on a collective or group level, such an employee may realize that it also took the collective efforts of other members of the organization to create a high performing environment, which catapulted the high performing employee to organizational stardom. Under such circumstances, the employee would revel in the justice of the situation but may yet worry about the fairness of it all, since they could not have achieved those heights without the collective efforts of others. Clearly, many HR policies, practices, and organizational strategies may well be affected in unintended ways by more clearly outlining the semantics of the innocuous words, "just" and "fair".

And the idea of what is "just" and what is "fair," in more recent memories, is becoming a global concern as multinational enterprises with far flung global operations are being forced to reckon with environmental concerns, pay issues, worker rights, social concerns, ethics, etc., which have had profound effects on the lives of many citizens in the host nations of operation, and whose views and framework for "justice" and "fairness" may be contextually dissimilar from those of the multinational enterprise particularly on the basis of their dissimilar perceptions of distribution and procedures in the allocation of resources and opportunities within either the "fairness" or "justice" domain. Indeed, Reithal, et al. (2007) had pointed to this possibility of OJ variables---procedural and distributive justice, also being influenced by cultural differences. Thus, without clarity, multinational enterprises run the risk of acting "justly" in order to enshrine equity, while their employees in host nations may find greater value in "fairness" where equality may be more valued, particularly if the political context is one that resembles authoritarianism more than it does a democracy. In a democratic context, "justice" may be more preferable than "fairness," for several reasons to include the impact of individual liberties and individualism associated with democracies, where equitable outcomes rather than equal outcomes may be most valued.

Thus, multinational enterprises who either choose to or are forced to adopt "fairness" in the allocation of resources and opportunities when matched against existing competencies and skills, under democratic conditions, could find such situation to either be problematic or counter-productive relative to their strategic goals and consequent fiduciary obligations to their stakeholders. Within the appropriate domain—fairness or justice, as determined by the multinational enterprise, remains the value of assessing the distribution and/or the procedures for allocating resources and opportunities. The impact of "fair" and just," when acknowledged and understood, on a research and practical level, or in various areas of society, government, and business, cannot be over-emphasized. Within the domains of "fairness" or "justice" the following questions become imperatives:

1. What resources or opportunities need to be distributed, and where, how, and to whom should the distribution occur?
2. What skill sets and competencies will be required to be matched up or aligned with the existing resources and opportunities?
3. What outcomes are being sought---equality or equity, and why?
4. How should programs be designed or policies formulated to align and match resources and opportunities against skill sets and competencies, within either a "fair" or "just" domain, in order to reach either an equal or equitable outcome?

Conclusion

This chapter made no claims about conclusively resolving the existing confusion in OJ research as it relates to distributive and procedural justice. However, it attempted to shine new light into the existing "blackbox" associated with distributive and procedural justice within the OJ domain, with the aim of re-orienting research towards focus on the semantics of "fair" and "just" and how the semantics of both terms could impact the current and future face validity and nomological validity of variables in OJ research. We concluded that "fair" and "just are not the same even though they share the same constructs. They lead to two distinct outcomes---equality or equity. Based on these differences and similarities, it was proposed that a new area of study called Organizational Fairness be developed while the current Organizational Justice research be rehabilitated to reflect the new thinking presented. In addition, another concept called Global Justice (GJ) was suggested to help with integrating the similarities and differences that exist between OF with OJ. These are by no means conclusive solutions because more questions may need to be asked in equal measure as new answers to such questions will also be needed. While most researchers have chosen to keep distributive justice and procedural justice either separate or integrated, this chapter takes neither side because it finds that the solution is to keep distributive justice both integrated and separate at the same time. Examples and illustrations were also provided to enhance our understanding of this new way of thinking of "fairness" and "justice" in terms of the "matching" and "alignment" of resources and opportunities against competencies and skill sets. This chapter further showed the semantic errors made when "fairness" and "justice" as terms are used interchangeably within the justice domain of OJ research. It is hoped that researchers and managers alike would heed to this call to rethink what it means to be "fair" and "just," while considering the impact of the outcomes of either---equality or equity, at the individual, organizational, and global levels of operation. It is also hoped this will begin a new journey for OJ research. The value of semantics and meaning in understanding and building concepts can no longer be ignored.

References

Bos, K. & Vermunt, R., & Wile, H. (1997). Procedural and distributive justice: What is fair depends more on what comes first than on what comes next. *Journal of Personality and Social Psychology, 72 (1)*, 95 – 104.

Bringberg, D., & Hirschman, E. C. (1986). Multiple orientation for the conduct of marketing research: An analysis of the academic/practitioners distinction. *Journal of Marketing, 50*, 161 – 173.

Cory-Wright, D. (1997). The meaning of words. *Reactions, 17 (12)*, 44.

Dano, F., Llosa, S., & Orshinger, C. (2006). Words, words, mere words? An analysis of services customers' perception of evaluative concepts. *The Quality Management Journal, 13 (2)*, 46 – 53.

Fellenz, M. R., & Fortin, M. (2008). Hypocrisies of fairness: Towards a more reflexive ethical base in organizational justice research and practice. *Journal of Business Ethics, 78*, 415 – 433.

French, R. B. (1999). Teaching, learning, and research: An exploration of the edge between words and experience. *Journal of Management Inquiry, 8 (3)*, 257 – 270.

Greenberg, J. (1990). Organizational justice, yesterday, today, and tomorrow. *Journal of Management, 16 (2)*, 399 – 432.

Hartman, S. J., Yrle, A. C., & Galle, W. P. Jr. (1999). Procedural and distributive justice: Examining equity in a university setting. *Journal of Business Ethics, 20 (4)*, 337 – 351.

Hauenstein, N. M., McGonigle, T., & Flinder, S. W. (2001). A meta-analysis of the relationship between procedural justice and distributive justice: Implications for justice research. *Employee Responsibilities and Rights Journal, 13 (1)*, 39 – 56.

MacCoun, R. J. (2005). Voice, control, and belonging: The double-edged sword of procedural fairness. *Annual Review of Law and Social Science, 1*, 171 – 201.

McFarlin, D. B., & Sweeney, P. D. (2001). Cross-cultural applications of organizational justice. In R. Cropanzano (eds.), *Justice in the workplace: From theory to practice* (pp. 67–96), 2nd edition. Mahwah, NJ: Lawrence Erlbaum.

Reithel, S.M., Baltes, B.B., & Buddhavarapu, S. (2007). Cultural Differences in Distributive and Procedural Justice: Does a Two-factor Model Fit for Hong Kong Employees? *International Journal of Cross Cultural Management, 7 (1)*, 61 – 76.

Skarlicki, D. P., & Folger, R. (1997). Retaliation in the workplace: The role of distributive, procedural, and interactional justice. *Journal of Applied Psychology, 82 (3)*, 434 – 443.

Sweeney, P. D., & McFarlin, D. B. (1993). Worker's evaluations of the ends and the means: And examination of four models of distributive and procedural justice. *Organizational Behavior and Human Decision Processes, 55*, 23 – 40.

Thibault, J, & Walker, L. (1975). Procedural justice: A psychological analysis. Hillsdale, NJ: Erlbaum.

Tomlin, P. (2012). On fairness and claims. *Utilitas, 24 (2)*, 200 – 213.

Tornblom, K. Y., & Vermunt, R. (2007). Towards an integration of distributive justice, procedural justice, and social resource theories. *Social Justice Research, 20*, 312 – 335.

Chapter 18
Family and Politics

Coauthored with: Mario E. Delgado
Rural Development Specialist/USDA

Society is one source of education for males and females alike regarding politics, leadership and service. However, family can be an even stronger influence on one's view of politics, leadership and service in society. This chapter explores some of these issues for personal reflection and provides recommendations on how society has changed along with its impact on the family.

Family and politics are related as members must care about each other in order for the unit to be functioning properly. As such, there must be integration of thoughts and coordination of strategic plans for better teamwork and execution. This chapter provides a philosophical discussion on the political systems in the United States and suggestions for improvements.

Integrating the Political System to Serve the Majority?
Most processes if not all and regardless of purpose, require specific sets of parameters to frame the range of actions needed to attain the desired objectives. Without a specific and limiting operational framework a process becomes inefficient at best, if not totally ineffective. Without limits it will ultimately collapse for lack of consistency and coherence. Furthermore, without clear principles and focus, the process can be serving the need and greed of a powerful minority elite.

The structural prerequisites, guidelines, and functional dynamics also apply to the management of political systems and their operations. Management skills are divided into technical, human, and conceptual areas. Due to the complex nature of our political systems, the most appropriate skill needed here is the conceptual skill as our leaders attempt to find the root causes for effective problem-solving. Unfortunately as the size and complexity of our political system have expanded, so have the operational liberties our politicians have been gradually granting to themselves to the detriment of the whole, and parts as well. In particular their actions have allowed the nation to falter into conditions that allow for:

1. *First*, too widely divergent if not irreconcilable political ideologies and objectives.
2. *Second*, additions and revisions to an almost infinite variety of laws and congressional operating procedures discrediting and debilitating the integrity of the political system.
3. *Third*, absence of an overriding set of national goals to filter and limit the priority typically given to parochial and special interests.
4. *Fourth*, political priorities are being set more in response to pollsters and polls than to ethical principles and values leading therefore to inconsistent and opportunistic decisions.
5. *Fifth*, the exponential expansion of laws promoted by the perverse incentive to grant prestige and influence to members of Congress according to the number of laws they have designed and help to pass.
6. *Sixth*, the overriding influence of materialism within both the general culture and the family unit are leading to permissive, short-term and mistrusting attitude across the board.

In general, our political ideologies are too divergent and the authority and liberties taken by our politicians in their role as legislators too great, to arrive at coherent and cohesive strategies that could benefit the nation as a unit. How can any system, democratic or not, thrive under such fickle foundations? How can we expect to solve a set of equations to their optimum value, when the constituent variables and functions are in a constant state of flux?

Such divergent and contradictory conditions must be resolved without delay, but not by addressing symptoms like more often has been the case. This is where the conceptual skills of management can become helpful for our leaders as they attempt to understand and differentiate the causes from the symptoms. Using the conceptual skills of management, our leaders can respond by taking the real causes to task. As a start, we must at least:

- *Re-structure* the entire national political system from top to bottom; at the national, state and local levels.
- *Reduce* the total number of politicians, also at the above three levels.
- *Re-orient* the political strategies and goals into a framework favoring national, state and local priorities in that order, and
- *Re-shape* cultural values from a materialistic to a moral content.

The materialistic nature of the culture has created a bigger gap between the rich and poor. Similarly, many rich individuals falsely claim that they are "job creators" and, through powerful lobbyists, ask to be given special "tax" incentives to grow their personal wealth. Due to such false perceptions and other "unearned" privileges that the super-rich get, wealthy people's income over the last 30 years (since 1980) in the United States has increased by 400% and the income of the bottom 50% of the Americans has decreased by 30%. Consequently, today, the top 1% of the wealthiest Americans tends to own over 30% of the assets in the country. The rich getting richer is not necessarily a good strategy for job creation because the rich are not necessarily job creators. Jobs are a consequence of an economic concept known as supply and demand. When consumers can buy more things for their consumption, businesses hire more employees. Rich people do not hire more employees if they cannot sell products and services. The profits of wealthiest people are often immediately deposited into their bank accounts and hedge funds. However, when average consumers become wealthy, many spend it and that cycle would eventually create more jobs. Therefore, it is the consumers and the middle class that help create jobs, and wealthy people should not be taking credit for it. Ultimately, it is basic economics: consumers or middle class citizens are the main engine for job creation.

All in all, if we don't *reduce, re-structure, re-orient, and re-shape as recommended above*, we will end up living more and more under a police state, within an atmosphere of siege, ruled by a council of industrial tsars and the super-rich minority, being served by an ever-expanding cast of political courtiers.

As The Human Decisions Model Goes, So Goes With the Cosmos

"Without stepping outside one's door, one can know what is happening in the world, without looking out of one's windows, one can see the Tao of Heaven" – Lao Tse. It has been our observation throughout the years that a significant of the fundamental principles and relationships between variables applicable to human behavior also correspond to equivalent functions in nature. The final impact of these principles does vary according to the scope of the tasks involved, but not the underpinning interdependence between the relevant variables. In other words, the laws final results may vary as the systems in question differ in scope, but the dynamics of the underlying processes will not, nor will the factors shaping the phenomena under review.

For example, the interplay and structures underpinning the human decision making process correspond with the equivalent action system for the Cosmos. Here we will attempt to demonstrate this point in the exposition that follows. Perhaps we ultimately do not need to look any further than inside of us and our phenomenology to discover universal principles and models permeating key aspects of the Cosmos. Lao Tse may have been more than poetic when he implied in the above proverb that by understanding our individual internal dynamics we can understand all else in the Universe as well. That is, that by expanding our knowledge of one's true nature and dynamics, we can also grasp the nature and dynamics of everything else including the Cosmos.

What follows is a comparison of the primary forces and flows between the human decision making process and the forces and flows connecting Quantum Theory with the General Theory of Relativity. We hope to be able to provide at least a glimpse on their correspondence in Values, Principle, Process, and Product. Let us use the *Human Decision Making Model* as the reference structure to base their correspondence.

Human Decision-Making Model
The structure of all human activities be they, actions, perspectives or thoughts is composed of four pivotal elements sequenced in a pre-determined and immutable flow. These elements are in order of appearance and internal impacts are:

Value(s) → Principle(s) → Process (es) → Product(s)

The Principle(s) or guide posts determine the component parts and framework of the processes and are derived from the Value(s) of the individual. The values represent the fundamental philosophical beliefs of the person over life and living in general. Examples are materialistic values, moral values and religious values. Values provide the energy and sustainability of the Processes and also determine the ultimate integrity of the entire Human Decision Making Model.

For example, in a decision making model anchored by Moral Values, the flow would look as follows in Table 18.1:

Table 18.1 – Moral Values

Values →	Principles →	Processes →	Products
Moral/	Love.	Giving.	Liberty
Spiritual.	(Uniting	(Sharing	(Human
(Trust&	Empathy)	Interactions)	Rights &
Clarity)			Cohesion)

On the other hand, Materialistic Values would generate a flow that would look as follows in Table 18.2:

Table 18.2 – Materialistic Values

Values →	Principles →	Processes →	Products
Materialism	Disdain	Taking	Domination
(Mistrust &	(Denigrating	(Exploiting	(Authoritarian
Manipulation)	Judgments)	Controls)	Stratifications)

The *Spiritual/Moral Values* set are the primary system of humanity. It exerts an innate strong pull in a direction that prevents the permanency of other lesser values system. The historical struggles in human history are an expression of the intellectual rejection of this truth and reality and have ultimately led to the periodic implosion of the lesser alternate approaches. And the same goes for the flows and dynamics observed throughout the Cosmos. Fortunately its realm, unlike the human, lacks the presence of obstinate egos and incoherent pursuits that would postpone the realization of its full constructive expressions like they do with the latter.

Cosmos Decision Making Model

Values

Values in the physical realm of the Universe or Cosmos are represented by the bath of radiation or cosmic microwave background together with its expressions of electromagnetic energy. Their combination provides the unifying force to the evolutionary process in the cosmos. They serve to bridge and coalesce the micro phenomena in Quantum Theory to the macro phenomena described in the General Theory of Relativity.

In the human realm, the bath of radiation is equivalent to the omnipresent spiritual essence present in nature and all its living organisms. In turn, the electromagnetic energy becomes equivalent to the constructive energy provided by emanating moral-ethical tendencies. Their combination provides the direction and stability to the evolutionary processes within the micro or individual and the macro or the groups and societies.

Principles

Principles in the physical realm are represented by the transformation of electromagnetic energy into gravitational waves with their inherent tendencies to attract and unite. They offer a pervasive orientation for connecting constructively all elements of matter.

In the human realm the gravitational waves are equivalent to our range of divine emotions such as feelings of peace, joy and love. The full range emanates from the spiritual essence of human nature. They exert a consistent pull towards thoughts, perspectives and actions consonant with the divine set of the full emotional range (from the Divine to the depraved ends).

There are many ways for humans to perceive and respond to life, just as it is for the Cosmos in response to its gravitational flows and formations. However, like with gravity in the Cosmos, the divine set of the range of emotions is an integrating primary drive as well. They are always making their presence felt regardless of the process in place at any one time.

Process

In the Cosmos, processes or methods of expansion and integration are generated by the inflation of the gravitational waves. These waves are both a manifestation of and the origins of Inflation. Inflation in turn promotes the transformation of small particles (micro) into large bodies (macro) as well as supporting the ongoing expansion of the Universe.

In the human realm, processes of expansion and integration are materialized via the gravitational pull resulting from acts of giving to and sharing with others. This constructive inflationary expression facilitates the formation and preservation of families, communities, societies and other large institutional bodies. Processes in the primary human realm also touch and make use of the full range of divine emotions.

Product

In the Cosmos the product becomes a synergistically expanding universe. A universe that is expressive of the integration of the laws within the Quantum and General Theories. A universe that is constantly connecting through the ubiquitous gravitational pulls as well as constantly expanding through the outreaching inflationary force exerted over its gravitational waves background. Aberrations are the exception and promote only temporary deviations from the Cosmos' relentless expansionary and integrating path.

In the human realm, the product is expressed by the innate and universal set of coordinated constructive human interactions. This is a path that is without ulterior motives. It evolves exclusively from the pure pleasure emanating from the divine range of emotions they elicit. Like the cosmos, aberrations in the application of the spiritual-moral principles will lead to destructive paths but only temporarily relative to eternity's infinite time and scope.

Table 18.3 – Cosmic Realm

Values →	**Principles** →	**Processes** →	**Products**
Bath of Radiation/ Microwaves (Positive Potentiality)	Gravitational Waves (Consistent Uniting Drive)	Inflation (Connecting, Growing)	Expanding Universe (Synchronized Dance)

Table 18.4 – Human Realm

Values →	**Principles** →	**Processes** →	**Products**
Spirituality (Positive Potentiality)	Divine Emotions (Uniting Drive/ Morality)	Giving (Connecting, Growing)	Expanding Humanism (Synchronized Dance)

The inflation or expansion of the primordial essence of the cosmos as well as of mankind are based on the *principle of unity or oneness* unity through the *process of giving without conditions*. It is the only stable path that integrates synergistically the small or micro (e.g. the individual and the atom) with the large or macro (e.g. nations and galaxies). Moreover, the micro in the form of the individual or a particle comes first as both the spirituality and radiation forces respectively originate at the smallest ubiquitous elements. Furthermore also for the large or macro to survive and thrive, individual quirks are side lined or short-lived by design and for the sake of unity for both models. This is done either proactively or learned reactively, as the small and the large are by design unavoidably integrated in an ever expanding interdependent cycle.

Ultimately the *act of giving*, with its accompanying divine set of emotions will prevail by its superior pleasure and attraction. Unfortunately, as of today humanity by its own blind choice, is living at an inferior lower quadrant of the expansive and inexhaustible spiritual universe. Unlike the cosmos that grows for the most part as designed, with minimal and self-correcting aberrations, we excel in denying ourselves the inexhaustible and enormous potential accessible to us since the beginning of our existence.

Emotional Complementarity
Human beings in general and inadvertently as well, lean on perpetuating throughout their individual lives the range of emotional states they learned to dwell in and respond to from early childhood and adolescence. Even if painful and destructive, those internalized set of emotions provide a sense of normalcy and familiarity conducive to their tolerance and rationalization. The tendency to validate reality through dwelling in familiar emotional states and accompanying perspectives, have been corroborated by tested psychological dynamics such as "confirmation bias", "selective perception" and "cognitive dissonance". Therefore the emotional mosaic we grow in and hence accept as normal and representative of life, becomes in turn a magnet for the evolution of our adult behaviors and perceptions of "real" life.

And now comes the explosive insight: *dysfunctional families* generate and reinforce destructive and unfulfilling, even hollow emotional states compatible with the set of emotions product of the *materialistic and acquisition oriented* values and lifestyle. Hence, in a culture where one if not both above perspectives are prevalent, a nurturing environment for the continuation and intensification of their influence becomes well established. Their interplay normalizes and also reinforces each other's influence and even relevance to the culture. This interplay continues until their socio-economic implications and unintended consequences destroy irreversibly the fibers of their founding culture.

What is the operational framework that brings these two apparently separate realms on a mutually reinforcing course?

This symbiosis is not hard to envision if we open our perspective to recognize the following two fundamental exchanges between their individual dynamics. First, the modern and highly specialized material- outputs-generating economic system demands almost complete dependence of the individual worker (employee and entrepreneur as well) on the system's ever expanding grasp. This takes place at the expense of the developmental needs of a sound family structure and of course of the personal needs of the individual worker too. Second, the dysfunctional family abounds with interpersonal dynamics that inflict psychological sufferings, if not also physical, on its members. Each member also attempts to drag every other member into their respective conditions, fitting hand-in-glove with the inconsiderate and unbalanced demands of the modern economic systems. Finally, both phenomena function in, and contribute to, an expanding conundrum of inferior and destructive emotions. Such quagmire helps validate each participant's by now well ingrained and familiar set of painful and self-destructive emotional realm

What could then be a way out of such implosive and self-reinforcing slippery slope?

The only way out is not by rationally discrediting their constitutions and dynamics, but by *replacing* their emotional justification with a set of values and behaviors superior in their emotional qualities and clarity. Such superior replacement factors in turn will promote autonomously the prevalence of macro institutions in support of the integrity and holistic well-being of the individual and the overall socio-economic system.

Like Families, Like Nations: Convergences at their Best

A family unit to be successful needs to share communalities between its members in three fundamental bonding factors: Values, Goals and Habits (Customs). It is not required as it is often proposed that its members share identical race and ethnicity. And so it goes with nations, even in a globalized framework with its free flows of populations across geographical borders. Therefore to obtain internal cohesiveness, for both families and nations, requires that their respective members share common values, goals and habits (customs).

But this is not all that is needed to sustain internal cohesion in both family and nation. A family unit even with bonding values, goals and habits (customs) in place, must also show continuous respect and frequent recognition (appreciation) for each member's identity and contributions in the realization of the common goals. And so it goes with nations in their recognition (appreciation) of the contribution from all its citizens, and respect for their well-being in their pursuit of the national goals.

Ultimately, in any close relationship, opposites after the novelty wears out do not attract but erode instead. Opposites undermine by definition the fundamental bonding (values, goals and habits/customs) and binding factors (respect and recognition). And so it goes with nations for which diversity for inclusiveness sake becomes a delusory and ultimately destructive endeavor. Diversity benefits a family and a nation only in ideas and not in ideals. It benefits when applied in the analysis of circumstances and proposed alternatives but not in ultimate design and direction. What consolidates family units and nations are complementary and not confrontational efforts and roles.

Finally, family units with immature members require a high degree of centralized controls to become and remain synchronized in design and direction. This is unlike families with mature and responsible members sharing the constructive sets of bonding and binding factors listed above. In these units self-control and constructive conduct are the norm. And so it goes with nations. On the one hand, the more incompatible and divided their populations and institutions are, the more central control is needed such as in autocratic and centrally-planned economic regimes. On the other hand, the more responsible and compatible its citizenry and institutions are, the more overall respect and recognition prevails. Such is the case in democracies and free and competitive market regimes.

So what is it to be? After all is said and done for a nation to attain and retain a minimal and non-intrusive polity, it must possess a citizenry willingly exercising judicious self-governance. And so it goes that such capacity and ability are found and developed first and foremost in the family unit.

Summary

As emphasized throughout this chapter, family and politics are similar in their goals as members must care about each other in order for the unit to be functioning properly. Therefore, there must be integration of thoughts and coordination of strategic plans for better teamwork and execution. This chapter provided reflections for personal improvements. Society is one source of education regarding politics, leadership and service. However, family can be an even stronger influence on one's view of politics, leadership and service in society. This chapter explored some of these issues and provided recommendations on how society has changed along with its impact on the family.

Chapter 19
Competitive Positioning through Strategic Alliances

By: An Quoc Nguyen
International School of Business, University of Economics Ho Chi Minh City,
Vietnam

Due to their socialization in sports and other childhood games, some boys tend to learn to form high performing teams that compete against others to win. Little girls, on the hand, are at times conditioned to be good to everyone by considering their needs and accommodating them through inclusivity. Some of such childhood skills are also transferable to the workplace as adults. As such, males tend to build strategic alliances by teaming up with others across the nation and country to gain benefits that they could not pursue on their own. As such, this chapter provides a little discussion about competitive positioning and strategic alliances to benefit both male and female managers in higher positions of the modern workplace.

Alliances are not a new concept; business alliances have always been part of social and political fabric, which has traditionally been dominated by males. As also pointed out by experts, strategic alliances are partnership between individuals and firms to contractually pool, exchange or integrate business resources for mutual gain. In addition, factors driving the increased prevalence of strategic alliances include moving into new markets, filling knowledge gas, pooling to gain operational economies, building complementary resource capability and speeding up new product introduction. Nowadays, in a very competitive environment, strategic alliances are considered a growing and significant mode of market entry. Contributing to the competitive advantage of an organization also has to do with positioning. Alliance formation could speed up competitive positioning and technological leadership in strategically important. Therefore, among several important aspects that obtain from strategic alliances, positioning is one the most significant tools for firms to consider when entering a new market and enhancing their competitive advantage.

Typical motives of strategic alliances

A few years ago, strategic alliances were considered as an option for corporate giants. Today, however, going alone is no longer a suitable alternative for some companies. Intensified foreign competition, shortened product cycles, soaring capital investment costs and ever growing new technologies are prominent applications of strategic alliances (Niren, William and Dennis, 1995). Firms undertake strategic alliances for many reasons: to enhance their productive capacities, to reduce uncertainties in their internal structures and external environments, to acquire competitive advantages that enables them to increase profits, or to gain future business opportunities that will allow them to command higher market values for their outputs (Webster, 1999). The strategic motives for organizations to engage in alliance formation vary according to firm-specific characteristics and the multiple environmental factors. This diversity has triggered the development of several classification schemes in the theoretical literature (elaborated from Agarwal and Ramaswami, 1992; Auster, 1994; Doz and Hamel, 1999; Doz et al., 2000; Harrigan, 1988a; Hennart, 1991; Lorange and Roos, 1993; Zajac, 1990): market seeking; acquiring means of distribution; gaining access to new technology, and converging technology; learning and internalization of tacit, collective and embedded skills; obtaining economies of scale; achieving vertical integration, recreating and extending supply links in order to adjust to environmental changes; diversifying into new businesses; restructuring, improving performance; cost sharing, pooling of resources; developing products, technologies, resources; risk reduction and risk diversification; developing technical standards; achieving competitive advantage; cooperation of potential rivals, or pre-emptying competitors; complementarities of goods and services to markets; co-specialization; overcoming legal/regulatory barriers; and legitimating, bandwagon effect, following industry trends.

Ohmae defined "Globalization mandates alliances, makes them absolutely essential to strategy. Uncomfortable perhaps-but that's the way it is. Like it or not, the simultaneous developments that go under the name of globalization make alliances-entente-necessary". There are several motives increasing prevalence of strategic alliances such as: moving into new markets, filling knowledge gaps, pooling to gain operational economies, building complementary resource capabilities and speeding up new product introduction (time-based competition). The level of cooperation between businesses seems much less influenced by internalized costs and benefits than by: the history of the partnering firms' relationships; the current market positions of each firm; their joint resource capabilities; and informational asymmetries relative to firms engaging in arm's-length market transactions (Dietrich, 1994). In other words, forming business networks and contractual or relational alliances is driven less by firms' retrospective economic rationalities than by their strategic intentions. Ultimately, according to experts, the variety of motives and drivers is enacted at four distinctive levels: organizational, economic, strategic and political. While seeking partnerships firms try to address internal organizational problems, they consider economic benefits;

engage in strategic positioning, or political maneuvering with governments and competitors.

Strategic alliance relationships and international marketing

The strategic alliance and its relational nature seem to be in debate among scholars in academic community (Janell, 2003). While some consider both vertical and horizontal to be within the domain of alliances, others believe only horizontal linkage is acceptable since vertical linkage represents the traditional buyer-seller. Some marketing perspectives suppose that strategic alliances are distinguished by the long term nature and commitment between buying and selling firm (Perks and Easton, 2000). From other marketing perspectives, supply chain relationships are considered alliances to be accepted by both parties to invest in future activities (Hoyt and Huq, 2000; Heide and John, 1990; Monczka *et al.*, 1998). Some other authors also pointed out that business to business marketing relationship takes on a variety of names derived from versions of symbiotic marketing, collaboration, consortia, joint ventures, linkages, alliances, networks and partnership (Varadarajan and Cunningham, 1995; Williams *et al.*, 1998). Business exchanges have transformed from a basis of transactions to a basis of relational capital, built on trust and commitment; and marketing has typically been responsible for implementing these relationships (Kothandaraman and Wilson, 2000). Therefore, whatever form, terminology or definition one chooses to accept, it is clear that alliances extend the connection and inter-relatedness of organizations, and thus are firmly embedded in the emerging paradigm of relationship marketing.

Market entry and positioning under strategic alliances

According to Varadarajan and Cunningham, entering new market, protecting of the home market and product positioning are those main motives of strategic alliances. This is supported by research about telecommunications industry (Sarkar *et al.,* 1999). Additionally, in a study of UK based international alliances, there are two main factors encompassing these points, one was based on competitive market power and other was on market development (Glaister and Buckley, 1996). Leveraging a firm's particular skills with the distinctive resources of its partners creates the opportunity for more effective positioning in the marketplace (Bucklin and Sengupta, 1993). The effect of the combination is to allow partners to take advantage of emerging opportunities and achieve more formidable strategic positions in a rapidly globalizing market (Sarkar *et al.*, 1999). Good products and strong products positioning are no longer sufficient to guarantee sustainable performance (Alidou, 2007). In the world of globalization and internationalization, two factors can explain this matter: the emergence of a summary of trends on the technology and information on the one hand and noticeable evolution of the structure of global competition on the other hand (Dunning, 1995; Tarondeau, 1993; Gugler, 1991).

Positioning also has to do with establishing alliances with strategic partners who can help convey the message of the essential nature of the service (W.David,

1997). An alliance, then, is a "union to promote common interests". It can also be a collaboration to find solutions that go beyond the capabilities of any one party. Finally, it can be a means of survival in competitive environment. Moreover, as discussed by Richard and Liden, companies need to combine competencies to enable them to have a strong global position in the markets.

If the intent is to achieve leadership rapidly in the new overseas market, the strategic alliances should quickly focus on innovative product and services with appropriate support. The players must foresee the competitive responds of the market towards the new entrants. Therefore, the entrance strategies should contain the following elements: focus on mainstream markets, resource leverage for rapid penetration entry, positioning to take the high and middle end of the market and integration of alliances partners into a seamless organization to deliver the offer. In brief, no matter how strong a single firm can be, when under the new formation of strategic alliances to enter a new competitive market, the players should much carefully in each of their movement in order to have proper strategies and rapidly take a solid positioning and therefore enhance competitive advantage.

Competitive advantage of strategic alliances

The most prominent theoretical outcome from an alliance is creating and sustaining a competitive advantage (Janell, 2003). Ivana and Davor imply that advantage stands for "to be in front" or better than others. The firm is said to obtain competitive advantage when it is doing better than its rivals or direct competitors. Doing better means that the profits of the firm are exceeding the industry average. In order for a firm to gain and sustain a competitive advantage in the marketplace, the conditions of each construct must be met, as they are both necessary and interdependent (Peteraf, 1993). Through extension, collaboration with a partner provides an opportunity to fulfill the requirements of a sustained competitive advantage. This implies there is the creation of value that is greater than that which each partner firm could generate on their own, within the boundaries of their limited resources. The effect of the combination is to allow partners to take advantage of emerging opportunities and achieve more formidable strategic positions in a rapidly globalizing marketplace (Sarkar et al., 1999).

There are three instances where alliances create the greatest degree of mutual value, and thereby sustain a competitive advantage in the marketplace. Alliances are most successful when the originating motives are positive, and the desire is to create new value, rather than an attempt to hide weaknesses, or merely exchange value, and the relationship provides a stream of follow-up opportunities (Day, 1995). Longevity has been found to be positively related to profitability, a parent's performance assessment of the alliance and favorable parental effect (Parkhe, 1993). Although it has been found that there are perceived differences in subjective performance based on the cultural orientation of the assessing partner, survival has the strongest and most significant correlation with subjective performance measures (Glaister and

Buckley, 1998). Yet, interestingly, one study of joint venture dissolution found that Japanese-US partnerships had greater longevity than US-US partnerships (Park and Ungson, 1997), which implies that country culture can be aligned to successfully achieve the goals of the alliance. Perhaps more importantly, performance has been found to improve with the depth of analysis of the proposed relationship on an ex-ante basis, and ex-post with the length of the relationship (Glaister and Buckley, 1999). Firms, like individuals, may have a disposition to trust. The idea that trustworthiness can be a source of competitive advantage. Barney and Hansen suggest that such a resource is enduring. Following Mayer, Davis & Schoorman, the trust disposition of a firm may be defined as a generalized willingness of a firm to trust external stakeholders and constituents. Some additional research supports the notion of firm trust disposition. Barney and Hansen also note that an organization's values and beliefs, including its trust disposition, may be supported by its reward and compensation system. Dyer reports that suppliers view General Motors, as an entity, as much less trustworthy as Toyota and Chrysler. A firm with a low trust propensity will tend to monitor its counterpart excessively. Such a firm will also have a low threshold of tolerance for even minor violations. A firm with a high trust disposition will be the opposite. Although some monitoring is desirable in partnerships, monitoring might become paralyzing if it is driven by an inherent propensity to distrust. The trust orientation of a firm may derive from a number of factors: leadership, past experience, the institutional context and the firm's mission (Alidou, 2007). Female leaders, who often lead with a transformational style of leadership, have the opportunity to enhance a firm's trust better than their male counterparts who tend to have a transactional style of leadership.

Conclusion and Recommendations

This section suggests that strategic alliances operation usually offer better results than the stand alone strategies. It also demonstrates that companies involved in strategic alliances gain more advantage than other types of businesses. These results allow both male and female managers to do better in the entire performance of their firms.

Without a proper combination of strategic alliances and positioning, a single firm will find it hard to enter a new international market. Strategic alliances can work for the benefit of a business to reduce development costs and speed up development timescales. They do however; require careful planning and monitoring, to ensure the business does not give too much away. As a result, strategic alliance can provide a powerful competitive advantage in new markets, cost, speed, knowledge, and technology access.

Following the above framework will provide an approach to developing successful strategic alliance which has the potential to improve the organization's strategic position dramatically, perhaps even to transform the company. Strategic alliance offers the parties an option on the future, opening new doors and providing unforeseen opportunities.

References

Agarwal, S. and Ramaswami, S. (1992), "Choice of foreign market entry mode: impact of ownership, location and internationalization factors", *Journal of International Business Studies*, Vol. 23, pp. 1-27.

Alidou, O. (2007), "Efficient Strategic Positioning in Developing Countries: The Case of North-South Strategic Alliances", *Problems and Perspectives in Management*, Vol. 5, No. 2, pp. 19-31.

Auster, E.R. (1994), "Macro and strategic perspectives on interorganizational linkages: a comparative analysis and review with suggestions for reorientation", *Advances in Strategic Management*, Vol. 1OB, pp. 3-40Ohmae, K. (1989), "The global logic of strategic alliances", *Business Review*, Vol 67 No.2, pp. 143-55.

Barney, J.B. (1991), "Firm resources and sustained competitive advantage", *Journal of Management*, Vol. 17, March, pp. 99-120.

Bucklin, L.P. and Sengupta, S. (1993), "Organizing successful co-marketing alliances", *Journal of Marketing*, Vol. 57, pp. 32-46.

Day, G.S. (1995), "Advantageous alliances", *Journal of the Academy of Marketing Science*, Vol. 23 No. 4, pp. 297-300.

Dietrich, M. (1994), *Transaction Cost Economics and beyond: Towards a New Economics of the Firm*, Routledge, London.

DI (2003), *The Interactive Firm: Network, Learning, Competition and Production*, The Confederation of Danish Industries, Copenhagen (in Danish).

Doz, Y. and Hamel, G. (1999), *Alliance Advantage: The Art of Creating Value through Partnering*, Harvard Business School Press, Boston, MA.

Doz, Y.L., Oik, P.M. and Ring, P.S. (2000), "Formation processes of R&D consortia: which path to take? Where does it lead?", *Strategic Management Journal*, Vol. 21, pp. 239-66.

Dunning, J.H., (1995), "Reappraising the Eclectic Paradigm in an Age of Alliance Capitalism", *Journal of International Business Studies*, Vol. 26, No. 3.

Glaister, K.W. and Buckley, P.J. (1996), "Strategic motives for international alliance formation", *Journal of Management Studies*, Vol. 33 No. 3, pp. 301-32.

Glaister, K.W. and Buckley, P.J. (1998), "Measures of performance in UK international alliances", *Organization Studies*, Vol. 19 No. 1, pp. 89-118.

Glaister, K.W. and Buckley, P.J. (1999), "Performance relationships in UK international alliances", *ManagementInternational Review*, Vol. 39 No. 2, pp. 123-47.

Gottinger, H.W. (2003), *Economy of Network Industries*. London: Routledge

Gugler, P. (1991), *Les Alliances Stratégiques Transnationales*, Institut des Sciences Économiques et Sociales de l'Université de Fribourg, éds. Universitaires de Fribourg Suisse.

Harrigan, K.R. (1988a), "Joint ventures and competitive strategy", *Strategic Management Journal*, Vol. 9, pp. 141-58.

Heide, J.B. and John, G. (1990), "Alliances in industrial purchasing: the determinants of joint action in buyer-seller relationships", *Journal of Marketing Research*, Vol. 27 No. 1, February, pp. 24-36.

Hennart, J.-F. (1991), "A transaction cost theory of joint ventures: an empirical study of Japanese subsidiaries in the United States", *Management Science*, Vol. 37, pp. 483-97.

Hill, T. (2000), *Manufacturing Strategy*, Palgrave, London.

Hoyt, J. and Huq, F. (2000) "From arms-length to collaborative relationships in the supply chain, an evolutionary process", *International Journal of Physical Distribution and Logistics Management*, Vol. 30 No. 9, pp. 750-64.

Ivana, P. and Davor, F., (2003) "Strategic alliances as source of retailers competitive advantage"

Janell, D.T. (2003), "Understanding alliances: a review of international aspects in strategic marketing", *Marketing Intelligence & Planning*, Vol. 21 No. 3, pg. 143.

Johansen, J. and Riis, J.O. (Eds) (2004), *The Interactive Firm: Pictures of Future Danish Production*, The Confederation of Danish Industries, Copenhagen (in Danish).

Kothandaraman, P. and Wilson, D.T. (2000), "Implementing relationship strategy", *Industrial MarketingManagement*, Vol. 29, pp. 339-49.

Lorange, P. and Roos, J. (1993), *Strategic Alliances: Formation, Implementation, and Evolution*, Blackwell Business, Cambridge, MA.

Monczka, R.M., Petersen, K.J., Handifield, R.B. and Ragatz, G.I. (1998), "Success factors in strategic supplier alliances: the buying company perspective", *Decision Science Journal*, Vol. 29 No. 3, pp. 533-78.

Niren, M.V., William, L.S. and Dennis, C.R. (1995), "An analysis of strategic alliances: forms, functions and framework", *The Journal of Business & Industrial Marketing*, Vol. 10 No. 3, pp. 47.

Parkhe, A. (1993), "Strategic alliance structuring: a game theoretic and transaction cost examination ofinterfirm cooperation", *Academy of Management Journal*, Vol. 36.

Park, S.H. and Ungson, G.R. (1997), "The effect of national culture, organizational complementarity, and economic motivation on joint venture dissolution", *Academy of Management Journal*, Vol. 40 No. 2, pp. 279-307.

Penniman, W.D. (1997), "Strategic positioning of information services in a competitive environment", *American Society for Information Science. Bulletin of the American Society for Information Science*, Vol. 23 No. 4, pg. 11.

Perks, H. and Easton, G. (2000) "Strategic alliances: partner as customer", *Industrial Marketing Management*, Vol. 29 No. 4, pp. 327-38.

Peteraf, M.A. (1993), "The cornerstones of competitive advantage: a resource based view", *StrategicManagement Journal*, Vol. 14, pp. 179-91.

Prahalad, C.K. and Hamel, G. (1990), "The core competence of the corporation", *Harvard Business Review*, Vol. 68 No. 3, pp. 73-91.

Richard , F., & Linden, B. (2008). *International marketing: An asia-pacific perspective*. Australia: Pearson Education Australia, No. 4, pp. 480-83.

Riis, J.O. and Johansen, J. (2001), "A strategic approach to develop agile manufacturing", in Gunasekaran, A. (Ed.), *Agile Manufacturing: The 21st Century Competitive Strategy*, Elsevier Science, Dordrecht, pp. 53-73.

Riis, J.O. and Johansen, J. (2005), "The interactive firm - towards a new paradigm: A framework for the strategic positioning of the industrial company of the future", *International Journal of Operations & Production Management*, Vol. 25, No. 2, pp. 202-16.

Sarkar, M.B., Cavusgil, S.T. and Aulakh, P.S. (1999), "International expansion of telecommunications carriers: the influence of market structure, network characteristics, and entry imperfections", *Journal of International Business Studies*, Vol. 30 No. 2, pp. 361-82.

Senge, P.M. (1990), *The Fifth Discipline: The Art and Practice of the Learning Organization*, Doubleday, New York, NY.

Stalk, G., Evans, P. and Shulman, L.E. (1992), "Competing on capabilities: the new rule of corporate strategy", *Harvard Business Review*, March/April, pp. 57-69.

Tarondeau, J.C. (1993), "Les Facteurs d'Internationalisation des Activités Industrielles", *Collection Economies et Sociétés*, Revue Française de Gestion, No. 19, pp. 55-71.

Varadarajan, R.P. and Cunningham, M.H. (1995), "Strategic alliances: a synthesis of conceptual foundations", *Journal of the Academy of Marketing Science*, Vol. 23 No. 4, pp. 282-96.

Webster, E. (1999), *The Economics of Intangible Investment*, Edward Elgar, Cheltenham.

Zajac, EJ. (1990), "CEOs' views on strategic alliances", paper presented at the Marketing Science Institute Conference on Managing Long-Run Relationships, Boston, MA.

Chapter 20

Wisdom in Words: The Language of HR Professionals

By: Eleanor Marschke
Nova Southeastern University

As organizational leaders, Human Resources Professionals have responsibilities that require insight, skills, wisdom, experience and a profound knowledge of their organizations. This chapter provides that Human Resources Professionals are contributors who honor a set of ethical duties, combining commitment to helping individuals and organizations to achieve excellence. They persuade follower's achievement and self-development while promoting development of groups and organizations (Caldwell, Truong, Linh, & Tuan, 2011).

Introduction

God created the world out of wisdom; therefore, the Human Resource Professional/Manager must create a work environment out of wisdom. Once at young age many kids were taught "Stick and stones may broke my bones, but words will never hurt me", the concept seemed to be true, but in all actuality it is far from the truth as words are very powerful and impactful in all forms, as words can bring life or death. According to Proverbs 18:21, death and life are in the power of the tongue. Dr. Piper (2009) delivers an interesting argument regarding words. He states, words carry immeasurable significance: The universe was created with a word; Prophets healed and cast out demons with a word; rulers have risen and fallen by their words; religious people have worshiped through words of song, confession, and preaching. Even in our technological age, politics, education, business, and relationships center on words (Piper & Taylor, 2009). As we mentioned, there is power of the tongue we can examine: What would homes, churches, schools and organizations be like if we used words with spiritual intentionality and eloquence, since the tongue is such a powerful force-for good or evil (Piper & Taylor, 2009)?

Within an organization, the lack of attention to the way words are being used in the workplace leads to bullying. Furthermore the affected individuals are demoralized; their behavior creates a toxic environment which impairs the organization's productivity. The role of Human Resource Professionals is to promote a bully-free workplace, recommend job applicants that prove civil and respectful, check references and put a deep emphasis in treating co-workers with dignity (Vega & Comer, 2005).

Too often many people speak without thinking or considering the person who is on the receiving end of those words coming out. In which it is always wise to be mindful that the words in which we use can either do enormous good or harm. Even without the intent of maliciously hurting others, the words we use can cause or penetrate a mass amount of impairment, as in an example of a Category 5 Hurricane sweeping its way across an island creating great destruction which could take an inordinate length of time of repair and restoration of that island.

Literature

God knows how powerful words are (Genesis 1), he spoke the world and life into existence. But God is so merciful (Psalm 103:14) and He knows how we are made which includes at times having trouble handing the responsibility and the power of words. When you truly know how impactful and influential words are, professionals must always remember your tongue has great power as it directs where you go (James 3:4); your tongue can destroy what you have (James 3:6); and your tongue displays who you truly are (Luke 6:45) (Warren, 2005).

In the book of James in the Bible, James talks more about the tongue than anyone else in the New Testament and if you notice all the chapters have a reference about managing the tongue. He mentions in chapter 3 verse 2 that if you are able to control your mouth, you are perfect, not in the sense of being sinless but in the Greek terminology of mature and healthy. When a person is sick and they go to the doctor and the doctor kindly asks you to stick out our tongue. The tongue reveals what is happening inside of you, not only physically but spiritually.

Aristotle is saying that "virtuous is to do the right thing, in the right way, in the right amount and at the right time;" however, when seen in a management context, virtues and positive moral rules try to guide the focus to worthy objectives and do not provide for correct judgments (Tullberg, 2012).

Your tongue directs where you go

There is power in your tongue as it has remarkable influence and control over one's life. We shape our words and our words shape us. Take a look at what you mostly talk about on a daily basis. The tongue is small and tiny, many people believe that the tongue is so small that it can does the less harm, not realizing it can do the most damage (James 3:5). Using a ship as an example, Look also at ships: although they are so large and are driven by fierce winds, they are turned by a very small rudder wherever the pilot desires (James 3:4). Likewise your tongue controls the direction of your life wherever you want to go and a little bit of a word or a phrase can influence the total direction of your life. The tongue is like a rudder that steers us. Your tongue is steering the week of your life (Warren, 2005).

Choices are made before results without the possibility of peeking into the future. When employees evaluate the work-family mix they are looking for the end results. The moral systems and their rules will be broken when the individual has to make one choice over another. Human Resources Professionals interfere to mobilize attractive concepts and to promote adjustments to worthy goals and authoritative instructions (Tullberg, 2012).

Your tongue can destroy what you have
Previously mentioned, a beautiful island with palms trees, exotic homes, and nice furnishings can be destroyed in an instant by a strong hurricane, just as the tongue can with hurtful or negative words. The tongue also is a fire, a world of evil among the parts of the body (James 3:5-6). It corrupts the whole person, sets the whole course of his life on fire, and is itself set on fire by hell. Gossip can be used as an example of fire, as it spreads quickly wreaking havoc all about. In that scripture James is saying that words can create a chain reaction. You can say something that you didn't mean to have any harm, but it can have devastating effects that are beyond your control. People can tame all kinds of animals, birds, reptiles, and fish, but no one can tame the tongue (verses 7-8). It is restless and evil, full of deadly poison. When he talks about poison, he is refereeing to the Greek meaning of snake venom, as just a few drops can be lethal. This statement is so powerful because your tongue can assassinate somebody within seconds (Warren, 2005).

Concepts are easily grouped into "good" or "bad" influenced by personal judgments about meanings of words and what they should include in order to fit the idea of what is "good" or "bad." Human Resources Professionals provide for assistance when conclusions have to be drawn based on different situations, allowing for concepts to be more descriptive and open to normative conclusions. To limit any influences, Human Resources Professionals provide for integrity, an important contributor to the good, source of pride, and self-esteem, fostering reflection and responsibilities (Tullberg, 2012). If organizations foster employee diversity and allow employees to choose something in line with their personality the employees would prove to create additional productivity.

Your tongue displays who you truly are
The words in which you speak reveal your character. Many people and professionals are very mindful of their character because their character speaks for itself, just as in comparison to someone buying house or getting a car, you are useless without credit. Your character displays what is really inside of you and your heart. From the same mouth come praise and cursing (putting other down). My brothers, this should not be. This is displayed as people saying one thing but acting contradictory. How can you become an effective leader, manager and professional if you are saying how people should talk and behave, but you in turn are doing the complete opposite (Warren, 2005)?

The good man brings good things out of the good stored up in his heart, and the evil man brings evil things out of the evil stored up in his heart. For out of the overflow of his heart his mouth speaks (Luke 6:45). It is said to be true that a person who has a harsh tongue has an angry heart, a person with a negative tongue has a fearful heart, a person with an overactive tongue has an unsettle heart, a person with a boastful tongue has an insecure heart and lastly but more importantly a person who is critical all the time has a bitter heart. Nevertheless, a person who speaks gently has a loving heart, a person who is always encouraging has a happy heart and most effectively a person who speaks truthfully has an honest heart (Warren, 2005).

The individual or collective capability for process alignment of moral awareness, character and conduct that demonstrates balanced and inclusive judgment related to moral results, rules, character and context is defines integrity capacity. HR departments with high integrity capacity will exhibit a coherent unity of purpose and action in the face of moral complexity. Human Resources Professionals who demonstrate high integrity capacity understand that this is a "professional asset" that constitutes the basis for sustained trustworthy relationships amongst stakeholders (Petrick, 2012)

Implications, Recommendations and Suggestions
In all things we do, we must always find room for improvement and solutions to problems. An effective Human Resources Professional / Manager should take several steps to achieving a more cohesive, positive, and supportive work environment for the organization and employees. Examining an example in which one of the most common mistakes in all organizations across the globe there is a lack of performance feedback and regular performance reviews, as many professionals have a hard time dealing with choosing the right words for their employees.

An organization's performance appraisal system impacts individual and organizational operations by prompting decisions regarding compensation and merit salary increases, training and development opportunities, performance improvement, promotion, termination, organizational climate, and financial management (Mulvaney, McKinney & Grodsky, 2012). An appraisal instrument serves as the tool to accurately discriminate outstanding performers from those who are below average. Research on performance appraisal reactions bas identified two general areas of interest: first, there is satisfaction with the appraisal instruments and fairness of the appraisal; second, there is a perceived fairness of the process and procedures used by the organization and in the distribution of the outcomes i.e. merit increases (Mulvaney, McKinney & Grodsky, 2012). More often than should, feedback and reviews are contrived if they occur at all. Unfortunately, mangers prefer to give the praises but tend to look over or not discuss the areas for improvement and stray away from conflict and then there are cases where some professionals sit on their superordinate in a seat of judgment. Most people struggle with telling the truth in love. Feedback and telling the truth is not just reserved for supervisors and annual performance reviews, but we have been privileged to be afforded opportunities with our words every day in our workplace.

As mentioned before words are truly powerful and using words in Human Resources there are great responsibility that comes with that, such as using wisdom in your words and speaking the truth in love. In the HR setting, the professional has to think of these four steps:

1. Understand and know my motives/purpose or rational.
2. Plan my presentation of communicating Step 1.
3. Provide an affirmation or declaration, which is always positive.
4. Risk all rejection.

Understand and know my motives/purpose or rational

Before opening your mouth to anyone, one must first know what their intentions are. They must identity the purpose of the topic of discussion and what are the hopes to be. Do not judge, or you too will be judged. For in the same way you judge others, you will be judged, and with the measure you use, it will be measured to you.

Mentorship programs provide for excellent opportunities for experience employees to give their time and assist younger employees with their careers. It is typically rewarding being able to give back using prior experience to make a difference in someone's career (Cabrera, 2012). HR's role is to identify those managers that lead by example and engage them into the mentorship programs, so they can set in motion positive reactions and inspire those around them to follow.

Communicating the purpose of the Conversation

The most important step is the preparation of how the conversation will end. This step determines the fate of the receiving end, as well as reveals your character and your heart as an individual. Intelligent people think before they speak; what they say is then more persuasive (Proverbs 16:23).

Conveying any message, written or verbal, represents one half of the communicating process. The other half is represented by the end receiver who has an equal role, although more difficult than the sender, as the environment adds to the difficulty of understanding what is the purpose of the conversation. Human Resources Professionals aim to satisfy the employees' needs and wants, therefore they actively participate in the way communication and sharing is done. They help employees understand that they are already in the context of a team and they should reflect on the countless ways in which communication occurs (Bertland, 2011).

Provide an affirmation or declaration

This is the point that reinforces your character and revealing the positive you have in your heart and the positive you see in others. Worry weighs a person down; an encouraging word cheers a person up (Proverbs 12:25).The six essentials of workplace positivity are: positive thinking, positive relationships, strength, empowerment, meaning, and well-being. Human Resources Professionals should use this framework and their personal character to enhance employee engagement and performance in order to achieve greater levels of organizational success (Cabrera, 2012).

A positive attitude is proven to provide a great competitive advantage for teams and organizations, as people who have a positive attitude have higher levels of engagement, perform better and are less likely to partake in counterproductive activities.

Table 20.1 – Godly and Ungodly Proverbs

PROVERBS	GODLY	UNGODLY
10:11	The *words of the godly* lead to life.	The *words of evil people* cover up their harmful intentions.
10:12	*Love* covers all offenses.	*Hatred* stirs up quarrels.
10:13	*Wise words come* from the lips of people with understanding	But *fools will* be punished with a rod
10:20	The *words of the godly* are like sterling silver.	The *heart of a fool* is worthless.
10:21	The *godly give* good advice	But *fools are* destroyed by their lack of common sense.
10:32	The *godly speak* words that are helpful.	The *wicked speak* only what is corrupt.
12:18	The *words of the wise* bring healing	*Rash words* are like swords of thrust.
13:1	A wise son *hears* his father instructions.	A s*coffer* does not *listen* to rebuke.
13:3	Those who control their *tongue* will have a long life.	A quick *tongue* can ruin everything.
13:10	Those who *take advice* are wise.	*Pride* leads to arguments.
13:18	If you *accept instruction*, you will be honored.	If you *ignore instruction*, you will end in poverty and disgrace.
14:3	The *words of the wise* keep them out of trouble.	The *talk of fools* is a rod for their backs
14:25	A *truthful witness* saves lives.	A *false witness* is a traitor.
15:1	A *soft answer* turns away wrath.	A *harsh word* stirs up anger.

Summary: Risking Rejection

At this point, it is very wise to use wisdom in how you deliver the truth, but it is very crucial that the truth is mentioned, as you do not want to glaze over any wrongs. Feedback is most important and must be verbalized. Love does not delight in evil but rejoices with the truth (Corinthians 13:6). Human Resources Professionals promote positive outlook in certain situations and discourage rejection. However, those who see rejection as temporary and based on specific circumstances tend to be better at persuading others (Pink, 2012).

Human Resources Professionals continue to have opportunities to expand and strengthen their role in helping organizations maximize productivity, govern more ethically, and compete more effectively. Human Resources Professionals have the obligation to prepare themselves to accomplish the goals of their organizations by refining their expertise about organizational goals, developing the skills of organizational members, aligning systems that are critical to the success of modern organizations (Caldwell, Truong, Linh, & Tuan, 2011), and creating a work environment out of wisdom.

We challenge and recommend each Human Resources Professional/Manager to use the book of Proverbs to juxtapose Godly vernacular as opposed to ungodly (Piper & Taylor 2009); see Table 20.1.

References

Bertland, A. (2011). The Limits of Workplace Community: Jean-Luc Nancy and the Possibility of Teambuilding. *Journal Of Business Ethics*, 991(8). DOI 10.1007/s10551-011-1156-7.

Cabrera, E. F. (2012). The Six Essentials of Workplace Positivity. *People & Strategy*, 35(1), 50-60.

Caldwell, C., Truong, D. X., Linh, P. T., & Tuan, A. (2011). Strategic Human Resource Management as Ethical Stewardship. *Journal of Business Ethics*, 98(1), 171-182. DOI 10.1007/s10551-010-0541-y.

Mulvaney, P., McKinney, P., & Grodsky, R. (2012). The Development of a Pay-for-Performance Appraisal System for Municipal Agencies: A Case Study. *Public Personnel Management*, 505-533, 41(3).

Petrick, J. A. (2012). Enhancing Ethical U.S. HRM Education and Practice: Integrity Capacity and HRM Professionalism. *SAM Advanced Management Journal*, 42-60, 77(4).

Pink, D. H. (2012). *To Sell Is Human*. Riverhead Books.

Piper, J. & Taylor, J. (2009). *The Power of Words and the Wonder of God*. Crossway.

Tullberg, J. (2012). Integrity-Clarifying and Upgrading an Important Concept for Business Ethics. *Business & Society Review*, 117(1), 89-121.

Vega, G., & Comer, D. R. (2005). Sticks and Stones may Break Your Bones, but Words can Break Your Spirit: Bullying in the Workplace. *Journal of Business Ethics (58)*, 101-109. DOI 10.1007/S10551-005-1422-7.

Warren, R. (Speaker). (2005). *Developing a Faith That Works For You: How to Manage Your Mouth – Part 8 of 15 James 3:1-12* [DVD]. United States: Purpose Driven Publishing.

Author Biographies

Navid Reza Ahadi is presently working as the Business Development Manager of a Management consulting company based in Bangkok. He left his home and family in Iran when he was 17 to pursue his passion for academic enlightenment. After arriving in Thailand, his first achievement was a diploma in Gemology from the Asian Institute of Gemological Science. He then began working in the Gemstone industry for a few years, while studying his Marketing Bachelor's in Bangkok University. Shortly after graduating he starts his new career in the area of digital marketing and Customer Relationship Management, quickly advancing to the position he currently holds today He actively continued to pursue his passion, balancing work and studies, earning him a MBA in Finance from Ramkhamhaeng University. Apart from his love of knowledge and devotion at work, Navid is also involved with several NGO's in Bangkok and supports them in his spare time for different projects mainly in education sector.

Wajma Aslami completed her Master's degree in Counseling Psychology. Her master's thesis focused on "Afghan Immigrant Parents with Daughters Seeking to Attend College Away From Home: Adlerian Group Counseling for Parents and Daughters" and she has co-authored several other articles on Afghans.

Qudsia Batool is a Civil servant in the department of social welfare and women Development since 1998 as well as visiting faculty in the university of AJ&K for the last five years. She received her Master degree in Business Administration from university of AJ&K (Pakistan) and Doctor of Philosophy in Management sciences from university of AJ&K(Pakistan). She has fifteen Research publications in the well-recognized international journals. Her area of research is HRM, HRD, Women in management, Leadership and women entrepreneurship. She has participated in the international conferences. She has represented Pakistan in the international conference on women empowerment at SUDAN.

Razia Begum is a lecturer of Management Studies and Human Resource Management at College of Home Economics, University of Peshawar Pakistan. She has done her M.Sc in Management Studies, MBA in HRM, and B.Ed. Razia taught various courses of HRM, Leadership, Organizational Behavior, small business management and Women Entrepreneurship to graduate and masters students.

Currently, she is engaged in the final stages of her PhD research titled "Personality Profiles of Successful Organizational Leaders". In the process of PhD, Razia has developed a standardized research scale to measure organizational leader's degree of successfulness, published two research papers while five are in the process of publishing. Razia also participated in numerous conferences and seminars, while presented three research papers in different international conferences.
She can be contacted via email at: razia-begum@hotmail.com.

Frank J. Cavico is a Professor of Business Law and Ethics at the H. Wayne Huizenga School of Business and Entrepreneurship of Nova Southeastern University in Ft. Lauderdale, Florida. He has been involved in an array of teaching responsibilities, at the undergraduate, master's and doctoral levels, encompassing such subject matter areas as business law, government regulation of business, constitutional law, administrative law and ethics, labor law and labor relations, health care law, and business ethics. In 2000, he was awarded the Excellence in Teaching Award by the Huizenga School; and in 2007, he was awarded the Faculty Member of the Year Award by the Huizenga School of Business and Entrepreneurship; and in 2012 he was again honored by the Huizenga School as Faculty Member of the Year. He holds a J.D. from the St. Mary's University School of Law and an LL.M from the University of San Diego, School of Law; and is a member of the Florida and Texas Bar Associations. He is the author and co-author of several books and numerous law review and management journal articles.

Mario E. Delgado, M.A., M.B.A., has been Adjunct Professor of Economics & Business Administration at Edison College in Fort Myers, Florida. He is also a Rural Development Specialist of the United States Department of Agriculture, facilitating access and process/underwrite applications for affordable housing ownership and rehabilitation programs. Professor Delgado conducts Latino outreach activities throughout Area 2 and provides support as needed State wide. He became familiar with Business & Industry, Community Facilities and Farm Services programs to provide a one stop capability in Rural Development Specialist/USDA outreach efforts. He also developed a strategic plan proposal for the State's Latino outreach mandate, successfully implementing it within his immediate area significantly increasing the number of Latino applicants and callers. Participate with SBDC (Small Business Development Center) and TAG (Team Agriculture Georgia) in the design and delivery of seminars to Latino owned small businesses and Latino farmers and ranchers. He can be reached through email at: medelgado2000@yahoo.com

Angelique Dorsett is currently a student at Nova Southeastern University studying Accounting and Business Administration. She previously attended Florida Agricultural and Mechanical University from 2000-2001, and completed an Associate's Degree in Accounting at Broward College in 2010. As a veteran of the United States Navy, she took advantage of using her Montgomery G.I. Bill to continue her education at NSU's Fort Lauderdale campus. After graduation she aspires to get CPA qualified.

Katie M. Gordon is employed with Florida Power & Light, a subsidiary of NextEra Energy, located in West Palm Beach, Florida, United States. Katie works for this Fortune 500 Company an Absenteeism Coordinator for more than 15 years. She received a Six Sigma Yellow Belt Certification in Process Management in 2012, is a licensed Mortgage Broker, and Certified Notary Signing Agent for several banks in the state of Florida, she is currently finishing her Masters in Leadership from Nova University located in Fort Lauderdale, Florida. Katie was born in Albany, Georgia and raised in West Palm Beach Florida, Katie can be reached through email at kg939@nova.edu.

Belal A. Kaifi completed a Post-Doctoral program in Business Administration with an emphasis in Management and Marketing at the University of Florida. Dr. Kaifi completed his Doctoral degree in Organization and Leadership at the University of San Francisco. He is currently a Fulbright Scholar Specialist which is sponsored by the United States Department of State, Bureau of Educational and Cultural Affairs. Dr. Kaifi has over 50 publications since 2008.

Janice M. Karlen, MBA, Ed.D. is a Professor of Business & Technology at the City University of New York - LaGuardia. She is currently the Director of Business Programs and a Prior Learning Assessment coordinator. Before joining LaGuardia, Dr. Karlen served as Vice President of the North Campus of Erie Community College, New York and Dean of Business and Personnel at Antelope Valley College in California. She has published many articles, spoken at conferences and on radio and television.

Maike Emmi Lina Koehler works in the Department of General Management at YES Pharma Services GmbH, an international Germany-headquartered pharmaceutical consulting and service company. Her focus lies on International Integration. Emmi has a Bachelor of Arts in Communication Design from University of Applied Sciences in Wiesbaden, Germany and an MBA in General Management from the Institute of International Studies, Ramkhamhaeng University in Bangkok, Thailand. Through her studies she combines a broad knowledge in both the creative and business area. Emmi was born and raised in Germany, however, has developed a passion for experiencing different cultures. She has lived in Australia & Thailand and is currently based in Philadelphia, USA. Emmi can be reached through e-mail at: emmi.lina.koehler@gmail.com

Eleanor Marschke earned her doctoral degree in Human Resource Management from Nova Southeastern University in 2008. Eleanor is employed at Thomas & Betts Corporation where for the last twenty eight years she has been a top performer in the sales department of this Fortune 300 Company which manufactures electrical construction products. Dr. Marschke's interest in Spirituality in the Workplace was the focus of her dissertation research. Dr. Marschke's website is www.spiriteducator.com where you can view her numerous publications on Spirituality in the Workplace, Sales, Worklife Balance, Health and ROI. Dr. Marschke can be reached at marschke@nova.edu

Crystal Ann Montfort is currently pursuing a degree in Finance at Nova Southeastern University. She plans on taking over family business in NYC when completed. She anticipates graduating in May 2015.

Bahaudin G. Mujtaba is Professor of Management and Human Resources at the H. Wayne Huizenga School of Business and Entrepreneurship of Nova Southeastern University in Ft. Lauderdale, Florida. Bahaudin is the author and coauthor of twenty professional and academic books dealing with management, diversity, business ethics, and cross-cultural management, as well as over 200 academic journal articles. During the past thirty years he has had the pleasure of working with human resource professionals in the United States, Brazil, Bahamas, Afghanistan, Pakistan, St. Lucia, Grenada, Malaysia, Japan, Vietnam, China, India, Thailand, and Jamaica. This diverse exposure has provided him many insights in ethics, culture, and management from the perspectives of different firms, people groups, and countries. Bahaudin can be reached at: mujtaba@nova.edu

Quoc An Nguyen completed his Bachelor in Medical Biotechnology in 2005 from University of Natural Sciences HCM city. An earned his Master Degree in Business Administration at the University of Québec à Montreal in 2014. Mr Quoc An Nguyen is currently doing some research in International Marketing and Business. An has over 8 years of experience working in the field of Healthcare as Sales and Marketing Specialists. In his daily activities, An interacts a lot with both technical science and business. An is currently running his own metal trading company with approximately 50 employees.

Daria Prause has a great background in classroom and virtual school management. Her first Master's degree is in Linguistics with major in teaching foreign languages (English and German) and cultures from a university in Russia. Daria traveled to more than 40 countries to learn about personal and working relationship and cultures at a workplace. In 2013 she immigrated in the US and decided to emerge more in a business side of leadership and does some research on human resources management, while finishing her MBA and conducting workshops on team building, conflict and time management.

Farzana Rahman Safi is Assistant Professor of Management and Human Resources Management at University of Peshawar's College of Home Economics in KPK Pakistan. Farzana has a passion to teach graduate courses of management. She worked as subject specialist for few years in various government owned institutions. Farzana holds a 'university Gold Medal' for securing first class first position in her master from University of Peshawar. Additionally, she is the recipient of 'XII Star National Woman Award' in education and teaching. Farzana completed a Master of Management degree from The Australian National University Canberra. Farzana, born in Peshawar of Pakistan, delivered numerous lectures, organized seminars, and participated in conferences at National level. Farzana is approachable at farzana_safi@yahoo.com

Kiran Razzaq is a student of MS at Superior University, Department of Business Administration, Lahore, Pakistan. At present, she is working on her thesis titled as "Consumer Resistance to Mobile Banking Adoption: An Empirical Analysis in Pakistani context" and key areas of her Research are Finance, Management, Business Education and Human Resource Development. She has participated in International Conference on Management Research (ICMR) 2012 and 2013 held by Superior University Lahore, Pakistan. Kiran has completed her Masters of Business Administration from Virtual University of Pakistan in 2011, with specialization in finance. She served Tez Gas Private Ltd. as an internee in 2010. She did B.com from University of Punjab, Pakistan in the year of 2008. She did her Matriculation

from Board of Intermediate and Secondary Education (BISE) Lahore. Kiran can be contacted through email at: kiran_pari41@yahoo.com

Tipakorn Seanatip (Tap) is a graduate researcher in the Faculty of Political Science and has a bachelor's of science degree from the Faculty of Humanities at Ramkhamhaeng University in Bangkok of Thailand. Currently, she is a full-time staff at the Institute of International Studies (IIS) of Ramkhamhaeng University, where she deals with students and faculty members from different countries who are completing their bachelors, masters and doctoral studies in Thailand. Tipakorn has worked in the restaurant industry of Thailand which provided her with experience to regularly interact with tourists from around the world. She speaks Thai and English and her graduate work is focused on political science at Ramkhamhaeng University. Tap can be reached at: avicenna_mylove@hotmail.com

Jatuporn Sungkhawan, D.B.A., is a strategic management professional with over 25 years of experience in multinational corporations. He has been associated with some of the world's largest companies to include agribusiness, financial service and management consulting. He is a university professor who teaches Strategic Management, Business Research, and Organization Behavior. He earned the Doctorate in Business Administration degree at Nova Southeastern University's H. Wayne Huizenga School of Business and Entrepreneurship, United States. He earned a Masters of Business Administration and a Bachelor's degree in Agricultural Economics at Kasetsart University, Bangkok, Thailand.

Ike Udechukwu is a faculty member at Shorter University where he teaches courses in management. He is published in journals such as Human resource Development Review, Public Personnel Management, and the Journal of Management and Entrepreneurship. His areas of research interest are management, African studies, leadership, productivity management, and employee commitment. E-mail: Udechukwu@hotmail.com

Nereida Valdes obtained her Degree in Business Administration. In 2010 she opened NVG Services, Corp offering small businesses with Bookkeeping, Payroll and Tax Service solutions. Nereida is pursuing a Masters in Taxation at Nova Southeastern University. Upon completion of the same she will obtain her CPA license.

Omar Wee-Ellis is currently pursuing a degree in Management at Nova Southeastern University. He aspires to work at the board level at a Forbes top 100

organization. Additionally he is planning to be a management consultant. Mr Wee-Ellis is graduating in 2016.

Memoona Zareen is a student of MS Business Administration from Superior University Lahore, Pakistan. At present she is working on her thesis titled as *"Mobile Money Service: Advancing Financial Inclusion of Unbanked Developing Population"*. Her major areas of research are finance, banking, money management and human capital development and keeps on participating in various national and international conferences on management and business research. She got certified in financial and accounting software packages from Pakistan Industrial Technical Assistance Centre (PITAC) in 2011. Memoona has completed her MBIT from Institute of Business and Information Technology, University of the Punjab, Pakistan in 2010 with major as finance and minor management and human resource management. She served MCB Bank Ltd., in 2009, has done her graduation from Queen Mary College Lahore, Pakistan in the class of 2007 and her HSSE examination from Board of Intermediate and Secondary Education (BISE) Lahore, Pakistan. She was born in the District of Chakwal, Pakistan. Memoona can be contacted through email at: memoona.zareen@gmail.com

Index

May you have the hindsight to appropriately diagnose gender challenges and opportunities, the foresight to solve them effectively while capitalizing on the prospects, and the insight to ask for help when appropriate!

www.ingramcontent.com/pod-product-compliance
Lightning Source LLC
Chambersburg PA
CBHW020605270326
41927CB00005B/178